A Fastnet Race almost defies satisfactory description. Anyone taking part will spend the duration of the race doing his damndest, eating and sleeping and seeing little of all that is going on. The spectator sees much less, and what is he to deduce from all he hears? Each competitor is dependent on the hull, gear, sails, navigator (an important man), skipper and crew. Who is to disentangle the effects of these factors (and that other one – luck) on each competitor's performance?

*Yachting Monthly*, September 1935

# Fastnet:
*the story of a great ocean race*

## Ian Dear

B. T. Batsford Ltd, London

ISBN 0 7134 0997 5

Filmset by Servis Filmsetting Ltd, Manchester and printed in Great Britain by Butler & Tanner Ltd, Frome, Somerset, for the publishers B.T. Batsford Ltd 4 Fitzhardinge Street London W1H 0AH

**Overleaf**   Dawn at the Bishop homeward bound during the 1975 Fastnet. This photograph was taken by Ambrose Greenway from the Swiss Admiral's Cupper, *On Dit*.

# Contents

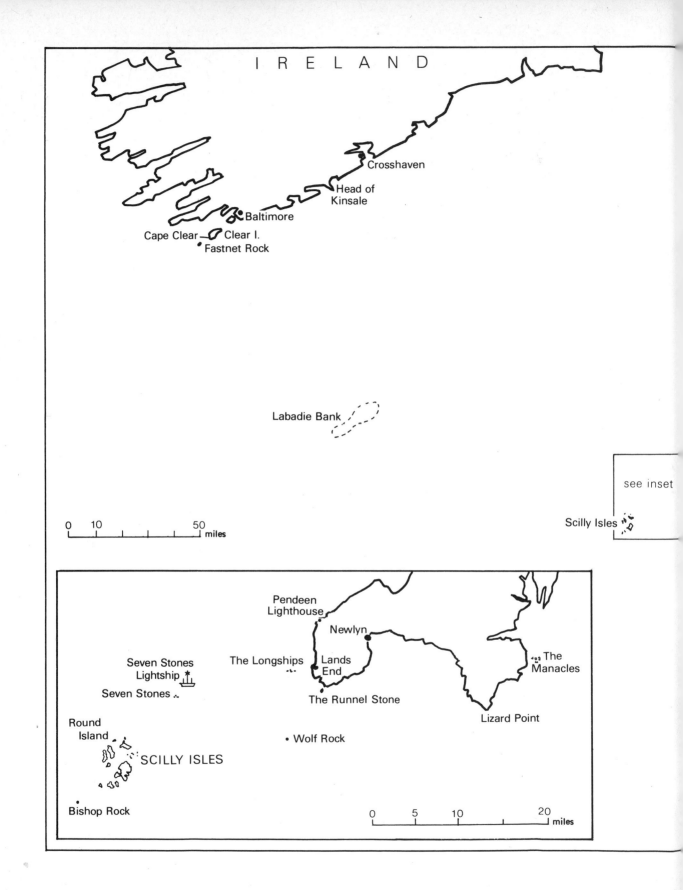

IRELAND

Crosshaven

Head of
Kinsale

Baltimore

Cape Clear — Clear I.

• Fastnet Rock

Labadie Bank

0  10        50
miles

see inset

Scilly Isles

Pendeen
Lighthouse

Newlyn

The Longships    Lands
End

Seven Stones
Lightship

The
Manacles

Seven Stones

The Runnel Stone

Round
Island

• Wolf Rock

Lizard Point

SCILLY ISLES

Bishop Rock

0      5     10        20
miles

# Introduction

I can think of no better way to introduce the Fastnet Race than by an article which appeared some years ago in *Yachting Monthly*, reproduced here by kind permission of the present editor, Des Sleightholme.

In the history of the Fastnet Race . . . one lesson stands out quite clearly, it is not a gambler's race.

Navigationally it is a simple course to follow, headland-hopping most of the way with two long legs aimed at prominent landfalls. As a race it is three races in one; the Channel leg beset by a complicated tidal set-up, the outward leg to the Irish coast when wind-shift tactics can win or lose the day and the return passage with the pitfall of a relaxing crew. It is often a hard race, sometimes an easy-weather race but never a simple race. Commander W.B. Luard, a veteran Fastnet navigator, [was] renowned for his navigational nose (an asset implying care for detail rather than some mystical olfactory gift). He has this to say of the course in general:

'More often than not the sovereign westerlies dominate the Fastnet course, with their backing and veering wind cycles as depressions . . . mostly centred north of the English Channel . . . approach and recede. Easterly winds, sometimes vicious, sometimes fickle, are less predictable; but in stable anti-cyclonic conditions often follow the fishermans' quip "like a kite: up by day and down by night". The interaction of day onshore sea breezes and evening offshore ones are also companions of fine settled weather.

Tidal streams, especially at springs, run sufficiently fast to demand exacting study. They can be the arbiters of victory or defeat. In westerly weather, which often gives the option of working down Channel either offshore or inshore in varying degree, an inshore course, though more of a gamble than one offshore, can, with a fair stream carried round prominent headlands – Portland, Start, the Bolts, Rame Head, the Dodman for example – bring a brave lift as the foul stream can then be partly cheated in the bays and bights.

Again the tidal streams turn earlier inshore than in the offing. If the winds keep faith, when beating, then a fair tidal stream can sometimes be held for up to 9 hours if the navigator knows his tactics.

A weather running stream, too, can bring in varying degree a threefold vantage at its best in windward work – favourable change in the direction of the apparent wind; increase in its velocity; and a closer course made good over the ground in relation to the true wind. These three benisons are at their best in light weather and spring tides – also winning conditions for the smaller class III boats.'

The weather during early August is famed for providing westerlies which are often strong to gale. It is a rare Fastnet Race which does not provide at least one blow. The succession of low pressure systems which advance upon the British Isles bring a constantly backing and veering wind and provide a series of tactical problems to be solved. For the most part a common problem is tackled the same way by everybody.

Upon leaving the Needles the fleet is often confronted by a choice of taking a starboard tack offshore or of a port tack inshore and thereafter working inside the Portland Race. With a forecast of a wind due to back and increase, that hitch offshore can mean a subsequent long port tack, with sheets eased, down channel, while the inshore people are sharpening up to make Start Point. If the wind backs just a little this is fine; if it backs a lot, so that the inshore boats can also crack sheets and still make Start, much of the offshore yacht's advantage is lost – she may even come off worst.

It is also a mistake to go too far offshore on that early starboard tack. Should the wind fail to back or worse, actually *veer* a shade, the race is virtually lost. The yacht will be down the spout. This is where gambles are too risky. A good Met man may bring it off though. Back in 1937 Capt. Franklin Ratsey took *Zoraida* far to seaward of the Scillies in search of a sou'wester he'd sniffed out. He was right. He picked it up and carried it far out ahead of the inshore fleet. (He later lost it all by losing his top-mast.) With a wind which fails to back as predicted and with inshore boats working their tides off and on, the offshore boat can usually hope for even odds at best.

The inshore course has a lot in its favour; here's what Derek Boyer has to say, he was co-owner with Denis Miller when *Clarion of Wight* was the 1963 winner:

'In '63 Adlard Coles in *Cohoe* gained a considerable amount of time by going right in at Portland Bill and thus dodging the foul tide.

Since that time I have myself been into the Bill and have found that if one is prepared to do this, the sea, from a boiling cauldron becomes almost like a mill pond even with strong south westerly winds.

The point therefore that I would like to make for the benefit of the cruising reader, is that when in the vicinity of the Bill in a foul tide, I suggest he takes courage in one hand and an echo sounder or large chart in the other and finds out for himself. I'm sure he will be very agreeably surprised.'

It must be noted that the boiling cauldron he mentions really does boil in fresh westerly weather and with a spring flood it is dangerous. A foul tide at Portland is a dismal eventuality which seldom seems to arise for the bigger boats but it is a setback which can afflict the smaller elements of the fleet. Says Adlard Coles:

'I think the first part down to Land's End is the most interesting and oddly enough often the roughest. The passage round Portland Bill is important because occasionally it pays to take the inside passage but sometimes it does not, depending on the hour of the tide and state of wind and sea.'

In 1959 it was a light air start. *Griffin II* was one of the yachts to scrape past Portland Bill just as the flood was beginning to run and she scraped past hugging tight into the shore and later just managed to catch her tide at Start. That race was also a refutation of the theory that in very hot weather (which it was) any wind that is going will be found close inshore. The West Bay theorists drifted windless.

Working the bays can pay off in terms of fair tide, but it is essentially a ruse for an attentive crew in a weatherly boat and there is always the chance that a wise man must be prepared to cut his losses quickly and get to hell out before he sticks there. It is often a case of knowing when to get *out* of bays rather than when to go into them.

The course out of the Rock usually involves either a wind shift or the promise of one – a vastly different matter. In 1963 a shift to the nor'west was promised. *Clarion of Wight*, the overall winner, was in the right place at the right time. Writes Derek Boyer modestly:

'In the 1963 Fastnet which *Clarion of Wight* won, our success I believe was mainly due to the fact that we stayed on the port tack for longer than we really should have done, and when we eventually did tack, the wind shifted in our favour so that we could lay the Rock. However, the point which must not be lost sight of is that the race was won by a very small margin against Adlard Coles in *Cohoe*. I believe it was 5 minutes which is not much over a rhumb line distance of 604 miles.'

He could, of course, have been left out on a limb with that big port tack; plotted on the chart however it still looks like the *making* tack.

On a dead beat to the Rock, the theory of the 5 degrees rule, tacking each time the course becomes unfavourable for the Rock by 5 degrees is a sound start but it is seldom that the wind stays so constant. Sooner or later it shifts. With the mark dead upwind any shift is welcome – unless one happens to be far out on what then becomes the *wrong* tack; the 5 degrees rule, with its ever-decreasing length of tack as the goal is neared shortens the chances of being stuck down-wind.

The promise of a shift however cannot be ignored and nobody would dare to do so. The accepted strategy of putting in a generous first leg towards the direction of the forecast shift and thereafter tacking towards the mark on the shift side of the direct rhumb line is safe providing it is not overdone.

Arrival at the Rock is always an emotional moment; it is often the point where a good race is lost due to relaxation of effort. Dick Carter, the winner with *Rabbit* in 1965, is probably the most qualified man in the game to comment:

'Intensity of concentration is essential to good performance in an ocean-race. But with the 600 mile Fastnet course this is doubly so. There are very few men (I have yet to meet one) who can keep at it 100 per cent of the time 4 hours on, 4 hours off without having lulls now and again. This underscores why ocean-racing is such a team effort. The boat must be kept at 100 per cent performance even though individual members of the crew may ebb and flow with their efforts. Someone in the crew must keep the drive.

This can be particularly difficult to sustain after rounding the Rock. Rounding the Fastnet is such an overpowering emotional experience it is somewhat anticlimactical to head out to sea again. There is a let-down. It can be aggravated by a sense that one is not doing very well in the race (one never knows for sure). The one comforting thought is that almost everyone else is feeling the same way. It is the time for redoubling efforts.

Thus the last part of the race, the return to Plymouth, presents great opportunity for crews that can rise to the occasion. This is the part of the race where most of the tactical errors are made, where one can lose the full advantage of a sudden shift in weather and where one generally is benumbed by ''battle fatigue''.

The race is not always to the swiftest.

The Fastnet is a ''thinking man's'' race. Whether tide-hopping in the Solent, ''playing'' the bays down to Lands End or guessing the weather in the Irish Sea, there is no let-up in the calculating of ones race strategy. Woe to the crew that stops thinking on that leg to Plymouth.'

Very very often the leg back to the Bishop is a reach or a run, often also it is a fast one; it can also end up with a landfall which (since the Scillies are a big target) while near enough for the slap-happy, can mean a missed tide for the racing man. The effects of surface drift can cause a miss of this sort.

Cmdr Luard [commented] on this draft:

'The existence of a steady current – the Rennell's current – setting north-westerly across the fairway of the English and Irish channels has now been disproved. An occasional one, after strong westerly gales, runs in this general direction, skirting the Chaussée de Sein northerly then turning north-westerly towards Cape Clear: but this mainly affects inward bound Atlantic ships. The surface drift from a strong south-wester, the important factor in the homeward run from the Fastnet Rock, can, if not allowed for, result in a landfall the wrong side of the Scillies. Its rate should be assumed as one fiftieth of the wind velocity; its direction as 40 degrees to starboard of downwind in the Northern hemisphere.

Gibbon once affirmed that the wind and waves were always on the side of the first navigators, a statement even the ablest Fastnet ones would sometimes greet with sardonic mirth.'

Bringing the Bishop abeam gives once more that fatal feeling of a race almost over; that this is a dangerous state to be in is emphasized by Adlard Coles:

'The part of the Fastnet course on which I have most often come unstuck is the last lap between the Lizard and the finish line. In 1961 I kept well inshore and I think fell back to fourth place by doing so. In 1963 I was determined not to make this mistake again so I kept well offshore. However, the wind was coming in gusts off the land (as Kim Holman, who is a Cornishman, told me afterwards) and there was much more wind inshore. This mistake cost me about 20 minutes and as I only lost the Fastnet Cup by 6 minutes my error made a considerable difference to the result. I think towards the end of a Fastnet Race the skippers and crews are probably more tired than they think and it is quite easy to throw the race away on the last lap. In 1963 I thought I saw some of the leaders heeling over to a good wind inshore although offshore it went light. My sight is not good and I wear glasses but oddly enough I was the only one who could see this wind offshore but I just did not trust my own vision so I did not act on it. It was only after the race was over that Holman told me that they were heeling over to a good breeze inshore and what I thought must be my imagination was in fact correct.'

Such are the fortunes of the Fastnet. It can be a desperate trial by endurance such as the '57 race, when American Dick Nye pumped his winning *Carina*, leaking from split and shattered planking, back over the line, or it can be one of those fickle drifters that end with a last wild and windy night for the small fry. It matters very little where the inexperienced owner, in it for the first time, ends up on the results list. He will learn more about fast passage-making in that one race than he will in years of short events or straightforward cruising.

# Early Days 1925—30

*The name of this great game is ocean racing, and it is also known as the king of sports.*

Weston Martyr

It was all started by a man called Weston Martyr. A well-known British amateur yachtsman, he had for some years been living in the United States and the Americans had introduced him to the Bermuda Race, an ocean race which had been started in 1906. In a letter to a British yachting magazine dated December 1924 Martyr proposed his countrymen take up this sport, for at that time it was quite unknown to them.

It is without question the very finest sport a man can possibly engage in; for to play this game at all it is necessary to possess in the very highest degree those hallmarks of a true sportsman, skill, courage, and endurance. The name of this great game is ocean racing, and it is also known as the King of Sports by those who understand how high are the qualities demanded by it from its followers. And they are right, for to take a small boat hundreds of miles out from the land to fight that implacable and relentless enemy the sea, requires, it seems to me, as much courage, for instance as the hunting of big game. To keep the boat *racing* day after day and night after night, through whatever weather may befall, with no possibility of escaping its fury except by fighting it, this calls for surely as great a nerve as the climbing of mountains, the saving dive of a full back amongst the charging forwards' feet, or the keeping up of one's wicket in a pinch.

In the United States, he said, a special type of boat was being developed to take part in ocean races. Mostly they were schooner rigged with a bermudian mainsail with most of the ballast being carried internally. These 'ocean racers' were usually about 45 feet overall, heavily built, but fast and comfortable. If the British didn't start taking an interest soon they'd never catch up, Martyr warned. 'As it is, I doubt very much if, even now, a British boat could compete successfully in, say, next year's Bermuda Race. We probably have boats capable of beating *Memory*, but have we six amateurs in this country with sufficient

experience in ocean racing to enable them to win against the crew which would sail the *Memory*? I doubt it,' and he went on to list a kind of questionnaire for any budding ocean racing hand.

Have you ever set a ring-tail in a hurry in the dark, and can you make it draw to advantage? How many kinds of 'fishermen's staysail' are there, and when are they most effective? Do you know how to organize a hot, sustaining, appetizing meal in a gale of wind, with everything battened down and the stove trying hard to stand on its head? How would you arrange for fresh air down below in bad weather, always remembering that it is impossible to rely on hatches, skylights, and portholes for ventilation? Do you fully realise the incredible amount of chafe that is continually going on in the rigging of a small boat at sea?

He implied that few British yachtsmen did know and that the sooner they got racing the better it would be for British yachting. A suitable course? Well, what about from the Solent, down the English Channel, across the Irish Sea to the Fastnet Rock, and back to Plymouth, a distance of some 615 miles?

This letter must have been read with intense interest by a lot of people, and when, in the next issue, Martyr announced that an American yacht was being built specifically to challenge British yachts to an ocean race in their own waters, correspondence and comment began to appear in other yachting magazines and in the general press. Most people seemed to think such a race an excellent idea, but there were detractors. The best known of these was Claud Worth, a founder member of the Royal Cruising Club and a highly respected cruising yachtsman, just the type of man who had been proving since the turn of the

1  E.G. Martin, the owner of *Jolie Brise* when she won the first Fastnet in 1925. He was a founder member of the Ocean Racing Club.

century that small yachts could safely survive the savage sea. But cruising, according to Worth, was one thing, racing in open water quite another. In *The Field* he wrote:

At the risk of making an unpopular suggestion, I venture to express a doubt which arises in my mind — are our latitudes suitable for a public ocean race? If two owners, experienced in ocean cruising, arrange a match involving several hundred miles of deep water, they know exactly what they are doing. But a public race might very well include some owners whose keenness is greater than their experience. If the weather should be bad, so long as there is a head wind they would probably come to no harm, for a good boat and sound gear will generally stand as much driving as the crew can put up with. But when running before anything approaching a gale of wind and a big sea in open water, conditions are very deceptive. A vessel of good shape and a reasonably long keel may run so easily and steadily that even an old hand, under cruising conditions, is apt to keep her running longer than is prudent.

Of course, one does not suggest that it is always necessary to heave-to when one gets a strong wind and a biggish sea. It requires much judgement to know whether a following sea has reached the dangerous stage. I have more than once been compelled very reluctantly to heave-to and watch a fair wind running to waste, and have soon after had reason to be very thankful that I was safely hove-to in good time.

But if one had been racing one would probably have been tempted to carry on, knowing that some other competitor might take the risk. These conditions might not occur once in a dozen ocean races, but the magnitude of the possible disaster should be taken into account.

In later years Worth moderated his opinion about a yacht's ability to run before a gale, but at the time he was obviously not only doubtful about ocean racing but did not like the proposed course either, and stated that he would prefer Vigo in Spain as the ultimate destination of the Ocean Race, as it was now being called in the press. But general yachting opinion was against him and the Fastnet course, after some discussion, was chosen. Worth, when asked why he was not entering his well-known yacht, *Tern IV*, replied: 'The course from Cowes round the Fastnet and back lacks the one great requirement of an ocean course. With the land close aboard for such a large proportion of the distance, any vessel might have entered on the chance of it being a light-weather race, as she could always give up and go in somewhere.'

Read now, after the disaster of the 1979 race, Worth's reasoning seems wrong, but over the next decade or so a great many of the entries for the Fastnet did run for shelter and frequently gave up once their anchor was down. And Worth was not alone in his opinion that the Fastnet was not a true ocean race. The doyen of American ocean racing, Alfred Loomis, did not think it was one either. 'It is a longshore event with a little jump of a hundred and seventy miles from Land's End, England, across open water to the Irish coast — and back again,' is how he described it in his book, *Ocean Racing*.

But by this description Loomis was not belittling the course. On the contrary, he had the greatest respect for it and likened it to the Grand National. 'The yacht that completes the Fastnet course in a bad year,' he commented, 'deserves all the praise lavished upon the horse that survives the hazards of the Aintree classic,' and added that if the Fastnet wasn't an ocean race in the true sense of the word it nevertheless 'has all the worst features of such a contest plus mental hazards that have to be experienced to be fully appreciated.'

The mental hazards he had in mind were twofold. In heavy weather it was, as Worth surmised, an easy race to quit but, as all the shelters were on the lee shore, almost impossible to re-enter; while in light weather the strain of trying to beat the tides and races as well as your competitors was, he made it sound, almost intolerable. 'In America we are accustomed at the start of a Bermuda race to battle the calms and the currents for twenty miles until we have rounded Montauk Point. But what can you say of an ocean race which endures for two hundred miles amid conditions peculiar — damned peculiar — to an inside waterway? In a soft Fastnet race owner and navigator vibrate between Brown's Tidal Streams and cold compresses.' Any modern participant would whole-heartedly endorse Loomis' comments, for the currents still run foul off St Albans Head; Portland Bill is still a nasty place when the wind is against the tide, with 'pyramidal waves, and holes between them big enough to swallow a house'; and the wind still has the irritating habit of heading a yacht just as it turns — after flogging down the Channel — for the Rock itself.

Though Worth and Loomis did not think the Fastnet a true ocean course, others disagreed. Sherman Hoyt, another distinguished American yachtsman during the 1920s and 1930s, for instance, called it 'the best and most sporting of all ocean race courses,' and George Martin, one of the founder members of the Ocean Racing Club, which was formed immediately after the first race, and the owner of the first winner, *Jolie Brise*, argued then and later that the Fastnet really was a true ocean race. In his book, *Deep Water*

*Cruising*, published in the 1930s, he countered both Worth's and Loomis' arguments strongly:

It has been said that the Fastnet Race is not an ocean race at all. This opinion, I think, is scarcely justified, since about three hundred and sixty miles are sailed out of sight of land and in water exposed to the whole drift of the Atlantic Ocean. As for the harbours of refuge, I personally am thankful that they are there, and I think that the history of the races which have been sailed provides convincing proof of the necessity for them. The climate in the North-eastern Atlantic is not sufficiently trustworthy to make places of refuge superfluous, or, indeed, anything but desirable. If competitors retire into them for inadequate reasons the discredit is to them and not to the course.

---

With the idea of an ocean race attracting attention a private committee of three, Weston Martyr, George Martin, and the editor of *Yachting Monthly*, Malden Heckstall-Smith, was set up to organise one. The course for such a race created much discussion and Weston Martyr had to fight for the Fastnet plan. A race round the Tuskar Light Vessel was one of the alternatives suggested but Martyr insisted that an ocean race had to have some ocean in it, and in the end the Fastnet course was agreed upon. The Yacht Racing Association gave its blessing and the Royal Western Yacht Club at Plymouth agreed to organise the finish. The start was moved from Cowes – as the Royal Yacht Squadron rather frowned upon the proceedings – to Ryde where the Royal Victoria Yacht Club fired the starting gun.

The course decided upon, the committee now issued the rules under which the race was to be run. It was to start on 15 August 1925 from Ryde and end at Plymouth, with the Isle of Wight and the Fastnet Rock being left on the starboard side. The race was open to any fully decked yacht of any rig which measured not less than 30 feet and not more than 50 feet on the waterline. Any entry had to sail in full cruising trim, and it was later decreed that each yacht had to carry a serviceable boat as well as suitable life-saving equipment. No restrictions were made on the number of amateur hands carried but 'no more paid hands will be permitted than can be normally accommodated in the fo'c'sle.'

The Boat Racing Association's system of measurement was selected to obtain a rating for each competing yacht but it was, in the words of the committee 'modified and adjusted to meet the special requirements of an ocean race.' Later, it was decided to ban yachts built to any IYRU class so that the race would not affect the entries to the West Country regattas which were taking place at the same time as the race.

By March 1925 there were already four entries for the Ocean Race, and by 1 July this had risen to 14 – including the American yawl, *Filatonga* – and eventually went as high as 16. But when the starting gun went at noon on 15 August the number had dropped to seven, *Filatonga* being one of the entries to fail to start. It was, perhaps, fewer than the committee had hoped for but they could also console themselves with the thought that the entries for the first Bermuda Race had numbered only three.

The seven starters all flew British yacht club flags but *Saladin*, a 33-ton Bristol Channel pilot cutter, was sailed by a Basque Spaniard, Ingo Simon, while *Jolie Brise*, a yacht built on pilot boat lines, had been constructed at Le Havre. From the start the Fastnet Race had an international flavour to it. The other five entries consisted of *Fulmar*, a 14-ton cutter built in 1901 as a yacht but on working boat lines, entered by the Royal Engineer Yacht Club; *Gull*, an 18-ton cutter built in 1896 by Camper and Nicholson and owned and sailed by an Irishman, H.P.F. Donegan; two Norwegian Colin Archer type ketches, *Banba IV* and *North Star*, owned and sailed by H.R. Barrett and M. Tennant respectively; and *Jessie L*, another Bristol Channel pilot cutter, owned and sailed by C.J. Hussey. All except *Jessie L* were gaff-rigged, deep-draft boats built for cruising.

Advice to these hardy pioneers had been flying thick and fast in the yachting press. Some of the most amusing came from an unnamed yachtswoman who explained at length what any lady member of any of the crews should wear. After sensibly advising the removal of any extras like jewellery, ribbons, ties, beads, and other ornaments, the writer, who obviously had an intense dislike of brown, suggested that essential pieces of wearing apparel should include 'two chiffon motor veils, in blue preferably (not brown, *never* brown on a boat), to go right over the hat and face if desirable, but secure the ends and don't let them wave abroad in the eyes of your neighbour.'

'White looks nice on board, but I don't advise it, as on sunny days I have noticed when sitting all day that the glare reflecting off your white knees is perceptibly more trying. Personally, I like the look of red, and it is a good colour for the eyes. A whole "get up" of red would be nice, but failing this blue serge "all the way". Let the skirt be of such a width as will permit of your stepping up (a long step) on board from a dinghy, and not too full, so that it blows at large, and rather on the long side for warmth.' Other essentials included 'three or four pairs of thick, white "fabric" gloves, long enough to prevent the wrists getting tanned, several pairs of stockings and heaps of handkerchiefs.

The only *brown* things you can ever wear with advantage on a boat are shoes, good strong Russia leather, and well-matched stockings.' Also recommended, quite seriously, was not one umbrella but two – as 'their greatest vice is their suicidal tendencies.' When in use 'it must be trimmed, like the sails, to the right angle so as not to hold the wind or get in the way.' Finally, and firmly, 'object to anyone who comes on board with brown long-shore waterproofs and make them go and get proper black or yellow oilskins. You don't want the look of the boat spoilt by the appearance of the people on board, which it certainly will be if they look all *brown*.'

A female reader of the yachting magazine in which this advice appeared, not unreasonably came to the conclusion that the writer of it could only have sailed in a yacht as a passenger and advised her lady readers to wear, not a skirt, but 'a pair of corduroy velveteen knickers' which were, she said cryptically, far safer. The knickers were a cross between plus-fours and riding breeches. The editor printed her letter but stamped on any doubts it might have cast on the soundness of the advice given by the writer of the article who was, he said tartly, one of the most experienced and well known yachtswomen sailing in the Solent! No one else seemed to think the advice anything other than normal but the military crew of *Fulmar* did later note that they were disappointed not to spot any lady ocean racer in 'plus-fours, galoshes, blue motor veils and holding an umbrella' on the deck of any of the other competitors at the start.

The noon start, made in fine weather and smooth seas, saw all seven yachts, led by *Gull*, quickly over the line, but the light winds from the ENE and the adverse tides soon had all the starters struggling to make headway. The short beat to No Man's Fort was succeeded by a reach to Bembridge, and then the yachts ran free once the Isle of Wight was cleared. The slower boats, *North Star*, *Jessie L* and *Banba IV*, suffered especially as the breeze fell off and the last named desperately rigged every sail her owner could lay his hands on. A trip was made out to the end of the spinnaker boom – a distance of some 30 feet – so that the raffee topsail could be set inverted as a water sail. Similar tactics were used on the other side to get the small jib-headed topsail set inverted on the main boom as a second water sail. An old reaching foresail was then set to fill with such airs as came off the spinnaker and another was set on the mizzen mast and boomed out with the boathook to do duty as a mizzen spinnaker. With all nine sails drawing, and looking something like a waterborne laundry line, *Banba IV* made some progress against the other two slower boats but after being becalmed that first night the three faster ones, *Jolie Brise*, *Gull* and *Saladin*, caught the

2   The first Fastnet, called the Ocean Race by the Press, was from Ryde on 15 August 1925. Here six of the seven starters can be seen at the line: *Jessie L*, *North Star*, *Jolie Brise*, *Saladin*, *Gull* and *Fulmar*.

breeze ahead of the others and left them behind. By 1430 *Jolie Brise* was nearly abeam of Portland with *Gull* inshore and slightly ahead of her and *Saladin*, five or six miles to seaward, just astern. *Fulmar* was dead astern and hull down, and the others were not in sight.

By Monday morning the wind had increased to a splendid easterly which had the three leading yachts tearing along. *Jolie Brise* was now in the lead and was abeam of the Eddystone at 0500 and off the Manacles by 0800, but she was being hotly pursued by *Gull*. As *Gull* approached the Lizard the crew were glad to be reassured by a yacht which had come out of Falmouth that only *Jolie Brise* was ahead of them, and from then on they considered the race between themselves and the French-built pilot boat. At this point *Gull* was carrying as much canvas as she could cope with – mainsail, jackyard topsail, yankee-jib topsail, and balloon staysail – and those on *Jolie Brise* who saw her vast spread of canvas admired the way her crew kept it all set in the stiff breeze. But they needed to drive her for, as *Gull*'s owner later remarked, *Jolie Brise* 'was going along as steady as a house with her spinnaker giving her a wonderful lift.' Donegan, struggling to close the gap, cut close in by the Lizard, and then gybed and reset his spinnaker in record time while Martin in *Jolie Brise* gave the Lizard a wide berth and took a leisurely 16 minutes to reset his. As a result, at the Runnelstone buoy the pilot boat was only ten minutes ahead. *Saladin* was no longer in sight but then, as the two leading boats headed into the

Atlantic, the wind dropped altogether and *Saladin* carrying a wind of her own reappeared. The others soon caught this breeze and first one and then the other would take the lead. On board *Jolie Brise* there was a feeling of irritation that *Gull* could not be shaken off but this was later replaced by a sense of companionship as the two yachts raced neck and neck. 'We were wonderfully evenly matched,' wrote Martin later, 'in those light airs; and to our great surprise, when a little breeze caught us, we felt it and gathered way as quickly as she did.' At one time the two boats were becalmed so close together that Martin feared they would drift into one another. The swell made both boats roll horribly and those on board could see how badly the gear was being strained by the spars swinging and banging about. As Martin watched his opponent he saw *Gull*'s topsail halliards part and he indicated to Donegan what had happened. 'Mr Donegan was at the tiller, and when he looked aft for a second he stood perfectly still, and then, with a gesture of splendid determination he took off his jacket and went forward to see to repairing the damage.' For a time *Gull*'s crew were only able to set her jib-headed topsail and as she had a nine-hour allowance over *Jolie Brise*, and had every chance of winning, this accident probably cost her the race.

As it was, *Jolie Brise* now got a light breeze and began to edge slightly ahead of *Gull* but the patch of calm into which the two leading boats had run had enabled both *Fulmar* and *Saladin* to catch up and by nightfall all four yachts were in sight of one another. By next morning *Fulmar* was within shouting distance of *Gull* though the only word which could be heard clearly was 'what?' This attempt at communication made the high-spirited Engineers' crew dry-throated

and hot. They thought about swimming but were deterred by the appearance of a large shark's fin about three yards from the yacht. 'The skipper leapt below and returned with two large revolvers,' one of the crew later related. 'The remainder of the crew having buried themselves flat, he proceeded to indulge in some of the most execrable shooting we have ever had the misfortune to witness. The presence of the revolvers on board remains unexplained, unless it was in anticipation of mutiny.'

Later, *Jolie Brise* and *Saladin* caught a breeze and moved away from the other two, leaving them rolling their masts out. On more than one occasion *Fulmar* drifted round in a full circle. *Jolie Brise* opened up her lead in the freshening breeze and by the time she rounded the Fastnet, at 1950 on the 19th, she was some 12 hours ahead of the next boat, *Gull*, which did not round until 0835 the next morning. Some two miles astern of her were *Fulmar*, which rounded at 0920, and *Saladin* which rounded five minutes later. The lighthouse keepers acknowledged the presence of *Jolie Brise* by waving a pilot-jack which the crew assumed meant they were first round. A spinnaker was hoisted but at midnight they were becalmed again till the morning when the wind backed to ssw and strengthened considerably. For the next 16 hours *Jolie Brise* averaged 8.1 knots, and from the Longships to the Lizard she averaged 8.7 knots. 'It was sailing such as one gets but seldom in a lifetime,' said Martin.

Just before *Jolie Brise* rounded the Rock the crew of the *Fulmar* made their first sighting of the Irish coast and put into operation what was known as the *Fulmar* method of reading the log after long calms. 'As it is rather unique and highly scientific it is worthy of description,' wrote one of the crew. '(a) first sight land,

(b) recognise it, if possible, (c) if you are the skipper or navigator, rush below with pencil, ruler and india-rubber and erase previous estimated position from chart, having first of all ascertained approximate bearing and distance from prominent shore object, (d) insert correct position on chart and hastily measure distance from last land sighted, (e) look up log reading and from this and real distance work out a percentage error for the log, (f) insert small cross on chart at a distance from the correct position depending on the credulity of the crew, (g) return on deck and inform the crew that the real position and the approximate position by dead reckoning coincide very closely.'

Out in front of *Fulmar* and *Saladin*, *Gull* soon had the wind that was speeding *Jolie Brise* to a notable victory and by late afternoon on the 20th she was lee rail under. Her owner was below making notes of the race. 'The cabin swing-table is doing its level best to assassinate me,' he wrote. 'I have been struck in the chest and chin, while the weighty box beneath is making frantic efforts to amputate one or both of my legs. My note-book is at one moment close to my face,

3  *Jolie Brise*, one of the most successful and consistent boats to race in the early Fastnets, which she won in 1925, 1929 and 1930, and came second in 1928. (*Beken*)

and in the next almost out of reach, and it seems hard to believe that the wretched article of furniture is only trying to obey the laws of gravity.'

The wind increased as the day drew to a close and the weather deteriorated but out ahead *Jolie Brise* missed the worst of it, though she went through some large seas at the Lizard as well as a rather nasty squall, and her log records that by 0500 on the 21st the wind was force 7. She then reduced to her headsails for a time before the wind went flat again and then came in light from the ENE so that the spinnaker could be set off the Dodman. A freshening breeze quickly took her to Rame Head where she was gybed and the spinnaker was carried almost to the finishing line which was crossed at 1445.

Further back *Gull* reported heavy rain and squalls and a big tumble of sea, and at one time the crew had to hand the staysail and lower the gaff to ease her. Not

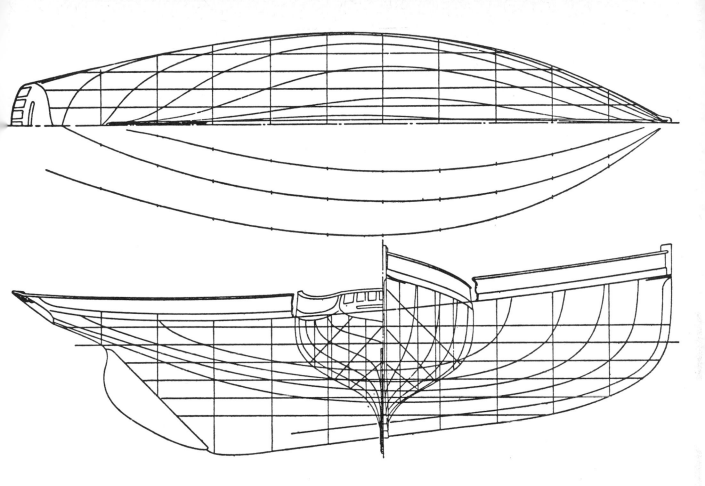

far behind her *Fulmar* hove-to for a while. But it was the slower boats – as was to happen so often in the future – which got the worst of the weather though initially their more leisurely gait, and the knowledge that they had no hope of winning, induced an atmosphere of relaxed enjoyment. *North Star's* dinghy was launched on the Monday so that fish could be obtained from a smack, and the next day it was launched again to visit *Jessie L* which lay becalmed nearby. Ahead of them *Banba IV* had a visit from a trawler whose skipper wanted to know what *Banba IV* was doing. One of the paid hands explained and the trawler skipper enquired who else the hand had on board with him. This produced a brooding silence but the question was eventually answered by another paid hand who said, *sotto voce*, 'a lot of bloody amateurs.' It was all very uncompetitive and enjoyable, and the only trouble facing the slower yachts at the time was whether their supplies would last. *North Star*, due to a leak, ran out of fresh water and was forced to catch rainwater when the weather broke. 'There were two vintages,' one of the crew

4   The original lines of *Jolie Brise* were never found but J. Laurent Giles, the designer, recorded them in 1928. LOA: 56 ft, LWL: 48 ft, beam: 15 ft 9 in, draught: 10 ft 2 in.

noted. 'The most nauseating, caught in a bucket at the foot of the spinnaker boom, was bottled and put aside in case of need. The remainder, from basins and oilskins, made excellent cocoa, though very unpleasant if drunk neat.'

But on the 20th the weather deteriorated and by the time *Jolie Brise* was crossing the finishing line the wind had increased to gale force for the three yachts still plugging their way towards the turning point. *North Star*, in fact, did not round until the morning of the sixth day, the 21st, and did so in driving rain and with a big ocean swell thundering against the foot of the lighthouse. *Banba IV*, having been hove-to during the night, was close behind but was then subjected to the full force of the gale which made her owner decide to run for the shelter of Baltimore. 'That is,' he later commented, if 'we did not lose the ship before we got there.' However, the wind moderated and a course

19

was once more set for Land's End with the owner's favourite piece of canvas, the square sail, set. During this heavy weather *Jessie L* gave up before rounding and put into Crosshaven under power.

While the slower boats were weathering this gale *Fulmar*, *Gull* and *Saladin* were having a close race of it between the Longships and Plymouth but at dawn on the 22nd with the Lizard abeam *Fulmar* was in the lead with the other two just in sight astern. In the last few hours *Gull* closed the gap considerably but *Fulmar* was second over the line at 1048 with *Gull* some three-quarters of an hour behind her. *Saladin* finished fourth at 1854. *North Star* finished next around midnight but was disqualified as a fierce ebb tide enticed her skipper to motor across the finishing line. The crew of *Banba IV*, made of sterner stuff, kedged when they arrived the next evening and retired below for supper. As they ate, a burst of cheering rang across the water from the clubhouse of the Royal Western — the response to George Martin announcing at dinner that the Ocean Racing Club had been formed. A breeze eventually took *Banba IV* over the line just before one o'clock in the morning, the buoy marking the line being found with the aid of a torch.

The first Fastnet Race was declared a resounding success by all the participants and *Gull*'s owner later wrote to Weston Martyr, who had sailed on *Jolie Brise*, that he'd been impressed with the atmosphere that the race had engendered once it was over.

I have raced a great deal and know the little petty feelings that sometimes prevail after the finish of an ordinary race. If one's boat has done excellently up to a point, and has then been pipped by horrible ill-luck by some rival, sometimes there is not a superabundance of joy. Contrast that with the congenial assembly in Plymouth, and do you not share with me the impression that the Ocean Race has merits beyond the most optimistic hopes of the originators, in that it brings out the best in us and creates a feeling of good fellowship amongst the competitors that no other class of racing is calculated to do so thoroughly and effectively.

Others obviously agreed with Donegan for not only was the Ocean Racing Club formed by popular acclaim but it was decided to race again in 1926. This, of course, brought up the vexed question again of what was the best course and *Banba IV*'s owner, H.R. Barrett, suggested that the country should be divided into four sections and that the race should be started each year from the home waters of the yacht which had won the previous year. It was an idea that appealed to Malden Heckstall-Smith and he thought

the east coast, the Channel, the Clyde, and the Forth, a suitable division and ideal areas from which to begin an ocean race. Other proposals were also put forward but after a good deal of discussion the Fastnet course was retained with the minor adjustment that in 1926 the start was to be made from Cowes, the Royal Yacht Squadron having obviously relented. On 1 February *The New York Times* reported that two American yachts, *Quita* and *Primrose IV*, were going to enter the race and at about the same time *Gull*'s owner urged that the British enter faster yachts. Otherwise, he warned, the Americans would win. 'Let me say,' he wrote, 'that I think we are rather inclined to overdo "seaworthiness." I know full well that I am laying myself open to strong criticism in expressing this opinion, but a race is a race for all that, and even though it lasts a week, an odd wet jacket is not likely to kill anyone.'

This comment probably was resented by most influential cruising yachtsmen, many of whom must still have eyed this new sport with a great deal of suspicion. Britain had a long tradition of building deep hulled, narrow-beamed craft, and yachtsmen brought up to sail these traditional designs in open water would have been strongly averse to changes just in order to make a yacht go faster. It took a decade or more for the true ocean racer to develop and even longer for the cruising attitudes of the majority of the crews to be eradicated. It was not until the 1960s, for example, that the traditional watch-keeping system of never disturbing the watch below except in an emergency was broken by the top-flight racing crews.

The Royal Engineers, at any rate, heeded Donegan's warning and acquired for themselves a much faster yacht, the 20-ton *Ilex*, designed by Charles Nicholson and built by Camper and Nicholson in 1899. Other entries that year included four which had raced in 1925: *Jolie Brise*, *Gull*, *Banba IV*, and *Saladin*. Besides *Ilex* there were four new entries: the American schooner, *Primrose IV*, designed by Alden; a new Fife cutter, *Hallowe'en*, owned by Colonel Baxendale; *Penboch*, a cutter owned by Robert Somerset; and *Altair*, a cutter owned — and raced — by Mrs Aitken Dick.

In the United States the Fastnet had obviously stirred some interest and though only *Primrose IV* eventually entered the race that year two young Americans, Warwick Tompkins and Alfred Payne, were so taken with the thought of crewing in the race that they paid their fares across the Atlantic on the off-chance of obtaining berths on one of the competitors. When Donegan heard that Tompkins had already sailed in the Bermuda Race and was a signaller he took him aboard and arranged a berth for Alfred Payne aboard *Saladin*.

The start was from Cowes on 14 August in sunshine and a smooth sea. The wind was moderate from the SW. *Jolie Brise* was first over the line after the gun had fired, followed by *Gull, Saladin, Primrose IV, Altair, Hallowe'en, Penboch, Ilex* and *Banba IV*. The American set a square sail and the rest hoisted spinnakers to starboard for the run down to the Spithead forts. From the forts it was a reach to Bembridge and as the wind became brisk the new bermudian-rigged *Hallowe'en* began to show the superiority of her rig and size and surged away from the rest of the fleet. This rather miffed the crew of *Saladin* which, up to that time, had been in the lead. Indeed they had hoisted a red ensign over the code letter T which in international code is an urgent two-flag signal meaning, 'do not pass ahead of me,' and were annoyed that not only *Hallowe'en* ignored it but *Jolie Brise, Gull, Ilex* and *Primrose IV* did as well.

It should be mentioned here that although *Hallowe'en* was a new boat she had not been built to the Ocean Racing Club's rule – which for 1926 had been altered slightly and simplified – and indeed more than one yachting journalist wondered whether Fife had ever even heard of it for *Hallowe'en* was severely taxed by it when racing in the Fastnet. She was first to finish that year in the remarkable time of 3 days, 19 hours, 5 minutes, a time which took many years to beat, yet she managed to finish only third on corrected time. The length of her overhangs and absence of deep bulwarks were two factors which worked against her and which resulted in her being the scratch yacht. A contemporary yachting writer commented that 'had Fife undertaken to build a yacht to fit the rule, he would have been able to design one which should easily beat *Hallowe'en* on time, though it does not follow that she would actually have been faster.'

The other yacht which drew a great deal of interest was naturally the American schooner. Owned by Frederick L. Ames of Boston, *Primrose IV* was a typical Alden design with a rounded bow and a short counter which resulted in very little overhang. This design, popular at the time in the United States, gave her a very good time allowance (over 28 hours on *Hallowe'en*) which both surprised and delighted her owner.

During the first night the wind came in from the WNW and the dawn was a red one – a timely warning of what was to come for some of the yachts. But at first

5 This was taken aboard *Saladin* during the second Fastnet. The owner, Ingo Simon, is at the wheel.

6 A converted Bristol Channel Pilot cutter, *Saladin* took part in the first two Fastnets, and again in 1929 when she came second.

the wind was maddeningly variable and at the Start *Saladin*, *Gull* and *Primrose IV* all got becalmed in the race which kicked up a nasty chop. Off Prawle in the dark *Saladin* was signalled by the Lloyd's station there. Prawle: 'What yacht is that?' Saladin: '*Saladin*.' Prawle: 'Are you in the Great Race?' Saladin: 'Yes.' Prawle: 'Good luck to you.' Saladin: 'How many yachts in race have passed ahead of us?' Prawle: 'We have not signalled any.' Saladin: 'American schooner *Primrose* just astern of us.' Prawle: 'Right. Good night.' Saladin: 'Good night. Thank you.'

Though the Prawle Point station had not spotted her *Hallowe'en* was in fact way out ahead and reached the Rock in the remarkably fast time of $61\frac{1}{2}$ hours rounding at 0100 on the Tuesday morning (16th). *Ilex* came next at 0830, then *Jolie Brise* at 1030 and *Gull* at 1415. There was then a gap of four hours before *Saladin* rounded at 1815, quickly followed by *Primrose IV* at 1830. During the day the wind had begun to rise and for the slower boats it was a slog up to the Rock. The nearer they got the harder it blew and at 2030 on the 17th *Banba IV* was forced to heave-to about 50 miles from the Rock. Visibility was very poor with flying patches of brownish-grey cloud overhead. *Penboch* within nine miles of the Fastnet lighthouse also hove-to for the night, as did *Altair*.

Those on the way back from the Rock also had a rough time. *Gull* was found to be leaking soon after she rounded and though she was pumped dry in 25 minutes the skipper suspected a leak. Not an encouraging thought with the night coming on, the glass falling rapidly, and the wind and sea rising. Then at 1830 on the Tuesday evening the stitching on the mainsail gave way and it had to be taken down and replaced by the trysail. It was then discovered that she was awash below again and it was decided to head for Baltimore.

By 2000 the wind and sea had risen considerably and the glass had dropped over three-tenths since *Gull* had rounded. It was a dark and stormy night and consequently no one could catch sight of the entrance light to Baltimore so Donegan was forced to bear away. By this time the seas had become enormous and *Gull* was taking them aboard heavily. The pump was working continuously but it could not cope and buckets were used. Eventually, they struggled into Crosshaven at 0700 the next morning and later found they had lost the caulking along the covering board and between the port deck outer planks. The American crew member, Warwick Tompkins, gave a graphic description of these few hair-raising hours.

The *Gull* was a plank-on-edge cutter of ancient vintage. She had a tremendous jackyard topsail, a terrific tiller, and a pack of wild Irishmen aboard

7 *Saladin* dried out. Her dimensions were: LOA: 49 ft, LWL: 43 ft, beam: 14 ft 8 in, draught: 8 ft.

8 *Gull* came third in the first Fastnet, but in the second she began to leak badly during a storm and was forced to put into Crosshaven in Ireland. 'She had a tremendous jackyard topsail,' wrote Warwick Tompkins, an American member of her 1926 crew, 'a terrific tiller, and a pack of wild Irishmen aboard her who flogged the life out of her.'

her who flogged the life out of her. . . . In thick weather we groped for Baltimore and when we got within what we estimated to be two miles and could not pick up the light we reluctantly gave up the heroic idea of beaching the *Gull* there, caulking her, and still finishing. (Yes, that's the sort of skipper and crew it was!) We hauled off for Queenstown (Cobh). We were close-hauled under trysail and storm jib with the wind coming down now from about No'east and that delightful Irish coast altogether too close under our lee. The seas were breaching clean over the old packet, and the spitfire jib – though we didn't know it till daylight – was pulling the runner eyebolt right out of the counter. We passed the Stag Rocks and they weren't more than two hundred yards to leeward; on the darkest, wildest sort of night they were plainly visible and audible, great and terrifying founts of spray just to leeward. This was possibly the closest escape I've ever had at sea and one of the few times my life has actually been in danger.

*Ilex*, too, had an eventful time when the wind rose. It was described light-heartedly enough by an intrepid crew member, but the Fastnet Race could on this occasion have easily ended in tragedy for the eventual winner.

On the way back from the Fastnet on 17/18 the wind became very strong, certainly gale force in

Gull

the gusts and it was decided that *Ilex* would move faster with a couple of reefs in the main. Accordingly, she was hove-to at 2330 and, like maggots from a cheese, the crew came on deck to reef. Reefing on a pitch dark night in a gale of wind is an exhilarating experience, certainly a rather novel one which, in the normal way, one does not lay oneself open to. Coming from the warmth below into a solid sheet of rain spray, with the shrill whine of a very high wind in the rigging and the welter of the sea with phosphorescent breaking wavetops all around was like coming into another world. Although the night was pitch dark, there was no need for light. All that was necessary was supplied by the extraordinary phosphorescence of the breaking water. The reefing proceeded according to plan until nearly completed when a sudden lurch and a wave sent overboard a hand who was aft on the counter. The ship being stationary, he had no difficulty in hanging on to the rail. The skipper, who was at the tiller, saw his predicament, made a dive to haul him out, and slipped over the side as well. The act of staying increased the midnight bathing party to three, a little variety being added by number three holding on to the main sheet instead of the rail.

All three got back on board, and so casually was the whole affair treated by them that some members of the crew did not know what had happened until the next day.

Of the other leaders the crews of both *Saladin* and *Primrose IV* discussed heaving-to during this dark and violent night, and *Jolie Brise* actually did so for five hours. The American schooner had blown out her balloon jib just after rounding the Rock and on the way back it seemed as if she might lose more than that. Luckily, *Primrose IV*'s canvas held and she had a magnificent run back to Plymouth, and on corrected time lost the race by only 13 minutes, 8 seconds to *Ilex* which finished at 2121 on the 18th over 12 hours after *Hallowe'en*. *Jolie Brise* was next in at 0404 but could manage no better than fifth place on corrected time, *Saladin* taking fourth place by over two hours.

But though these leaders had had a rough run back it was – as was to happen so often in the future – the smaller, slower boats which suffered the most. Long after *Hallowe'en* had crossed the line at Plymouth *Banba IV* and *Penboch* renewed their struggle to round the Rock, but *Altair*'s crew decided they'd had enough and made for the safety and comfort of Baltimore. For three days nothing was heard of her and two destroyers were dispatched to search for her. But eventually her owner telegrammed to say she was safe. *Banba IV* eventually made it round the Rock at

1230 with *Penboch* some 50 minutes behind her. *Banba IV* set off like a scalded cat and had the Longships abeam 25¾ hours after rounding the Rock. *Penboch*, however, was in no such hurry and after blowing out her second jib it was decided to heave-to again and have some tea. 'The state of the boat below was beyond description,' wrote the skipper who described the motion of his boat as being rather like that of a terrier shaking a rat, 'everything being on the floor in a saturated trodden mass of food, blankets, and broken glass.' However, once the crew had sorted themselves and the boat out *Penboch* got under way again and finished under six hours behind *Banba IV*.

So ended the second Fastnet Race. *Hallowe'en* had confounded her critics by coming in first in an incredibly short time and without losing her mast. However, the new bermudian sail, which had behaved so well throughout the race, for some reason went berserk near the finish. It tore its slides off the track, parted the halliard and clattered down onto the deck, and *Hallowe'en* had to finish under her trysail. Later, she was converted to gaff rig, or 'conventional rig' as it was then called. Perhaps the horrific stories which circulated after the race of the problems the crew had reefing her during it were not exaggerated.

---

If the 1926 race had its rough moments the 1927 one may possibly have had one or two calm ones. If it did, the 15 starters didn't notice them. The weather had been bad all that summer and it was decided by the committee to postpone the race if necessary. But when the boats came to the line at 1130 on Saturday, 13 August, the wind had dropped below gale force, though the day was dark, with heavy rain falling. Of the old-timers *Ilex* was at the starting line again, along with *Altair*, *Penboch* and *Jolie Brise* (under new ownership). *Saladin* had entered but did not start. The newcomers included two American schooners, *Nicanor* and *La Goleta*. *Nicanor*, an Alden schooner, had arrived in Cowes having just broken the Trans-Atlantic sailing record for her class, the passage from Boston to the Scillies having been made in 20 days, 7 hours. She must have seemed a formidable opponent to the motley collection of British yachts competing against her – motley because they included *Saoirse*, described variously as a square-rigged staysail schooner, a 'sketch,' or 'the smallest barquentine-rigged yacht afloat'; two cutters, *Tally Ho!* and *Content*, both of which were modelled on the Falmouth Quay punt; *Shira*, which followed the design of a Loch Fyne fishing boat; and *Maitenes*, a German designed-and-built ex-10 metre.

Diverse and original as these yachts were, interest again centred on the American entries. *La Goleta* was

9 *Ilex*, the 1926 Fastnet winner. The Sappers have never missed a Fastnet yet and they raced *Ilex*, with varying success, between 1926 and 1939.

also an Alden-designed schooner, but she was slightly smaller than *Nicanor* and had been built in England for her American owner, Ralph St L. Peverley, who was living there. She had only just been finished, and the Fastnet was her first race. She was to leak badly throughout it.

*Shira* was first across the starting line followed by *Penboch*, *Jolie Brise* and *Spica*. Although the wind at the beginning had dropped to a moderate southerly by the time the fleet had reached St Catherine's it was blowing hard. By then *Jolie Brise* was leading, with *Tally Ho!* second and *Nicanor* third. *Saoirse* went out into the Channel in the hope of getting a fairer wind but the others kept inshore and slugged into the wind which had veered to the sw kicking up a nasty sea. By 1530 *Penboch*'s crew decided it was time to reef and while they were doing this *Morwenna* and another yacht passed them running back to Cowes. It was

known later that *Morwenna*'s dinghy had shifted on deck and had crushed one of the crew. The other boat was probably *Shira* which sprang a leak early on.

By 0400 the next morning *Tally Ho!* had the Portland light abeam. *Nicanor* was ahead to windward, *Jolie Brise* was close to the shore off Teignmouth, *Ilex* was abeam and *La Goleta* was on the weather quarter. However, in the next four hours the smaller American schooner made a lot of progress and by 0800 *Tally Ho!* was a long way astern and *La Goleta* split tacks with her fellow American, *Nicanor*, but *Nicanor* gained in the next few hours by standing out while *La Goleta* stayed inshore. The wind was less strong at this time and the sea had moderated. For a while *La Goleta* was able to carry her topsails but by the afternoon the wind had increased again. This obviously suited *Tally Ho!* because she began to close with *La Goleta* and off the Start passed her. By dawn the next morning, Monday, she was three miles to the westward of the Eddystone lighthouse, with the wind blowing in very fierce gusts from the NNW. She had already overtaken *Nicanor* and *Ilex* but *Jolie Brise* was still ahead. Suddenly, just as *Tally Ho!* was approaching the Manacles, her crew saw a yacht approaching them. 'To our surprise it turned out to be the *Jolie Brise*,' wrote Lord Stalbridge, the owner of *Tally Ho!*, after the race. 'We could not think what had happened, but surmised that the weather was too much for her off the Lizard, and this proved to be correct. She sailed close to us and when we asked her what it was like she said she had had to heave-to and that it was too bad. Now was our chance, as, knowing from experiences in a gale in the Bay of Biscay what a wonderful sea-boat the *Tally Ho!* was, and also confident in our sails and gear, we thought that by reefing her down and making things ship-shape we might be able to weather the Lizard, and if so would catch the tide and be a tide ahead of any of our competitors who failed to do so.'

This the crew proceeded to do and though one big sea hit her, which made her shudder from stem to stern and sent spray clean over the mainsail, the Lizard was weathered by 1600. As it was obvious that none of the others had been able to catch the tide, and as the wind had backed round to the NW and had increased in strength, it was decided, rather than face a foul tide and a head wind off the Longships, to run into Newlyn roadsteads for the night. That same night *La Goleta* hove-to under the lee of the Lizard and bided her time.

The rest of the fleet, however, dropped out of the race one by one. Faced with a gale force headwind and rough seas they gave up rather in the manner in which Loomis and Worth had feared competitors within easy reach of shelter would. Loomis later stated that he thought *Jolie Brise*'s retirement, or defection as he called it, was a tragedy. She had made, he said, a fair start towards becoming a national institution, like the King's yacht, *Britannia*. Her withdrawal from the race was, he said, a blot on her escutcheon. The new owners of *Jolie Brise*, however, did not seem unduly repentant about their action. The crew, they said afterwards, had not a dry rag between them and none of them had had any appreciable sleep since leaving Cowes.

*Penboch* did not even get as far as the Lizard. Knowing there would be a big sea off Start Point the owner had tried to get out into the Channel. But as the shore was left behind, getting to windward became harder and harder. *Penboch* crashed into every wave, dipping her bowsprit half its length into the water. She clawed her way to windward too slowly to catch the tide round the Start so her owner decided to take her into Dartmouth to rest the crew and wait for a favourable tide. But the wind increased as they lay at anchor, and they never re-entered the race. *Thalassa*, which lost her staysail on the Sunday and her second

jib on the Monday, at least tried to get back in the fray after putting into Torquay to get her sails repaired. But after hitting what her owner described as a 'super squall' he came to the conclusion it would be impossible to weather Start Point, and put into Dartmouth. *Nicanor* also started again after putting into Falmouth for a day but then had to give up after breaking a gaff. *Nellie* and *Saoirse*, after tacking across the Channel, found themselves, three days later, more or less where they'd started from, and both decided discretion was the better part of valour. They were among the first of many Fastnet competitors who found that it rarely pays to go out into the Channel.

The editor of *Yachting Monthly* happened to be on board *Saoirse* with his wife, Peter, and the latter protested indignantly over the decision to retire. 'We let her steer in the end to work off her disgust at "giving up the ghost",' said the editor, who, incidentally, added to the number of labels on his host's boat by deciding she was not a yacht at all but a windjammer. 'Steering was heavy work for the following seas towered high above the helmsman's head. But the skipper left Peter at the wheel, "because," he told the rest of the crew, "she's the best helmsman I've got".' Other retirements included *Spica*, with a leak; *Altair*, with a split mainsail; and *Ilex*, having also sprung a leak and had her headsails blown away.

The experience of *Maitenes*' crew is perhaps typical of the appalling conditions that faced the yachts that year. Reefing under such conditions became a major undertaking. Her owner, W.B. Luard, wrote:

We crawled for'ard in a blackness that turned to pitch, clinging to rails and rigging as she dived into seas. We had to battle and fight, grope and fumble, shout and yell. The doctor, at the helm, handled her consummately. We settled halliards and manned the roller gear. A shout from aft, flung to leeward by the wind, faded to a whisper, and Graham, tearing for'ard, cried that the sail was split by the clew. . . . We pulled, we hove, we strained, we tugged, we shortened down inch by inch, foot by foot, then the pawl, slipping, destroyed, in a flash, two rolls before we realised what had happened. We cursed, swore, attacked the job again with the desperation of despair. In the bows, Lister and the squadron-leader struggled to shift jibs, working to their waists in water. Caught suddenly by a screaming gust, it took charge, thrashing like a flail with loud volleying cracks. They fought its flogging fury, scrambling and muzzling it into passivity. By the time they had set the small jib, we had rolled her down to

10 This photograph of *Tally Ho!* was taken 11 years after she won the 1927 Fastnet, but her rig remained essentially the same.

two reefs; and the whole crew, clinging to the kicking boom, rove a preventive lacing, and hardened it down for a full due. Two hours had passed – two hours that seemed like minutes.

*Maitenes*, unburdened of some of her canvas, now moved splendidly, but then, after sheltering for several hours under the lee of Berry Head, a new crisis developed off the Start.

A succession of overwhelming blows, unleashed from the heart of the storm, exploded upon the ship. She heeled till the water swirled over the cockpit coaming, then righted suddenly. It was over before we realised what had happened: the

mainsail had ripped from leach to luff. Out of control, we paid off broadside to the seas, with no steerage way. An immense comber, reeling from the blackness, towered high above us. We held our breaths. The ship rose on its side. 'Hold on for your lives,' I shouted, and the next moment we were flung on our beam ends. A wall of water hit our exposed bilge, and we careered over till we thought we should capsize, the whole crew clinging like mad to anything solid. Then we were flung back, turning stern to the sea.

A knockdown in modern ocean racing is not too uncommon – no less that 48 per cent of the 235 owners who replied to the RORC's questionnaire after the 1979 race said they experienced one during that race – especially one which does not go beyond the horizontal. But for a yacht to suffer a knockdown in those days, when yachts had long, deep keels and were of a very much heavier displacement than the modern ocean racer, must have been a most unusual and disturbing event for the crew. Yet they refused to give up, and bent on a trysail. But when dawn came – 'a heavy dawn, full of spit and malice' – it was obvious they were making no headway, so they ran back and anchored under the lee of Start Point. All day the gale raged, and all that night, but by dawn it had eased and once more *Maitenes* was pointed west. But at dusk that day they were becalmed off Plymouth and all that night they drifted aimlessly with the tide. The next day was Wednesday, and the sun shone briefly. Then at noon the glass started to drop again. A council of war was held and it was decided that with the weather again deteriorating they had little chance of getting to the Fastnet Rock under trysail, and it was decided to abandon the race. At Plymouth they were told they'd been given up for lost.

The storm left three yachts in the race, *Tally Ho!*, *La Goleta*, and *Content*. But *Content* was soon the victim of bad navigation. 'We have been most unfortunate in having to retire through nothing more serious than a defective compass,' explained Lord Cranbrook, one of the crew, afterwards, 'and were it not for the fact that the owner was not aboard, we would have in all probability trusted to our luck and continued in the race.'

Many years later one Fastnet crew said they found it a positive advantage to be without their skipper! But perhaps in those days if you got lost in a boat which didn't belong to you the polite thing to do was retire, which is what *Content*'s skipper did when he found himself some 50 miles off course when the Irish coast was sighted. Up to that time *Content* must have had a fair chance of winning the race. With only two other boats left racing, she had been three hours behind *La*

*Goleta* off the Longships which meant she had about 17 hours of her handicap in hand over the American schooner and not much less in hand over *Tally Ho!* Loomis, who was the navigator on *La Goleta*, later dismissed Lord Cranbrook's excuse for retiring and put the blame fairly and squarely on *Content's* nagivator. 'The atrocious landfall is ascribed to a compass error, but the run from Land's End to Fastnet is only 170 miles and to miss it by 50 miles means an error of nearly two points. Prior to taking departure from the Longships *Content* had to beat to westward for 200 miles, closing with definite landmarks every few miles, and how a compass error of two points during these four days of beating escaped the attention of the navigator is beyond my comprehension.'

Whatever the reason for *Content's* retirement, *Tally Ho!* and *La Goleta* were left to battle it out between them and what makes the 1927 Fastnet such a memorable race is that is just what they did. 'In the whole history of yachting in British waters,' commented one magazine afterwards, 'there has never been so hard a fight between two yachts over so long a course and under such weather conditions.' They raced neck and neck from the time they passed the Longships on the outward journey till they crossed the finishing line at Plymouth within 50 minutes of one another.

Having spent the Monday night anchored in Newlyn roadsteads *Tally Ho!* was under way the next morning by 0630 in a moderating wind, and all that day, after passing the Longships where a big sea was still running, they beat out into the Irish Sea, but by 2200, with the wind now backed to the SW, they were at last able to lay the rhumb line course for the Rock. At dawn on Wednesday a white sail far astern was sighted. At the time *Tally Ho!*'s crew thought it was *Nicanor*. By 1500 she was abeam of them in a fine reaching wind, but too far away to identify. Later, she altered course and passed ahead of *Tally Ho!* to the west. By now the weather had begun to deteriorate again and the visibility was so poor that though the Rock was reckoned·to be only three miles away it could not be seen and there was no sight of land. However, shortly afterwards the lighthouse lit up and the vague outline of the land could then be seen. The schooner to the westwards had in the meantime altered course and at 2200 came alongside and hailed *Tally Ho!* To the Englishmen's surprise it was not *Nicanor* but *La Goleta*, and they then knew there was no one ahead of them. *Tally Ho!* drew slowly ahead of *La Goleta* and at 0120 on Thursday morning she rounded the Rock, about quarter of a mile in front of the Americans.

The glass on *Tally Ho!* now registered a low 29.3 and it was obvious to Lord Stalbridge that they were in the centre of a depression. 'I fear that standing into a lee shore in thick weather and a falling glass,' wrote Lord Stalbridge about rounding the Rock that night, 'was not an act of great seamanship. However, you cannot make omelettes without breaking eggs; we were out to win the Fastnet race if we could, so we were out to take some chances, and luckily they came off. No sooner were we clear of the Fastnet, than it began to blow hard from the NE, and from 2 to 4 a.m. that morning I think we had as big a bucketing as at any time, as the wind was against the sea. Yet we had to drive her along for all we were worth, not only to beat *La Goleta*, but to get sea-room. And drive her we did, more under water than over I fear, but by 4 a.m. it had got too bad and we had to heave-to and reef again.'

Up to the time of rounding the Fastnet Rock *La Goleta* had had as rough a time as any of the other yachts. Yet, despite persistently leaking decks, she stayed at sea while the others sought refuge, though on the Tuesday the crew took her into Mounts Bay and dropped all sails in order to tighten the new rigging which had been badly stretched in the gale. After rounding the Rock, and knowing they would have to have *Tally Ho!* five hours astern at Plymouth if they were to win, *La Goleta*'s crew hung on to as much canvas as they dared for as long as they dared. Two men clung to the wheel during this hair-raising passage back to the English coast and at one point they logged 14 miles in an hour and 20 minutes. Complete disaster nearly struck during this run back when one of the crew, W.S. Tallman from Pittsburgh, was washed overboard. 'At the time the schooner was logging ten knots,' wrote Weston Martyr, who was on board, 'and I expect Mr Tallman understood perfectly that the race could not be stopped at that stage for any man overboard, even if he did come from Pittsburgh. In any case he must have got a mighty good grip of something for it took six strong men and a watch tackle to get him back again. He came back smiling too with his cigar still between his teeth. But the lower half of him was stripped and both his sea boots had gone.'

At 1700 that day *Tally Ho!* was abeam and then she dropped behind. But *La Goleta*'s crew were finding it harder and harder to keep driving her at such a pace and by 2000 it became clear she was carrying more canvas than was good for her. For two more hours they hung on, but at 2200 it was decided to douse the reaching jib and the main topmast staysail. 'This meant running before a small hurricane and some tremendous breaking seas with three hands out on the bowsprit,' Weston Martyr commented. 'To jibe is simple under such conditions and to jibe or broach-to then meant three dead men. They stowed that jib and Loomis says he has never in his life seen such a

11 Alfred Loomis took this photograph on board *La Goleta* during the 1927 Fastnet, the year when only two boats completed the course.

together (they really did, for this once) contrived to give us the rottenest spell of weather I have ever encountered.'

wonderful piece of helmsmanship as the owner perpetrated on that occasion. Al was in a good position to judge too. He was on the bowsprit.'

After running by the lee all that last night in order to clear the Runnelstone, *Tally Ho!* was still in sight the next morning, and the Americans then knew that barring accidents they were beaten. Nevertheless, they averaged eight knots from the Runnelstone to the finishing line and crossed exactly 42 minutes ahead of the British yacht. But *Tally Ho!* won on corrected time by just over four and a quarter hours.

Loomis later compared the rigours of this race with those of the Bermuda Race. The latter he called a joyous dash from the temperate zone of Long Island to the tropical climate of the Bermudas. The Fastnet, on the other hand, 'is a desperate trek to the North Pole, around it and back among the ice floes of the Irish Sea to a finish in the sub-Arctic zones of Plymouth. As to the strength of wind I regretfully give the palm to the six days of the 1927 Fastnet Race. I say regretfully because, being patriotically minded, I hate to admit that any other country can offer worse weather than we have in America. But England and Ireland working

It would have been reasonable to suppose that after the rigours of the 1927 race there might have been some lack of enthusiasm about the Fastnet fixture the following year. But not a bit of it. For the first time a French boat, *L'Oiseau Bleu*, entered the race, as did two American schooners, *Nina* and *Mohawk*, both of which had recently completed the Trans-Atlantic Race to Spain. Additionally, there were nine British yachts: *Jolie Brise* and *Ilex* came to the line once more, and there were five new entries. These were: *Lassie*, a 29-ton, narrow-hulled yawl; *Neptune*, a large cutter known for her heavy weather performance; *Amaryllis*, a yawl which had once cruised around the world and which was now owned by the Royal Naval College, Dartmouth; another yawl, *Noreen*, a converted 12-metre which, of course was at her best in light weather; and three cruising cutters, *Magnet*, *Mamango*, and *Viking*. All the entries had a minimum waterline length of 35feet as the Ocean Racing Committee had decided, after the heavy casualty list of the previous year, that the smaller yachts had been too severely punished for them to be allowed to enter again. Instead the Channel Race was instigated by the Club, and this proved a most successful fixture for the smaller yachts.

Interest was again focused on the two American entries, and on *Nina*, a 50-foot LWL double staysail schooner* in particular, for she was revolutionary in design and already had an awesome reputation for speed, having won the Queen of Spain's Cup in the Trans-Atlantic Race to Santander earlier in the summer. Owned by Paul Hammond, a well-known American yachtsman, *Nina* had been designed by Starling Burgess to the Ocean Racing rule governing the Trans-Atlantic Race. She was built for the express purpose of winning races. This was an entirely new approach to the sport so far as the British were concerned. Yachting journalists were still prone to report the Ocean Race under the cruising section of their magazine and while it was considered great fun to race whatever yacht you happened to own at the time, to build one especially to win races seemed, to some Englishmen at any rate, to be taking the whole thing rather too seriously. To be truthful a lot of English yachtsmen's ideas on sportsmanship were as outmoded as their yachts so far as ocean racing was concerned and in *Nina* there appeared for the first time in British waters the concept of the all-out ocean racer. But it was not only the new concept which jarred with some Englishmen but the amount of money which had been lavished on *Nina*, and there were the usual mutterings at yacht club bars about the almighty dollar trying to buy success. In fact, *Nina* was very costly by the standards of the day but most of the money had gone in getting her built quickly and in the special fittings in which both her designer and owner liked to indulge.

*Nina* was certainly lavishly fitted out and though equipped with 11 two-gear winches on deck and four ratchet mast winches she had to have a crew of 11 to handle the complicated rigging and canvas, many more than would have been carried on a British yacht of comparable size. Another British member of the crew, B.R. Waite, later described *Nina*'s rig in some detail.

*Nina* set a jib and boom staysail, the latter called a jumbo, in her fore triangle. Aft of her mainmast a Bermudian mainsail. Between the two masts a variety of sails of all sorts of shapes and sizes can be set. . . .

When Advance adopted the staysail rig in America, her owner commenced his experiments with a staysail hanked to a stay running from about four feet above the deck on the after side of the foremast, to about two-thirds of the way up the fore side of the mainmast. This sail was quite naturally christened the 'Advance' staysail. When the sail plan of *Nina* was got out, this sail was called by its old square-rigged name, the mainstaysail, but the designation of 'Advance' was given to those of the upper staysails which were quadrilateral. *Nina* carried a large selection of staysails. They were: the short hoist upper staysail, the Queen, the Advance, Heavy Advance, Wide Advance, Vanderbilt, the Balloon maintopmast staysail, generally known as the Golwobbler, and the main balloon staysail, now known as the Nina.

A description of these sails is more easily achieved by sketches than by words; the accompanying sketches may assist the reader who may care to try and sort out the various staysails carried by this remarkable boat.

[Fig. 12] shows the small triangular Queen set above the main staysail. It will be noticed that this latter sail and also the jumbo are boomsails and work on a horse.

In [Fig. 13] the working Advance is shown, the larger Advance, the heavy, and wide, being shown dotted. Below these Advance staysails a Vanderbilt is set. This sail has its luff run up on a track in the usual Bermudian fashion, the head is set flying, the main staysail halyard being used, and the foot is loose.

The Vanderbilt can only be used to advantage on a reach; since it has to be set on the lee side of the mainstay.

[Fig. 14] shows the main balloon staysail on *Nina*; the tack of this sail is run out on the jib outhaul, the throat is hoisted to the foremast head on the lee bightstay, and the head sent up to the main top by the staysail head halyard. This sail is still in the experimental stage from all accounts, and the sheeting to the mainboom has not proved very satisfactory. . . .

The dotted sail in [Fig. 14] is the normal balloon main topmast staysail, shortened to Golwobbler by the crew of *Nina*. Both these sails are made of balloon canvas, and in quite a light wind it is necessary to take the single sheet to a winch.

The start to the 1928 race took place in a moderate westerly breeze with *Ilex* first over the line a couple of

*note: Although described as a schooner Sherman Hoyt who skippered her in the 1928 Fastnet later wrote that she was no such thing, adding that it was just as well, given the amount of criticism flying around of *Nina*'s rig after the race, that at the time this was not known. 'Under the Universal Rule,' he wrote, 'a schooner's mainmast shall not be stepped farther forward than 55 per cent of her waterline length from the forward end of the waterline. *Nina*'s mainmast is a very few inches forward of that point. Hence, while technically not a schooner, neither was she a sloop, with less than 62 per cent of her sail area aft of the mainmast; nor a yawl nor ketch, with her tallest mast the aftermast. Perhaps Alfred Loomis's designation of her as "a two-masted cutter" described her rig correctly.'

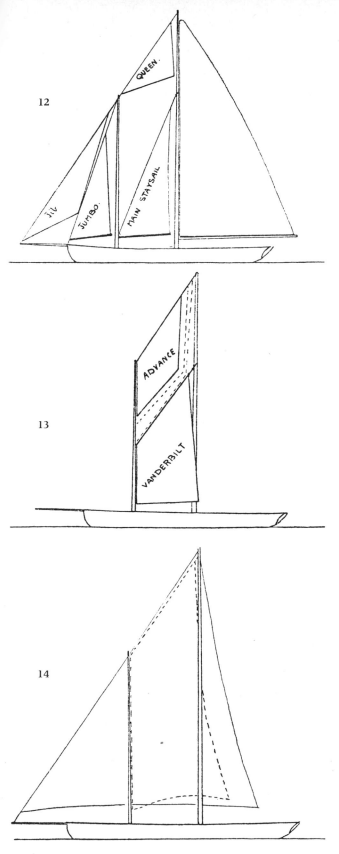

12

13

14

lengths ahead of *Neptune, Mohawk, Nina* and *Jolie Brise. Viking* lagged badly and did not cross the line until four and a half minutes after the gun had gone. At Ryde pier *Neptune* had a lead of nearly two minutes from *Mohawk*, the whole fleet, with every stitch of canvas aloft, making slow progress against a foul tide. At this point *Nina* was six-and-a-half minutes astern of the leader and Weston Martyr, who was on board, began to wonder about the much vaunted schooner.

At first we aboard *Nina* did not like the look of things at all. For *Ilex, Neptune*, and *Mohawk* ran away from us steadily; *L'Oiseau Bleu* passed us to windward; *Jolie Brise* slipped through our lee; while *Lassie* came up from astern and went ahead, going two feet to our one. Off Ryde Pier *Nina* was in seventh place, six and a half minutes astern of *Neptune*. To me this seemed very dreadful. I turned a troubled face toward our skipper (no less a personage than C. Sherman Hoyt) and he, observing me, smiled a most tranquil smile and winked. Then, 'Wait awhile,' he said. I waited. As we neared the eastern end of the Wight our skipper aroused himself from, apparently, a pleasant dream. He uttered commands, and for some minutes my attention was engaged in battling with acres of balloon maintopmast staysail and in setting something called a 'Broad Advance' in its stead. When I came to I found *Nina* sailing at seven knots right into the eye of the wind, and I looked around for our competitors. Incredible as it may seem there were no competitors there! It is true there was a sail or two in sight. *Mohawk* was hull down on our lee quarter and beyond her, if you looked hard enough, you could see some scattered sails. But as competitors, *qua* competitors, the other boats had faded right out of the picture as soon as *Nina* came on the wind.

Sherman Hoyt, who had been asked by Hammond to take *Nina* on the Fastnet, as he himself had to return to New York, must have been acting the reassuring skipper in front of his English crew member for he had never sailed *Nina* before the race and had had only two days in which to familiarise himself with the radical rig. Weston Martyr also did not mention that some of *Nina*'s initial tardiness was caused by an unnamed British entry which persisted in luffing the American. 'With some 650 miles to go,' wrote Hoyt afterwards, 'he would put his helm hard down without warning and shoot for us. Naturally we would have to respond in some confusion and drop further back. Fortunately in one of his later attempts he found one of his compatriots between us, and was most thoroughly and emphatically cursed out as an unspeakably silly fool.' *Neptune* also tried luffing the

other American entry but promptly broke her spin-naker outhaul. There was also trouble on *Nina* in the navigator's department. Hammond had asked War-wick Tompkins to join *Nina* from Paris as navigator but he and Hoyt did not hit it off. Someone forgot to wind the chronometers and they were restarted inaccurately, and later the skipper's confidence in the navigation was not enhanced when he was given a fix which placed *Nina* some 40 miles inside the French coastline. Hoyt later related in his memoirs that during the first night at sea an unfortunate gybe all standing swept away the yacht's one and only taffrail log, and that he then took over the navigating which had to be done by dead reckoning. (Waite, however, says that the log was not lost until they were nearer the Rock and as his was a contemporary account it is probably the more accurate of the two.)

During the race the crew of *Nina* changed staysails no less than 23 times — not unusual nowadays to change headsails that number of times but so unusual in 1928 that every account of the race mentions this fact — and quite a proportion of these must have been made as the American schooner sailed down channel towards the Longships at which point she became becalmed. Later the wind came in from the south and more sail changing took place with the jib, jumbo and

15   The start of the 1928 Fastnet. From left to right: *Neptune*, *Mohawk*, *Nina*.

heavy Advance being lowered and replaced with the Golwobbler and a balloon jib, and a course was then laid for the Seven Stones. The lightship was passed at 1145 on the Friday, 48 hours after the start, and *Nina* was close enough to it for some of the crew to lob oranges and apples aboard it, and this led to an amiable argument on the respective merits of cricket and baseball. As one of the baseball enthusiasts managed to hit *Nina*'s mainsail while trying to throw a piece of fruit the 200 yards to the lightship the British crew members claimed that this proved cricket was far superior.

By 2200 that night *Nina* was over the Labadie Bank and soon after the wind increased. Out of sight of land and without a log Hoyt must have found the problem of pinpointing the Rock quite a headache. Later he wrote:

The only other method we had of reckoning our speed was by a gadget worked in some mysterious manner by valves, trapdoors or mirrors, I forget exactly which. It recorded the speed in miles per hour on a dial in the cockpit. Unfortunately, the dial never registered less than six and a half in a calm, and worked up from that to a maximum of nine. Far be it from me to cast aspersions on this output of science, but being unable to grasp the principle on which it worked, and finding no one on board who did, we were perforce obliged to fall back on our sense of smell to find the Fastnet. Careful calculations, or perhaps one should say wild guesses, were made every half hour as to our mean speed, and by 0700 a rift in the clouds let a little ray of sunshine through, which showed up the white lighthouse on the rock right under our bows. We sent our name by semaphore to the keeper on the rock, and he, stout fellow, flagged back the good news that we were first round.

Without the log it was difficult if not impossible to gauge the distance made good but a course was set for the Runnelstone or as close to it as the wind allowed. At 1210 *Mohawk* was passed making for the Rock 'snoring along under balloon canvas for the mark, and a fine sight she made with a bone in her teeth and the sun on her canvas.' Early on the Sunday the wind fell light again and became variable, but in the afternoon a squall came up which brought heavy rain with it. The wind, however, refused to settle and *Nina*'s course, as well as her sails, had to be changed several times. But by the evening it began to blow steadily from the west and with balloon jib, wide Advance, whole mainsail, and a spinnaker set *Nina* started making a steady ten knots and this she maintained until Plymouth Sound was entered. Here, the skipper, his temper already probably frayed from navigating, had difficulty in finding the finishing line which ran between the flagstaff on the King's Harbour Master's house and North Drake's Island buoy. Hoyt wrote:

This involved threading our way several miles up the harbor, in which I had never been before, and working our way up a zig-zag channel with more blinking 'boys' than I ever expect to have to identify. Of course it was night, pitch dark, and blowing a moderate gale. To add to my perturbation, I, who had never before had to resort to glasses, suddenly discovered that in the dim light I could barely decipher the indistinct print of my Admiralty chart, and where in hell was North Drake Island? Poor Martyr and Waite tried to explain to me that 'North Drake's Island Buoy' meant a 'boy' north of Drake's Island, and that there was no such thing as North Drake's Island which I was vainly trying to locate on the chart. Eventually, with me completely exhausted and in a very bad temper, *Nina* was greeted with a gun from the shore and we had apparently to me, and certainly to the satisfaction of my two-Englishmen, finished in the lead.

In fact *Nina* crossed the line some 18 minutes after midnight on the Monday morning, and won the fourth Fastnet by over five hours on corrected time from the other American entry, *Mohawk*.

Some of the other competitors ran into trouble very early on. The French yacht, *L'Oiseau Bleu*, clung grimly to *Nina* when the latter left Spithead and this tenacity attracted the attention of those on board the American schooner. 'This little ship,' commented Waite later, 'was putting up an amazing performance, our French friends were certainly driving her, and it was a gallant sight to see her forefoot leaping out of the water as she plugged into the head seas. We were allowing *L'Oiseau Bleu* $9\frac{3}{4}$ hours, and had their ship been as stout a vessel as her crew were gallant seamen, given ordinary luck, this craft would have been a very real danger to us.' But luck — that essential ingredient for any Fastnet winner — was not with them and the fierce pace set by *Nina* soon began to tell on the French entry. A small leak off St Catherine's — caused by grounding at some point early in the race — became a really serious one off the Needles, and *L'Oiseau Bleu* had to retire. *Lassie* also hit trouble early on. Before even passing St Catherine's the tack wire parted while the crew were sweating down on the topsail tack tackle, and a little later the topmast split when the hook on the weather shroud tackle parted. The topsail and flying jib were handed and the broken topmast eventually housed. This seemed to have little effect on her speed and she managed to hold her own with *Jolie Brise* whose crew later reported that *Lassie* seemed actually to increase her speed with less canvas.

When lighter weather came the next day *Lassie*'s topmast was hoisted six feet or so, so that the flying jib could be set but the going was slow and the Lizard was not abeam until 0600 on the third day. To urge her along the crew managed to rig the topsail on a small spar normally used as a storm spinnaker boom, and when the balloon spinnaker needed repairing it was patched with a napkin. The crew showed their resourcefulness in keeping *Lassie* going as fast as possible but on the Saturday, the fourth day out, the spinnaker was kept up too long and, in a sudden gust that shifted two points, it was taken aback and flung aft. The sail was ripped into tatters and the boom broke. Poor visibility made navigating difficult and at 0935 on the Sunday a fishing boat was hailed and a bearing on the Fastnet Rock was requested. Much to the relief of the navigator the bearing proved identical to *Lassie*'s course, and 15 minutes later the lighthouse loomed out of the mist — a white, desolate pillar. It took until 1230 to round, however, as the wind was now light and contrary, but once *Lassie* had turned for home it freshened and steadied, and the distance from the Rock to the finishing line was covered in 34 hours,

40 minutes. This gave *Lassie* a very creditable sixth place on corrected time.

*Neptune*, ahead of *Lassie*, rounded the Rock on the Saturday in less clement weather and accompanied by what, as one of the crew recorded, appeared to be gunfire. 'August 18: the wind remained on the quarter all day and by evening we were hoping to sight the Fastnet, but with a falling barometer, heavy rain, and very poor visibility we were feeling very doubtful. It was spotted, however, when nearly abeam, and at 2330 we rounded the rock, thus completing the first stage of the race. No sooner had we done so however than the report of a gun, and in a few minutes another, gave us a considerable fright, but to our great relief it turned out to be merely a fog signal.' *Neptune* eventually finished third behind *Nina* and *Mohawk*, but dropped to fourth place on corrected time.

*Ilex*, like *Lassie*, also broke her topmast but nevertheless managed to finish fifth, and was also placed fifth on corrected time. *Mohawk*, after coming in second, was beaten into third place on corrected time by *Jolie Brise* despite the latter being becalmed in Mounts Bay for several hours on the way to the Rock. *Magnet*, *Amaryllis*, and *Mamango* were the Thursday tail-enders. In fact there seems to be doubt whether *Mamango* finished at all and it is probable that, like *Noreen*, *Viking* and *L'Oiseau Bleu*, she retired.

It had been a mixed race for weather, with variable winds and poor visibility, and then strong winds towards the finish for the leading boats which obliged both *Jolie Brise* and *Neptune* to take in two reefs some 30 miles west of the Longships. But the race undeniably belonged to *Nina* and on corrected time she was over five hours ahead of *Jolie Brise*. If *Mohawk* had not attempted what was to become that well-tried but rarely successful tactic of close reaching across to the French coast instead of hugging the British one she might have given her fellow American a closer battle. But, as was to happen so often in the future, when *Mohawk* tacked back across the Channel 11 hours later the crew found themselves almost in the same position as when they'd started. But they then drove her hard and still managed to round second, seven hours behind *Nina*. A remarkable performance under the circumstances. *Neptune*, too, with better luck, could have given *Nina* a close race for at the Lizard she was only two hours behind the American boat which on corrected time meant they were just about level pegging. But at Land's End she was becalmed for ten hours against *Nina*'s one.

*Nina*'s win caused a spate of correspondence and articles in the yachting press. Weston Martyr opened it by writing an article headed 'Why the Americans Win – and How We Can,' and provocatively calling the Fastnet Cup the *Nina*'s Cup. 'Next year,' he trumpeted, 'we have got to beat the *Nina* and any of *Nina*'s sisters which will surely be built to defend the *Nina*'s Cup. We have got to do this thing, if only for the sake of our credit and our self-respect. And the only way we can do it is to go about the business with even more spirit and determination than the Americans showed this year.'

This provoked a long letter from the American owner of *La Goleta*, Ralph St L. Peverley, who revealed he was more English than most Englishmen in his sporting attitudes. Read now, his arguments seem those of Colonel Blimp, but he had many supporters of them when he stated that the Fastnet Race should be preserved for those cruising yachts which wished to race occasionally, and that 'racing machines,' as he called them, should be definitely discouraged. Otherwise, he warned, the Fastnet could degenerate into a stale duel like the America's Cup, 'until perhaps a bad year like 1927 comes along and there is an accident that will kill the sport of ocean racing.' In the light of the 1979 race, he has perhaps been proved right to a very limited degree but it is difficult to see how he hoped to preserve the race, and its atmosphere of jollity and comradeship, in the form in which the early ones had been sailed. *Nina* exposed the fallacy that the Fastnet could be preserved for those who prized 'splendid comradeship and good fellowship' above speed and the will to win, and many people did not like the fact that she had done so.

The controversy aroused that old man of the sea, Uffa Fox – though of course he wasn't old in 1928 – who promptly designed an ocean racer which he was sure would beat *Nina* and confessed in a letter that when he first read Weston Martyr's renaming of the Fastnet Cup he had wanted to punch his nose. 'My racing flag is, as you know, the skull and crossbones, which means that we are fighters out for someone's blood.'

The feelings of American yachtsmen reading this correspondence are not hard to imagine and it was not long before Sherman Hoyt wrote to the editor of *Yachting Monthly* on behalf of them. 'I feel that you should be told frankly what an unfortunate effect certain articles and letters have had over here on yachtsmen generally and particularly on those who have the future and good of ocean racing most closely at heart,' and went on to give a long and reasoned explanation of how and why *Nina* was built and raced. His letter was placed before the Committee of the Ocean Racing Club who were quick to respond, and their feelings about Sherman Hoyt were quickly established in the first paragraph of their reply. 'I have been asked by my Flag Officers,' wrote the Hon. Secretary, 'to inform you that you have been unanimously elected Rear-Commodore of the Ocean Racing

**16** Paul Hammond's radically designed *Nina*, the first American yacht to win a Fastnet. Sherman Hoyt skippered her in the 1928 race and she was an easy winner.

Club,' and the letter then went on to disassociate the club from opinions expressed in some parts of the yachting press which it dubbed 'ill-informed, prejudiced, and even unsportsmanlike.' Far from discouraging the building of boats to ocean race, it was the club's hope, the letter stated, that more would be built both in Britain and in the United States. Thus the pattern for the future was set, but that did not prevent hostility towards the new sport of ocean racing being openly expressed in the press, often from influential people. Brooke Heckstall-Smith, for instance, was Secretary of the Yacht Racing Association, and he wrote a most critical article about ocean racing in *The Daily Telegraph*.

The fact that there were no American entries for the 1929 race could have been the end result of this heated correspondence. But it is more likely that the cause of their absence was because no Trans-Atlantic Race took place that year. Whatever the reason, their non-appearance, and the fact that the weather was com-

paratively moderate, made it a less spectacular race than its predecessors. However, it was still international in content as there were two French entries as well as eight British ones. The two French yachts were *Guerveur*, designed like a La Rochelle Pilot boat, and a bermudian schooner, *Vega*, owned by Georges Baldenweck whose name was to reappear repeatedly on the pre-war Fastnet entry lists. Among the other entries were several familiar names: *Jolie Brise* had been entered again and having once more changed hands, now being owned by Robert Somerset who had previously campaigned *Penboch*; and *Saladin*, *Ilex*, *Neptune* and *Amaryllis* all came to the line again. There were three new British newcomers: *Grey Fox*, a yawl, a Bristol Channel Pilot cutter called *Cariad*, and a new bermudian rigged cutter, *Maitenes II*, entered by W.B. Luard.

Of these *Maitenes II* was the most interesting for though she was not built to the ORC rule she was certainly built with the Fastnet Race very much in mind. Some 50 feet overall, she had a high 75-foot mast and had been built in France at Carantec. She is described well by Douglas Phillips-Birt in his book *British Ocean Racing* as 'an advanced idea of a fast cruiser with moderate length of overhangs and fairly short keel. She was heavily and economically constructed with an iron keel and inside ballast, and initially was over-canvassed, with her big area of sail set in a Bermudian rig, a tall solid mast carrying two headsails having the jib set from a bowsprit.' But though the most advanced design in the race, *Maitenes II* did not fare well as she was not well tuned.

The race started on Wednesday, 14 August in a light westerly breeze which had the starters hoisting every possible sail. The 12-metre fleet coming the other way caused the first boat across the line, *Neptune*, to gybe all-standing, much to the amusement of the others that followed her. *Maitenes II*, fourth across the line, took the lead after 20 minutes before being overtaken by *Saladin*, *Jolie Brise*, and *Neptune*. A duel began between *Neptune* and *Maitenes II* which the latter had to break off when her jib traveller, too lightly constructed, flattened out in a squall and left the sail thrashing to leeward. One reef was taken in while repairs were carried out and *Maitenes II* dropped back. By 2130, with the whole fleet standing out on the starboard tack to get the benefit of the tide, *Neptune* and *Jolie Brise* were reckoned to be five miles to windward, and *Maitenes II* never regained the lead. The wind continued to be mainly light to the Lizard.

Most of the fleet chose to stand out into the Channel but four yachts, *Neptune*, *Jolie Brise*, *Ilex*, and *Maitenes II*, continued to hug the coast. At dawn on the Friday the crew of *Ilex* spotted *Saladin* on the port quarter and the official times at the Lizard were: *Neptune*, 0530; *Jolie Brise*, 0600; *Maitenes II*, 0700; *Ilex*, 0730; *Saladin*, 0800. 'The much debated question as to whether the fuss and bother of tide-dodging down the coast in light airs pays against the bold policy of getting right out into the channel, remains an open one,' commented a crew member of *Ilex* after the race. 'In 1926 *Ilex* made for open water and it paid handsomely. This year we tide-dodged. Did it pay? Quien Sabe? At any rate, we did not lose much by it.' The light weather, however, suited *Saladin* well so even though she was the limit boat, with a handicap of 17 hours, 15 minutes, 15 seconds over the scratch boat *Guerveur*, she could be expected to be up with the leaders. But the others which kept out undoubtably lost time by doing so. *Grey Fox* was not abeam of the Lizard until 1000 with the scratch boat not arriving at

17  The 48-ton French yawl, *Guerveur*, owned by Baron de Neufville, was the scratch boat for the 1929 Fastnet but finished last – and so late that her time was not officially recorded.

18  The crew of W.B. Luard's new bermudian cutter, *Maitenes II*, just after the start of the 1929 Fastnet.

19  The start of the 1929 Fastnet in a mild NW wind. From left to right: *Saladin*, *Grey Fox*, *Cariad*, *Amaryllis*, and the two French entries, *Vega* and *Guerveur*.

this point until 1045. The remaining two starters, *Cariad* and *Vega*, lagged even more badly behind and did not pass the Lizard until 2115 that evening.

By noon *Saladin* had Land's End abeam and the wind from the sw began to harden. Up to that year the wind had blown mostly from that direction once the starters had set a course for the Fastnet, giving them a reach to the rounding point. But this particular year, as it was to do so often in the future, tradition and comfort were shattered when the wind veered and headed the fleet. 'At nightfall we found ourselves plunging into a rising sea, close-hauled on the port tack and steering NNW,' wrote Weston Martyr who was on board *Saladin*. 'Before the darkness hid them we saw *Neptune* and *Jolie Brise* standing up like a couple of churches, eating out to windward of us and fore-reaching fast. Abeam, but well to windward, was *Ilex*, while astern, and apparently making heavy weather of it, *Maitenes* showed her tall stick naked above a three-reefed main.'

The new bermudian cutter and her crew were in fact having a very rough ride and revealing that neither were really in prime condition to tackle a race like the Fastnet, even in a comparatively light year. 'The Colonel discovered that the compass adjusting magnets had shifted,' wrote Luard in a description of the race on board *Maitenes II*, 'though he swore he remembered their former positions, and they were resecured; a staysail sheet lead sheered in its seating; another followed suit; we looked at our runners with awe and rove preventers; the chart table was soaked; the after cabin buried under wet sails; Barrett stretched on a lee berth, ashen, lifeless; and the Major in sorry plight – struggling against a mingling of sickness and trench fever.' To make matters worse for the hapless crew a heavy, breaking sea was running, steep and unpleasant.

*Maitenes II* had a very uncomfortable 36 hours before reaching the shelter of the Irish coast, and before getting there her mainsail was torn and one of her crew had broken his toe. As the Rock was approached the crew could see the tear in the mainsail growing and it was a race as to whether it would split right across before the Rock was rounded. Luckily it didn't and immediately *Maitenes II* was round, the main was dropped and frantic repairs began. Seeing *Maitenes'* sail being lowered, those on *Grey Fox* thought she'd hit the shallow patch two cables NE of the Rock and rounded herself in a 'wide sweep worthy of a battleship.'

By the time *Maitenes II* and *Grey Fox* rounded, at 1930 and 1950 respectively on the Sunday, *Jolie Brise* was over 22 hours ahead, having rounded at 2100 the previous evening, with *Ilex* second at 0640 the next morning and *Saladin* third at noon. A man with a megaphone told those on board *Saladin* this news and then added, 'It's lucky ye are to be on top of the water.' 'Why?' shouted the crew. 'It blew that hard yesterday it nearly sunk *us*!' was the reply.

The man with the megaphone must have been off duty when *Ilex* rounded for their communications with the lighthouse were much more tenuous. One of the crew wrote the following:

As we approached the rock, our distinguishing flag hoisted, we fired a verey light. A black dot appeared on the balcony of the lighthouse, placed himself where we could only see one of his arms and guess at the other, and started to semaphore. All available brain on *Ilex* was turned on to reading, and good guesswork filled in the gaps in a string of letters and turned it into *Jolie Brise*. So far, so good; but all the crew of *Ilex* could not read the rest, and we gave it up. Undeterred, Black Dot continued to work himself up to a peak of signalling frenzy, and eventually collapsed against the balcony rail, registering disapproval. Meanwhile, one member of the crew was having a pleasurable morning. Hoot, having roped in a suitable assistant, had got out the signal flags and a book of the words, and was looking like an advertisement for a flag day. Up went a vast string of flags to the cross-trees. No sooner were they up than up fluttered the answering pennant from the lighthouse. Black Dot had recovered. Things were looking up. The only beings who appeared at all disconcerted with the rapidity of the reply were our signalmen, who were now burrowing like moles into the book of words again. The ship drifted placidly towards the rock.

'What kind of shock will we get as to our position from the lighthouse,' I wondered. 'This flag business seems a slow process; however, our message must be nearly through by the length of the hoist.'

At this moment someone inquired what message we had hoisted. 'I have just sent the general signal "what!"' explained Hoot, still rushing anxiously through the pages of the code book. There is no doubt that such a signal is a great temptation to a lighthouse keeper who has had nobody to talk to for the last two months. Black Dot reacted with energy and goodwill but with complete lack of success. He might as well have burst into Gaelic. Perhaps he did. With the rock abeam we had gleaned nothing.

20  Cmdr H.F. Nash's new 34-ton cutter *Cariad* carried a squaresail at the start of the 1929 Fastnet. She retired before rounding the Rock and was never entered for the race again.

'But—' began the Busy Bee, and that was as far as he got. A hoarse noise from the lighthouse silenced him and startled the gulls. It sounded like 'Hullo!' It *was* hullo. We had established communication. As the one who talked the most and did least I was deputed to shout back. Our conversation ran something like as follows. (The reader must picture the yachts drifting past the light, minimum distance two hundred yards, gradually increasing):– 'Hullo!' from the lighthouse. 'Hullo!' (me) (pause). 'Hullo!' (pause). 'Hullo!' (pause). '*Jolie Brise* passed 9pm . . .' (rest of sentence lost. 'What?' (me). 'Hullo!' (lighthouse). 'Hullo!' (me) 'You are next.' 'When did *Neptune* pass?' (me, strain on larynx getting severe). 'Try semaphore' (lighthouse). 'Can't read your semaphore' (me). 'Wow!' (tone of deep disgust from lighthouse). At this point my larynx threatened rupture, and the vocal communication was suspended *sine die*.

As we foregathered to discuss the news a voice was heard from our signal halliards. 'Has he answered yet?' it said. There flaunted from the cross-trees a string of flags. Slightly flushed, our signalman was preparing another signal. 'No, he has not answered,' we said without enthusiasm. 'What have you asked him with that little lot?' 'They mean "when",' said our signalman proudly.

Having at least established that *Jolie Brise* was nine hours ahead of them the crew of *Ilex* were faced with the problem of trying to whittle this down to under two, the allowance that *Jolie Brise* gave *Ilex*. A spinnaker was set, and the chase was on. *Neptune* had obviously not rounded – she had in fact retired as had *Vega* and *Cariad* – but when *Saladin* was passed outward bound for the rock at 0800 the next morning, followed later by a rather bedraggled *Maitenes II*, it was clear to the Sappers that there was a danger behind as well as in front. They managed to keep their boat running at an average of six knots up to the Longships but then the wind began to drop and by 2300 on the Monday night *Ilex* was forced to kedge off the Lizard. But *Jolie Brise* managed to keep well ahead of the failing breeze and crossed the line at 1835 on the Monday evening, a clear winner. If the wind stayed light *Ilex* still had a chance of taking second place but by the Tuesday morning it had freshened considerably and reached the yachts further west a long time before it caught up with *Ilex*. Consequently *Saladin* saved her time and came second on corrected time while *Ilex* squeezed into third place on corrected time just half an hour ahead of *Maitenes II* which was fourth.

Though there were some minor gear failures during the race and some reefing had to be done it could really be termed a fair-weather Fastnet which is something the 1930 race could never be called. In fact it is something of a toss-up whether it was worse than 1927 or not. The wind was probably not as strong for so much of the time but it was at its most awkward so far as the fleet were concerned. It was a headwind down to the Longships which was normal; when it veered so that it stayed as a headwind to the Fastnet, which had happened the previous year; but then it swung round to the east once the yachts had rounded giving most of them a long beat back as well. Fog also made the course hazardous, if not downright dangerous. The race was described by the designer, Laurent Giles, who was aboard *Maitenes II*, as being 440 miles of windward work, mostly in hard winds or gales and vicious channel seas, and 160 miles to leeward, mostly in a gale. It's not surprising that over half the starters retired.

The Americans were back again in 1930, represented by Ralph Peverley's Dutch-built steel schooner, *Lelanta*, as were the French with Georges Baldenweck again entering the fray with his new bermudian cutter, *Ariel*. Apart from these two all the entries were British, and all had been on the Fastnet before: *Jolie Brise*, *Maitenes II*, *Ilex*, *Amaryllis*, *Neptune*, *Viking*, and *Magnet*. *Amaryllis* and *Neptune* shared the honour of being the scratch boats, and there were nine starters in all.

The small number of entries provoked comment in the yachting press and some questioned the future of the Fastnet. 'Bobstay' in the British magazine, *Yachting World*, predicted that the newly instituted Santander Race, which attracted more entries, would soon oust the Fastnet in popularity. 'No one wants to go and see the Fastnet Light,' he wrote, 'but many yachtsmen may be attracted by a visit to the North of Spain. It seems fairly obvious that a race with the prospect of shore attractions at the end will always draw more entries than one which is round a purely artificial mark. After a gruelling test of boat and man it is far more pleasant to rest and recuperate in Santander than amidst the more sombre surroundings of Plymouth.' 'Bobstay' also raised the old question of too much windward work, again not really understanding that before a pleasant finishing place and not too much hard headwind work the ocean racing man has always wished to pit his skill and stamina as much against the elements as against his competitors. 'Bobstay' was just another yachting journalist with the cruising mentality judging something he didn't really understand.

There was a fresh westerly wind blowing when the yachts came to the line at 1130 on 12 August, and no sooner had the yachts hoisted their spinnakers for the

21 Mr H. Newglass's 33-ton ketch, *Grey Fox*, was another 1929 starter which raced in only one Fastnet. She finished fifth.

short run through Spithead than a violent squall descended. Some crews managed to drop their spinnakers in time but both *Jolie Brise* and *Neptune* had their spinnaker booms broken.

As the yachts hardened onto the wind to round the Isle of Wight topsails were soon doused and mainsails reefed. *Neptune* was again being driven hard by her Naval crew and she soon took the lead, but the pounding she took beating into the wind and sea began opening her up. The crew stuck to their task for as long as they could but eventually they had to run for Plymouth, leaking badly and with a broken tiller, and *Jolie Brise*, still carrying a whole mainsail, took the lead. She passed Plymouth at 2130 on the 13th. She then stood offshore and passed the Lizard at 0100 about seven miles from land, and at this point it was decided to take in one reef. It was as well that the crew did so for off the Seven Stones the wind increased and a second reef was taken in. While this was being done a lot of water came aboard.

Meanwhile, *Maitenes II*, now without her bowsprit and fitted with a shorter, hollow mast that meant she carried less canvas, chose to hug the shore hoping to find smoother water. It was a gamble, but provided

the tides round Portland Bill, Start Point and the Lizard were saved it seemed worth taking the chance. The gamble was taken and proved worth it but the second night out was a wild one with the crew taking two, then three reefs in the mainsail and carrying only a stormsail forward. Luard wrote:

The wind, steadying for a short time at south-west, blew true and hard, then veered, point by point, in heavy rain squalls and screaming gusts. We made Mevagissey, beat to the Dodman, then hauled off for the Lizard. During the middle watch it was blowing a moderate gale, and in the morning watch the strength of the wind rose steadily to a fresh, strong gale; but the sea was amazingly smooth. The ship stormed west like a thing alive, smothering herself with spray and spume. As we approached Black Head the short-lived gale started to blow herself out in blinding rain squalls, the wind roaring off the land as from a gully, droning and ululating in the shrouds, blotting out the Lizard light only a few miles distant.

At the Lizard *Maitenes II* was some five hours behind *Jolie Brise*, and in second place, but then she had to put in at Newlyn to repair her mainsail and this lost her six valuable hours. *Ilex* was abeam of the Lizard at 1730 on the same day, with *Amaryllis* next at 0140 the following morning. Then there was a long gap before

41

*Viking* was abeam at 1700, and somewhere astern of her were the others except for *Neptune* and *Magnet* which had already retired, and *Lelanta* which had run for shelter in Plymouth Sound.

Out in front *Jolie Brise* had to cope with a dying wind half-way across the Irish Sea and by 1130 on the 16th she was more or less becalmed, and it was not until 2015 that evening that she rounded the Rock. However, once round it a fine reaching breeze sprang up which blew for 12 hours before it backed abruptly and began blowing hard from dead ahead. This lasted till evening when she passed *Viking* still plodding towards the turning point, and soon afterwards the fog descended. Hearing the fog signals from the Seven Stones on one side and the Longships on the other, *Jolie Brise*'s navigator managed to grope his way back into the English Channel, and the Lizard was abeam at midnight on the 17th. From the Lizard it was a run back to Plymouth and she crossed the finishing line at 1818 on the 18th, the winner for the third time of the Fastnet Race.

Behind *Jolie Brise*, *Maitenes II* and *Ilex* fought it out for second place. *Maitenes II* had an exasperating time of it with winds that continually headed her, blew hard when they weren't anticipated, and refused to blow at all when she had been well reefed down in readiness for the expected increase in wind. The weather forecasts which the crew received on their wireless was the cause of much of the confusion and proved to be consistently inaccurate. Still not an uncommon feature of racing in the Fastnet, though overall the forecasting has been pretty accurate.

But despite these vagaries the crew of *Maitenes II* were delighted that their boat seemed to be holding her own with *Ilex* which at noon on the Saturday was seen a long way behind on her port quarter. Near the Irish coast the wind became fickle, and rain, poor visibility and then fog prevented the crew from spotting the Rock. At around 1000 the fog lifted slightly and much to their chagrin the crew sighted *Ilex* homeward bound. The fog then came down again but the lighthouse not only sounded its fog signal but displayed its light as well and this enabled *Maitenes'* crew to grope their way around the mark which was rounded at 1235, some three-and-a-half hours behind *Ilex*. By this time the wind had gone around to the east and *Maitenes II* started tacking along the rhumb line course to the Longships. But by 0615 the next morning the wind had again changed direction and was blowing first from the west and then from the NW. A spinnaker was set but quickly had to be dropped as the wind rose rapidly to gale force. In a description of the race for the readers of the American magazine, *Yachting*, Weston Martyr wrote:

Now was the time to reef, but they did not do it, as this fair wind at last was a gift from the gods which they did not care to waste. It was soon a case of the old, old story – carrying on too long. By 1400 there was so much wind and sea that they dared not bring the boat into the wind to get the mainsail off her. They had to carry on – with a full mainsail, dead before a north-west gale, force 8 to 9, the boat logging $9\frac{1}{2}$ and 10, two men at the helm, oil bags over the bows and half-a-dozen warps and two buckets towing astern. It must have been a hairy sail – especially as this was the moment chosen by Kirkpatrick to fall overboard. I have not been able to get quite to the bottom of this business. The rest of the crew swear that Kirkpatrick fell overboard, that they had to work like mad lightning to get him back, and that it took the whole lot of them to do it. Kirkpatrick, on the other hand, says he just went aft to read the log and his foot slipped and so he had to get aboard again via the main sheet. I dunno. By 1700 in some tremendous squalls, the boat became practically unmanageable and the crew began to get anxious about their landfall. I am not surprised. A full gale dead aft, a lee shore somewhere ahead, night coming on and the boat running away with them! However, just before

dark they managed to sight Cape Cornwall, by 2200 the Longships was abeam and *Maitenes* was soon tearing along in smooth water under the lee of the land. By 0130 the Lizard was abeam, and there, not daring to jibe in the middle of that wild night, they 'stayed' round and fled on the other tack into Plymouth, arriving just in time for breakfast.

The only thing Weston Martyr doesn't mention to his American readers is that Luard had a man standing by with a knife in case the mainsail had to be cut at the tack and let rip, as rounding up under such conditions would almost certainly have meant losing the mast. It must have been quite a trip but they gained three-quarters of an hour on *Ilex* – which had had a more sedate run, her crew having managed to drop her mainsail and set a trysail – between the Lizard and the finish, and on corrected time finished a healthy 4 hours, 20 minutes ahead of her. She also made up nearly two hours on *Jolie Brise*.

The only other yacht to finish the race was *Amaryllis*, which broke her topmast 50 miles from the finish, *Viking* having given up 30 miles east of the Fastnet when her mainsail split and *Ariel* returning to Plymouth after her forestay had carried away 20 miles to the west of the Longships. It had been quite a race, and it had taken the winner a week to complete it.

22  The start of the 1930 Fastnet. The two left-hand boats are *Neptune* and the American schooner, *Lelanta*, and the two right-hand ones, *Maitenes II* and *Ilex*. The two centre ones cannot be identified and probably the right-hand one is only an onlooker. Way out ahead of the starters it looks like the Big Class, which included the King's *Britannia*, is also racing.

# America's Decade     1931–9

A member of the RORC had once said, regretfully rather than bitterly, that the only way for the British to win the Fastnet again was to shoot Sherman Hoyt with the starting gun. It was now evident that Olin and Rod Stephens would have to be lined up in front of it with Sherman.

       Douglas Phillips-Birt in *British Ocean Racing*

In 1931 two landmarks in the story of the Fastnet occurred, one much more important than the other. In October of that year the Ocean Racing Club was granted the Royal Warrant and from then on was known as the Royal Ocean Racing Club; and the American yawl, *Dorade*, owned by Rod and Olin Stephens, appeared at the starting line for the 1931 Fastnet, and won it with consummate ease.

That the appearance of *Dorade* must be seen as being the more important of the two events is not meant in any way to belittle the Ocean Racing Club's new status, the granting of the Royal Warrant implying as it did that the new sport of ocean racing had at least been accepted in some quarters. But the appearance of *Dorade* is something of a watershed for the Fastnet Race. And though the Americans did not win in 1937 or 1939 their influence on the Fastnets which took place up to the outbreak of war was a lasting one. The 1930s was America's decade. Up to that time the number of competitors had been sparse and those that entered were perhaps still attracted more by the novelty of the race than by an inherent desire to race for the sake of racing. *Nina* had been an exception to the rule; but after *Dorade* it was the appearance of a cruising yacht at the line for a Fastnet Race that proved to be the exception. That symbol of the early Fastnets, *Jolie Brise*, raced in 1931, but it was the last time that she entered and the 1930s saw the steady development of yachts that were built for ocean racing yachtsmen who also wanted to cruise, as opposed to yachts built for cruising yachtsmen who occasionally entered a race for the hell of it.

For the 1931 season a new rating formula was introduced and was to remain unchanged for many years. A new rigging allowance was also brought in to encourage two-masted entries, and before *Dorade* had even appeared on the horizon yachting journalists had scented a change in atmosphere. 'Has the day of the pilot cutter gone?' wrote one. 'I mean as a potential winner of an ocean race. I think it has,' and he went on

to point out that ocean racing in the United States was producing a highly specialised type of yacht designed by men like Starling Burgess, L. Francis Herreshoff and Frank Paine who also turned out yachts for the defence of America's Cup.

*Dorade* was very obviously one of these new generation yachts. Designed by Olin Stephens, a young, up-and-coming designer who was to dominate the yacht designing scene for many years, *Dorade* had a waterline length of 37 feet 3 inches with the rather narrow beam of 10 feet 3 inches, and her displacement of $14\frac{3}{4}$ tons was considerably less than what in Britain was thought normal for this length of yacht. She was, wrote Phillips-Birt, 'the most important step yet taken in the yachtsman's search for his own type of fast seagoing vessel.'

But though interest probably centred on *Dorade* if only because of her remarkable win in the recently completed Trans-Atlantic Race, there were other new entries that year which must have attracted a lot of attention. To start with, the Trans-Atlantic Race had lured over three American schooners, *Amberjack II*, *Water Gypsey*, and *Mistress*, the last being designed and skippered by Sherman Hoyt but owned by George E. Roosevelt; and two cutters, *Highland Light* and *Skal*. Never before had there been such a formidable array of American talent in British waters and this invasion must have caused much comment and curiosity. The French also fielded a newcomer, *Brise Vent*, as well as a 1930 entry, *Ariel*. Two new British newcomers were a Nicholson-designed cutter, *Patience*, the scratch boat for the race, and the Shepherd-designed cutter *Lexia*; and *Ilex*, *Maitenes II*, *Amaryllis*, *Jolie Brise*, *Neptune*, *Viking* and *Noreen* were again at the starting line on Tuesday, 11 August when the gun went at 1100.

It was a boiling hot day with no wind and all the yachts, except *Highland Light*, kedged close together waiting for a breath of wind and for the tide to ease.

**23**  *Dorade*, seen here kedged at the start of the 1931 race, also won in 1933.

*Highland Light* continued to lie at her moorings on the wrong side of the line – and was recalled! After 35 minutes *Neptune* managed to creep away, followed ten minutes later by *Ilex*, *Dorade* and *Noreen*, but the last of the 17-strong fleet, *Ariel*, did not manage to make any headway until 70 minutes after the gun.

The winds continued light and westerly for the first 48 hours and it was a fluky business trying to make headway as the yachts made their way down channel, but those who kept close inshore did somewhat better than those who chose a mid-channel course. *Neptune* and *Jolie Brise* went further out than most and *Mistress* followed them, Sherman Hoyt assuming that if the skippers of these two didn't know what they were doing no one did. But there was – and is – much more to the Fastnet than simply following the yacht ahead and by the time the fleet passed the Lizard, *Neptune*, the first of the three to have it abeam, was some four hours behind the leader, *Water Gypsey*. Later, *Jolie Brise*'s owner, Bobby Somerset, explained his error which had led *Mistress* so badly astray. 'We banked on the wireless reports as to weather,' he stated, 'and we were deceived. As events proved we stood too far to the south'ard.'

All except *Viking*, which passed at 1115 on the Friday, had the Lizard behind them by Thursday night by which time there was quite a heavy sea running, and a freshening SE breeze enabled everyone to hoist their spinnakers. By early evening the wind had increased and there was much debate on board the yachts as to how long their spinnakers could be kept hoisted. In some cases this problem was solved for the crew because the gear gave way. On *Patience*, which was duelling with *Highland Light* at the time, the spinnaker boom snapped right in the middle and the spinnaker shot up into the air and wrapped itself firmly around the topmast stay some 70 feet above deck, where it kept blowing out in great balloons and threatened to snap off the top of the mast. With the spinnaker pulling at this height the stability of the yacht was badly affected and she began to roll badly. For a moment things must have looked bleak for the crew but luckily the rolling motion unwound the spinnaker and it blew clear. It was quickly lowered and stowed away, and a reef was put in the main for good measure. This was soon increased to two and then three as the wind steadily increased and veered. *Highland Light* also broke her spinnaker boom and experienced the same problem with the spinnaker as *Patience*, but it, too, unwound itself when the yacht began to roll badly. Another casualty was *Ilex* whose topmast went again – someone said the Sappers must have had to carry a golfbag full of them so often did this happen – but her crew ingeniously rigged the spinnaker boom in its place and used the remains of

24  *Dorade*'s sail plan. Her dimensions were: LOA: 52 ft, LWL: 37 ft 3 in, beam: 10 ft 3 in, draught: 7 ft 8 in.

25  The start to the 1931 Fastnet was in boiling-hot sun and a flat calm. Here a group of competitors can be seen creeping towards the Spithead forts after being kedged at the line for at least three-quarters of an hour. *Mistress* is in the background, then from left to right: *Maitenes II*, *Ilex*, *Dorade* to weather and astern of *Ilex*, *Lexia*, *Noreen* and *Patience*.

26  *Highland Light*, one of the two American cutters to take part in the 1931 Fastnet. She came fourth.

the topmast to boom out the spinnaker.

The crew of *Maitenes II* were having an especially difficult time shortening the yacht's bermudian sail down and so they decided to run under the lee of the Cornish coast in order to reef. Her owner recorded:

At 2030 we came about, lee rail well under, and ran off, with the wind freshening fast. Half an hour later we had the lighthouse a cable away to starboard, but we held on a short while longer to clear some shoal patches before heaving-to and shortening down. Then, without any real warning, we seemed to be in the middle of a veritable *pampero*. It started to blow so hard that we could do nothing with her; the wind came cascading and zipping off the high hills, hurtling down gullies

and crevices, churning the sea white, whipping solid belts of spray from the surface. The ship lay over and reeled; we dodged her through a succession of vicious squalls and blinding rain, thinking each one would dismast her. Before we knew what had happened Pendeen light flashed on the bow, towered overhead, and disappeared in driving murk.

Eventually, the comparative safety of St Ives Bay was reached, a sheltering collier was missed by a matter of feet, and the anchor let go. Over 45 fathoms of cable, in a depth of eight fathoms, had to be paid out before she would hold. More reefs were put in and the tired and wet crew put to sea again at dawn. Infuriatingly, the wind immediately moderated away from the shore and it was then realised, from the moderate swell encountered, that the gale they'd been forced to shelter from had been a purely local one which they would have escaped if they'd stayed well away from the land.

Though *Water Gypsey* had parted her spinnaker guy 'with a crack like a 6-inch gun' at the Lizard she still retained the lead and, while the wind was still aft, reached higher than the other yachts so that when the wind began to veer she was able to follow it round without having to tack to the Rock which is what everyone else had to do. This tactic put her in a very strong position and though reduced to a trysail for a

time she had a very fast run to the turning mark, rounding first at 1024 on the Friday, just two minutes ahead of *Patience* and ten ahead of the remarkable and much smaller *Dorade*. While the others had reduced sail – and *Noreen* had split her mainsail and retired – *Dorade* had pressed on under full canvas.

*Mistress*, which rounded fifth at 1305, had nearly lost two of her crew in the Channel while they were trying to reef the mainsail. The boom had swung out with the men still clinging to it and they had narrowly missed being washed away when they had been dunked waist-deep into the steep sea that was running. Then while crossing the Labadie Bank the Americans had nearly been run down, an ever-present fear of any Fastnet skipper. A fleet of trawlers bore down on them, their lights as George Roosevelt described it, making the area look like Times Square. At the time, *Mistress* was running by the lee with her large fisherman's staysail as well as her spinnaker set, and was, as one of her crew, Anthony Heckstall-Smith, described it in his book *Sacred Cowes*, 'rolling her guts out in a huge, angry following sea.' With little or no room to manoeuvre, frantic efforts were made to attract the trawlers' attention so that they would alter course. But the trawlers had their nets down so that they could not manoeuvre either, and they blew their sirens in warning. As the crew fought to get in the spinnaker Roosevelt nearly gybed *Mistress* all-standing. To add to the confusion it soon became obvious that one trawler in particular was on a direct collision course with the yacht. One of the crew wrote later:

The skipper fired off a verey light, and for a few seconds the pink flare glowed in the sky and illuminated the scene. *Mistress*'s decks running with water, her crew, black figures, all staring towards the trawler rolling and plunging through the seas. Then all was dark again. Someone shouted, 'She's running us down! Bear away, man, bear away! But for God's sake don't gybe her!' Riding on a great wave the trawler's bow looked as high as an ocean liner's. We had to bear away three to four points to clear her. We all but gybed. It was a nasty experience, and we sailed on, hurling abuse at that trawler and all others upon the sea. We hoped he'd catch no fish and told him so, and other things besides.

The leaders now set off back to the English coast on a close reach in poor visibility and with the wind still blowing hard. In these conditions a good landfall was essential and four of them, *Patience*, *Highland Light* (fourth round at 1126), *Dorade* and *Mistress*, did make good ones with the Longships well under the lee bow so that they were able to ease sheets and make for the

27 The scratch boat, *Patience*, at the start of the 1931 race.

Lizard without any problem. But *Water Gypsey* lost valuable time – perhaps as much as two hours – when her navigator mistook the Pendeen Light for the Longships and bore *Water Gypsey* away up the Bristol Channel. Her owner, Sam Wetherill, was asleep at the time but some sixth sense woke him and he went on deck feeling all was not well. He brought the schooner on to the wind at once and managed to weather the Longships without tacking, but then ran into a tide rip which whisked the yacht within 200 yards of the rocks.

'The seas came aboard from fore and aft and both sides at once,' wrote Weston Martyr later, 'and Sam sat in the cockpit, trying to steer with the water up to his neck.' The skipper himself said that it was the worst punishment he had ever taken in a sailing craft and he thought the boat would be knocked to pieces or the whole rig ripped out of her. It was a nasty moment but *Water Gypsey* weathered the rocks and extricated herself from the rip, and went on to finish third and take second place on corrected time.

While these faster boats were plunging home at an average rate of over eight knots (7.2 knots in the case of the smaller *Dorade*), the rest of the fleet was having a very rough time of it indeed. *Amberjack II*, which eventually finished on the Tuesday, reached the Rock

28 *Water Gypsey*, seen here at the start of the 1931 Fastnet, was the first to round the Rock that year, but was beaten into second place by *Dorade* by just over eight hours on corrected time.

early on the Friday morning but then spent six hours trying to get away from its lee. The owner, Paul D. Rust Jr, said:

It was blowing so hard, that we could not shorten sail, and when it started to blow we heeled over with such a tremendous lurch that before we could close the hatches the seas rolled into the cockpit and flooded the bunks, washing our tinned food supply away and drenching our clothing and blankets. All of us were on deck, with the exception of our cook, who remained below bailing as hard as he could with a bucket. . . . All the time we were drifting closer to the perilous lee shore of the Fastnet Rock. The men ashore kept making the signal 'JD' to us, telling us we were sailing into danger, but we knew that as well as, or even better than, they did. We were so close to the rock that we could see the crosspieces of the windows. Indeed, at one time we could not have been more than two or three hundred yards off the rocks. At last, after such a night as I do not want to meet again, we were able to shorten sail, and with three reefs in the mainsail and a storm jib

we crept out of danger inch by inch, all of us pretty well exhausted. It was still blowing a gale, however, with tremendous seas running. In fact, it seemed that the weather became even wilder, and we could do nothing but run before the storm.

*Amberjack II* struggled back to the English coast and made a landfall in the area of Padstow Bay. There she was greeted by a motor boat which came out from Portreath. 'Five of you not yet reported,' the motor boat owner shouted to the Americans. 'All the others are in except *Maitenes*. She lost her mast and foundered. It's in the paper.'

*Maitenes II* had, in fact, done no such thing though what did befall her was sufficiently tragic. Having ripped her mainsail near the Fastnet she rounded the Rock under trysail and a reefed storm staysail but was soon forced to heave to and remained so through all of Saturday afternoon and way into the next day. At 0400 the next morning it was still blowing hard, a good force 9 according to *Maitenes'* skipper, and seas were occasionally breaking aboard and filling the cockpit. More than once they broke half-way up the trysail. At 0900 a particularly vicious squall hit her and she broke through the top of a high wave and lay abeam to the seas for a moment before swinging back into the wind. This was viewed with 'serious apprehension' by those on board as well it might. By 1000 the wind had risen to force 10 and at 1145 the

49

**29** Two 1930 starters, *Maitenes II* and *Ilex*, taken at the start of the 1931 race.

boat was overpowered by another vicious gust which nearly laid her on her beam ends. It was then decided to get her to run before the wind under bare poles. A sea anchor was bent onto a 3½-inch warp, and eight bags, filled with fish oil, were placed along her sides. Knives were placed in handy positions ready to cut away the trysail in case it stuck, and the boat was the paid off and the sea anchor streamed astern. This manoeuvre was successfully accomplished and the trysail lowered, and *Maitenes II* ran before the wind though not without difficulty.

What happened next is best described by the owner in his own words.

A short time later, at 1245, Colonel Hudson [the co-owner of *Maitenes II*], who was clearing an oil bag by the after starboard stanchion, was thrown overboard by a violent lurch of the ship. We threw a lifebuoy as soon as possible, and I swung her off in the hope the sea anchor warp would ride towards him, that possibly he might be forced into the drogue itself, and that somehow we might be able to haul him in. He succeeded in grasping the warp, but it was torn from his hands and, encumbered by sea-boots and oilskins, he sank at once. The steepness of the seas had again increased and they were breaking heavily. From time to time

we were pooped and the ship became more difficult to handle. The loss of Colonel Hudson was a great blow to all hands, and I realised that some of my crew were nearing physical exhaustion – a serious matter – though their behaviour was splendid. The ship was steering roughly east, the wind again having veered, and making six or seven knots. Force of wind 10.

*Maitenes II* was now over the Labadie Bank and with the sea steep, confused and irregular – Luard's description of it is very similar to those given by skippers in the 1979 race when they were in the same general area as *Maitenes II* – and she was again pooped several times. A trawler, whose attention had been attracted, now semaphored that a further gale had been forecast and it was then decided that risking the lives of the exhausted crew further could not be justified and the trawler was requested to take the yacht in tow. This was eventually achieved though not before the trawler's boat had been overturned and lost – luckily the men in it scrambled aboard the yacht – and the trawler itself had fouled *Maitenes II*, damaging her superstructure and rigging.

30  *Noreen*, seen here at the start of the 1931 race. She raced in the 1928 Fasnet, as scratch boat, but failed to finish. She did not finish in 1931 either.

Years later Luard commented how amazingly local the bad weather had been and that had he not been over the Labadie Bank he was in no doubt that he could have weathered the storm without undue worry. From his comments Luard obviously thought that the bank, which he described as 'notorious,' caused the confused seas though modern scientists say it is too deep to have other than a minimal effect on wave patterns.

Although *Maitenes II* suffered the worst in the storm none escaped its effect entirely. *Ariel*, which rounded at 1000 on the Saturday, at least managed to sail out of the vicinity of the Rock but then got caught 20 miles off the Scillies and was hove-to for 32 hours. *Viking*, near the Rock on the Friday night, was forced to heave-to until the Monday, when she rounded. On the way back her exhausted owner nearly ran her on to the Seven Stones and then to cap it all she ran into another gale off the Lizard and had to heave-to yet again, this time for 24 hours. She eventually crossed the line five days after the first boat home, but at least she finished, which is more than she'd managed to do in either 1928 or 1930. On board her this time was a

young naval officer, John Illingworth, and he apparently persuaded the elderly owner, Lindsay Fisher, to continue despite an announcement on the wireless, while *Viking* was still 70 miles from the turning mark, that the first boat was already home. Altogether Illingworth was to participate in 14 Fastnets and post-war was to have a profound affect on the ocean racing scene. Perhaps this, his first Fastnet, sailed in a large cumbersome cutter, which went to windward in a seaway 'like a cow in a bog,' and whose mainsail was so stiff it was like reefing plywood, influenced his own thinking when designing ocean racers. It was certainly an uncomfortable ride that year and Illingworth records in his book, *The Malham Story*, that the crew had to have pillows on top of their heads as well as under them to avoid being cracked against the deck head by the boat's violent motion.

While all the slower yachts had a rough passage, the 1931 race was in marked contrast to earlier heavy-weather Fastnets in that only two yachts, *Maitenes II* and *Noreen*, retired. The rest just plugged on and eventually reached Plymouth.

Apart from the weather, which was appalling throughout, except for the first 36 hours or so, and the tragic loss of Colonel Hudson, the 1931 race will always be remembered as being one of the closest ocean races ever sailed. The times of the first six boats to pass the Lizard homeward bound on the Saturday were: *Patience*, 1030; *Highland Light*, 1040; *Water Gypsey*, 1050; *Dorade*, 1110; *Mistress*, 1210; and *Lexia*, 1410. This showed what a phenomenally close race it was, boat for boat. But it was to become closer still as the yachts raced for the finishing line – which, much to Sherman Hoyt's relief after his difficulties in 1928, now ran from the outer breakwater at Plymouth – and *Patience*, under reefed mainsail, reaching staysail, and yankee jib topsail, shook out her reef when she saw *Highland Light* beginning to creep up on her. At Rame Head *Patience* was only 150 yards ahead of the American schooner but managed to set her spinnaker quicker a mile from the finish and crossed the line one minute and 18 seconds ahead of *Highland Light*, a distance of 200 yards separating the two yachts. For the last half-mile both were running by the lee in a 25-knot wind.

Just 20 minutes behind *Highland Light* came *Water Gypsey* and then, much to everyone's amazement, *Dorade* crossed having saved 19 hours of her 20-hour allowance, and 24 minutes behind her came *Mistress*. On corrected time *Dorade* won easily, by just over eight hours, with *Water Gypsey* second and *Mistress* third. The last comment in *Mistress*'s log was 'gosh, what weather,' and Sherman Hoyt said later that it was the toughest race he'd ever been in. The course was 615 miles: *Amberjack II*'s log read 903.

The 1931 Fastnet was immediately recognised as a classic race by the press but 'Solent' in *Yachting World*, after stating that ocean racing had now firmly established itself, went on to decry the daily papers for calling it an international event, which, he said firmly, was 'contrary to the ethics of the sport.' That the Fastnet Cup should be raced for on a national basis was, he implied, quite wrong. Remembering the Admiral's Cup the article reads quaintly today, to say the least, but it shows that the future of ocean racing no longer seemed in doubt and only the best means of pursuing it were a matter for speculation. 'Solent' also raised the question of a common rating rule between Britain and the United States, something which E.G. Martin also raised in *Yachting*, adding that the two countries should co-ordinate their racing programmes as well. In the same magazine Sherman Hoyt, obviously invigorated by his summer in *Mistress*, rhapsodised on the thrills of the sport while roundly condemning the constant alteration of the rating rules in both countries and warning that ocean racing must not become too refined. 'Ocean racing is here to stay,' he concluded. 'It may not appeal to all, and interest in it will wane if it becomes too technical and standardised. Let us try not to surround it with too many finicky and "oldmaidish" safeguards and limitations, or it will lose its appeal.'

Lest by his comments the modern reader should conclude Hoyt was anti safety regulations it is worth noting what he had to say about Colonel Hudson's death. 'My practice, foolishly deemed by some to be a sissy precaution, on insisting upon the use of a life line attached to any crew member working on an exposed deck, had not been observed, and resulted in the death of a gallant gentleman.'

Despite an informal meeting between the Commodore of the ORC, Malden Heckstall-Smith, Olin Stephens and Sherman Hoyt, after the 1931 race, no common rating formula was agreed between the ORC and the Americans, and in the following year the CCA (Cruising Club of America) drew up its own formula which was quite different in principle to the ORC's.

As Douglas Phillips-Birt pointed out many years later in his book, this failure to reach agreement at least had the advantage, so far as the British development of the sport was concerned, in retaining the ORC rule which was formulated so that a yacht could be measured at its moorings. Without such simplicity of application, Phillips-Birt remarks, it could have been difficult to measure the large fleets of the immediate post-war era.

Though a common formula was not adopted, a co-ordinated racing programme was, and after 1931 the Fastnet became a biennial fixture alternating with the Bermuda Race.

With the popularity of ocean racing now apparently assured, and with the minds of more British yachtsmen adjusted to the fact that the sport called for a new type of yacht and a new attitude to racing it, it would not have been unreasonable to suppose that the 1933 Fastnet would attract a large entry. But it did not and at one time it looked as if those staunch supporters of the Fastnet Race, the Royal Engineers, would be the only British entry, but eventually two other yachts besides *Ilex* turned up at the line. These were *Lexia*, which had come fifth in the previous Fastnet, and an old Nicholson designed cruising cutter, *Flame*.

Such a paucity of British entries brought scathing comments from the columnists and Weston Martyr suggested that the RORC should substitute the Fastnet for a punt race on the upper Thames, providing at least one silk cushion for each member of the crew. His comments were not well received by the more serious – or should one say, earnest – sections of the yachting press which maintained that courage was not what was lacking but the resources to build the right yachts with which to beat the Americans. It was the same argument as that used whenever the British were beaten in America's Cup races and it was equally disingenuous. The fact was that the Americans were better at ocean racing than the British and until the British got down to doing something about it they would continue to be beaten by the Americans over the Fastnet course.

The American entries for the 1933 race were also three in number: *Dorade*, skippered by Rod Stephens with Sherman Hoyt aboard, was at the line again as were two schooners, *Grenadier* and *Brilliant*, which had sailed from Boston and City Island respectively. *Grenadier*, owned by two young brothers, Harry and Sherman Morss, was another in the long line of successful Alden designs. *Brilliant*, owned and sailed by Walter Barnum, had come from the board of Olin Stephens. Both yachts proved to be formidable opponents, but not as formidable as *Dorade*. Apart from a limitation being put on the size of spinnakers and headsails, and the introduction of a propeller allowance, the innovations for the 1933 race was a different course and a start before instead of after Cowes Week. The course that year was westwards through the Needles Channel to the Fastnet Rock and back leaving the Nab Tower to port and finishing at the Spithead forts, a distance of 720 miles. The starting date was fixed for July 22 which would give the competitors time to do the race and be at Cowes Week.

The 1933 start was very like that of 1931, taking place in an almost flat calm. *Grenadier* was first across

31 The British cutter, *Lexia*, finished fifth in the 1931 Fastnet.

the line, followed three minutes later by *Dorade*, and for the first hour these two seemed to be the only ones able to keep any sort of steerage way. They ghosted into a half-mile lead while *Lexia* and *Flame* simply drifted together into a close embrace and *Ilex* bounced over a reef off which she was only shaken on a falling tide by the very determined efforts of her crew. Altogether, it was not one of the Fastnet's most distinguished starts, but off Lymington a breeze came up and the fleet settled down to some serious racing. *Dorade* now led, followed by *Grenadier*, *Flame*, *Lexia*, *Brilliant* and *Ilex*, but there was only about ten minutes between the lot of them.

During the first night the wind dropped and *Dorade* drifted into the swift east-going stream off Portland Bill. *Lexia* did the same and was carried so close to the rocks that her crew were forced to start her engine. Though now disqualified she carried on for the fun of it and was third round the Rock behind *Dorade* and *Flame*, both of whom had been keeping close company and forging ahead in the light airs that prevailed. The wind was so paltry that *Dorade*, despite being close hauled the whole time, found it paid her to carry her balloon jib for about 80 per cent of that time. *Flame* rounded the Rock at 1820 on the third day out, followed by *Dorade* at 2045. Then came *Lexia*, at 0130 the next morning, followed by *Grenadier* at 0205, *Brilliant* at 0405, and *Ilex* at 1550 having been becalmed for rather longer than any of the others on the way to the turning mark.

The wind remained light on the homeward leg until the Longships was reached and then a firmer breeze set in. At the Lizard, with *Flame* leading *Dorade* by $2\frac{1}{2}$ hours, the American yawl was as much as 12 hours ahead of her compatriots, but the stronger wind set the two American schooners really moving and as it was a westerly they got it before the leaders did. While the gap was beginning to close its speed of narrowing was increased by the fact that *Dorade* kept missing the tides off the various heads. For instance, off St Catherine's she was only an hour and 20 minutes astern of *Flame*, but then the tide began to set against her and, though her log never registered less than seven knots from St Catherine's to the Nab, *Flame* finished over six hours ahead of her, and *Brilliant*, 12 hours astern at the Lizard, finished only 49 minutes astern of her. Despite this, *Dorade* won easily – by several months one journalist remarked sourly – on corrected time.

The race between *Brilliant* and *Grenadier* was closely fought and they performed, as one commentator noted, more like a couple of New York 'forties' during a Saturday afternoon race than two large schooners completing a 720-mile ocean race. Try as she might *Brilliant* could not catch *Grenadier* as they churned up-channel at over ten knots. So, as Alf Loomis who was on board described it,

*Brilliant*'s board of strategy went into action and decided on desperate measures. Taking in our spinnaker, we reached sharply in toward the Wight shore, adding distance, diminishing our speed, taking the last of the ebb on our starboard bow, but gambling everything on being the first to enter the flood stream around St Catherine's. . . . *Grenadier* was now four miles ahead, and with spinnaker in was reaching in to the Nab Tower. But then the break came. *Grenadier* stopped moving through the water, and the tide set her slowly westward. The young flood, fanned by a new westerly, extended no more than two hundred yards from the beach, took us in its kindly grip. We hugged the breeze and we hugged the shore until a careful reading of the current diagrams indicated that we were in the branch setting directly toward the Nab. We squared away for the tower and – most satisfactory episode in many years of ocean racing – jibed around it a quarter of a mile ahead of *Grenadier*.

*Brilliant* held on to this cleverly achieved lead and crossed the line just two minutes and 24 seconds ahead of her rival. But on corrected time *Brilliant* could do no better than fourth, with *Grenadier* taking second place and *Flame* a well deserved third. Though rated badly under the RORC rule, for a 33-year-old yacht, skippered by a man twice that age, to beat home all the other entries by six hours was quite an achievement.

A new trophy, the *Jolie Brise* Cup, was first raced for in 1933. Later the number of trophies and prizes awarded after a Fastnet Race proliferated at such a rate it would be tedious to explain the purpose of each. But the method of awarding the *Jolie Brise* Cup that year was so novel as to be worth recording. It was Bobby Somerset's idea that the cup should be awarded to a yacht which had entered the Fastnet even though, because of the handicap system, it had no chance whatsoever of winning. Each yacht, therefore, was given a handicap. This entailed each competing owner allotting all the entries except his own what he thought was the right time allowance to enable each yacht to win. A mean of all these allowances was then taken and alloted to each entry in addition to their ordinary

**32** The lines and sail plan of *Grenadier*, a 1933 American starter. Her dimensions were: LOA: 59 ft 10 in, LWL: 43 ft, beam: 13 ft 8 in, draught: 8 ft 2 in.

**33** *Grenadier* and *Dorade* at the start of the 1933 Fastnet, which, as can be seen, also took place in hardly a whisper of wind.

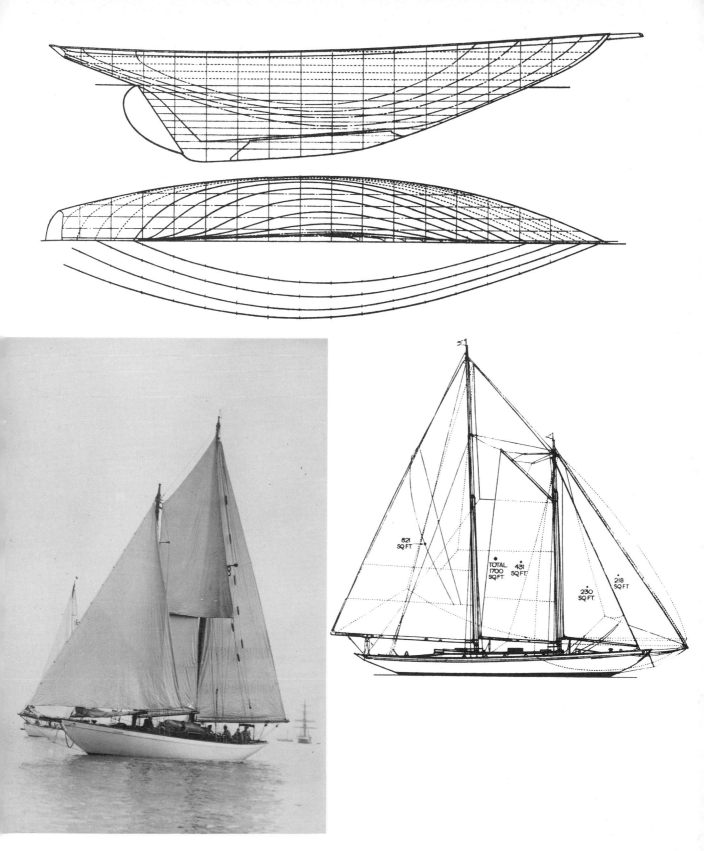

55

handicap. After the 1931 race *Dorade* must have been given a very low handicap time indeed by the owners. If so, they still, and literally, under-rated her, for in 1933 she won not only the Fastnet Cup but the *Jolie Brise* Cup as well.

The race over, the recriminations began. Articles headed 'Has the Fastnet Race Failed? Perhaps the test is too severe,' and carrying messages of gloom and despondency started appearing in the yachting press and elsewhere. The editor of *Yachting Monthly* wrote flippantly that 'rumours that the RORC will abandon the Fastnet Race, that the rating rule will be altered to allow for age of gear and seaworthiness of hulls, or perhaps that the Fastnet Rock is to be raised and placed in the Solent, have each had their advocates,' and added, on a more serious note, what others had already said in one way or another. '*Dorade* is a splendid specimen of the type of craft which makes the best use of the RORC rule, the type of yacht, indeed, that the rule encourages. All will agree without doubt, that *Dorade* is a beautiful creation, and for cruising in the longer seas of the Atlantic and up and down the eastern seaboard of the States she is no doubt admirably suited; but this lovely ship does not represent the ideal for cruising in our Narrow Seas under all the conditions which are peculiar to our climate for nine-tenths of the season. British yachts-men need a heavier, beamier and appreciably slower type of ship if they are to cruise with reasonable

**34** Another 1933 American starter, the schooner *Brilliant*, at the line. Behind her is *Ilex*.

**35** *Rose* was already pretty ancient when she came to the line for her first Fastnet in 1935. Built in 1899, she was given to the RAYC by Col. C.F. King in 1936 and the club raced her in the 1937 and 1939 races. Her rig was complicated even by the standards of the day, no less than 19 halyards and purchases leading to the mainmast.

comfort around the coasts of Great Britain,' and so on and so forth. In short, the old cruising hands were making a last-ditch stand. Or perhaps, as one American commentator pointed out, the British were just being their usual perverse selves and were making a loud noise about the Fastnet being finished as an ocean racing fixture, because the rule encouraged the wrong sort of boat, in order to make sure British yachtsmen would rally round what was by now an institution. This would ensure that not only would there be another Fastnet but that it would be a successful one.

---

In fact that's just how it did turn out, though the reason for the increased entries in the 1935 race was probably because the British yachting mind, slow in stays, as it were, had at last changed tack and the country now began to produce yachts which, even if

they didn't actually beat the Americans, looked as if that were their intention. So the Fastnet that year produced no less than 13 entries from the home country as well as three French yachts and one American. Admittedly, the average age of the British contingent was 21 years, but statistics, especially averages, never tell the whole story, so it should be added that nine of them were bermudian rigged (still quite an innovation) and that some of them had double-clewed jibs, the very latest in fashion and first used in America's Cup races the previous year. More important, five of them were less than two years old. The club, bowing to mounting criticism of the handicap system following the two previous Fastnets, penalised these newer boats more severely; and where before the club had stipulated that Lloyd's scantlings must be used – a worthy intention but hardly practical with the increasing number of foreign entries, many of whom paid no attention at all to Lloyd's requirements – each yacht now had its own scantling allowance.

*Ilex*, now rerigged as a Bermudian cutter and no longer looking like a loser, was at the line again. Apart from *Thalassa*, a 1927 entry, she was the only British starter to have previously entered a Fastnet. However, the cruising faction were still represented: Claud Worth's old Fife-designed, gaff-rigged ketch, *Maud*, had been entered, for instance. *Maud* had been held up to an earlier generation as being the perfect cruising boat. 'She was as handy as a gimlet,' Worth wrote of her, 'and would wriggle through a narrow channel like a Una boat. . . . She proved weatherly for a ketch and an exceptionally safe sea boat.' But amongst a new generation of yachts she proved to be hopelessly inferior in speed, comfort and weatherliness, and retired before the Lizard was even reached as did *Banba* (no relation to *Banba IV*), another yacht of ancient lineage. A third starter which had no serious hope of doing anything except perhaps keep afloat was *Amy*. Built in 1887 she had been chartered for the occasion by a crew of naval officers who obviously just wanted to compete for the fun of it. *Amy* was not very flatteringly described by a crew member of another yacht as 'old-fashioned, neglected-looking, with faded tanned canvas that looked in poor condition, and her topsides were in need of paint.' A lot of people though the RORC should not have allowed her to start, but she eventually managed to complete the course without sinking. Perhaps it was as well that it was another light-weather Fastnet.

The Royal Navy were also represented that year by the recently Hong Kong-built ketch, *Tai-Mo-Shan*. Though built primarily for cruising, she had the same look about her as the new cruiser-racers but did not have enough wind to show her paces and came 13th on corrected time. Like other Fastnet entries of the 1920s

and 1930s – *Foxhound* and *Jolie Brise* are two other examples – *Tai-Mo-Shan* is still afloat and giving her present owners a lot of fun. The author saw her at Puerto Andraix, Majorca, in August 1980, in spotless condition.

Not to be outdone by the Senior Service, the Royal Air Force entered a boat for the first time, a bermudian sloop called *Emmeline*. But she, too, had an undistinguished race coming ninth on corrected time, just in front of *MacNab*, a new cutter which also failed to show her paces in the light weather that prevailed.

Other entries included an old Soper-designed yawl, *Rose*, which did well in the early stages, but then faded; the French schooner, *Hygie*, which also suffered from the lack of wind; *Brise Vent*, another French entry and a veteran of the 1931 race; *Carmela*, a brand new cutter but an old-timer in style; *Kismet III*, described as a converted 15-metre with a 12-metre rig; and *Isis*, a new French cutter owned by Georges Baldenweck. But interest centred on the new American Stephens-designed yawl, *Stormy Weather*, and two new British boats: *Foxhound*, a Nicholson-designed cutter, and the 72 foot steel yawl, *Trenchemer*. *Foxhound*, built for Mr Isaac Bell, an American living in England, had not been designed specifically to the RORC rule, though she had been constructed with it very much in mind. On the other hand *Trenchemer*, built for an Englishman also called Bell, based on plans entered by Olin Stephens in a Royal Corinthian Yacht Club design competition, had been specifically constructed to the RORC rule, the first yacht to be so built.

But *Stormy Weather* was the favourite. Larger than *Dorade* by about a foot on the waterline, but beamier by over two feet, she was without the earlier boat's flared topsides. Owned by Philip le Boutillier and skippered by Rod Stephens, *Stormy Weather* arrived, like *Dorade*, with a formidable reputation, having just won the Trans-Atlantic Race to Bergen.

The start in 1935 reverted to an August date, Wednesday, 7th. As this clashed with Cowes Week, the start was from Yarmouth and this shortened the course – westwards through the Needles Channel, round the Fastnet, finishing at Plymouth – to 585 miles. The gun went at 1500 on the first of the ebb, with a light wind from the SSW making it a close fetch down the Solent. It was a somewhat chaotic start as everyone crowded for the weather berth and this resulted in *Hygie* hitting *Kismet III* in spectacular fashion, her bowsprit sticking out beyond *Kismet's* starboard quarter. However, both sailed on apparently undamaged. Later the French schooner ran aground on rocks near Fort Victoria and was not refloated for half-an-hour. *Amy* fell in irons at the line, which caused frantic alterations of course amongst the other competitors, and *Trenchemer*, to quote an eye-witness, was tearing about like a hunting porpoise, smooth and swift, with apparently little regard for the direction of the wind or anything else. There was, *Trenchemer*'s skipper remarked, probably more breaches of YRA rules in the last five minutes before the gun of that particular race than in any other period of yacht racing.

*Stormy Weather* was first across the line after the gun, narrowly missing *Trenchemer* in a port and starboard tack incident. 'The excitement of that first half-hour was intense,' wrote one of *Trenchemer*'s crew, Iain Rutherford, in his book *At the Tiller*, 'with the whole fleet jostling off Yarmouth pier and gradually stringing out after the starting gun had unleashed us on our 600 miles race. We all held out towards the Needles on the port tack but only *Foxhound* and *Kismet* managed to pass the Narrows without going about. The order there was *Kismet*, *Foxhound*, *Trenchemer*, *Stormy*, and *Carmela*, with the others, including *Tai-Mo-Shan*, well astern.'

*Kismet III* did well to take the lead so early as she'd made rather a late start, but once she got going her light weather rig drove her through the rest of the fleet at a tremendous pace. It was going to have to if she was to have any chance of winning for the Rule had heavily penalised her long overhangs and fine racing hull. *Foxhound* went well too, pointing higher than *Stormy Weather* and footing faster too. Both these yachts carried genoas while *Trenchemer* set a staysail, double-clewed jib and a rather large jib topsail. A yachting commentator remarked on the extent of the influence of America's Cup J-class on the setting and pattern of the headsails of these leading boats, a visible sign that the combined influence of the out-and-out racing yacht and the ocean cruiser were merging into a new type, the cruiser-racer. But it was to be some years before this new type adopted the high aspect ratio mainsails of the J-class, did completely away with bowsprits (though several entries in 1935 were without them), began setting the mast further aft to allow for more powerful headsails, and, finally, setting these headsails from the masthead. Some of these developments, all originating from the J-class, came about before the Second World war, which put an end to the Fastnet for eight years, but others had to wait until after it.

The leaders, along with *Carmela* and *Thalassa*, slowly drew away from the rest of the fleet and when night fell *Kismet III* and *Foxhound* were becalmed under St Alban's Head, while *Stormy Weather* crept past them offshore. *Trenchemer*, having missed the tide round Portland, was forced to kedge for an hour before a light air came in from astern enabling her spinnaker and large mizzen staysail to be set and some

progress made. Dawn found *Kismet III* in the lead again, well to seawards, while inshore *Foxhound*, *Stormy Weather* and *Trenchemer* were all more or less together. But after another day of fickle breezes and calms *Stormy Weather* once more took over the lead with Start Point abeam. Astern of these leaders were *Carmela*, *Isis*, *Rose*, and *Ilex*, with the rest of the fleet strung out well astern. Just as dusk fell on the second night out a stronger breeze came off the land which had *Stormy Weather* heeling nicely and shot *Rose* ahead of *Foxhound*. *Trenchemer*, having trouble with her sheets through continually changing sails, dropped back. Later her navigator, W.B. Luard, who had owned *Maitenes II*, gave a lecture on the race and criticised the almost non-stop sail changing which took place, his comments – though appropriate at the time no doubt – showing how ocean racing has changed in the last half-century.

A well-known designer had charge of our sails. He had never been ocean racing before, and forgot that frequent sail changing is not always a virtue. Sometimes, when we were doing as well as possible, he would come up and say, 'I think we'd better have the double-clewed jib down and put up the double-clewed yankee'. We would start to do this and the jib would jamb. We would spend half an hour getting it down, and would perhaps have added quarter of a knot to our speed. Then, half an hour later we would hand the yankee and replace it with some other sail – perhaps the genoa jib. And so it went on. Ultimately, I reckoned that we lost six hours this way.

However, with the Lizard abeam at 0325 *Trenchemer* was still third behind *Stormy Weather* and *Kismet III*. Behind her came *Rose* followed closely by *Foxhound*, and, further behind, *Carmela*, *Emmeline*, and *Ilex*. Friday was another light day, with the leaders trying to find the best course to pass Land's End and head for the Rock. *Trenchemer*'s crew, suspicious of the weather forecast which predicted SW winds, decided to stay south. But when at 1500 both *Kismet III* and *Stormy Weather* went about onto the port tack *Trenchemer* followed suit though she later tacked again when both the leaders continued to stand to the north in the hope that the wind would back. Rod Stephens said afterwards that this was a mistake. *Trenchemer*, her steel hull causing compass trouble, could not take full advantage of this tactical error, but *Foxhound*, holding closer to the rhumb line course, did, and in a freshening NW breeze which later backed a bit but not enough to free *Kismet III* and *Stormy Weather*, she rounded the Rock first at 1425 on the Saturday having gained 3 hours 35 minutes on the American yawl and 1 hour 45 minutes on *Trenchemer*.

In sight astern of *Foxhound* was *Trenchemer*, heeling error on her compass having taken her too far west, but of *Kismet III* and *Stormy Weather* there was no sign. But then they were both spotted beating along the Irish coast approaching the Rock from the north. *Kismet III* rounded at 1447 and *Stormy Weather* at 1500. *Foxhound*, approaching from the opposite direction, gybed and rounded third at 1455.

The freshening breeze during the night had caused some problems though it never exceeded force 5. *Kismet III* had tried to reef by putting a tackle on the tack of the mainsail but the sail had ripped almost right across, and *Thalassa* and *Ilex* both carried away their bobstays. *Thalassa* was badly delayed by this mishap and rounded the Rock some 16 hours after the four leaders. However, the Sappers' boat soon made up for lost time in the strengthening wind and was passed by the leaders on the way back from the Rock only some seven hours behind them.

With the wind now abeam of her, *Foxhound* went like a train but she could not hold off the bigger boats, *Kismet III* and *Trenchemer*, and they both soon passed her, with the smaller *Stormy Weather* dropping back into fourth place. At this point it looked as if *Foxhound* really had a good chance of winning, but then – as so often happens in the Fastnet – she made a landfall too far north and, with the wind falling light again, dropped out of the running, just as *Stormy Weather* was creeping back up to the other two leaders. *Trenchemer*, close behind the leader, *Kismet III*, passed the Seven Stones at 0845 on the Sunday having averaged over nine knots from the Fastnet. She then picked up a fair tide, and with a falling wind was abeam of the Lizard at 1400. At that point *Kismet III* was ten minutes ahead of *Trenchemer* and *Stormy Weather* only an hour and 40 minutes astern, with *Foxhound* now lagging by six hours. Later Luard, aboard *Trenchemer*, wrote:

From this point to the finishing line formed the most exciting part of the race. We hoisted a genoa jib as a light weather mainsail, and, with the large mizzen staysail catching every light air, the spinnaker set in various positions, slowly overhauled *Kismet*, our masthead angle increasing from observations aboard her from 29 to 45

arriving a few minutes before 1600. On corrected time *Stormy Weather* won by the substantial margin of six-and-a-half hours from *Trenchemer*. *Ilex* sailed a magnificent race under her new Bermudian rig and came third, followed by *Foxhound* and, in fifth place, *Kismet III*. *Rose* was another to be treated harshly by the rule and on corrected time she dropped to 11th place.

It was America's year again, with the Stephens brothers showing they could design and race a yacht like no one else, and *Yachting Monthly* ended an article on the ninth Fastnet with fitting praise for *Stormy Weather*'s crew and their methods. 'To see the work they were engaged in the day before the start, and in the evening to see the spotless condition of the yacht (as though she carried two paid hands) was literally awe-inspiring.' 'No temperament, no nerves, and no end of vitality,' was someone else's comment on the young Americans.

By the time the next Fastnet rolled around in 1937 ocean racing had become a sophisticated sport in which many nations took part, with the Fastnet now the apex of a series of races where the base was forever broadening. The Channel Race had been started in 1928 as an annual event, then followed the races to Dinard, round the Haaks and Maas light vessels, and the Heligoland and Plymouth-Belle Isle races, and so on. In 1937 no less than eight ocean races took place, giving the crews and yachts taking part unrivalled experience which would stand them in good stead for the Fastnet. No longer did a few dedicated cruising men – probably not, like their yachts, at the peak of physical fitness – come to the line to take part in the Ocean Racing Club's single fixture. Instead, in 1937, a record entry of 29 yachts from five countries came to the line, most of them superbly equipped and manned by experienced crews. Significantly, the fleet had been divided into two, a racing division and a cruising division, and the number of cups to be won had more than doubled, to five.

'By 1937,' wrote Douglas Phillips-Birt, 'design for offshore in British waters had been transformed. The new type of fast cruiser was generally approved. Overhangs, short keel, moderate displacement, and bermudian rigs no longer struck chill into the heart of blue water sailors.'

Of the British entries, 18 in number, there were three new outstanding newcomers: *Bloodhound*, a sister-hull to *Foxhound* but rigged as a yawl; *Ortac*, designed by Robert Clark, a young newcomer to the sport; and *Maid of Malham*, designed by Laurent Giles but incorporating many of the new radical ideas of her owner, John Illingworth, who, in the 1935 Fastnet had skippered *Thalassa*.

**36** The first boat home in 1935 was *Kismet III* (No. 1, seen here in another race). Described as an ex-15-metre with a 12-metre rig, she was penalised too heavily under the RORC rule to come better than fifth on corrected time.

minutes. But we could not draw level, being, perhaps, half a mile astern at dusk, the two ships making little or no way against the westerly stream. For over three hours we battled to gain feet, the ship pointing badly under her genoa set on the mainmast, though we had made, in furtive and stealthy light airs, to within two cables of *Kismet*, which, in a few minutes, felt the first breath of a light land breeze that failed to reach us.

This land breeze carried *Kismet III* over the line first at 0200 on the Monday, with *Trenchemer* next nearly an hour and a half behind her. *Stormy Weather* came in third about 14 minutes after *Trenchemer*, followed by *Foxhound* – which, to add to the miseries of her crew making a bad landfall, had been becalmed for eight hours off the Lizard – 12 hours after that. *Rose* came in fifth and *Ilex* sixth, there being an interval of just over an hour between them with *Rose*

Of these three, *Maid of Malham* was the closest to being the progenitor of the post-war ocean racer, and though her hull was light displacement and contained some surprising features like a sawn-off counter and a cutaway keel it was her rig which stirred controversy. In fact, though it was Giles' first ocean racing design, Illingworth had chosen him over two more venerable gentlemen, Mylne and Fife, because he did not like the preliminary design submitted by the former – it included a bowsprit – nor the latter's insistence that he design the sail plan as well as the hull. So while Illingworth was happy to let Giles get on with the hull he knew what kind of sail plan he wanted – and intended getting it. Giles had sailed with Illingworth and they obviously got on together, and though Giles probably grumbled a bit – 'you buggers with fixed ideas are awful,' Illingworth records him saying – Illingworth's notions of a radical sail plan, and how the cabin of a cruiser-racer like *Maid of Malham* should be laid out, were in the final design.

A description of the *Maid*'s accommodation is interesting when it is compared with what must have been common practice when she was built and what is normally done today. A *Yachting Monthly* writer wrote:

The accommodation has been planned with certain definite requirements in view. The owners hold that the saloon, which must seat the full crew of eight, should be as far aft as can conveniently be arranged; that the hatch should open directly out of the cockpit and not directly into the saloon; that there should be a proper chart table outside the saloon and handy to the cockpit, with space for the watch on deck to shelter, and facilities for cooking; that there shall be as many bunks as possible outside the saloon (three in this case), and one of them should be fully bulkheaded off but really handy to the cockpit; that finally there shall be sleeping accommodation for the whole crew of eight in harbour. All of which takes a good deal of arranging on a 35-foot waterline.

The waterline length, incidentally, was chosen by Illingworth not so much because it was the minimum length allowed for the Fastnet at that time but because Illingworth had persuaded several owners all to build a similar length to guarantee some close racing. This group quickly became known as the 'thirty-fives.'

The crux of the *Maid*'s radical rig was that the working headsails were set from the masthead, something Illingworth, starting with *Thalassa*'s sail plan, had been working on for some years. Though adopted by Robert Clark for *Ortac*, other designers still made sure that the forestays for the working headsails were fixed at the traditional point to the mast, which on a gaff rig was the main upper cap. The new Bermudian one-piece mast had made this point entirely theoretical but most designers still clung to it, *Maid of Malham* and *Ortac* made sure they did so no longer.

Setting the working canvas from the masthead created a more powerful, higher aspect ratio sail which logically meant the mainmast being stepped further aft. This in turn led to a smaller, higher aspect mainsail and a shorter boom. Away, too, went the traditional Bermudian mast which, following the lines of its gaff-rig predecessor, still tapered elegantly to a point, for it was now essential that the strength of the mast be carried right up to the masthead. *Maid of Malham*'s hollow spar looked very much less elegant than others, but it was far stronger.

Not content with the revolution he had wrought, Illingworth then elaborated on the headsail arrangement by having two positions for the forestay. With working sails the after forestay position would be used, but in heavy weather with only a working jib set the forward one would be. As this now gave the *Maid* twin fore top stays, twin forestays and, in most places, twin halyards there appeared on the foredeck a rash of tack levers, which, the yacht's designer commented tersely, made that part of the boat look like a goods station shunting yard. Illingworth later admitted that the arrangement was over-complicated. But he was learning all the time, and though he did not win the Fastnet in 1937 he won it twice later on.

The course for the 1937 Fastnet was again altered, the fleet for the first time being obliged to leave the Scillies to port after rounding the Rock before finishing at Plymouth.

Interest in the race was intense and bookmakers were offering the following odds: *Bloodhound*, *Maid of Malham* and *Ortac*, 8–1; the Stephens designed American entry, *Elizabeth McCaw*, and the large Fife designed *Latifa*, 10–1; *Stiarna*, a sister-hull to *Bloodhound* but cutter-rigged, and the Stephens-designed Dutch yawl, *Zeearend*, 12–1; the German wishbone Ketch, *Senta*, another German yacht, *Roland von Bremen*, which was the winner of the 1936 Trans-Atlantic Race, another Nicholson-designed cutter, *Firebird X*, and *Trenchemer*, 16–1; and so on down through the complete list of entries until the older cruisers were reached where the odds offered were 100–1 or more. An ex-15 metre, *Pam*, was scratch boat and bottom of the bookmakers' list at 125–1. They were right. She finished last.

A moderate northerly breeze greeted the starters which crossed the line on Saturday, 7 August. *Elizabeth McCaw* and *Saladin* were recalled, but only *Saladin* responded and everyone must have sailed the race wondering whether the Americans would be disqualified. According to the rules they should have been but the RORC committee decided against doing so as they considered a matter of seconds made very little difference in a race over 600 miles long.

Uffa Fox was at the starting line that year and recorded the scene.

There was a good deal of yelling at the weather end of the line from *Zoraida* and *Pam*, for the dinghy on the mark barge to be pulled up. Of those at this end of the line *Asta* made the best start, with Ikey Bell's *Bloodhound* close up on her weather quarter, but it was *Zoraida* who lugged out for the weather berth and the slack water over on the northern shore, the others holding their course down through the strength of the tide. When *Zoraida* had crossed the line her crew hauled in her mainsheet and stole out to the weather of the fleet. Of those who took the eddy tide under the RYS (Royal Yacht Squadron), Michael Mason's *Latifa* led the way soon after the start, with John Gage's *Stiarna* second, *Maid of Malham* third, the gaff boat fourth, and the American yawl fifth. . . . Once Egypt Point had been reached Michael Mason, with a strong lead, luffed across for the northern shore, and when there had a strong lead from the rest of the fleet. Being a RYS member he was bound to put his faith in the Squadron eddy, and it did not fail him, and I really enjoyed seeing him right out ahead of all the fleet.

The breeze came and went and then hardened slightly at nightfall when the leaders were already off Start Point, and *Latifa*, still in the lead, was abeam of the Lizard at 0420 and just managed to avoid the new flood tide which caught the rest of the fleet. *Trenchemer* came next, at 0515, ten minutes ahead of the German Navy yacht, *Asta*, which was followed by *Firebird X*, *Bloodhound*, *Elizabeth McCaw*, and *Striana*. *Maid of Malham*, which could reasonably have been expected to be up with these leaders, did not pass the Lizard until 0930. But she was well bunched with two other 'thirty-fives,' *Ortac* and *Phryne*. All except *Zoraida*, *Trenchemer* and *Zeearend*, whose crews gambled on a predicted westerly and therefore kept going so as to pass the Scillies to starboard, now made for the Longships.

The westerly came on the Sunday night but *Latifa* was first round the Rock at 1330 on the Monday, followed by *Stiarna* and *Elizabeth McCaw*. Then came *Zeearend*, her gamble of passing south of the Scillies obviously having paid off (for various reasons it didn't for the other two). When *Zeearend* rounded the fog was so thick that the crew never saw the light at all. But they could hear the breakers in about the right spot and sailed around them, and got confirmation of their position when they heard Irish voices high

37 In the 1937 Fastnet, Michael Mason's new yawl *Latifa* came home second behind the one American entry, *Elizabeth McCaw*. She was second home again in 1939 and after the war she came first in her class in the 1947 race. She raced again in 1949 and 1951 then disappeared from the Fastnet entry list until she reappeared in 1975.

above them coming through the murk.

*Asta*, rounding third, left too fine a margin between herself and the Rock and was nearly swept onto it, but the tide just carried her clear. Later, *Asta*'s skipper, Lt Cmdr Baron von Lepel, said it was as much luck as skill that they missed being driven ashore.

*Maid of Malham* got to within four or five miles of the Rock but then a failing wind and a contrary tide held her up and she did not round until after 2300. 'By midnight,' wrote one of the crew, 'we were a mile or so from the Rock, and to the south, but the fog was very thick, and the light invisible. We could hear the rattle of the gear aboard a yacht close by, but could not see her. We set the double spinnakers [these were only allowed during the 1937 season and Illingworth was the only one who really made any effective use of them] and lowered the mainsail, but what with the swell and almost complete lack of wind our speed was almost nothing.'

The next morning a wind did eventually set in, a force 2 or 3 from the sw, and *Maid of Malham* made good time until becalmed once more off the Eddystone and this ruined any chance of her winning. 'We lay there all night in an almost glassy calm,' wrote Illingworth. 'I trimmed and retrimmed the sails trying to get her going in the almost fallen breeze. The breeze had to last two more hours to blow us happily into Plymouth, and as it turned out easily to win the Fastnet, but as I say it was not to be; the wind went to nothing and we spent the entire night halfway between the Eddystone and the shore, trimming the light ghosting masthead genoa without any avail and simply drifting about.'

At dawn, still working hard to get his boat going, Illingworth went to sleep standing up on the foredeck, slumped into one of the lower shrouds and woke up just in time to prevent himself falling overboard.

*Latifa*, seven hours ahead of the next two boats, *Elizabeth McCaw* and *Stiarna*, at the Lizard was also caught by the lack of wind and lay becalmed for no less than eight hours off Rame Head almost in sight of the finish. While *Latifa* lay wallowing in the swell, the American yawl managed to sneak ahead and ghosted across the line, followed by *Latifa* 14 minutes later, and then *Stiarna* 36 minutes after that. Fourth across was *Zeearend* which beat *Bloodhound* to the line by just one minute.

There had been several duels during the race but probably the closest fought was between *Elizabeth McCaw* and *Stiarna*. 'We were always in very close company with *Trenchemer*, *Firebird*, *Bloodhound*, *Asta* and *Stiarna*,' said *Elizabeth McCaw*'s skipper, 'Ducky' Endt, who, having sailed in the 1928, 1933 and 1935 Fastnets, was an old hand at tackling the course, 'but our great tussle was with *Stiarna*. We were at the Lizard going west within half an hour of one another, and at the Fastnet were ten minutes astern of her. On our way to the Bishop Rock we overhauled her and managed to keep ahead. During the last few miles we carried our spinnaker though the wind was not really free enough for it to be much good.' Weston Martyr, however, thought it was Endt's work with the spinnaker that won the American yawl the race. 'He literally pulled her along the last fifty miles with a little piece of string made fast to the spinnaker boom instead of the heavier guy and trimmed the spinnaker to a hair.'

But it was *Zeearend* which won on corrected time from *Stiarna* by just under two hours, and everyone agreed that her owner Kees Bruynzeel had sailed a faultless race by making excellent landfalls in the poor visibility and somehow keeping his boat moving in even the lightest zephyr. 'She is a good boat,' said one of the crew when asked how she'd won. 'When there is wind, she goes fast. When there is no wind, she goes a little slower.'

Two of *Zeearend*'s main opponents, *Trenchemer* and *Bloodhound*, made bad landfalls – *Trenchemer* made hers on the wrong side of the Scillies – while others just could not keep their yachts moving in the light conditions, and the Dutchman outsailed 11 larger boats and beat *Maid of Malham*, the third boat on corrected time and perhaps the greatest threat to her, by over four hours on corrected time. *Banba*, which finished remarkably well in eighth place, deservedly won the Hong Kong Cup awarded to the first cruising boat on corrected time. *Asta*, sixth back, won the *Jolie Brise* Cup for being the first cruising boat home. *Ilex* won the Inter-Regimental Cup. *Tai-Mo-Shan* was the only entry to retire as she had to put ashore a sick member at Queenstown.

---

The entries for the 1939 Fastnet underlined the change that had taken place in ocean racing This time the fleet was split into three divisions, Open, A and B. Which yacht was put in which division was explained in the *Royal Artillery Journal* in equestrian terms for its still predominantly horse-minded readers:

Open Division: Steeple chasers
A Division: Genuine hunters
B Division: Cobs

B Division was for real old hookers, clumbungies as they were called, and though three were entered for the race only one, *Forban*, started and she was one of the three yachts which did not complete the course that year. With only five starters out of the 26 belonging to A Division, the race was dominated by the 'steeple chasers' and a good proportion of them were new boats.

Despite war being less than a month away the Germans were at the line again with three starters. *Nordwind*, the new Kriegsmarine Bermudian yawl that had been built to the extreme limit allowed, 60 feet, was their most powerful entry, and the Luftwaffe had sent across another, smaller, yawl, *Walkure*. And there was a new *Roland von Bremen*.

The Dutch had two entries, the new de Vries Lentsch Bermudian cutter *Olivier van Noort*, owned by A.W. Goudriaan, and *Zeearend*, the 1937 winner, still owned and raced by Kees Bruynzeel.

The French had one entry, Georges Baldenweck – by now something of a Fastnet fixture – again appearing at the starting line with *Aile Noire*, the yacht he'd designed specially for the 1937 Fastnet.

With only six foreign entries in the Open Division – there were no Americans that year – the 1939 Fastnet was dominated by British yachts. Interest centred on Ted Gore-Lloyd's Bermudian sloop, *Benbow*; a Bermudian yawl, *Lara*, owned by Kenneth Poland; the Bermudian cutter, *Mary Bower*, which was a near sister ship of *Ortac* which was not racing that year;

38  *Griffin* sailed in the 'A' Division in the 1939 Fastnet. She later became the RORC's first club boat.

39  The first boat home in 1939 was *Nordwind*, owned by the Kriegsmarine. She completed the course in the fastest time since *Hallowe'en* in 1926. Under British ownership she also sailed in the 1953 Fastnet.

and another Bermudian sloop, *Erivale*. All of them had been designed by Robert Clark.

Other new entries in the Open Division included the Fife-designed *Evenlode*, *Morva*, *Joyrena*, and the Hong Kong built Bermudian cutter, *Golden Dragon*, designed by her owner, H.S. Rouse. Veterans of the 1937 Fastnet included *Maid of Malham* (being sailed by the Royal Naval Sailing Association in the absence of Illingworth on duty abroad), *Bloodhound*, *Stiarna* and *Latifa*.

The most interesting entry in A Division was a new gaff cutter, *Griffin*, owned by the RORC's Admiral, E.G. Martin, and destined to become the club's first boat.

The course was again changed, being from Ryde westwards through the Needles Channel with the Scillies being left to the north on both the outward and homeward legs. The finish was again at Plymouth.

The gun for the 11th Fastnet went on 5 August at noon with the wind fresh from the north, gusting quite heavily at times in rain squalls. It looked as if, for a change, it was going to be a heavy weather race. But the squalls did not deter most of the crews breaking out genoas or yankees over reaching staysails as the line was crossed, first by *Stiarna*, closely followed by *Maid of Malham* and *Zeearend*. This excess of canvas soon had its first casualty when 'a real snorter of a

squall,' as one eye-witness described it, hit the fleet as it reached through Cowes Roads, and *Benbow* lost her big balloon jib.

After a poor start *Latifa* began working her way through the fleet and was soon abeam of the scratch boat, *Nordwind*, but at the Needles the German yawl led the fleet. This short run established for *Latifa*'s crew that *Nordwind* was the boat to beat, not on corrected time for *Nordwind* was giving the British boat something like four hours, but boat for boat, and a battle developed between these the two largest yachts in the race which began at the Needles and did not finish until Plymouth. During this time they were never more than a mile apart.

As the Needles was being passed by the rest of the fleet, *Aile Noire* crossed the starting line having somehow got stuck on the Brambles sandbank.

During the night and the early hours of Sunday morning the wind backed steadily. *Latifa*, in these conditions, managed to get her nose ahead of *Nordwind* while *Bloodhound* and *Benbow* kept close on her tail. These four got past Start Point before the wind headed the rest of the fleet which *Latifa*, at least, did not then see again. Monday morning saw the German yacht in front and off the Scillies she was two miles ahead when she tacked to give the Skerries a wide berth. *Latifa*, however, kept close to them as one of the crew knew the area well, and when the rain squalls had cleared the British boat was again in the lead, by two miles. All that day the two great yachts fought it out with *Benbow* hanging on grimly in third place. At this point *Bloodhound* had dropped out of sight astern.

The wind now headed the leaders and they picked up the Irish coast near the Head of Kinsale, 40 miles to leeward of the Rock, and had to beat up to it. For some reason – perhaps it was a navigating error – *Benbow*, which had been closing up on *Latifa*, now hoisted a spinnaker and changed course for the coast. This left *Nordwind* and *Latifa* to fight it out for the honour of rounding the Rock first, an honour which now carried with it the *Elizabeth McCaw* Trophy, a handsome silver reproduction of the Fastnet Rock and lighthouse. Alf Loomis who was on board *Latifa* wrote:

*Nordwind* closed with the coast to leeward of a clump of remarkable rocks known as the Stags, and tacked away. We carried on, looking for the header that we hoped would let us up on the opposite tack. It did not come and we tacked to starboard, *Nordwind* drawing ahead in a freshening air. In again we went on the port tack, still looking for the lead wind. No dice. Out, and in, almost to the mouth of Baltimore Bay in the lee of Cape Clear. About to starboard, and at last we found what we'd been seeking. Tumbling down from mountainous shoulder of Cape Clear Island came the wind in lusty favoring squalls. Mike, at the wheel, luffed out of the sharpest of them, with *Latifa* eating up to windward of *Nordwind* like a 12-metre. But *Nordwind* soon saw what we were up to and tacked in to share our fun. It looked for some minutes as if we had regained the lead but when, presently, we drew away from the Cape and the wind failed, there sat *Nordwind* on our starboard beam not 200 yards distant. As we lay becalmed, *Latifa*'s extremely efficient crew snaked a larger jib topsail out of the locker and doused the one we had been carrying (a number two over a jibstay genoa). *Nordwind* began to follow suit but, in the few instants in which our masthead stay was denuded of sail, the wind came in again. We were now two miles from the Fastnet Rock, looming up in the late afternoon light, and the uppermost thought in the minds of everybody was the Elizabeth McCaw Trophy. *Nordwind* went out to get it and, as soon as the wind reached us, we tacked to get it from her. She covered us and before she was filled away Mike tacked again – twelve-metre tactics with a vengeance, after 360 miles of ocean racing! But the moment came when

40  The Luftwaffe boat, *Walkure*, tacking away to avoid the shallow patch near the Rock, while duelling with *Rose*.

41  The crew of *Rose* are all on deck as she cuts between the shallow patch and the Rock. By doing this they beat *Walkure* round the Rock. The original caption for this shot said that the Luftwaffe later got their own back by bombing the RORC clubhouse!

42  The 1939 winner, *Bloodhound*. (*Beken*)

short tacking ceased to offer even the chance of escape. *Nordwind* laid for the Rock on the starboard tack and our only hope rested in the possibility that the tide would set her down and cause her to pass to leeward of it and round the

first boat home. It was this prize that the two biggest boats concentrated on for they knew, with the much smaller *Bloodhound* only two hours astern, the Fastnet Cup was beyond the grasp of either of them. In the race back the German yawl first of all blew out her spinnaker and then *Latifa* lost hers when it wrapped itself around the upper spreaders and disintegrated. Smaller spinnakers were set by both boats and in a wind that strengthened to 20 knots, building up a disordered sea, they rolled down towards the Bishop. With *Nordwind* still ahead *Latifa* passed the Bishop at 1300 on the Tuesday, but then the wind faded and it took the British boat nine hours to cover the 45 miles between the Lizard and the finishing line. She eventually crossed at 0501 on the Wednesday, about 33 minutes behind *Nordwind*.

However, the breeze freshened once more for the other leading boats and *Bloodhound*, five hours behind *Latifa* at the Lizard, made up half of this time and finished only 20 minutes behind the third boat, *Benbow*, which crossed at 0719. All first four boats had beaten the previous record held by *Hallowe'en* since 1926 but they were being closely pursued by other competitors and it was not certain for some time who had won the Fastnet Cup. *Zeearend* came second on corrected time and missed the main prize — which went to *Bloodhound* — by only an hour and five minutes. *Roland von Bremen* finished at 0826, a good enough time to push *Latifa* into fourth place with *Benbow* fifth. Immediately behind this second group came the Dutchman, *Olivier van Noort*, and the British *Erivale*, having fought as close a battle round the course as *Nordwind* and *Latifa*. They had rounded the Rock with *Olivier van Noort* a little way ahead, but on the run home, and always in sight of one another, *Erivale* crept into the lead and finished just two minutes ahead though on corrected time she lost to the Dutch boat by 22 minutes.

Behind these two came *Lara*, eighth on corrected time, followed by *Evenlode*, which had made a bad landfall, *Nordwind* tenth, and *Aile Noire*, which had sailed a remarkable race after so poor a start, 11th.

But some of the stars had failed to shine: *Maid of Malham* never showed at all, while first-class yachts like *Phryne*, *Mary Bower* and *Stiarna* also had a poor race, the last blowing out no less than five sails before finishing 18th.

Though no American yacht was present in 1939 the Americans could still claim victory of a kind. Ikey Bell, the owner of *Bloodhound*, was American, and the second boat, *Zeearend*, had been designed by Sparkman and Stephens.

other way. She avoided this by careful sailing, almost scraping the barnacles from the weather side of the Rock as she slipped past and we rounded several yards outside her wake, five minutes astern.

*Nordwind* rounded the Rock at 1920 on the Monday evening with *Benbow*, third, an hour behind. *Bloodhound* rounded fourth at 2105, followed by *Lara* at 0145 the next morning, *Olivier van Noort* (0255), *Evenlode* (0845), *Erivale* (0952) and *Roland von Bremen* (1011).

By the time *Roland von Bremen* had turned the mark the wind and sea had risen appreciably and *Benbow* soon lost her heavy spinnaker while *Bloodhound* lost two of hers. But the fight was now on to win another of the new trophies, the *Erivale* Cup, awarded to the

# CHAPTER THREE

# Post-war Pioneers    1947–59

Having signed ourselves on for the Fastnet
We wish to see down in the Log
The 'vittals' our Captain sees us get,
And a fair distribution of grog.
Five meals a day is the least we
Expect to have dropped in our 'tums',
While of spirits, as part of our dietary,
Neat whiskies, neat gins and neat rums.

We ain't over anxious to labour,
But realise the ship must be manned;
So we'll put in our eight hours daily
And for sixteen will quietly get canned.
The Captain may eat at our table,
He's a sociable sort of a chap,
Provided he minds of his manners
And keeps a tight hold on his trap.

Articles for crew of *Thalassa*, from *To Sea in Carpet Slippers* by A.C. 'Sandy' Sandison

Ocean racing in Britain began again in September 1945, a handful of yachts completing the Channel Race to Dinard escorted by a destroyer to make sure they avoided any minefields. But as the Americans wanted to hold the Bermuda Race in 1946 it was decided not to hold the first post-war Fastnet until the following year. Before it took place the minimum waterline length for a Fastnet entry was reduced to 30 feet and a change in classing entries was decided upon. No longer would class divisions be decided by length alone but would be based on rating as well. For the 1947 season there were three classes: Class I, which was for yachts of a minimum LWL of 38 feet and below 60-foot rating; Class II, for yachts of a minimum LWL of 27.5 feet and below 38-foot rating; and Class III, for yachts of a minimum LWL of 19 feet and below 27.5-foot rating. This meant that only yachts in Classes I and II were eligible for the Fastnet.

The two years from the end of the war to the 12th Fastnet in 1947 was a time when considerable re-adjustment took place in British society. In ocean racing, as elsewhere, it became apparent very quickly that the more leisurely, monied pre-war days had gone forever. No longer could the sport be dominated by the large expensive cruiser/racer, with its complement, however small, of paid hands. The future lay in the small, light displacement, relatively inexpensive yacht and men like H.G. 'Blondie' Hasler, with his 30sq. metre *Tre Sang*, and Adlard Coles with his first *Cohoe*, soon proved that these smaller, light displacement yachts were both safe and fast offshore, and they were an inspiration to those who were determined to go ocean racing on a small budget.

However, the most startling advance in ocean racing design came with Illingworth's Class II cutter, *Myth of Malham*. While his earlier boat, *Maid of Malham*, had had revolutionary ideas incorporated into her construction, *Myth of Malham* turned inside out everyone's idea of ocean racing design and at the same time exposed yawning gaps in the RORC rule.

At the end of the war Illingworth had found himself in Australia, and had helped found the Sydney-Hobart Race, winning the first one in 1945. The following year he sailed *Latifa* in the Bermuda Race before returning to England determined to build a new yacht. Laurent Giles was consulted and work on the design of the new boat started. Twice the designer drew a set of lines and twice they were rejected by Illingworth who, this time, was not content just to revolutionise the sail plan and rigging of ocean racers, but their hulls as well. The third set of lines he accepted, apart from eradicating a steep tumble home the designer had added to her quarter in an effort to make her more attractive. Then Illingworth announced to the no doubt astonished Giles that he intended to cut off both the bow and the stern above the waterline, leaving the lines under the water untouched; and that he was going to put a transom just above the waterline in the bow and one two feet or so outside the waterline at the stern. It is not recorded how Giles took this news but, as Illingworth has recorded in his book, *The Malham Story*, he was a very patient man. He did, however, say that 'when John Illingworth commissioned my firm to design his new ocean racer in 1946 I took good care to plant the responsibility for her behaviour at sea firmly on his shoulders,' and added that *Myth of Malham* justified Illingworth's judgement amply and ably. 'She is absolutely at home on the high seas,' said Giles.

The result of this partnership was a light displacement boat with a high freeboard, straight sheer, sawn-off ends and an extraordinary rounded bow which drew as many adverse comments as the rest of the boat

**43** *Myth of Malham* in a calm patch plainly showing her rounded bow. One yachting journalist called her 'a dreadful-looking monstrosity'. But she won the 1947 and 1949 Fastnets and revolutionised yacht design.

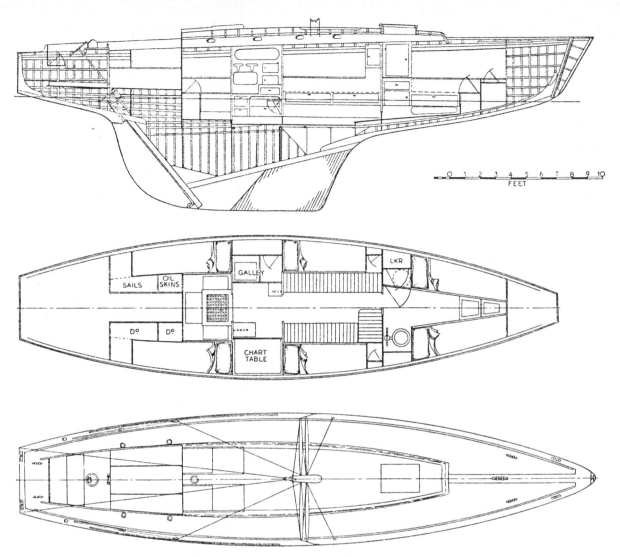

44 The plans of *Myth of Malham* showing her false bow, her neat accommodation, and how far aft the mast was stepped.

put together. It was detachable because both Illingworth and Giles suspected that with the appearance of *Myth* the RORC rule would have to be altered, and they wanted, when long overhangs were no longer penalised so severely, to be able to add a more graceful bow to her. *Myth* was not by the standards of the day – perhaps by any standards – a pretty boat. A commentator in *Yachting* called her 'a dreadful-looking monstrosity,' but her straight sheerline and short overhangs cleverly evaded the depth and length measurement of the RORC rule. Her sail plan too was arranged with the quite legitimate intention of evading the RORC rule, which penalised the foretriangle of a yacht's sail plan lightly, putting the burden on the mainsail area. But as Illingworth wanted large overlapping headsails it suited his purpose to have *Myth*'s mast stepped only just forward of amidships which resulted in a mainsail which measured only 14 feet at

its foot and which had a very high aspect ratio of 3:1. 'I don't call that a 'mainsail,' Giles protested to Illingworth, 'it's just a flag abaft the mast', and in a rather restrained review of the yacht, *Yachting World* called the sail plan 'quite the most extreme example we have seen in this country.'

*Myth of Malham* was built in Scotland and finished just in time to take part in the Clyde Fortnight where she was quick to show her close windedness. She then won a race from Rosneath to Portsmouth and the Channel Race in quick succession, and entered the Fastnet as one of the entries to be most feared. Humphrey Barton, one of Laurent Giles' partners and a regular member of Illingworth's crew, wrote with wonderment of his first day aboard her.

The first unusual feature I noticed about the *Myth* was the two companion hatches placed side-by-side and divided by a narrow piece of coach roof on which were mounted the mainsheet lead block, winch and cleat. This proved to be a great success. In fine weather we always had both hatches open; in rough weather the windward hatch was closed. The long deep cockpit, divided into two by a bridge deck on which were mounted the mainsheet slide and a telescopic gallows of John's design, reminded me of *Maid of Malham*. It had been the original intention to have wheel steering in the after cockpit but there had been no time to fit this. Instead we had a short tiller in the forward cockpit. The sheet winches were designed by John and there were two on each side of the cockpit. On the extreme outer edge of the covering boards were the sliding sheet leads running in tracks. The sheets for all headsails led through these to blocks further aft and thence forward to the winches.

The rigging of the mast, which is placed almost in the middle of the boat, is a little unusual in some respects. There are two staysail halyards, two jib halyards (mast head), spinnaker halyard, main halyard and spinnaker boom lift. Headsail halyards lead to top-action bronze winches on each side of the mast. Both the forestay and masthead forestay are single; the former can be released by a lever situated under the fo'c'sle floor. Preventer backstays are double, there being one to each quarter. Runners are single part and are set up by levers to John's design. The fore and aft rigging is kept at a fairly high tension to ensure reasonably straight luffs to the headsails.

Lying flat on my stomach on the fore deck I hung over her extraordinary rounded nose to see what was happening lower down. Apart from noisily pushing up some water and spray, and sometimes throwing spray ahead of her, there appeared to be nothing very unusual. Then I noticed two jets of water streaming from two holes in the fore-foot every time she rose to a slight swell. This was really most strange; in fact I could hardly believe my eyes. As a partner in the firm that designed the yacht I should perhaps have known all about it but in point of fact I had little or nothing to do with designing her. It had been a fearfully busy winter and each of us had been so occupied at his own particular job that there just had not been time to take in all that was going on around one.

'John,' I asked, 'why does your ugly duckling have two jets of water streaming from her fore-foot every time she lifts her nose?'

'That is easily explained,' he replied. 'As you know, the false nose bolts on to a water-tight bulkhead. On deck there is a short steel tube for'ard which carries the ends of the lifelines. This tube has two large slots on its forward face. Air passes down this tube into the false nose. At the top of the bulkhead are four large holes which can in an emergency be plugged – you will see the corks hanging from brass chains if you go below and look. Air finds its way aft through these holes and will, I hope, provide enough ventilation. Any water that might get down through the tube would eventually have filled up the nose had we not drilled two holes in the fore-foot to allow it to drain off.'

*Myth* was full of such inventive touches, and she proved to be one of the most revolutionary designs ever to appear in a Fastnet Race.

There were 27 starters for the first post-war Fastnet, ten in Class I and 17 in Class II, a highly satisfactory number considering the course had not been raced over for eight years. It was also an international event with the Dutch being represented in Class I by *Zeearend*, the 1937 winner, and in Class II by *Olivier van Noort* and *Corabia II*. The Irish were represented in Class II by *Aideen* as were the Danes (*Marama*) and the Norwegians (*Peter*). Most of the other, English, entries had raced in pre-war Fastnets: *Latifa, Bloodhound* – now owned by a future ROKC Commodore, Myles Wyatt – *Neith, Benbow,* and *Lara* were all in Class I, while *Phryne, Erivale, Maid of Malham, Thalassa, Griffin* and *MacNab* were all Class II. New to the race were *Theodora, Orion,* and *Rulewater* in Class I and *Gauntlet, Concara, Goodewind,* and the Sappers' new boat, *Seamew,* in Class II. But old-timers like *Rose* and *Ilex* were not at the starting line when the gun went at 1400 on Friday, 8 August.

The start was off Southsea, with one end of the line being marked by a buoy and the other by a destroyer, and the course, also for a change, was eastwards round the Isle of Wight, with competitors being allowed to pass between the Scillies. The wind was very light from the east and *Myth of Malham*, for one, had a bad start being blanketed by the destroyer. Nevertheless, Illingworth managed to luff the beautiful *Benbow* to a standstill, much to the disgust of the owner's wife, who shouted, to Illingworth's amusement, 'Get out of our way, you ugly little boat.'

By the Bembridge Ledge buoy 'the ugly little boat' had overhauled most of the fleet and lay fifth behind *Zeearend, Latifa, Bloodhound* and *Benbow*. '*Latifa* went through the fleet in a six-knot breeze like a train of cars,' wrote Alf Loomis who was aboard Kenneth Poland's keel-centreboard yawl, *Lara*, 'closely followed by the lovely *Bloodhound* and *Benbow*, and pretty soon we saw the fabulous *Myth of Malham* laying the port tack for the Wight shore.'

There had been a good deal of speculation aboard *Lara* – and almost certainly aboard nearly all the Fastnet entries – about *Myth of Malham*, and as Illingworth had kept her under wraps, as it were, before the race, little was known about her. On *Lara* someone said that when she appeared it would be in the guise of a secret weapon, springing fully manned and canvassed from the deck of a submerged submarine. 'She went like smoke,' said Loomis, 'and, although she draws more than seven feet, played the reefs off Bembridge at least a mile closer than I would have enjoyed doing. Which is one reason, the tide being now ahead, that she rounded the Bembridge buoy in company with competitors almost twice as big as she.'

The older yachts, however, had a struggle to keep going westwards against the tide. But the sun was out and *Griffin*'s account of this part of the race reads like a holidaymaker's diary. Not tough Fastnet going at all. But when the Bishop was cleared two-and-a-half days later the yachts met a nasty cross chop which set them rolling in a particularly unpleasant corkscrew motion. Progress was painfully slow and for many it was not until the Wednesday morning that the Rock was sighted. *Griffin*'s crew, having sailed for the last three or four days with hardly a sail in sight, rounded the Rock with 11 other yachts though by this time the leaders, *Latifa* – which had rounded first to win the Elizabeth McCaw Trophy – *Zeearend*, *Bloodhound*, *Myth of Malham* and *Benbow*, were well on their way home. *Neith* was first of this group of 12 to round, at 1130, then came *Olivier van Noort* and *Marama* at 1230, *Aideen* at 1240, *Peter* at 1250, *Theodora* at 1300, *Maid of Malham* and *Thalassa* at 1320, *Goodewind* at 1405, *Gauntlet* at 1445, and *Griffin* and *Concara* at 1535.

The wind was free for the leaders on the return trip but then it headed them when they entered the English Channel. *Myth of Malham*, after some minor compass trouble which had put her too far south at the Bishop, spent a bumpy 18 hours beating into a fresh easterly. Near the finish this died and as *Myth* drifted along the army began some target practice, and the yacht only narrowly escaped being hit. The language, according to one of the crew, was frightful. The line was crossed at 2317 on 14 August, 6 days 9 hours 17 minutes out from Spithead, and although it had been a light weather race Illingworth later noted that *Myth* had averaged just over six knots from start to finish. She finished fifth behind *Latifa* (2124, 13 August), *Bloodhound* (1109, 14 August), *Benbow* (2222, 14 August), and *Zeearend* (2228, 14 August), but on corrected time she was easily the winner from *Latifa* by nearly six hours.

The rest of the fleet struggled in over many days: *Lara* and *Phryne* both had a bad race and finished well down as they both had mainsail trouble. *Gauntlet*, the last boat to finish, took ten days to cover the course. At least she got there. Others – *Rulewater*, *Concara*, *Goodewind*, *MacNab*, and *Seamew* – found the going too slow and retired. But one old-timer, *Thalassa*, had a good race coming third in the Class II cruiser division, and her log shows that her crew, Thalassians they called themselves, had a good time too, for, intermingled with comparatively normal entries which showed they were becalmed, were comments of a more general nature.

|  |  |
|---|---|
| | *12 August* |
| 0830 | Flatters. |
| 0930 | Harry Flatters. |
| 1030 | Fanny Adams. |
| | *13 August* |
| 1900 | Dinner taken: Fried chips, baked pollack and codling in milk with sage, garlic and tomatoes, cheese sauce, peas, baked potatoes, peaches, beer, gin, whisky and rum. |
| | *14 August* |
| 1000 | Rear view of two members of crew performing their ablutions on the after deck rather reminiscent of the more colourful apes at Regent's Park. Any complaints about the comparison would more justifiably emanate from the apes. |
| | *15 August* |
| 1245 | Beer and spirits holding up well in spite of considerable punishment and pessimistic 'forecast of Captain.' |
| | *16 August* |
| 0500 | Tobacco situation which has been getting a little strained today temporarily relieved by Captain Baker who being aroused from his slumber at 0500 dived into some secret recess and produced a packet of 20 and issued one each to Port Watch and Navigator. Issue deferentially received! Captain Baker rather surprised at being treated so politely became suspicious and endeavoured to hide the packet. |

It can be seen from this extract that Thalassians had a healthy disrespect of their skipper, Alan Baker, and a healthy liking for the good things in life. It was all part of the Thalassian way of life which Sandy Sandison, *Thalassa*'s cook and a regular crew member, boiled down to two things in his book *To Sea in Carpet*

*Slippers*: 'a) race *Thalassa* as hard as possible on every possible occasion, and b) extract in the doing of this the maximum amount of fun and enjoyment,' which included eating well, very well, drinking deep, and not taking anything, or anyone, especially the skipper, seriously. *Thalassa*'s crew were probably fairly typical of the younger post-war generation of Fastnet yachtsmen who, perhaps to their infinite surprise, had managed to survive the war and were hell bent on celebrating this fact by living life to the hilt.

---

With *Myth of Malham*'s design kicking a hole in the RORC rule it is not surprising that by the next Fastnet, in 1949, it had been revised in an attempt to close the gaps so brilliantly exploited by Illingworth. It was decided that all yachts built after 1 January 1940 would have to be rerated. The new ratings were to be calculated by certain additional measurements and mathematical formulae which were formulated to plug the gaps without affecting much, if at all, the ratings of most of the ocean racing fleet. It was also decided to introduce allowances for yachts which had less than the maximum drafts allowed for a boat's waterline length.

This revision of the rule was intended to be only temporary until a completely new rule was drawn up, and while it may have stopped people thinking that *Myth of Malham* was a rule-cheater it certainly did not stop her winning the 1949 Fastnet in as convincing a fashion as she had in 1947. In fact, *Myth* very nearly did not appear at the starting line in 1949, and it was only because one of Illingworth's crew, Mary Blewitt, 'bullied' him into it, as he described it in his book, that Illingworth got her afloat at all that year. 'You are a bloody fool to leave the best ocean racer in the world ashore with the Fastnet coming on us,' she said to him succinctly.

Sadly, *Myth* had no way of proving she was the best in the world that year as, again, no Americans were entered, and without them nothing could be proved. Nevertheless, there was some pretty stiff competition amongst the other starters which included, in Class I, *Gulvain*, an aluminium constructed cutter, 43 feet LWL, and a logical development of *Myth of Malham*; and in Class II, *Fandango*, at 33 feet LWL a smaller version of *Gulvain*. She had the larger boat's reverse sheer but was built of double-skinned mahogany. Both were brand new and both looked flyers, *Gulvain* just having won the Cowes-Dinard Race. But neither had been tested in heavy weather. Another new Class II yacht with a lot of potential was the Gunners' new yacht, *St Barbara*, while old-timers included *Latifa*, *Bloodhound* and *Erivale*. Altogether there were 29 starters, nine of them in Class I and 20 in Class II, the latter including two Dutch yachts, *Olivier van Noort* and *Corabia II*; one French entry, *Farewell*; and the Argentinian yacht, *Joanne*.

The start, which had reverted to the Royal Yacht Squadron line at Cowes, was on Saturday, 6 August. The course was slightly altered, being through the Needles Channel to the Scillies, which could be left on either hand, round the Fastnet and then back to Plymouth, leaving the Scillies to port. The wind was a moderate westerly at the start but the weather forecast was ominous. But even before it came on to blow accidents started happening. Off Hurst Castle, *Sea Feather* lost her mast in the bumpy seas and very shortly afterwards so did *Ortac*.

*St Barbara* began her long and distinguished Fastnet career well as this extract from her log indicates. 'At 1015 we were away to a good start and at once took the lead from the whole fleet. The wind was westerly and moderate which meant a beat down to the Needles. The weight of wind was just right for the large genoa and the ship romped along beautifully with the lee rail down. Gradually we increased our lead on the *Myth* who was second away and rather more quickly on the remainder. Eventually *Bloodhound* came up and passed us but not until Yarmouth was nearly abeam.'

That first night the wind stayed moderate westerly, around force 4 or 5, but the dawn was a red one and the wireless predicted a SW gale which would veer west later. On *Myth of Malham* the glass fell with such extraordinary swiftness that the navigator, Mary Blewitt, had difficulty in persuading Illingworth what was happening. Navigator: 'Tell the skipper the glass has fallen one-tenth in the last quarter of an hour.' Pete: 'Maria says its fallen one-tenth since last reading, sir.' Skipper: 'Impossible; she must mean one-hundredth.' Pete: 'Skipper says you must mean one-hundredth.' Maria: 'I don't mean one-hundredth. I mean one-tenth.' Pete: 'She means one-tenth, sir.' Skipper: 'Tell her to look again.' Pete: 'Maria, Skipper wants you to look again.' Maria: 'Tell him I said one-tenth and mean one-tenth.'

With the big boats like *Latifa*, *Bloodhound* and *Mariella* – at 68 feet overall the largest yacht in the race – well ahead, *Gulvain* had Start Point abeam at 0730 on the Sunday morning, having stood out across the Channel during the night. She overhauled both *Myth of Malham* and *Corabia II* in a freshening wind, and was closing up on *Joanne*. At 1000 she passed the Argentinian and with the Eddystone abeam was logging 9½ knots. But it was too good to last for the new and untried boat and as the wind and sea began to rise, and the glass to drop, small gear failures began to occur and this made the crew cautious in what sails to set. By afternoon she was under a single headsail though still making 7 or 8 knots. At 1530 she had the Lizard abeam in a nasty tumbling sea. The visibility was poor but *Mariella* was spotted making for shelter with her mainsail split. Then at 1730 came disaster for *Gulvain* when the stainless steel rod which connected the forestay to the release lever below decks parted with a sound like gunshot. The staysail immediately flogged itself to ribbons and the mast began whipping about in the most alarming manner. It was now blowing force 8, gusting to force 9, and the gale was driving *Gulvain* straight onto the lee shore. It must have been a very nasty moment for the crew but luckily the wind then veered just sufficiently for them to be able to hoist a no. 3 jib and creep round the Lizard and into Falmouth. One of *Myth*'s most dangerous rivals was out of the running.

Meanwhile, *Latifa*, having passed the Lizard at 1130 under trysail and storm jib, passed the Runnelstone at 1310, but was then forced to double-reef her trysail and heave-to for some hours. Behind her *Bloodhound* was reduced to a headsail and her mizzen, and then to just a spitfire jib. *St Barbara*, in fourth place behind *Myth of Malham*, also hove-to as did all the others behind her. These amounted to only a dozen or so as already there had been many retirements caused by sea-sickness and gear failure. The crew of *Fandango*, perhaps *Myth*'s only other serious rival, were crippled by sea-sickness, and retired; *Olivier van Noort* broke her rudder and was towed into Plymouth by a cable ship; *Golden Dragon* broke her tiller; *Farewell* broke a crosstree and put into Brixham; *Helgoland*, *Eostra* and *Corabia II* all had sail trouble of some sort or another; while *Phryne* was plagued by both gear failure and sea-sickness. It was a long list, longer, perhaps, than it should have been but post-war restrictions were still in force and keeping a yacht's gear in A1 condition was probably a struggle if not impossible.

While all these retirements were taking place behind her, and almost all the rest were hove-to, *Myth* kept going under a double-reefed mainsail and a staysail. What's more, in a full gale and extremely poor visibility, Illingworth decided to follow *Bloodhound* – which was being navigated by no less a person than the Hydrographer of the Royal Navy – through the gap between Land's End and the Scillies. It was a calculated risk but Illingworth had great faith in his navigator and in his American direction-finding set which was getting good bearings of Round Island and from the RDF station at the northern end of the Scillies. But it was, as Illingworth admitted, anxious work tacking inside the Scillies in a full gale with the visibility down to a hundred yards at times, but eventually they were through beyond the Seven Stones Reef. Here the wind eased back to force 6 or so,

and, hard on the wind, with a small jib set forward of the staysail, Illingworth set a course for the Rock. *St Barbara*, however, was more cautious, a sensible reaction in the circumstances but one which was later regretted as her fair log reveals.

At 1800 DR put the ship 5 miles SSE of the Lizard. We had been running on dead reckoning since losing the Needles having sighted no land from which to take an accurate fix, and after over 24 hours there is always the possibility that it has become inaccurate. Consequently, rather than close with the coast in bad weather and poor visibility to pass between the Longships and the Seven Stones, the skipper decided to stand off to the south and keep an offing until the weather cleared a bit. Unfortunately as it turned out this decision cost us several hours allowing *Latifa*, *Bloodhound* and *Myth* to get way out ahead.

By 0700 on the Monday all *Myth*'s reefs had been shaken out and she was making $6\frac{1}{4}$ knots in a sea that was still very lumpy. Then at 1015 that morning the helmsman shouted out that the spreader had come adrift. The crew off watch below, knowing that the lee spreaders were always free to pivot on the mast fittings, merely shouted back that that was what it was designed to do. 'Yes,' came the reply from the helmsman, 'but not at the inner end.' This brought everyone up on deck very quickly and it was seen that a lower spreader had come adrift from the mast. Two crew members were sent aloft and emergency repairs made, and at 1445 on the Tuesday *Myth* rounded the Rock. The lighthouse keepers flashed that *Latifa* had passed at 0930 that morning and *Bloodhound* at noon. To be under three hours behind *Bloodhound*, a very much larger yacht, seemed to *Myth*'s crew to be almost too good to be true, and by this time she had stretched her lead over the next yacht, *St Barbara*, to nearly 12 hours.

A blue nylon spinnaker was now hoisted for the run home and the other female member of the crew, Pam, took the helm. Just as the spinnaker halyard was about to be made fast *Myth* gave a big, lurching roll which sent a crew member, not a large man, sailing up the mast. Fortunately, he not only managed to hang on to the halyard but was able to hook his feet under the lower crosstrees, and when *Myth* rolled back again Illingworth tailed his 14 stone onto the end of the halyard and the man dropped back on deck. 'That'll

**45** During the war the Gunners' boat, *Rose*, was hit by an incendiary bomb, so it was decided to build a new boat. The result was the highly successful *St Barbara*, which took part in every Fastnet between 1949 and 1965, before being relieved of her duties by *St Barbara II*.

be an effing good warning to you to be more careful when hoisting a spinnaker in force 6,' said Pam to her skipper.

*Myth* was now doing 9½ knots, more than her theoretical maximum speed. This soon proved to be too much for the spinnaker boom and it broke. Repairs were made and a smaller spinnaker set, but the head of it soon pulled out and it was replaced with a large yankee. By 0400 the wind had eased and the large blue spinnaker was reset, and the Bishop was abeam at 1430, but at nightfall the wind began to rise again. One of the crew wrote:

By 2300 we were doing seven knots, by midnight eight knots, by 0100 nine knots and by 0200 ten knots! That was quite the most fantastic piece of sailing I have ever experienced in my life and all the members of the crew said the same thing. The visibility was only about one mile, it was as dark as pitch without any horizon or stars or lights to be seen, so that the helmsman only had the glowing compass card to steer by. We were tearing over the water, leaving a wake like a destroyer, the water fanning up from the bow as if we were being towed at twice our maximum speed. As each wave came up from astern we started to plane and remained for long periods (15 seconds or more), poised on the top almost as if we had developed wings. You could feel the ship quivering and vibrating under the strain and we blessed the stout double masthead preventers which took the enormous pull of the spinnaker. How the nylon stood it I don't know, for we were being drawn through the water far in excess of theoretical maximum speed – there was something awe-inspiring, almost frightening about the whole thing.

Eventually, after *Myth* had nearly broached-to twice, the entrance to Plymouth harbour was reached and in driving rain the spinnaker was at last doused and a jib and staysail set, and *Myth* crossed the line at 0447 on the Thursday morning. Only two boats were ahead of her: *Latifa* had finished at 1725 the previous evening and *Bloodhound* at 2335. On corrected time *Myth of Malham* won by over eight hours from *Bloodhound*, the Class I winner, with *Latifa* third. The only other two yachts to finish in Class I were *Theodora* and the Sappers' *Avalanche of Aldershot*, an ex-German 100sq. metre. The first took nearly nine days to finish, the second just over 11 days. *Avalanche* had ripped her mainsail and finished in light winds under trysail while *Theodora*, an old Bristol Channel Pilot cutter, was similarly delayed by not having one of her sails left untorn.

Class II fared better with six yachts finishing, but

the last boat over, *Galahad*, reported using her engine when she had to put in to Baltimore and was therefore disqualified. *St Barbara* came second in Class II behind *Myth of Malham*, and crossed the line at 1926 on the Thursday evening. *Joanne* came next at 0533 the next morning and was placed third on corrected time. Almost 24 hours later *Sea Otter* arrived but nearly four days passed before the next Class II boat, *Griffin*, crossed having taken 10 days and 2 hours to complete the course. It was calculated afterwards that she had sailed 800 miles to cover the 615-mile course.

So out of 29 starters only nine officially finished, gear failure and sea-sickness taking its toll. The race had shown the superiority of *Myth of Malham* and had drummed home the fact to a new generation that after a series of light-weather Fastnets and a world war a yacht's gear and sails – and her crew – had to be in top condition if a heavy weather Fastnet was to be safely completed.

It was a lesson that was driven home by the 1951 Fastnet which some yachting journalists subsequently labelled a classic race but which really merely underlined that to finish the Fastnet in a hard year you had to be good. There were 29 starters again but this time no less than seven countries were represented. To everyone's delight the Americans were back once more, Kennon Jewett bringing his 41-foot LWL ketch *Malabar XIII* on from Spain, having won the Havana-Santander Trans-Atlantic Race. Rod Stephens was back too, skippering the new Swedish yawl, *Circe*, designed by his brother Olin. Those who could remember the Fastnet Races of the previous 20 years

knew it was an unbeaten combination.

Owen Aisher later wrote of *Circe*:

Every detail had been thought of, nothing superfluous. The boat looked naked; one had to put quite a lot of time into examining everything to see whether he (Rod Stephens) really had got enough halyards and pieces of string to take him anywhere. He had – just! I was very impressed with the thin topping lift he had to the boom, merely something capable of holding it up; no runners, masthead rig, not cumbersome; little emergency runners if they had to rig staysail or spinnaker staysail from the upper cross trees; for these there was a stay which was brought into the mast (very neat) behind a groove! Only one halyard. This was to serve for the staysail or small spinnaker, etc., whereas we carried the spinnaker staysail halyard and the staysail halyard. Further the size of the block he had was obviously inadequate, apparently. The general result was, as mentioned, that the boat looked naked. Nevertheless, as we all know, she was thoroughly efficient and good enough to win – certainly good enough to hold *Bloodhound*, although there is a difference of 6 feet on the waterline.

From Holland came an old favourite, *Olivier van Noort*, and Kees Bruynzeel's new plywood-hard-chined sloop, *Zeevalk*, designed by E.G. van de Stadt. 35-foot LWL, *Zeevalk* was an extreme example of the new light displacement yacht in the tradition of *Myth of Malham*, *Fandango* and *Gulvain*, and displaced about one-third of a conventional yacht of similar length. Someone said she was the largest sharpie ever

**46** The 1951 start took place in a gale and the starters were well reefed down when they came to the line. Not all the yachts in this photograph are identifiable but the one on the extreme left of the picture is *Overlord* (430) and the one on the extreme right *Circe* (376). The yacht with tanned sails in the centre is *Fandango* (111). The dark hulled boat to windward and slightly ahead of *Fandango* is *Jocasta* (659) while the white yawl to leeward of her is *Thalassa* (136) and astern of her is *Erivale* (236) and *Iolaire* (182). (*Beken*)

built. France was again represented by *Farewell*, Eire by Douglas Heard's new Uffa Fox-designed Flying Thirty, *Huff of Arklow*, and for the first time there was an Australian entry, *Waltzing Matilda*, owned and sailed by Phil Davenport and his wife. To complete the list of foreign entries there were three yachts, *Lively*, *Aegir X* and *Kranich*, from Kiel which were manned by British servicemen.

The pick of the new English boats that year were Geoff Pattinson's Class I sloop, *Jocasta*, and *Yeoman*, a Class II Nicholson-designed yacht which could be rigged either as a sloop or a cutter. She was owned and raced by Owen Aisher.

Those that had appeared at the starting line before ranged from the highly successful *Bloodhound* to the old *Thalassa*, and included *St Barbara*, *Fandango*, *Erivale*, *Latifa*, *Lara* and *Foxhound*, the last racing for the first time in a Fastnet Race since 1935. In all it was an impressive line-up and the race was eagerly anticipated. The only notable absentee was *Myth of Malham* as Illingworth, a serving Naval officer, was abroad.

The start was not until 1600 on Saturday, 11 August and the weather was dreadful. The wind was from the sw, force 7 gusting to 8, and the rain was lashing down. 'Life on shore could hardly have been more depressing,' wrote Douglas Phillips-Birt with the feeling of someone who has experienced what he is describing. 'The old narrow streets dripped under persistent rain from a sky loaded with grey and apparently weary of summer. . . . On the parade the full weight of the south-westerly met you, laced with unceasing rain. And the Fastnet was due to start in a few hours. You simply did not *want* to go ocean racing that day. Better Cowes; better to see the Week out to its dregs; better even to go home and work, though that would perhaps be putting it too strongly.'

Originally, it had been decided to send the yachts eastwards round the Isle of Wight but the day before it was decided to send them westwards through the Needles Channel and delay the start till 1600 so that the fleet would have the ebbing tide under it. Perhaps this was an unfortunate decision for the wind from the sw came in gusts of 40 knots or more and, blowing against the tide, kicked up a very nasty sea. To add to the competitors' discomfort the pouring rain brought mist with it which cut down the visibility drastically. Wrote Alf Loomis, who was aboard the American entry, *Malabar XIII*:

I had never seen outward conditions less propitious for the start of a race of any kind. If it wasn't raining cats and dogs I don't know what it was raining. The anemometer on *Malabar*'s mizzenmast head was buzzing steadily at 25 to 30, and slid up to 35 and better in the puffs. It seemed a very good idea when I saw them tying in reefs in the main and mizzen (even though, as I am told, *Malabar* had never reefed before) and preparing to set the number two jib. Around us as anchor was weighed and our competitors came into motion in the pouring rain we saw single reefs, double reefs, furled mizzens and other evidence of an increase in wind velocity. It increased. *Circe*, with Rod Stephens at the helm, got the start, and, so far as I was concerned, was welcome to it.

*Bloodhound*, second over the line, drove between the new Class II sloop, *Phizz*, and the shore, just shaving the rocks along the western edge of Cowes roadstead and possibly giving the starting officials the fright of their lives. Behind *Bloodhound* came *Lara*, and, in fourth place, the much smaller *Yeoman*, still miraculously carrying a whole mainsail. 'I think everyone thought we were crazy,' *Yeoman*'s skipper Owen Aisher commented later, 'but we had a very small mainsail.' *Latifa*, on the other hand, was already under trysail and a spitfire staysail. *Huff of Arklow* and *Olivier van Noort* were over before the gun, and were recalled.

Out of the lee of Egypt Point the wind freshened and immediately gear began to fail. The clew of *Malabar*'s jib let go, forcing the American yacht to drop back while it was taken in and replaced by the boom staysail. Once this was drawing the Americans set about catching up the rest of the fleet but as the innermost buoys of the notoriously dangerous Shingles bank were being approached it was decided that another reef had to be put in the mainsail. This was about to be done when, with the sound of what Loomis described as the roll of theatrical thunder, the bottlescrew belonging to the main lower shroud parted and the mast snapped in two places. Luckily, no one was hurt and the wreckage was quickly cleared, but *Malabar XIII* was in imminent danger of being blown onto the Shingles. The engine was started and the boat turned, but then the engine packed up and refused to restart, and it was decided to anchor. Shortly afterwards, the Yarmouth lifeboat came out and gave the luckless Americans a tow into harbour.

While all this was happening the Shingles again nearly claimed a victim, for *Jocasta*'s steering broke near the bank's sw corner. The breakage put the yacht about and she was actually driven over part of the bank before control of her was regained with a jury tiller. She carried on, but several others didn't, and before open water was even reached *Erivale* retired to the Hamble when her main boom began coming apart and *Huff of Arklow* turned back when a jib halyard block pin sheared, and cleats began to come off her mast. *Farewell*, *Phizz*, *Aegir X* and *Rebel Maid* all had problems of one sort or another and were forced to retire as well. *Huff of Arklow* made repairs and restarted, but the others stayed in harbour. Dick Broom, the owner of Illingworth's old boat, *Maid of Malham*, decided that things were going to get worse before they got better and opted for sheltering for the night. He found a good anchorage under Hurst, and *Thalassa*, *Lively* and *Foxhound* did the same. As no one aboard *Foxhound* had ever set a trysail before, the owner, the Hon. Mrs Pitt-Rivers, organised some sail drill before weighing anchor some six hours later.

While these four lay at anchor what remained of the rest of the fleet punched their way down channel against a gale of wind which soon caused more retirements. *Tilly Twin*, a reverse-sheer cutter designed by Laurent Giles along the lines of *Myth of Malham*, *Gulvain* and *Fandango*, retired to Cherbourg with rigging trouble, and both *Bloodhound* and *Latifa* had casualties amongst their crews. On *Bloodhound*, the skipper, Myles Wyatt, was thrown violently across the cockpit smashing the tiller and several of his own ribs. *Bloodhound*, under an emergency tiller and with her skipper lashed firmly into his bunk, carried on, but *Latifa*, with one of her crew similarly injured,

**47** Rounding the Rock in *St Barbara* during the 1951 Fastnet. She finished third in Class II.

returned to Cowes. On the Sunday, having got going again, *Lively* split her mainsail and retired to Weymouth. *Griffin* split hers as well and developed a leak into the bargain and she made for Plymouth. *Fandango*, which had been smoking along, and up to Start Point had been leading the fleet, had to retire to Brixham when the inboard end of an upper crosstree sheared.

So the list grew, but some carried on regardless though *Thalassa* sensibly anchored for the second night running under the lee of the western arm of Weymouth Bay, and her crew tucked into a morale-raising hot dinner carefully prepared by ocean racing's best-known cook, Sandy Sandison. While the Thalassians were putting away soup, roast leg of lamb, and duff pudding, *Overlord*, the Sappers' new boat, left the race to get a new backstay runner block – she later rejoined – while *St Barbara* sheared the main shaft of one of her jib sheet winches and had to

complete the course leading both sheets to the remaining winch.

At Start Point, after *Fandango* had dropped out, the leaders were *Circe*, *Bloodhound* and *Yeoman*, but by the Lizard the Swedish yawl had dropped back into third place. *Bloodhound*, with the Lizard abeam at 0545 on the Monday, now took the lead with the remarkable *Yeoman*, still with a whole mainsail, only 15 minutes behind her. Next came *Circe*, abeam at 0800, being hotly chased by *Jocasta* just four minutes behind her, with *Zeevalk* fifth.

In a letter to a friend in which he described the race, Owen Aisher said he regarded Bruynzeel as his most dangerous rival.

The Dutchman in *Zeevalk* was the real enemy. How the hell he got along with his floating streamlined kitchen cabinet the night it was really blowing hard, I cannot imagine. All kinds of boats got into trouble, but I must say *Yeoman* was most comfortable and really going. I believe if the wind had held strong she would have been first round the Fastnet, because, when we got to the Lizard, *Bloodhound* was two miles ahead of *Circe*, and they were just behind us, but *Jocasta* claims to be just ahead of us. I would not know about this, but I do know just after we saw *Bloodhound* we had to bear away slightly to let the Dutchman cross us, which seemed to us unbelievable. This really sobered us up! From then on it was a ding-dong battle. Somehow we got away from her and knowing that at night we must lose sight of her in any case, we split tacks and hoped that our guess would be better than Bruynzeel's. I believe anyway she was not so good in light weather as *Yeoman* and as a result of this, we managed to get to the Rock about $1\frac{1}{2}$ hours before her.

In fact the gale blew itself out very quickly and the wind died almost right away and became variable. In these conditions *Circe* showed what a magnificent light weather boat she was by drawing right away from *Jocasta*, overtaking *Yeoman* and *Bloodhound*, and establishing a lead which she hung on to grimly until almost up to the Rock. But this leg of the race was a painfully slow one and while most of the leaders were able to keep moving some of the others further back could not. *Olivier van Noort*, for instance, was becalmed for 18 hours. *Circe*, too, found a patch of calm for a while in the middle of the Irish Sea. But then Rod Stephens took a dip over the side, as 'this was the best way I knew to start up a breeze,' and gradually *Circe* began to make headway. At the Rock she and *Bloodhound* were close together but approaching the turning point from opposite directions. There was hardly a breath of air and at one point the British boat was forced to kedge when only 100 yards from the turning point but eventually she rounded what Rod Stephens calculated to be about one boat's length ahead of *Circe* and took the Elizabeth McCaw prize by a matter of 30 seconds or so. They crossed within hailing distance and then both set off for the Bishop on a close reach. To the north the crew of *Maid of Malham* saw the two leaders rounding, the first yachts they'd seen for nearly two days. Two hours later they were made spellbound by the appearance of *Yeoman*. 'What an amazing performance!' commented *Maid*'s skipper. 'Were we going to see the rest of Class II on her tail? Thank goodness that was not to be, we saw only one other large vessel before dark which seemed to confirm *Yeoman* was hours ahead of the small fleet.'

*Yeoman* was, indeed, hours ahead of her class and in the fickle winds that now prevailed she began steadily to draw level with the leaders, but never quite managed to overtake them.

The crew of *Jocasta*, having just escaped being wrecked on the Shingles, had another frightening experience when they hit a rock while rounding in the very light airs. She slid off but then was twice driven back onto the rock, before finally managing to get clear. Luckily, she was not damaged. On the leg back to the Bishop her navigation proved to be more accurate than that of the two leaders – both of which were using Consol – and she rounded the Bishop first. Close behind *Jocasta*, *Bloodhound*, *Circe* and *Yeoman* were *St Barbara* and *Kranich*, the latter being somewhat disabled when a tin of grease was upset below turning the whole yacht into a skating rink.

The last leg to Plymouth saw the three leaders racing neck-and-neck up to the finish under spinnakers, being hotly pursued by the smaller Class II boats like *Yeoman*, *Zeevalk* and *St Barbara*. After the Scillies Rod Stephens' expertise with the spinnaker began to tell and *Circe* again took the lead and held it until she crossed the finishing line with an elapsed time of 5 days 7 hours 31 minutes. *Bloodhound* was only 11 minutes behind her, with *Jocasta* third, 42 minutes behind. But it was the smaller Class II boats that put up the most remarkable performances, with *Yeoman* crossing the line fourth in an elapsed time of 5 days, 10 hours, 26 minutes. *St Barbara* was in next, in an elapsed time of 5 days, 11 hours, 29 minutes and *Zeevalk* was sixth over the line in an elapsed time of 5 days, 12 hours, 48 minutes. On corrected time *Yeoman* was the overall winner from *Zeevalk* by two hours and 21 minutes, and she also won her class, while *Jocasta* was first home in Class I on corrected time with *Circe* second. Third place in Class I went to *Olivier van Noort* which just squeezed ahead of *Bloodhound* on corrected time by under five minutes.

48   Owen Aisher at the helm of *Yeoman III*, the 1951 winner.

49   The 1951 winner, *Yeoman III*. Her dimensions were: LOA: 48 ft 6 in, LWL: 35 ft, beam: 10 ft 9 in, draught: 7 ft 6 in.

In the light of the performances put up by the smaller boats in the 1951 race it began to be argued that the LWL limit for the Fastnet should be lowered. With their very successful Class III yacht, *Loki*, in European waters for the 1953 season the Americans lobbied strongly for this change, and that year the RORC ruled that Class III boats were now eligible to compete in the Fastnet. The introduction of better construction techniques with modern materials, and the proliferation of man-made fibre sails, combined with post-war economies which obliged more and more yachtsmen to campaign smaller boats, made this a sensible decision.

But lowering the LWL limit did not bring a flood of extra entries. In fact Class III, with nine starters, had the smallest number of entries of the three classes which altogether totalled 38, including representatives from the United States, Sweden, Germany, Holland, Belgium and France. The United States especially fielded a strong team with a Bermuda Race winner in each class. The biggest of this trio was the 57-foot sloop, *Gesture*, designed by Sparkman and Stephens, and owned and skippered by Howard Fuller, and the winner that year at Cowes of the New York Yacht Club Challenge Cup. In Class II there was *Carina*, a 46-foot Rhodes-designed yawl owned and skippered by Richard Nye, which came to the line with the Cowes-Dinard Race and the Britannia Cup already under her belt. *Loki* was the Class III representative, a 38-foot Sparkman and Stephens designed yawl owned by Dr Gifford B. Pinchot.

For the first time the fleet was large enough to be started by class. The largest yachts started at 0945 on Saturday, 8 August and were followed by the other two classes at quarter-of-an-hour intervals. *Bloodhound*, with a fluky easterly behind her, was first across in Class I, but *Gesture* had her spinnaker hoisted first. Despite the staggered start the light conditions soon had the smaller yachts in amongst the larger ones and before the Needles were even reached the Class II Belgian entry, *Wyvern II*, was amongst the Class I tailenders, and *Loki* was well up with the Class II entries.

While the bulk of the fleet were nearing the Needles the tide changed sweeping *Foxhound*, *Marabu*, *Kailua* and *Overlord* to the north of the sw Shingles buoy which had to be left to starboard. They kedged and then had to tack back against the tide which lost all of them about an hour by which time *Loki* was through Class II and catching up with Class I. This caused the crew of *Favona*, the eventual winner, to shrug their shoulders and say, 'That's that,' so superior did the beamy American yawl with her large sails seem.

Once past the Needles *Bloodhound* increased her lead and followed by several other Class I boats she stood out from Portland to escape the foul tide. Only *Marabu* of the bigger boats took the inside passage and though at first she made little progress this manoeuvre later helped her get amongst the leaders who had a fast reach down to the Lizard but were then becalmed off Plymouth. *Fandango*, in Class II, still had Portland Bill light in sight astern at 0200 on Sunday morning, nine hours after having it abeam, and most of her class were around her struggling to make some headway, with Class III faring no better.

'The truth is that one is never totally becalmed in the English Channel,' wrote the navigator of Adlard Coles' Class III *Cohoe II* of that first night, 'but you can be so nearly so that the work needed to keep her moving is far more strenuous than in coping with a gale. These conditions pay big dividends to those who know best their in-shore tides and have learnt where to find that little breeze which blows along the coast and perhaps only stretches a couple of cables out to sea.'

It was off Portland Bill that *Cohoe II* started her duel with two other Class II yachts, *Rum Runner* and *Alexandra of Itchenor*, a duel which lasted till the finishing line. In fact, in all three classes there were races within the race with two or three yachts in the same class fighting it out boat-for-boat. *Favona* and *Lothian* were two more Class III yachts which disputed every mile between themselves, while in Class I *Bloodhound*, *Foxhound*, *Jocasta*, *Gesture* and *Lutine* were all grouped together over most of the course. Having made little or no progress off Plymouth these

50   The 1953 winner, *Favona*. (*Beken*)

51   *Bloodhound* leading the fleet after the 1953 start in a light easterly. (*Beken*)

leaders were not through the Scillies until dawn on the Monday and by nightfall that day *Foxhound* had taken over the lead. The next morning one of the Class I entries, the 1939 Erivale Cup winner, *Nordwind*, now under British ownership, was forced to give up because of rigging trouble, one of the two retirements in this light-weather race.

At about the time the big boats were heading for the Rock the smaller ones were still struggling to get the better of a foul tide off the Lizard in variable winds and Class II were strung between the Lizard and Land's End. *Fandango*, doing better than most of her class, passed the Lizard at 0130 on the Monday morning and by noon was through the Scillies, and, with the wind having veered, pitching through some very long swells on the starboard tack, just laying the course for the Rock. *Uomie*, the ultimate Class II winner, was by this time 12 hours ahead of *Fandango*, and was fighting it out with a couple of other Class II yachts, *St Barbara* and *Carina*. The wind was all over the place but by mid-morning on the Tuesday it was giving *Uomie* a six-knot run under her spinnaker until the wire luff rope parted forcing emergency repairs tc

be made. Despite the delay this caused, she was still ahead when she next sighted *Carina* some 20 miles before reaching the Rock; but the latter, tacking downwind to keep her mizzen staysail filled, seemed to be gaining. Soon *Uomie*'s crew saw the first evening flash of the lighthouse and headed straight for it with *St Barbara* not far behind. *Uomie* was eventually round first in Class II, rounding at midnight in conditions that were so quiet that her crew could hear the whirr of the lighthouse motors. *Carina* rounded an hour later while *St Barbara* was still two miles astern of her, but most of Class II did not reach the Rock until the middle of the day and on the Wednesday *Fandango*, for one, was given the magnificent sight of the Class I leaders, *Bloodhound*, *Foxhound*, *Jocasta*, *Gesture* and *Lutine*, running back from the Rock in line abreast. *Foxhound* had managed to retain her lead up to the rounding point but at the mark *Bloodhound* managed to creep ahead and rounded just three minutes ahead of her sister hull, at 2059 on the Tuesday evening, with *Gesture* third at 2120.

Meanwhile, the American Class III yawl, *Loki*, had been having a remarkable race, and had not only outstripped her own class but most of Class II as well, and was hot on the heels of the Class II leaders when she rounded at 0737 on the Wednesday morning only 37 minutes behind the Class II Dutch flyer, *Zeevalk*, with the Class III boat, *Right Royal*, not far astern of

her. At that time *Loki* was ten hours ahead of *Favona* on corrected time and looked a likely winner, but she later got becalmed off the Wolf Rock and finished in third place overall. *Right Royal* did well on the leg back to the Bishop and caught up with *Loki*, but then she too got becalmed and though she came in second in her class behind the American yawl on elapsed time she could only manage sixth place in Class III. *Cohoe II* had the swiftest return for a Class III boat, catching up six hours on *Loki* and an hour and a half on *Favona*, a depression on the fifth day of the race bringing her the kind of winds she liked. 'At least the conditions allowed us to remember it really was a Fastnet Race,' recorded one of the crew. '*Cohoe* was hard on the wind, force 5, with a 12-foot high swell and a tide running across the wind.' Some yachts, he said, had claimed after the race that they had rounded the course without getting their decks wet, but *Cohoe II* was not amongst them. Even in a light-weather year it seems that the Fastnet keeps the worst of the weather for the smaller boats.

Behind *Loki*, *Favona* and *Lothian* were still locked in battle. One of *Favona*'s crew recorded:

As we made the land at the point of Cape Clear Island, *Lothian* came up on the starboard tack and put about in our wake. She did not like the sea that was building up, but was sailed full and travelled very well. We must have made five tacks together before we came to the Fastnet, each ready to come about the moment the other tacked. *Favona* concentrated on keeping between *Lothian* and the Rock, and may have been a bit pinched in doing so. *Lothian* gradually closed the gap until, at 1718 by the ship's clock, the Fastnet lighthouse was close aboard to starboard and *Lothian* was a boat's length away under our lee. The surface of the water was white from the backwash off the Rock, the lighthouse keepers shouted their Irish approval of the scene, and then we both bore away, jibed, and were round. The keepers signalled the same time for both boats.

*Lothian*'s spinnaker was hoisted immediately and she drew ahead, but when *Favona* followed suit the gap was soon closed. But then the bad cross swells – all that remained of a storm off Rockall – caused *Favona*'s spinnaker boom to dip into the sea. The foot of the spinnaker filled with water and the shackle to the spinnaker halyard block promptly parted, and the sail had to be rehoisted on a jib halyard. It was an awkward run that night for the two small yachts for the seas were confused, but nevertheless *Favona* managed to average $7\frac{1}{4}$ knots for the next seven hours before the wind eased and backed. During the forenoon *Lothian* was spotted some four miles ahead and though the gap was closed during the day *Lothian* finished 23 minutes ahead of *Favona* to come second in the fleet overall behind her rival as well as second in Class II.

Ahead of this close-fought battle between *Favona* and *Lothian* the Class I leaders were still involved in their own tussle. After rounding the Fastnet *Bloodhound* retained the lead from *Foxhound*, but then *Gesture*, in third place, managed to overtake *Foxhound*, and behind these three *Lutine* began to gain ground inch by inch. By evening the wind had died and all night long the leaders inched forward under their spinnakers with *Lutine* and *Gesture* and *Jocasta* right alongside each other. At the Bishop they all stood inshore except for *Lutine* which stood out more into the Channel. This tactic paid off for she caught a better breeze and temporarily took over the lead until *Bloodhound* caught her up at the Lizard, went ahead, and crossed the line first in a time of 5 days, 7 hours, 9 minutes. But going out into the Channel had enabled *Lutine* to save her time and though she finished 18 minutes after *Bloodhound* she was first in Class I on corrected time, with *Jocasta* second and *Olivier van Noort* third.

Behind *Lutine* and *Bloodhound* which were fighting it out for the Erivale Cup for the first boat home were *Gesture* and *Jocasta*, locked in an equally close contest.

At the Lizard *Jocasta* led the American by three minutes and at one point they were close enough together to indulge in a luffing match. However, *Jocasta* just managed to hang on to her lead and crossed the line a mere five seconds ahead of *Gesture*.

In Class II *Uomie* led the way back with *Carina* about five miles astern of her and with *St Barbara* two miles astern of *Carina*. Throughout the Wednesday night the wind freshened from the sw and *Uomie* was overtaken by both *Carina* and *St Barbara*. Yet at first light, to the surprise – and delight – of *Uomie*'s crew, *Carina*, which eight hours before had been five miles ahead, was now seen to be five miles astern, which showed how patchy the wind was. During the early hours of Thursday, *St Barbara* increased her lead over the other Class II boats but *Uomie* managed to retain her lead over *Carina*, finishing 25 minutes ahead of her at 1203, some two and a quarter hours after *St Barbara*. On corrected time *Uomie* came first in Class II – and fourth in the fleet – with *Carina* second and *St Barbara* third.

The results of the 1953 race showed that it was a small boat race, with eight of the first nine boats on corrected time belonging to Class III, and with the tiny *Favona* having a better elapsed time between the Fastnet and Plymouth than *Bloodhound*, which, on corrected time, could do no better than 12th place overall.

---

Two years later the weather pattern repeated itself when a fleet of 46 boats came to the line at Cowes on Saturday, 6 August, in a moderate sw breeze which never at any time during the race exceeded force 4. However, what the wind failed to provide by way of strength it made up for in direction by being on the nose for some yachts not only all the way to the Rock but all the way back again too. But for the Class I yachts it was a fast race and the eventual winner of both the Elizabeth McCaw and Erivale trophies, *Mare Nostrum*, finished the course in the third fastest time ever recorded, 3 days, 22 hours, 48 minutes, 34 seconds. A Spanish entry, *Mare Nostrum* was designed by Sparkman and Stephens and skippered in the race by an American, Woody Pirie.

But the Americans were also represented strongly with their own yachts, with entries again in all three classes, interest centring on designer Raymond C. Hunt's Class III cutter, *Harrier*, and Richard Nye's new yawl, *Carina II*. Built in Germany, and complete with bowsprit and bumkin *Harrier*'s large area of canvas made her hot favourite for the Fastnet Cup in the light airs which were forecast. Crewed by the owner and his family she had already distinguished

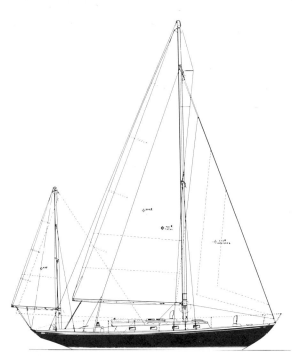

**52** The sail plan of the Class III American yawl, *Loki*, which came third in her class in 1953, the first year Class III yachts were allowed to enter the Fastnet. Her dimensions were: LOA: 38 ft 1 in, LWL, 26 ft, beam: 9 ft 7 in, draught: 5 ft 8 in.

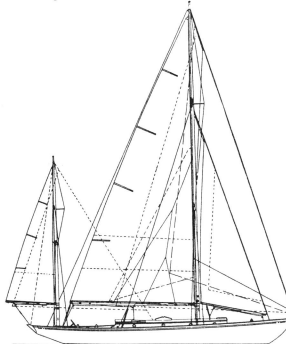

**53** The sail plan of *Carina*, the American yawl which came second in Class II in the 1953 Fastnet. Her dimensions were: LOA: 46 ft 4 in, LWL: 34 ft, beam: 11 ft 5 in, draught: 6 ft 6 in.

herself during Cowes Week, but unfortunately one of her bottlescrews parted early in the race and she was forced to retire. *Carina II*, like her predecessor a Class II boat, went like greased lightning and not only led her own class by miles but was rarely out of sight of Class I and well deserved her overall win. Again designed by Phil Rhodes she was beamier and longer than the earlier *Carina* and had already proved she was a good performer by first of all winning the Trans-Atlantic Race and then scooping prizes like the Britannia and New York Yacht Club cups at Cowes. For the Fastnet a stopper had been put on her centreboard tackle to prevent the plate dropping the last foot, and this reduced her rating by nearly 18 inches. It proved to be a winning move, but early on in the race it seemed as if it might have been a mistake, for during the first day she sagged away badly to leeward of most of her competitors.

The start, as was now customary, was staggered. In Class I, the first away, *Lutine* just beat *Foxhound* across the line with *Bloodhound* and *Gladeye* close behind them. The start for Class II was more scattered, especially for those inshore, as a cruising yacht towing a dinghy on a long painter – a traditional appearance for a Fastnet start, apparently – chose that moment to sail through the fleet. However, *Fandango*; the new Clark-designed steel cutter from Holland, *Zeezwaluw*, with her designer on board; *Carina II*; another new Dutch yacht, *Vrouwe Emilia*; *Maid of Pligh*; *Griffin*; and *Theta* were all away close together. *Glance* was over the line early and had to return. Thinking the recall gun was for him Huey Long in *Ondine* also turned back, though he had not been over at all. (Now American owned, *Ondine* had previously raced in the Fastnet as a Swedish entry under the name of *Kay*.) Soon after she restarted *Ondine* had another stroke of bad luck when she passed the wrong side of the Middle Shingles buoy and had to tack back to round it correctly. This left her a long way behind the rest of her class, but thereafter she was sailed impeccably and was only half an hour behind her closest rival, *Carina II*, at the Lizard. She had not altogether lost her Swedish connections as aboard for the race was the Swedish designer, Knud Reimers.

The start for Class III was also scattered but among the first to get away were *Harrier*, *Planet*, *Cohoe II*, *Lapwing* and *Eloise*.

Just west of the Shingles, *Mare Nostrum*'s mainsail halyard came adrift and the mainsail came halfway down the mast. She was forced to stay on the port tack until repairs had been carried out and therefore got close inshore while the rest of the fleet kept on the starboard tack to get the benefit of the ebbing tide. However, the wind now veered and unexpectedly gave *Mare Nostrum* a better lift, and she shot into the lead, and stayed there. With the wind now free the run to the Lizard was fast for all classes but by the Runnelstone it had begun to die, and most of Class III were caught there by a foul tide and a fading breeze. *Favona* just caught the tide, however, as did *Lothian*, *Right Royal* and *Casella*, with the Swedish cutter, *Honey*, also just squeezing through in time. John Illingworth, back in the race for the first time since he won it in 1949, was sailing his new minimum waterline yawl, *Mouse of Malham*, and he took her between the Runnelstone and the Longships to within what Adlard Coles described as a few mouse lengths of the rocks. *Cohoe II* followed and both yachts came out several miles ahead and to windward of their immediate Class III competitors.

Out ahead the Class I boats were having a magnificent sail, the veering wind making them harden their sheets to keep on the rhumb line for the Rock. *Mare Nostrum* was still in the lead followed by *Foxhound*, *Bloodhound*, *Lutine*, *Marabu*, *Jocasta* and *Circe*, with the smaller *Carina II* not far behind. The wind continued to veer and by the time the leaders neared the Rock the wind had headed them. But *Mare Nostrum* was round at 2200 on 8 August, having taken 2 days 7½ hours to complete the first half of the course. She was the only yacht to round that day. Behind her *Foxhound* and *Bloodhound* were having their by now traditional duel with the former's cutter rig having a slight advantage in the head winds over her sister ship's yawl rig. Alf Loomis who was aboard *Foxhound* wrote:

A break in the wind came when we were within 20 miles of tacking distance for the Fastnet and put us on the port tack with *Bloodhound* right on top of us. There followed a spot of helmsmanship by our talented skipper which may have lasted six, eight or ten hours – one loses track of time when Ray Pitt-Rivers is up to her favorite trick of outsailing the sister hull of divided rig – and presently *Fox* was on top and *Blood* was tacking away for a lucky break. The lights of the Irish coast went on, finding us closer to the Fastnet than to Galley Head, and when we were inside a line between the two and could barely distinguish in the twilight the wicked rocks known as The Stags to leeward of us, we also tacked to starboard. I wish I had had the nerve to counsel holding on until we were within smelling distance of the rocky coast as we did in daylight in *Latifa* in '39. But I was partly consoled when we rounded the Rock to port two hours and 20 minutes behind *Mare Nostrum* and 15 minutes later passed *Bloodhound* still plugging to windward.

Within three hours *Bloodhound*, *Carina II*, *Lutine*,

54 The Italian yacht, *Mare Nostrum*, seen here outward bound through the Needles Channel after the start of the 1955 Fastnet, was the first boat home that year.

*Jocasta*, *Ondine*, *Circe*, *Cyane* and *Marabu* were also homeward bound, and the run to the Bishop for these leaders was an exhilarating one. *Foxhound*, for instance, covered 150 miles in exactly 20 hours. *Mare Nostrum* managed to keep this wind with her to the finishing line which she crossed at noon on the Wednesday but for the others the last leg from the Bishop to Plymouth was painfully slow. *Foxhound* spent 12 frustrating hours drifting under a cloudless sky before she covered the last 47 miles to the line which she crossed at 1748 nearly six hours after *Mare Nostrum*. Behind *Foxhound*, *Lutine* – the eventual Class I winner – was forced to kedge for a short time, while *Jocasta*, *Circe* and *Ondine* – always well up with her class-mate, *Carina II* – simply drifted around in circles, but eventually *Lutine* crossed at 2110, some three-and-a-quarter hours after *Foxhound*, closely followed by *Bloodhound*. Then came the remarkable *Carina II*, over at 2158, followed an hour-and-a-half later by *Circe*. Then came *Jocasta*, with *Ondine* close behind her. On corrected time *Carina II* won by just under 48 minutes from *Ondine*. Although the larger boats had carried a fair wind at least at the Bishop, for

the smaller ones it came on the nose as soon as they'd rounded, and for them it was a slow race. And later the fitful breezes and adverse tides tended to make the Class III boats all pile up at points like the Bishop, the Lizard, and Prawle Point, and it wasn't until the Friday morning that any of them crossed the line. But then six did within 15 minutes of one another: *Mouse of Malham*, *Rondinella*, *Favona*, *Alexandra of Itchenor*, *Annasona* and *Planet*. *Mouse of Malham* came out on top of this heap to win Class III after a very close tussle with *Rondinella* which came second on corrected time.

*Mouse of Malham* − irreverently called *Bat of Balham* by some − was a remarkable little boat which displaced only $2\frac{1}{4}$ tons. One part of her design in particular was a precursor of the modern ocean racer, for Illingworth had had her built with a separate skeg and rudder and a short fin keel, which ten years later was to become all the rage. For some reason this innovation was not accepted at the time and Illingworth, who by now was a full-time yacht designer, dropped it from later designs. Illingworth, writing about her design in his book, said that she had crept through every tiny loophole in the RORC rule, 'but she was completely seaworthy, which is the final criterion, at least for a designer's conscience I think. I took a lot of trouble with her rig: a yawl rig with two headsails forward, a tiny mainsail and eventually an

enormous mizzen staysail, the latter nearly 30 per cent larger than the mainsail. I had gone back in detail through the RORC records and found that many of the races are won on the reach. A boat must be able to get to windward decently, of course, but reaching and running really count.'

Unfortunately, for Illingworth there was hardly any reaching in the 1955 Fastnet − Loomis reckoned there was about six minutes of it! − which made his win in Class III a remarkable achievement.

---

Two years later Illingworth was back again, this time with *Myth of Malham* (which he now jointly owned with Peter Green) despite the fact that a radical modification to the RORC rule now gave *Myth* a less advantageous rating. Ever since *Myth* had appeared it became inevitable that at some point the rule was going to have to be changed. A completely new formula for measuring had at last been devised which resulted in the penalty for long overhangs being reduced, and the foretriangle measured at 100 per cent instead of 85 per cent to take into account that a much larger proportion of a modern yacht's sail area was carried forward of her mainmast than had previously been the case. Rerating now put *Carina II* and *St Barbara* in Class I and *Right Royal* in Class II.

The 1957 race was one of the most memorable in the history of the Fastnet, ranking alongside 1927, 1930 and 1949. A contemporary article on the weather during it was titled 'A Gale at the Start, A Gale at the End, with Nothing Much Different in Between,' and that was about how it turned out, with two depressions passing over the area within a few days of one another. The second depression brought even stronger winds than the first, and being hot on the heels of the first it did not allow the wind to moderate much or for any length of time.

There were slightly fewer starters than in 1955 – perhaps the weather forecast had dampened the ardour of some of the entries – but 41 came to the line, a sufficient number for one of the yachting magazines to say that the start must have been one of the most impressive in the history of ocean racing for not only was the wind blowing at least force 7 from the wsw but there were again a large number of entries from overseas. As an added interest an American team of three boats were competing against a similar British team in a series of races which culminated with the Fastnet. The winning team was to be awarded the Admiral's Cup, so called because it had been donated by *Bloodhound*'s owner, Sir Myles Wyatt, who was Admiral of the RORC at the time, and by John Illingworth, Peter Green, Geoffrey Pattinson, who owned *Jocasta*, and *Uomie*'s owner, Selwyn Slater.

According to one of *Bloodhound*'s crew, the cup had been presented by Wyatt and the others to sharpen the competitive spirit of British owners, but later Wyatt was to say that he regretted the effect the Admiral's Cup had had on the sport by making it so cut-throat. This was an understandable reaction. But if there hadn't been an Admiral's Cup something similar would have been introduced because, with hindsight, it was surely inevitable that ocean racing would go the way of so many other sports which had once been gentlemanly pursuits – golf, tennis and, more recently, cricket are examples – so that big money, heavy promotion and publicity, and sponsorship by big business, as well as a ruthless dedication to winning, was bound to become an accepted fact of life sooner or later. Without at least some of these ingredients the sport could very well have died. The fact that it boomed instead during the 1960s and 1970s must at least in part be due to the Admiral's Cup.

As a member of the American Admiral's Cup team *Carina II* was at the starting line again along with her other two teammates, Bill Snaith's *Figaro* and G.W. Blunt-White's *White Mist*. Opposing them were *Myth of Malham*, *Uomie* and *Jocasta*, the British team going into the Fastnet with an eight point lead. But as the Fastnet counted triple points the competition was still wide open.

Other entries that year included two Frenchmen, three Dutch, three Germans and two Swedes. The British contingent included old-timers like *Lutine*, *Bloodhound*, *Jocasta*, *St Barbara* and *Evenlode*. *Yeoman*, the 1951 winner, was back again under new ownership, the RORC, and a new name, *Griffin II*, while two newcomers, *Cohoe III* and *Drumbeat*, looked likely winners in their respective classes, III and I. *Drumbeat*, designed by *Harrier*'s owner, Raymond C. Hunt, was a 40-foot LWL cutter with twin centreboards. *Cohoe III*, a 26-foot LWL sloop, was a rather more conventional design which reflected Adlard Coles' desire for a heavy weather boat. He could not have chosen a better race in which to test her qualities.

Before the start Illingworth went to the race committee and suggested the fleet leave the Isle of Wight to starboard so that it did not have to go through the Needles Channel, his reasoning being that a disabled yacht could easily be driven onto the Shingles Bank in the high winds that were blowing, and the crew lost. It seemed a sensible enough suggestion in view of what had happened to *Jocasta* and *Malabar XIII* after the 1951 start, but Illingworth's suggestion was not taken up though in future sailing instructions for the race included the alternative start should the race committee decide the weather was too rough to put the fleet through the Needles Channel. So in a wind which Illingworth reckoned was force 9 the three classes set off the Fastnet at quarter-of-an-hour intervals.

Almost at once the retirements began with *Overlord*, which now belonged to the Royal Army Service Corps Yacht Club, returning with a broken jibstay, and before long almost half the fleet had been forced to turn back for one reason or another: *Kormoran*, *Evenlode* and *Santander* all returned to Cowes, *Kormoran* with backstay trouble, *Evenlode* with rudder trouble, and *Santander* with a serious leak caused by a broken keel bolt. Then *Drumbeat* dropped out having stripped five of her six winches as did *St Barbara* with the same problem, and *Galloper* retired having had to fish out a crew member from the Channel. *Black Soo*, a remarkable Class III light displacement boat whose heavy weather mainsail was no larger than a 14-foot International dinghy's, was one of the last of the long list of retirements. She got within 75 miles of the Rock but then her electrical system packed up and when her owner heard the forecast which predicted the second gale he sensibly turned back.

The flog down through the Needles Channel was a test that year for any yacht and crew, but *Myth of Malham*, with two reefs in her main and a largish storm jib, went particularly well despite the appalling conditions. Her progress was being carefully watched

**55** The winner in 1955 and 1957 was Dick Nye's *Carina II*. She just failed to make it three in a row when she came third overall, but first in her class, in 1959.

by Peter Green's wife through binoculars and later she assured Illingworth that she had seen the forefoot of *Myth*'s ballast keel shoot clear out of the water as the yacht threw herself through the steep, broken sea. E.P. de Guingand, on board *Carina II*, reported a similar incident when he saw the ex-12-metre *Vanity* leap out of the sea and expose several feet of her keel aft of her mast. *Bloodhound* was first through the Needles Channel followed by *Lutine* and *Evenlode* but there was no let-up in the wind and by evening it was obvious to those left in the race that it was going to be a wild and uncomfortable night with the seas off Portland breaking heavily. In his book *Heavy Weather Sailing* – the Bible for most British yachtsmen – Adlard Coles gives a vivid description of what it was like that first night at sea.

On deck all was dark except the friendly orange glow of the compass and the reflections of the navigation lights. The cold regular four white flashes of Portland Bill lay on our starboard bow. The watch on deck were secured by safety harness,

and they needed it, for every sea broke aboard forward, and in the gusts the yacht lay far over.

Down below the aft end of the cabin was like a half-tide rock. As each sea struck the cabin top forward it came streaming aft, flooding through the aft hatch and a cabin door which had broken, as that year we had no spray hood. Both quarter berths were flooded and the chart table unusable, so I had to spread the sodden chart on the table at the forward end of the saloon.

Navigation was a whole-time job as we were skirting Portland Race, with the spare man on deck taking hand bearings on Portland lighthouse. It was also physically difficult, as I was thrown about so much. If the chart was left for a moment it would shoot across the cabin together with the parallel rulers and dividers on to the lee berth. Progress was desperately slow, as it always is when rounding a light, but hour by hour the bearing changed and I was able to plot each position a little west of the last one.

Regularly the yacht needed pumping. Masses of water found its way into the bilges. The seas must have been getting through the cracks edging the cockpit lockers, and spray through the cabin hatch, through the broken cabin door and through the ventilators.

The Swedish yacht *Elseli IV*, sailed by Gustav Plym, the son of the great Swedish boatbuilder, August Plym, also had a tough time negotiating the Race. The spinnaker pole was swept overboard – a mishap which later almost certainly cost the Swedes first prize in Class III – and the eyebolt holding the tackle for the jib halyard snapped. Later it was found that no less than seven planks had been split during the heavy pounding the boat took during that first night at sea, but luckily the damage was relatively superficial and did not cause a severe leak. When *Elseli IV* eventually emerged on the other side of the race the yacht's English navigator turned to Plym and said: 'Sir, may I congratulate you on being one of the few to have succeeded in passing through Portland Race in a south-westerly gale.' It had certainly been a wild passage during a night that Plym described in his book *Yacht and Sea* as being like a naturalistic painting of a subject he had never seen before. 'The clouds were thin enough to let the full moon shine through and give sufficient light to show every detail on the yacht clearly,' he wrote. 'The wind blew the tops off the breakers, mixing the salt spray with the rain from quickly passing showers. It felt like needles hitting the skin to face the wind, and the breath was nearly taken away. The screaming sound in the rigging was like the shriek of a woman in despair.'

Later that night Plym was forced to drop his mainsail because it had become damaged and *Elseli IV* rode easier under the trysail which was hoisted.

The German yawl, *Inschallah*, was not as fortunate as *Cohoe III* and *Elseli IV* in riding out the combination of high winds and the Portland Race, and had her doghouse windows smashed in by a breaking sea. She fired distress rockets and was towed to safety by a lifeboat, adding to the list of retirements which eventually totalled 29 leaving only 12 boats in the race, and few of these escaped damage. *Figaro*, for instance, blew out her spinnaker at one point. Bill Snaith was below eating his breakfast when it happened but his sailmaker, Ed Raymond, was on deck. A crew member poked his head down the hatch and said that the spinnaker had blown out. 'Tell Ed that's his bad luck,' said Snaith without pause, 'I haven't paid for it yet.'

The leaders at the Lizard were *Carina II*, *Jocasta*, *Griffin II*, *Elseli IV* and *Cohoe III* – even though she put into Dartmouth for $3\frac{1}{2}$ hours when the tide off Start Point was missed – and for a time the wind for these front runners began to ease. *Carina II* ate up the miles to the Rock making seven knots in the force 4 wind and she rounded at 1400 on the Tuesday followed by *Kay* and *Jocasta*. Once round, the Americans set their big spinnaker and a mizzen staysail and the Kenyon log leapt up to ten knots, and as the wind freshened once more *Carina II* began to surf occasionally. As the wind climbed towards gale force again, the light weather sails were doused until she was making around eight knots under main and staysail alone. Rain squalls were making the visibility poor but the Bishop Light was picked up just a few minutes before sunrise on the Wednesday morning and was passed a quarter of a mile off. The wind now died and there were some anxious moments aboard that it might be lost altogether, but with the big spinnaker and the mizzen staysail reset *Carina II* carried the gentle breeze to the finishing line which she crossed at 2000 on the Wednesday having averaged 8.3 knots round the whole course. The victory was well deserved for Nye had welded a first-rate, if pretty wild, crew around him. They even had a war cry when things got bad to drive them on. 'Is every man a tiger?' Nye would roar. 'Grr . . . grr . . . grr,' roared back the crew. They were indeed tigers, every one of them, and they made sure *Carina II* was driven at maximum speed over every inch of the course.

While thrashing out through the Needles Channel *Carina II* had fallen off a wave and cracked several frames which had caused quite a severe leak. This meant she had had to be pumped out the entire way round, but as they crossed the line Nye called out: 'All right, boys, we're over now, let her sink!'

Four others in Class I finished: *Kay*, *Jocasta*, *Lutine* and *Bloodhound*. Five also finished in Class II: *Myth of Malham*, first in the class by over two hours on corrected time from *White Mist*, with *Figaro* third, followed by *Griffin II* and David Maw's new boat, *Bluejacket*. But only two managed to finish in Class III, *Cohoe III* and *Elseli IV*, and once the former had left the shelter of Dartmouth to make the tide off Start Point these two fought a close duel which lasted all the way round the course.

In the period between the gales *Elseli IV* had managed to draw away from the British boat, her masthead genoa pulling magnificently, but when the strong winds returned *Cohoe III*, now carrying full sail and showing what a marvellous heavy weather boat she was, soon closed the gap and both yachts arrived off the Irish coast at about the same time. Adlard Coles, however, tacked inside the Stag Rocks, thereby gaining a few vital miles by getting the fair tide earlier and benefitting from the smoother water under the lee of the land, and *Cohoe III* rounded at 1340 on the Wednesday just 20 minutes ahead of the Swedish yawl. Despite a NW gale warning *Cohoe III*'s crew set her spinnaker and *Elseli IV*'s her large genoa, and both boats began their hair-raising ride for the Bishop.

As the wind rose the Swedish yawl started to surf occasionally and her speed hit 11 knots at one time. It was an experience, wrote Plym, that none of the crew had ever experienced before in such a relatively large yacht. 'When she rode up on a wave,' he said, 'speed increased so rapidly that we had the sensation of falling. During this acceleration the rudder seemed to be locked, and the helmsman felt that the boat was steering herself. The bow wave splashed up against the back of the mainsail and on the windward side the spray reached half way up the spreaders. It was fascinating and, to tell the truth – slightly terrifying.' But *Elseli IV* was not driven off course by the quartering seas which forced *Cohoe III* to tack down wind to keep her going under spinnaker at maximum speed. At times indeed she was sailing far in excess of her theoretical maximum. With the British yacht travelling faster but having to cover a greater distance than the Swedish one made the two about equal over the leg and they arrived together at the Bishop in seas which Plym described as high breaking mountains of water. On the final leg to Plymouth *Elseli IV* broached-to twice and at one time she was forced to lower her mainsail to avoid being pooped. But later the winds moderated and she was able to reset it, but without her spinnaker on this final run to the finishing line she was at a definite disadvantage and though rated higher than the British yacht she finished half-an-hour behind *Cohoe III*. For over 500 miles these two had fought a remarkable race. Most of

56 John Illingworth reckoned that it was blowing force 9 at times at the start of the 1957 Fastnet. The Swedish Class III boat, *Elseli IV*, seen here just after the start, was one of the very few to finish that year. (*Beken*)

the time they had been separated by only a few miles and were in sight of one another much of the time. After the Swedes had crossed the line a sail appeared out of the darkness to leeward. 'Good morning,' called out *Elseli IV*'s English navigator, 'Who are you?' '*Cohoe III*. Good morning. And who are you?' '*Elseli IV*.' 'Well done, *Elseli*.' 'Well done, *Cohoe*.' Well done, indeed.

Although *Figaro* came third in Class II, Francis Chichester thought she should have done better. Chichester, who had taken part in the 1955 Fastnet in his own yacht, *Gypsey Moth*, had elected to navigate on *Figaro* for the 1957 race and later he analysed astutely the factors, each small in themselves but having a cumulative effect, which hampered her from being driven at maximum speed. In his autobiography, *The Lonely Sea and the Sky*, he wrote:

It is easy to be wise after the event, but there are some things which slowed us down. Firstly, I believe that Bill and his crew had been celebrating the winning of the New York Yacht Club Cup on their last night in Cowes. We were late over the starting line, and when on leaving the Needles I asked for the starboard tack to take us out into the Channel, Bill said, 'Can't we sail the other tack (towards Swanage) which looks less rough?' The navigating instinct is a very tenuous affair, and I could not give a good reason why the Swanage tack should not have been equally good. So we took it, but as it turned out it cost us many hours of racing time.

American yachts favour 'points' reefing, which undoubtedly sets the sail better than roller reefing. *Figaro*, however, had a big pram hood over the companion way, and it was difficult to get at the mainsail boom to reach the sail; the hood was not substantial enough to stand on. As a result, we were reluctant to reef, reefed too late, and later, when the wind abated, we were equally reluctant to unreef, and unreefed too late. Another drawback was that the yacht was stuffed with experts. Everyone tended to exercise his own special expertise. Bobby wanted to demonstrate his latest method of gybing, which cost us time unsnarling the spinnaker and repairing the damage. Ed liked to harden in the foresails, unconsciously demonstrating how strong they were. He had five men hardening in the jib sheet, using two big winches. They were marvellous sails, but often hardened in too flat for the best speed.

However, to have finished at all in 1957 was in itself quite an achievement, and *Figaro*'s third behind her compatriot, *White Mist*, in Class II, combined with *Carina II*'s repeat of winning overall as well as her class, gave the Americans victory over the British in the race by 33 points to 27. But this was not quite enough to snatch an overall victory for the Admiral's Cup which was won by the British team by the narrow margin of two points.

In 1959 the Admiral's Cup was thrown open to all nations. The Americans did not field a team but the French and the Dutch did. The Italians entered a yacht, the Sparkman and Stephens designed yawl, *Mait II*, for the first time and there were also two Americans, two Swedes and a Belgian at the start line. *Mait II* must have had one of the most high-powered crews ever to put an ocean racer round the Rock. She was crewed by 11 Italians, no less than seven of whom were Olympic yachtsmen, and she was navigated by Francis Chichester. Alas, she had an undistinguished race, being beaten by two Class II boats on elapsed time, and coming seventh in Class I and 34th overall.

Richard Nye, with *Carina II*, was back again trying to make it three in a row. The British, however, had entered some powerful competition which included established Fastnet entries such as *Evenlode*, *Lutine*, *Marabu* and *Bloodhound* in Class I, *Myth of Malham*, *Bluejacket*, *Right Royal* and *Griffin II* in Class II, and *Cohoe III* in Class III. But it was probably the newcomers that were the biggest threat to Nye's ambitions. Selwyn Slater had entered a new Class I yacht, *Ramrod*, and in Class II Ren Clarke's *Quiver II* looked very competitive. Class III newcomers included *Danegeld*, *Pym* and *Belmore* which if the weather stayed light could prove dangerous. Interest, however, centred on the Swedish Sparkman and Stephens designed yawl, *Anitra*, owned and sailed by Sven Hansen. A Class II boat, *Anitra's* varnished topsides and superb construction attracted many envious glances before the race.

The Dutch Admiral's Cup team included a new Class I yacht, *Zwerver*, which won the Britannia Cup that year, as well as two old favourites, *Olivier van Noort* and *Zeevalk*, but the French fielded a team of entirely new yachts so far as the Fastnet was concerned: *Eloise II* (F. Herve), *Marie-Christine II* (J-C Menu), and *St Francois* (G. Craipeau). Unfortunately, all the French team were affected by broken gear and were forced to retire.

Although the Americans were not as strongly represented in 1959 as they had been in some years, the fleet that came to the line at Cowes on Saturday, 8 August, were, without doubt, the cream of the world's ocean racers, and they were about to be faced with what one of the yachting magazines called one of the most exacting races ever held with the weather dishing up everything except snow. But it was a light easterly when the gun went for Class III which that year started first, with about $1\frac{1}{2}$ hours of a foul tide to run. *Danegeld* was first across with *Meon Maid II*. *Rondinella* and *Maze* made for the mainland shore as did the rest of the class except for *Griffin II* which opted to stick to the Island side. In Class II, after being first across, Illingworth also decided to work the Island shore, but later crossed and had the misfortune to run aground off Beaulieu for a short time. The most spectacular start in Class I was made by *Drumbeat* which, with her centreboards up and her masthead spinnaker drawing, crossed the line very close to the shore by the Royal Yacht Squadron about ten seconds after the gun.

The three classes were soon mixed up, with the bigger yachts moving quickly through the smaller ones. Off Yarmouth *Danegeld* was in the lead but then *Drumbeat*, having made up half an hour against the tide, overtook her. At Hurst the fleet was bunched together and it was then seen that *Griffin II*'s tactic of working the southern shore had paid off for she was in second place. But *Drumbeat* was first through the

Needles Channel and the first to catch the fair tide and a new reaching wind, but later, in the fickle winds and foul tide that caught nearly everyone off Portland, she lost the lead and never regained it. A couple of miles from the Shambles Lightvessel she, in common with most of the fleet, was forced to kedge in 20 fathoms, the anchor warp being lengthened with the help of mooring lines and the genoa sheets. However, the big Swedish yawl, *Anna Marina*, just made the tide at Portland as did *Griffin II* and *Anitra*, an advantage which subsequently enabled the latter two to beat the rest of the fleet by a substantial margin on corrected time and gave *Anna Marina* the Erivale Cup.

Most of the smaller yachts now tacked inshore with the hope of picking up a land breeze, but when *Carina II* was sighted becalmed between Anvil Head and St Alban's Head they went out again. It was a dark, moonless night with a lot of fog about but the next morning the sun rose in a clear sky. It became boiling hot before a haze set in which before the end of the day again turned to fog. The experiences of the crew of *Tilly Whim*, a Class II Laurent Giles designed sloop, must have been typical of what was happening to most yachts at that time. 'By breakfast time we had the Shambles diaphone abeam. This dismal sound was to dominate us all day. To kedge or not to kedge: we could get no clue from the invisible land, nor from the various yachts in sight, of which only *Right Royal*, *Petasus* and *Moonlight II* were definitely recognisable. During the afternoon we brought the Beme up on deck to listen to a Vivaldi concert and bathed over the side: the yacht's forward motion was barely perceptible.' Astern of Class II, the Class III yachts *Danegeld*, *Cohoe III* and *Lora* were all struggling to keep way on in the lightest of airs, and got swept into Portland Race for their troubles. It proved, as one crew member recorded, a most instructive experience but they were all eventually ejected into Lyme Bay where they were joined by *Claire de Lune* and *Evenlode*. The five yachts then drifted slowly westwards until the tide once more set against them and they were forced to kedge. By afternoon the visibility was down to 20 yards and another miserable drifting night was suffered with drizzle helping to make tempers even shorter. Dawn found *Danegeld* kedged under Start Point in pouring rain and between the gaps in the mist about a sixth of the fleet was identified from her decks.

But not everyone suffered these miseries. Having caught the tide at Portland *Anna Marina* kept well out and caught the one off the Start as well and by 0235 on the Monday morning she was past the Lizard despite having logged minus eight miles during one four-hour watch when the tide was foul. There was then a gap of four hours before *Griffin II* passed the Lizard and another of five hours before *Anitra* had it abeam. Two-

and-a-half hours behind the new Swedish boat was *Carina II*, still well in the running for another overall win. By this time the fog had cleared for the leaders but was replaced by heavy and persistent rain which improved the visibility hardly at all, and in the afternoon thunderstorms began to develop. Then, with only a dozen or so yachts west of Prawle Point, the wind suddenly increased to force 5 or 6 from the SW, and dismasted *New Dawn*. *Vashti* summoned help by radio telephone and stood by the crippled yacht until it was safely escorted into Salcombe. At about this time the only other American entry in the race besides *Carina II*, the Class II yawl, *Jen*, also became a casualty when one of her spreaders carried away and she was forced to withdraw. Ironically, *Bloodhound*, taking part in her last Fastnet, had already retired because of the lack of wind which was now causing the damage.

The fleet was now well spread out with the leaders close hauled on the port tack making for the Rock while the rest were still struggling to round the Lizard. But *Danegeld*, and the others around her, at last caught the stronger wind – and the thunderstorms – and passed a very wet Monday night illuminated by almost continuous lightning. 'The rain lashed one's face and dripped down between towel and neck,' wrote one of *Tilly Whim*'s crew members who thought that night the only true period of unrelieved misery in the race. 'Helmsmen made sure that they did no longer

57  The sail plan of *Anitra*, the winner of the 1959 Fastnet, which was designed by Sparkman and Stephens for the Swedish yachtsman, Sven Hansen. Her dimensions were: LOA: 48 ft 5 in, LWL: 33 ft 6 in, beam: 12 ft 4 in, draught: 6 ft 11 in.

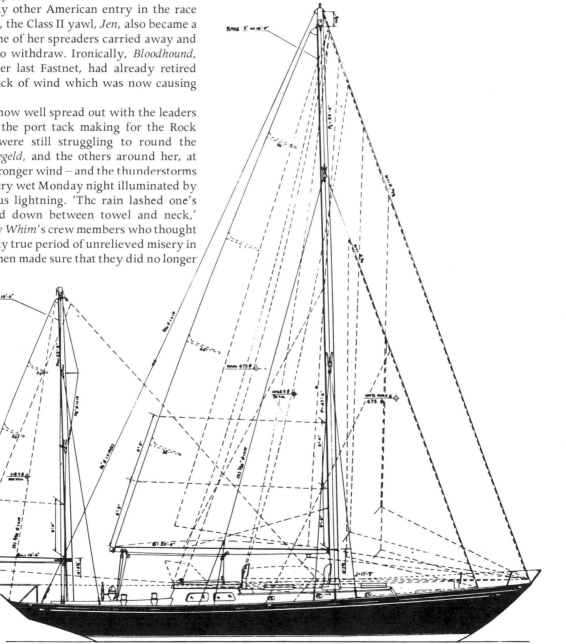

**58** The start of the 1959 Fastnet. *Anitra*, the eventual winner, is on the right of the picture. To leeward of her and astern of her are two French Admiral's cup boats, *St Francois* (9CR/F1) and *Eloise II* (1489). Sail number 1055 belongs to *Moonlight II* which came in fifth in Class II. (*Beken*)

than their regulation half-hour turns before huddling back under the shelter of the doghouse. The Eddystone's bearing changed agonisingly slowly.'

The Lizard was passed by most during the Tuesday forenoon and by the afternoon *Danegeld*, for one, had the Wolf Rock abeam. By that time *Anna Marina* was almost up to the Rock which she rounded at 1905 on the Tuesday evening followed by the new Dutch cutter, *Zwerver*, 35 minutes later, with another Dutchman, *Olivier van Noort*, third, two hours after that. *Griffin II*, which had been doing magnificently, lost valuable time near the Rock by going too far to the east and having to tack up to the mark. Nevertheless, she was only four hours behind the leader when she rounded and was heading the fleet on corrected time. *Anitra*, the eventual winner on corrected time, was six hours behind her at this point.

Only a handful of other yachts rounded on the Wednesday. They included *Lutine*, *Ramrod*, *Marabu*, and the Class III cutter, *Pym*. *Drumbeat* was the 13th boat to round, at 1835, and the crew were disgusted to

learn from a bystander in a motor boat that *Pym*, rating 25 feet to *Drumbeat*'s 35, had rounded 20 minutes earlier. *Danegeld*, the eventual Class III winner, did not round until 0200 on the Thursday in company with five others. 'The night was hideous with the glare of the light, the wash of the waves, the cries of seabirds and the execrations of humans as spinnakers were doused and jennies set to the steadily mounting breath of a fresh southerly wind,' wrote one of *Danegeld*'s crew members. The shipping forecast in fact mentioned gales but added fog and calm at the Scillies for good measure. Those further back hoped the gale would push them forward while the calms would hold back the leaders and this is indeed what happened until the wind caught up with those in front and gave them an exciting, not to say hair-raising run from the Lizard to the finish in poor visibility. During this last leg Francis Chichester, conning *Mait II* through the murk, decided to play safe, as by then the Italian yacht had nothing to gain by taking risks, and decided to make a landfall at the Eddystone Light. It was, he decided, the only sensible thing to do as the Italian crew were given to lengthy conferences which did not encourage quick decisions, and as he needed to be only 400 yards out in his dead reckoning to put *Mait II* on the rocks at the entrance to Plymouth Sound instead of over the finishing line he wasn't going to risk putting the yacht in a position which might need instant action to save her.

Anitra's English navigator, Michael Richey, was also faced with a lee shore and no visibility, but unlike Mait II, which was well behind the Swedish yawl both boat for boat and on corrected time, Anitra had everything to lose. Richey turned to Sven Hansen and said: 'If my navigation is correct, we shall make Plymouth breakwater (the finishing line) and win the race, but if it isn't we shall pile up on the rocks outside. It's your yacht, you decide.' Hansen told Richey to go ahead and Anitra won the Fastnet Cup, arriving sixth in the elapsed time of 5 days, 8 hours, 39 minutes. The five yachts ahead of her were all Class I boats. Anna Marina was the first boat home in 5 days,

1 hour, 46 minutes and she was followed by Zwerver, Olivier van Noort, Lutine and Carina II, the American boat just failing to take overall honours by 51 minutes on correct time. Pym was first home in Class III some 21 hours after the overall winner, but both Danegeld and Faem beat her on corrected time and she dropped to third place with Cohoe III fourth.

While the leaders were crossing the line or approaching it the rest of the fleet, as seemed customary, now got hit by high winds. The predicted force 8 blew from the south and rose to force 9 in places. The larger boats missed the worst of it – though Drumbeat was forced to drop her mainsail at one point as was Moonlight II – but the tailenders were hit quite hard and the last yacht, Rummer, took eight days to finish.

# CHAPTER FOUR

# Modern Times      1961–77

On a beat to windward, any crew below was woken up on each tack and moved to windward bunks. If on deck, they sat birds-on-a-branch style, facing outwards with their feet dangling over the weather side – although with their torsos in the strictly legal position *inside* the life-lines. There was no time to enjoy this business of sailing.

> Paul Antrobus describing the crewing methods on board the 1973 Admiral's Cup boat, *Frigate*, in his contribution to *Ocean Racing Around the World*

It is rather arbitrary to elect 1961 as the year the Fastnet entered modern times. But it was the start of a new decade, and one which was to see an amazing growth in the sport of ocean racing as well as a new, tough, professional approach to it; that great symbol of a previous era, *Bloodhound*, was no longer at the starting line; and by 1961 the Admiral's Cup had established itself as a major international yachting trophy for which, that year, no less than five countries competed.

The United States fielded an Admiral's Cup team once more, and joined France, Holland and Sweden in trying to wrest the cup from Britain. The number of starters in 1961 almost doubled to 95, with entries from four countries other than those participating in the Admiral's Cup series. The days of a handful of entries, crewed by a band of amateur enthusiasts, were gone forever but it must have delighted the survivors of those early Fastnet Races to see *Flame*, a 1933 entry, at the line once more. Around her were the most powerful fleet of Class I ocean racers ever seen, with Kees Bruynzeel's huge new ketch, *Stormvogel*, and the even bigger American schooner, *Constellation*, dominating them. Two of the American Admiral's Cup team, *Windrose* and *Cyane*, were Class II newcomers, but the third member, *Figaro*, had represented the United States in the first series in 1957 with rerating now placing her in Class I. Veterans in Class I included *Zwerver*, *Griffin II*, *Lutine*, *Olivier van Noort*, *Marabu*, *St Barbara*, *Ramrod* (under new ownership), and *Drumbeat*. New to the class because of rerating but not to the race were *Myth of Malham*, again representing Britain in the Admiral's Cup, and the 1959 winner, *Anitra*, which was representing Sweden. Altogether there were 24 starters in Class I.

Class II, with 38 starters, included new yachts like *Assegai*, *Rapparee*, and the first of Ron Amey's highly successful string of *Noryemas*, as well as established names like *Bluejacket*, *Right Royal* and *Pym*, the last now elevated from Class III. Class III had 33 entries

but this was quickly reduced by one before the gun went when *Faem*, on the port tack, was rammed by another Class III yawl, *Capreolus*, and was forced to retire with a large hole in her topsides. The course was the same as usual – through the Needles after the start from Cowes, leaving the Scillies on either hand, rounding the Rock on either hand, and returning to Plymouth leaving the Scillies to port – and the start, on 5 August, went smoothly for Classes I and II. But in Class III there was some confusion when, just before the gun, the guardship started firing a Royal Salute for *Britannia*, which, with the Queen on board, was just leaving Southampton. Some yachts mistook the Salute for the gun and went over the line, and the start became a shambles.

The wind, force 4 to 5 from the wsw that touched force 6 at the Needles, had the fleet tacking vigorously out through the Needles Channel with *Stormvogel* in front. But having passed the Needles *Stormvogel*'s main halyard broke and it took three valuable hours to repair it, making her owner's wish to beat *Nordwind*'s time in the 1939 race a remote possibility. The Swedish yawl, *Dione*, also had halyard trouble and lost time, and *Drumbeat* had to land an injured crew member when a winch abruptly failed and hit him on the kneecap.

Towards evening the wind dropped and veered a couple of points to the north, but it was a fine clear night and with *Zwerver* now in the lead the fleet beat steadily down channel. Success on this leg depended more on the crews' ability to drive their yachts to windward at night than on any particular gambit, but most tacked well out into the Channel on the starboard tack and then tacked back into Lyme Bay when the tide turned foul. Sunday dawned bright and clear with the wind right on the nose, blowing between force 3 and 5, and that night the visibility was so good that Alf Loomis, navigating *Lutine*, could see the looms of Start Point, the Eddystone and the Lizard all at the same time.

59  *Flame*, a 1933 entry, leading the Class I fleet at the start of the 1961 Fastnet. Astern of her is the German *Ortac*, *Ramrod*, and *Drumbeat*. (*Beken*)

By dawn on Monday the wind had dropped away for the leaders and the strung out fleet began closing up. *Zwerver*, still in the lead, could not round the Lizard against the foul tide. *Figaro*, in the same area as the Dutch yacht, had a view of the promontary for seven long hours before a breeze came in from the ESE and filled her huge spinnaker, sending her past *Stormvogel* and in hot pursuit of *Zwerver*.

The American Admiral's Cup team had, incidentally, altered their sail plans gambling that the weather would be light. They had taken quite severe penalties under the RORC rule for shipping extra large genoas and vast spinnakers for which they had had built extra long booms, and had reduced their mainsail areas in order to get back a little rating. So far the gamble had worked and the United States was leading in the series by 13 points. And with the wind now light the Americans were well placed.

The lack of any real breeze began mixing the classes, with Ren Clarke's new *Quiver*, number three in the line, well ahead of some of the bigger Class I boats like *Constellation*, while *Galloper* and *Viking of Mersea* were two well-placed Class III entries.

Soon, however, the wind began to increase for the whole fleet and backed, and the weather forecast predicted that a small but intense depression over West Finisterre would pass over the Isle of Wight early the next morning. All day Monday the wind increased with the yachts careening along under spinnaker, some wave-riding at above their maximum hull speeds. Towards evening the visibility decreased badly as rain squalls came in and the wind rose to force 7. By this time *Stormvogel* making 12 knots had taken over the lead and was half-way to the Rock with the huge *Constellation* hot on her heels. Further back the Class II leaders, *Quiver III*, the French Admiral's cupper, *Marie-Christine III*, and *Windrose*, were safely through the gap between Land's End and the Scillies but the Class III leaders, headed by *Belmore*, heavily reefed and with a heavy-weather jib goosewinged to starboard, were only just approaching it. Behind *Belmore* were *Galloper*, *Cohoe III* and *Alcina*, and all these four were not only well ahead of the rest of their class but in front of half of Class II as well.

Between 1800 and midnight on the Monday the barometer dropped half an inch and the wind for the leaders shifted from ESE to NW but did not go beyond force 7 in strength. But for those still in the area between the Lizard and Land's End it piped up to force 9 at times, and in rain and lightning of near-tropical intensity, and in mounting seas, some yachts carried on under bare poles. *Bluejacket*, for instance, fore reached for $5\frac{1}{2}$ hours under bare poles for the first time in her racing career.

The centre of the depression reached the area just before midnight and Erroll Bruce, aboard the Class II yawl, *Rapparee*, described the scene vividly.

Many of the yachts were becalmed with the rain falling vertically in the beams of a torch; white horses reared only from habit as the gale suddenly ceased. Then even the rain stopped, and a patch of star-lit sky appeared overhead. This was the storm centre. We were in this calm for 40 minutes, tossing about in steep waves with no steerage way, while another unidentified yacht lay uncomfortably close. Many other yachts felt the calm for just a few minutes, and some were in this state when the midnight weather report informed them that the depression was overhead and deepening; severe gales were forecast for many areas, and this was the lull before the gale would pipe up from a direction immediately opposed to that from which it had last blown. It was a peculiar feeling to be sitting quietly in the middle of a gale centre, calculating the best action in the gale which must strike at any moment. Half the crew were asleep but lest we should feel too secure on the still airs, our mate of the watch mentioned that the last time he had been caught off a lee shore in a gale ocean racing, the crew had been forced to abandon ship, seeking safety on board a rescuing warship. The Seven Stones, as we talked things over, were seven miles to leeward in the expected north-west gale, but I decided it was not necessary to shift to storm canvas in this lull, hoping that the depression was moving too fast to give us a protracted gale.

When the wind arrived it was from the NW and came in vicious cold squalls up to force 9 which had *Rapparee* pounding on the new waves which were building, and to reduce speed Erroll Bruce had some of the weight of the staysail taken on to the weather sheet. But *Rapparee* was still making $5\frac{1}{2}$ knots with her lee rail under. John Illingworth, racing the Class III cutter, *Arabel II*, which he'd designed, was also in the eye of the storm for a while and reported force 9 winds once the new gale came in. As all his winches but one had packed up by this time he must have had a strenuous race and he did well to finish ninth in his class. Adlard Coles said that the new gale was one of the most violent, if brief, storms he'd ever experienced up to that time in those waters and five miles north of the Wolf Rock *Cohoe III* broached-to. The spinnaker, which the crew had kept hoisted in the hope that they would sail beyond the worst of the

storm, promptly blew out and the halyard was let fly to relieve the strain. The pressure had been so great, however – Adlard Coles reckoned it to be in the area of two tons – that it bent the steel bolts which held the sheet blocks and drew them half-an-inch through the toe rail and the planking below, causing half-inch fractures in the upper plank. In *Heavy Weather Sailing* he later wrote:

Everything was blotted out by rain. The gap between the Longships and the Seven Stones Lightvessel is 12 miles wide. We set a compass course and raced in the gathering gloom seeing nothing at all, though we must have passed near the Seven Stones Lightvessel (where the tanker *Torrey Canyon* came to grief in 1967) before emerging into the open sea in the Irish Sea approaches. The barometer touched its lowest at about midnight and the wind veered to SSW, followed by a veer to NNW two hours later.

I shall always remember that night. It was intensely black. The rain was absolutely torrential and the visibility nil. The wind was exceptionally strong and gusting well above gale force.

These strong gusts, however did not last long enough to build up a sea and though 63 knots was recorded at the Lizard at one point the wind soon moderated to force 6 or 7 from the SW by which time *Stormvogel* was up to the Rock, she and the other leaders, *Zwerver*, *Myth of Malham* and *Figaro* never having felt its full force. *Stormvogel* rounded at 1048 on the Tuesday morning, followed by *Zwerver* three hours later. Then came *Figaro*, *Lutine*, *Constellation* and *Myth of Malham*, but it was the smaller *Quiver III* which led on corrected time at this point when she rounded at 1919 at the same time as the bigger *Myth of Malham*. In Class III *Belmore*, followed by *Cohoe III*, lost the lead to *Galloper*, the latter going to the front of her class before the Fastnet after somehow having managed to carry her genoa throughout the gale until eventually the halyard carried away. With 12 rolls in her main *Galloper* had anticipated the change in wind direction by going 40 miles to the west of the rhumb line, and this enabled her to fetch the Rock on one long port tack without having to short-tack along the Irish coast as many boats had to do. This tactic paid handsome dividends and she was 15th to round the Rock and first in her class ahead of *Belmore*, *Cohoe III* and *Vashti*. Most of the fleet, however, were less fortunate and before the Rock no less than 30 yachts retired, six more were forced to heave-to, and another six had to run off before the wind. One of those that ran before the gale was *Pundit* and she ended up nine miles west of the Bishop, while *Wishstream*, which did the same thing, finished up

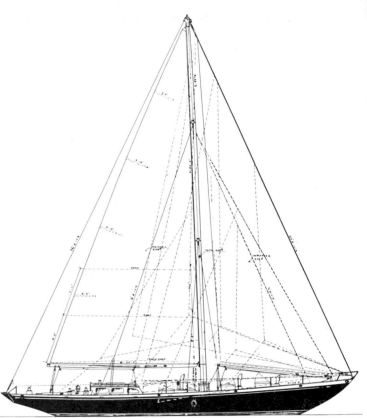

60  The Dutch Class I yacht, *Zwerver*, a 1959 entry when she came fourth in her class, was the 1961 Fastnet winner. (*Beken*)

61  The sail plan of the 1961 Fastnet winner, *Zwerver*, designed by Sparkman and Stephens. Her dimensions were: LOA: 56 ft 9 in, LWL: 39 ft, beam: 11 ft 9 in, draught: 8 ft.

back at the Wolf Rock and took 15 hours to regain her original position.

Once round the Rock the ten leaders in Class I, plus the Class II yachts *Quiver III* and *Windrose*, had a magnificent run to the Bishop, with *Stormvogel* passing it at 2328 that night. The wind stayed with the Dutchman on the last leg to Plymouth and she finished at 1513 on the Wednesday having taken 3 days, 21 hours to complete the course and missing *Nordwind*'s record by some five hours. *Constellation* was in next followed by another Dutch yacht, *Zwerver*, and then the wind died. *Zwerver* had been well back before the Bishop and had had to tack downwind to carry her spinnaker. She had a hard, fast race for during the storm she'd been knocked down twice, 30 miles ESE of the Rock, and had been forced to heave-to for five hours. But then she averaged 9.3 knots between the Rock and the Bishop and though

during this leg she lost time to *Anitra*, *Figaro*, *Myth of Malham* and the Class I *Springtime*, on corrected time she was an easy overall winner by about 4¾ hours.

After rounding the Rock fifth *Figaro* hoisted her extra large spinnaker and increased her speed by a knot. Heavy rain-squalls made the crew wonder whether they'd been wise to hoist it but they hung on to it until the inevitable happened. 'We pushed our luck too far,' commented Norris Hoyt, one of the crew members, who then went on to describe how *Figaro* helped win the Admiral's Cup for the Americans that year.

At 1000 we caught a 40-degree shift in a rainsquall, were knocked beam-ends, and couldn't get her to pay off with the helm against the stops. The giant spinnaker eased itself with a great sigh, 100 feet of vertical and horizontal daylight, and a crisp rattling of fragments. The mizzen staysail, set upside down for effectiveness in light air, tore out some 25 feet in sympathy. Bill Snaith tore out some hair and made eloquent remarks about good judgment. And within an hour the stern horizon was blossoming spinnaker domes. Plainly, only the big bag held the treasure. We set up a sewing circle, and for five hours we stitched madly – mizzen staysail in the cabin and spinnaker in the cockpit – three stitching, two holding, and one threading. I took pictures, cooked, ran errands, Bill Snaith, cigar a-la-Churchill, steered. When we set both sails they held, and we began to lose the bubbles again. When the statistics were in we'd stood off the British resurgence and won the cup. In effect *Figaro* stitched her way to victory.

The other two American Admiral's cuppers had their problems as well, *Windrose* breaking her boom and *Cyane* her tiller, but in the final placings on corrected time *Figaro* was third in Class I while *Cyane* was ninth, and in Class II *Windrose* was second behind *Quiver III*. Up to the Bishop *Quiver III* had had the race in the bag having at that time no less than three hours in hand over *Zwerver*. In Class III *Galloper* was equally favourably placed being well ahead of the eventual winner, *Belmore*. But then the wind died leaving *Zwerver*'s main rivals slatting their mainsails off the Lizard. *Quiver III*, for example, took nearly 14 hours to cover the last 47 miles and on this last leg alone lost five hours to *Zwerver* – and the Fastnet Cup.

The breeze, when it at last came, wafted in from the NE and then backed north and strengthened. It gave most of the fleet a fine sail home but some yachts, including the luckless *Galloper*, *Drumbeat*, the German-owned *Ortac*, and *Silvio*, ran into an unreported storm on the Thursday morning. It blew force 8 from the NE, dismasted *Ortac*, took *Drumbeat* aback, and caused *Galloper* to overstand badly and lose the Class III prize, the Foxhound Cup.

It had been a typical Fastnet, with frustrating calms and unpredictable weather. As the RORC report on the race commented, you had to be both good and lucky to win in 1961.

---

On 10 August 1963, a large crowd saw the start of what was to be the greatest Fastnet Race in the history of offshore racing. Greatest because of the number of starters, 125, the quality of the yachts, and the interest engendered by the struggle for the Admiral's Cup between six teams, France, Germany, Great Britain, Holland, Sweden, and the United States. Britain emerged triumphant and for the first time for ten years a British yacht won the Fastnet Cup and the British team recaptured the Admiral's Cup from the USA.

These words, written by a correspondent of a British yachting magazine with understandable hyperbole, illustrates well the delight with which a British victory was received for though the 1963 race was a good one it was no classic.

Top British ocean racing yachtsmen started the 1963 season with a new determination. The loss of the Admiral's Cup to the Americans and the continuing string of wins of the Fastnet Cup by foreign yachts had put them on their metal and competition to gain a place in the Admiral's Cup team was rigorous. This was encouraged by a new system of selecting the British team. Previously, it had been chosen by the selection committee of the RORC on merit, but in 1963 rigorous trials were instituted and a considerable number of new yachts were built for them. *Musketeer*, built for the then RORC Commodore, Peter Green, by Camper and Nicholson, was a front runner as was Sir Max Aitken's new Illingworth and Primrose designed cutter, *Outlaw*, whose one-inch thick cold-moulded 48-foot hull only displaced 14 tons. A near sister to *Quiver III* was built for Ron Amey, *Hephzibah* for *Vashti*'s owner, Maurice Laing, and Olin Stephens' first design to the RORC rule, *Clarion of Wight*, for Derek Boyer and Dennis Miller. Miller was a comparative newcomer to ocean racing but a lot more was going to be heard of him after the 1963 Fastnet for he was amongst the new breed of owners who were to bring to ocean racing within the next few years the 'all or nothing' approach that finally levered the sport into the modern era in Britain. Miller and Boyer were a successful partnership which had campaigned *Pym* as a new boat. But then he and Boyer decided to go their separate ways for the 1961 season. This proved an unsuccessful move so they joined forces again to build a new Admiral's Cup contender for the 1963 season. They both agreed to go to Olin Stephens for the design of the new boat because, Miller remarked, he was the only designer neither of them disliked! Whatever the reason it proved a good choice.

But despite the increasing competitiveness the designs of British boats and the men who raced them were still strongly influenced by the attitudes of the past. It was an era of transition and most owners still built with an eye on the second-hand market if they were selling and on family cruising if they weren't. This made interiors important as Paul Antrobus pointed out in his contribution to *Ocean Racing Around the World*, and Camper and Nicholson, for one, gave a great deal of thought to them. 'Their idea,' wrote Antrobus, who was a regular member of Ron Amey's crew in the 1970s, 'was to provide dry and comfortable accommodation below for the off-watch crew and to provide excellent galley facilities so that, conditions allowing, food could be served in as civilised a style as possible. Many yachts carried a permanent cook, and crews sat round a saloon table to eat. When you consider this was probably built of solid mahogany, it comes hardly as a surprise to know racing men have now discarded this extra, needless weight and are content to eat off their laps!'

But in the early 1960s yachts were still built for the

crew to sleep and eat in comfort – in Baron de Rothschild's huge *Gitana IV*, which was to break the record in the 1965 Fastnet, the crew often dressed for dinner which was served by stewards – and for the owner to cruise with his family without the spartan living conditions below that weight-conscious ocean racing men soon introduced. 'British boats used to be heavier and stronger than American yachts,' Antrobus quotes Rod Stephens as saying, 'presumably as a result of building to Lloyds specification. We used to reckon they were all right in a blow, just slogging through that short chop you get in the Channel, when finesse didn't matter too much. You only had to look at the fittings (winches, blocks, cleats, mast fittings). They were heavy, inefficient, like something off one of the old J-class. If you wanted decent fittings then you had to get them from the USA.'

The 1963 start was in traditional Fastnet weather, a force 6 from the west with the forecasters predicting it to veer to the NW just about the time the leaders were due to round Land's End and head for the Rock. Alan Hollingsworth, the skipper of the Class III boat, *Deseret*, wrote the following in his book *Crewing Offshore*.

We reach up the line with three rolls down and the working jib in a mill of yachts like feeding-time in a fish-pond. We shoot under the stern of a Class I giant and an American voice from under a ten-gallon dayglow sou'wester calls out 'Real Fastnet weather, eh Bud?' as a green growler sends spray shooting to our crosstrees. At the base of the Squadron Castle a jet of grey smoke ejaculates noiselessly and before the sound has reached us we are across the line with the sheets bar-taut. Tack and tack again and the heavier gusts lay her flat, the lee scuppers running green. 'Change to No.2,' I yell and provoke a frenzy on the foredeck until the smaller sail is up and drawing hard. Tack and tack again and the first hank parts from the foresail luff followed swiftly by two more, popping like buttons on a fat boy's vest. Another foredeck frenzy and we are down to No.3 but she is sluggish under the tiny sail. The watch below, sodden now like us all, sits damply on the heaving cabin sole furiously reseizing the headsail hanks on No.2. We change again in the ugly Hurst channel seas, falling into the holes with a crash that makes the crockery leap from its fiddles. The navigator, grey-faced and sweating, comes up with the tacking plan for the Channel leg and dives compulsively for the lee-rail. We turn our eyes from his misery and glue them on the foresail luff as we gather way from tacking yet again. A waterlogged foredeck hand, his teeth chattering

like castanets, retches violently as he winches home the sheet. Six days to go. For an instant I wonder why we came, but dismiss the unworthy thought as we clear the Bridge buoy and punch laboriously seawards into the gathering dark. . . .

Alf Loomis, again navigating in *Lutine*, wrote afterwards that American long-range weather forecasters had predicted a 150-mile-an-hour gale on 12 August – Loomis' reports in *Yachting* were always full of amusing over-statements – which created a lot of ill-will amongst the American contingent, apparently, as it caused them a lot of worry for nothing. For, after the wild start so evocatively described above, at the Rock for many boats there was only what Loomis described as an Irish hurricane, ie a wind that blew directly up or down a mast at a rate of no knots whatsoever.

*Lutine*, that year, did not make a particularly good start, but, as Loomis reported, 'at least we kept away from the milling horde directly off the Royal Yacht Squadron at Cowes where calls for water and crash of splintering wood mingled with the roar of gun and wind,' and this time he was not exaggerating for Britain's biggest hope to retrieve the Admiral's Cup, *Clarion of Wight*, was involved in a port and starboard incident at the line with *Primevere*. One of *Clarion*'s spinnaker poles was snapped and a small hole was made in her deck. Illingworth, who was skippering *Primevere* but was not at the helm at the time, called for water but later lost the protest over the incident. It was as well that he did because at the beginning of the race Britain was trailing Sweden by four points in the Admiral's Cup series and if *Clarion of Wight* had been disqualified the Cup would almost certainly have stayed outside Britain for another two years. As it was, the collision did not incapacitate her and she went on to win the Fastnet Cup and helped Britain reclaim the Admiral's Cup.

More serious was another collision between *Oberon* and *Rondinella*, both British, in which the latter was badly holed and dismasted. Both withdrew and soon after the start another British yacht, *Starfire of Kent*, was forced to withdraw when her steering gear broke and she hit the Shingles. *Witte Raaf* went aground off Cowes and was another early casualty.

One of the American Admiral's cuppers, *Figaro*, also met trouble at the start when the wind blew overboard her life-raft which then inflated itself and floated away. In the process of retrieving it, the American yacht's mainsail was torn, but after this poor beginning *Figaro* excelled herself and eventually won her Class. *Outlaw*, one of the Admiral's Cup team, also had problems when the gooseneck sheered before the gun went and she crossed the line under headsails only. However, repairs were soon made and *Outlaw* began slamming her way down the Needles Channel.

Damage to gear was not the only hindrance the yachts suffered. The number of active members of the crew of *Marabu* soon dwindled alarmingly as sea-sickness took its toll. Perhaps they had ignored John Illingworth's strict advice of 'no red meat, no fried foods and NO ALCOHOL' before a race.

'When our cook, a good lady from the admiralty, announced her intention of cooking a meal involving a rather over-dead chicken (or was it a sea-gull?) from a recipe headed *Cordon Bleu*,' recorded a surviving crew member afterwards, 'a few more faces turned a healthy shade of emerald green, and then we were three.'

Doubtless, *Marabu*'s crew were not the only ones afflicted by sea-sickness as the fleet, led by Mrs Sally Langmuir's yawl, *Bolero*, *Stormvogel*, and the new Swedish yawl, *Capricia*, headed for Portland with the force 6 gusting to force 7 still dead ahead and kicking up a very nasty sea. Adlard Coles in his new fibreglass 36-footer, *Cohoe IV*, designed by Camper and Nicholson, worked close inshore and took the inside passage at Portland. This worked wonders and he jumped into second place on corrected time behind *Bolero*, with *Capricia* third and *Clarion of Wight* fourth.

The wind eased slightly during the night and by Plymouth *Stormvogel* had taken over the lead from *Bolero* which was having trouble with her mainsail track. When the crew had tried to unreef the mainsail it was found that the track had come adrift from the mast and, despite anchoring to try and sort out the problem, she was forced to continue with her main reefed to the Rock. However, once she'd rounded her skipper, Peter Bowker, found an ingenious solution to the problem by rigging a line from the mast head aft, and on this improvised jackstay the upper part of the mainsail was set flying. It worked, but *Bolero* by then was out of the running.

Another of the big new boats, *Capricia*, also had trouble when her main halyard parted in the vicinity of the Eddystone Light. *Capricia* was able to keep going because her designer, Olin Stephens, had had the foresight to provide a spare one. His brother Rod swarmed up the mast and soon put things to rights, a not unremarkable feat for a man who was 50 at the time!

Other, more serious, accidents now increased the number of retirements: *Assegai* lost her mast off Bolt Head, *Corabia* lost hers off the Longships and a large tanker ran *Micronette* down near the Eddystone. Reports were mixed on how badly damaged she was but it was bad enough to force her to retire.

Way ahead of most of the fleet *Capricia* and *Stormvogel* were rounding Land's End early on the Monday morning with *Outlaw* not far behind them.

*Figaro* was also well up but another Class I boat, *Avrion*, missed the tide at the Lizard as did many others. *Quiver III* was doing well until her forestay bottlescrew snapped. Miraculously, although the weight of the mast was all on the luff of the genoa, the luffwire held and a new bottlescrew was fitted.

At the Seven Stones *Outlaw* was in the lead with some of the smaller boats like *Cohoe IV*, *Clarion of Wight*, and Peter Green's new *Musketeer* edging in behind the bigger leaders. Others had dropped back by this point having tried unsuccessfully to work the tides inshore. Conversely, *Musketeer* had done well by standing out after Start Point, working the tides off Plymouth and catching the first of the flood off the Lizard. But at 1930 that evening it was *Cohoe IV* which was leading on corrected time.

It was this leg, from the Seven Stones to the Rock, which held the key to the 1963 race and those that took the port tack benefitted when the wind backed as predicted to the NW. *Clarion* kept well to the east of the rhumb line as did *Cohoe IV* and *Capricia*, while *Musketeer* made short boards up the rhumb line and *Outlaw* made long ones. *Lutine* went right the other way and passed south of the Scillies. As a result she did not round the Rock until $15\frac{1}{4}$ hours after the first boat, *Capricia*, and finishing in the bottom half of her class on corrected time.

The wind on the Tuesday was patchy and after *Capricia* rounded at 0914 that morning there was quite a gap in time, two hours, 41 minutes, but not in distance, before the second boat, *Stormvogel*, rounded. Then came *Bolero* (1328), the German Admiral's cupper, *Rubin* (1455), the Swedish Class I boat, *Vagabonde* (1515), which was also an Admiral's Cup entry, and *Carina II* (1604), this year being sailed by Richard Nye's son. The large gaps in the rounding times showed the holes in the wind and as the afternoon progressed it began to fade right away, though *Clarion of Wight* managed to squeeze round at 1724 and at this point was the leading boat on corrected time.

This fickle breeze affected some yachts more than others. For example, both *Glenan* and *Najade*, French and Dutch Admiral's cuppers respectively, had been ahead of *Lutine* on the beat up to the Rock because of the latter's tactical error of passing south of the Scillies. But it was the Lloyd's Yacht Club boat that rounded first, at 0030 on the Wednesday morning, followed by *Glenan* at 0210 and *Najade* at 0430. Later in the morning the Swedish boat, *Kay*, outward bound, passed close to the leader, *Capricia*, on her way back to the Bishop. Arne Frisell, the son of *Kay*'s owner, was aboard *Capricia* and as his father was anxious to know how *Capricia* was doing he asked where *Capricia*'s great rival, *Stormvogel*, was. Arne

**62** The Hon. Max Aitken's Class I yacht *Outlaw* under storm spinnaker. She was a member of the British Admiral's Cup team in 1963, finishing that year's Fastnet sixth in her class.

*Figaro*, having kept close company since the Rock and covered 123 miles at an average of 7.8 knots, suddenly found themselves at lunchtime on Wednesday rolling around off the Scillies. But it was a slow run back for most of the fleet. *Lutine*, for instance, logged only 30 miles in the first nine hours after turning the mark, but 50 miles from the Bishop the wind freshened and this carried her to the Lizard when it again became light and variable in direction. Eventually *Lutine* crossed the finishing line some 17 hours after the winner of the Erivale Cup, *Capricia*, which finished at 2221 on the Wednesday evening with *Stormvogel* second and *Bolero* third. On corrected time these placings were adjusted to 17th, 29th and 20th in Class I respectively. It was not a year for the big boats.

The smaller boats, however, were doing surprisingly well, being favoured by the light weather conditions. *Cohoe IV* was well up on the rest of her class, and on most of Class II as well, when she rounded at 0312 on the Wednesday morning, with the small amateur designed Class III French sloop, *Pen Ar Bed*, also well up with the bigger boats and rounding at 1122. Another French Class III boat doing well at this point was *Astrolabe* which rounded at 1150. Ahead of the fleet on corrected time *Clarion of Wight* reached the Bishop at 2230 on the Wednesday with her closest rival, *Cohoe IV*, reaching the same point at 0340 the next morning. *Pen Ar Bed*, still well up on corrected time, had the Bishop abeam at 1030. On corrected time all these boats did amazingly well overall: *Clarion of Wight* won overall honours beating *Cohoe IV* into second place by a mere six minutes, with *Pen Ar Bed* taking third place and another Class III boat, *Belmore II*, taking fourth. *Astrolabe* took sixth place overall, fifth place going to the Class II boat, *Camelot*. The first boat in Class I, *Figaro*, could only manage tenth place overall, which just showed how the wind after the first couple of days had favoured the smaller boats.

But the weather still had something up its sleeve for the rest of the fleet and during the Thursday a depression came up channel causing problems amongst the slower boats. Spinnaker sheets parted and sails tore. The Sappers' boat, *Ilex II*, was even forced to heave-to just short of the Bishop. Altogether there were nine retirements in Class III, 12 in Class II and three in Class I, including the Count of Barcelona's new yawl *Giralda* which, with spinnaker set, ran aground on some rocks near the Bishop and had to use her engine to extricate herself.

The Americans did especially well in Class I with *Figaro* winning the Founders Cup and *Carina II* taking second place. *Baccarat* and *Dyna* were fourth and fifth behind the German sloop, *Rubin*. But though *Figaro* and *Dyna* did well the third member of the American

jerked his thumb over his shoulder and everyone on *Kay* then knew that *Capricia* was almost certain to be the first boat home.

'Watching her go by under the great lift of her spinnaker,' wrote author Ernle Bradford who was aboard *Kay*, 'we felt a little indolent, perhaps even rather guilty, for we had just caught a mackerel! In a boat of *Kay*'s displacement we hardly felt a mackerel-line made much difference, but I tried to imagine the horror that would be shown by the skippers of some light displacement boats if one suggested putting out a mackerel-line in the middle of a Fastnet race. . . .'

*Kay* eventually rounded the Rock the next morning in an almost dead calm and counted 13 other yachts also trying to drift round. Once pointed for the Bishop, however, the wind increased and logging ten knots *Kay* even overhauled one of the American Admiral's cuppers, *Windrose*, and managed to hold onto this lead and crossed the line about six minutes ahead of the American boat.

As the smaller boats were rounding the leaders ran into a calm patch off the Bishop and *Outlaw* and

Admiral's Cup team, *Windrose*, could only manage 22nd place in Class II and this enabled Britain to win back the trophy.

Gear failure in 1963 was not nearly so frequent as in earlier years but when the crew of *Belmore II* submitted their analysis sheet of the race they reported that their No.1 spinnaker, in common with many others, had been blown out. They also recorded a more unusual gear failure, 'the Captain's cranium after fall below causing slight concussion necessitating his being put ashore for hospitalisation, the race being carried on without him.'

To lose your skipper might be regarded by some as a drawback, but *Belmore II* had gone on to come third in her class and fourth overall, and under the heading 'General remarks including factors most affecting boat's performance' on the analysis sheet, one of the crew had written, 'get rid of your skipper, somehow.'

---

In 1965 a new element arrived in the Fastnet Race: the Australians came. There had been, of course, Australians in the Fastnet before 1965 but for the first time they were challenging for the Admiral's Cup. They brought with them a new kind of professionalism and determination which provoked a mixture of admiration and suspicion amongst their British counterparts. They arrived in England early and sailed and trained hard. They were tough, ambitious, and uncompromising in their will to win, and showed British yachtsmen just how amateur they still were in their approach to training and sail evaluation. As a result the three Australian team yachts, *Freya*, *Camille of Seaforth* and *Caprice of Huon*, all performed well in the earlier races in the series. The 13-year-old *Caprice of Huon* in fact did brilliantly, winning the Britannia Cup, the New York Yacht Club Cup, and winning her class in the Channel Race, and at the start of the Fastnet Australia was only 14 points behind the leader, Britain. Other teams were entered by Holland, France (led by Eric Tabarly in *Pen-Duick II*), Sweden, Ireland (for the first time), Germany and the United States. The British built eight yachts to compete for the three places in their team, and the practice of building for each new series now began to take on a pattern, with *Quiver IV* and *Noryema IV* taking over from the earlier boats of the same name and, like their predecessors, winning berths in the team. The third member of the team was Dennis Miller's sloop, *Firebrand*, his season in *Clarion of Wight* having convinced him that advances in the sport could be made if an owner were sufficiently ruthless and dedicated – and rich. He therefore made another amicable split with his partner Derek Boyer and again went to Olin Stephens for a new design. The result was

*Firebrand*, a boat Rod Stephens was later to see as a turning point for ocean racing in Britain. But it was not her hull that was so revolutionary but her rigging, combined with Hood sails.

The development of large foretriangles and small mainsails had been hindered up to that time by the limitations of wire rigging and wodden masts which made it impossible to make the forestay sufficiently rigid to take more powerful headsails. But rod rigging and metal masts, combined with Ted Hood's powerful masthead genoas, broke through this barrier and Miller took full advantage of these new developments. *Firebrand* also had another innovation, a bendy boom whose curve was altered by having the mainsheet run through a series of block along its length and then onto the deck. The sail could then be flattened in a fresh wind by winching in the mainsheet, or allowed to curve in light weather by checking it. The same principle applied to *Firebrand*'s Hood headsails which had rope 'stretchy' luffs instead of wire. Sail trimming now became as exact an art as tuning the engine of a racing car. It required a totally dedicated crew, but Miller had that as well – 'a determined bunch of ruffians who would give up all else for a season's racing' was his description of them – and there's no doubt that they drove *Firebrand* with skill and verve, and she came to the line for the 21st Fastnet with eight wins already under her belt.

But despite *Firebrand*'s advanced design the yacht of the year in 1965 was a small Class III amateur-designed American sloop called *Rabbit*. Owned and designed by Dick Carter *Rabbit* was 24-foot LWL and 34 feet overall, and was built by the Dutch builder, Franz Maas of Breskens, who also built and designed another successful Fastnet entry that year, *Tonnerre de Breskens*, which came second in Class II. *Rabbit* had a metal mast – also designed by Carter – with an internal halyard arrangement. It was built by Ted Hood who commented to Carter that 'even the 12-metres don't do it like this,' which, considering how much development money is poured into the America's Cup yachts, shows how far ahead of his time Carter was. Below the waterline, *Rabbit* was equally radical, Carter having given her a spade rudder about three feet aft of her fin keel and a trim tab on the keel itself. This split configuration, used by Illingworth on *Mouse of Malham*, reduced the area of wetted surface and was soon to become standard practice. But in 1965 it was radical indeed.

The number of starters for the 1965 race was again a record, 151, but the weather for once, was beautiful, a light breeze sending the fleet towards the Needles under an almost cloudless sky. In fact the weather during the entire race was in complete contradiction to its usual pattern, this time providing a run to the

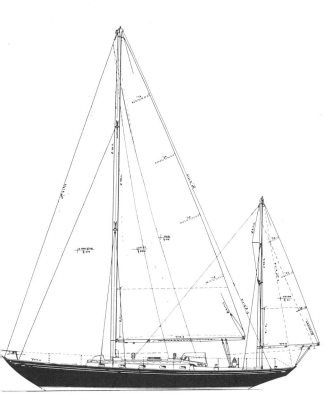

Rock and a beat back. It was all upside down, as someone said at the dinner after the race, in honour of the Australians' first visit.

Class I started first at 1830 with the remains of a foul tide running against it. The Italian yacht, *Al Na'ir III*, with Rod Stephens at the helm, was first across the line after the gun in Class I, with Olympic helmsman Gordon Ingate putting the Australian Admiral's cupper, *Caprice of Huon*, over first in Class II, *Caprice* being closely followed by *Noryema IV* and *Firebrand*. In Class III both *Islay Mist* and *Green Highlander* made good starts but *Tjaldur* was over the line and had to return. She then found she had no wind and had to kedge for a while before setting off in pursuit of the fleet.

Baron de Rothschild's huge Class I yawl, *Gitana IV*, starting at the windward end of the line, was soon in

**63** The sail plan of *Figaro*, the Class I winner in 1963. Her dimensions were: LOA: 47 ft 1 in, LWL: 33 ft, beam, 12 ft 2 in, draught: 4 ft 5 in.

**64** The Australians fielded an Admiral's Cup team for the first time in 1965 and *Caprice of Huon* was its most successful yacht, coming fifth in Class II in that year's Fastnet.

the lead, her huge 2700 sq. foot quadrilateral genoa, for which she carried a substantial penalty, drawing beautifully. In a force 2 or 3 which had a northerly hint in it she fetched down the Solent at 8 knots or so and cleared the Shingles without tacking, closely followed by *Zwerver* and *Quiver IV*. *Marabu*, involved in a luffing match with *Evenlode*, went the wrong side of the Shingles buoy and had to return to pass it correctly.

With the tide due to turn foul at Portland at 0145 the next morning many laid off a course which took them either outside or through the race and it was touch and go whether even some of the bigger boats would make the 35 miles in time. But the wind hardened slightly and gave a fine reach before eventually backing to give the smaller Class III boats not only a foul tide at the Bill but a headwind as well. But then it dropped again and left many near the Start waiting for a lift and only a few, which included *Rabbit*, escaped the foul tide. Freddie Kemmis Betty's yawl, *Aloha*, with Alf Loomis on board pen at the ready, was one of those that elected to stay inshore and paid the penalty for doing so. *Quiver IV* took the seaward tack which proved the correct tactic and yachts like *Fanfare*, *Musketeer*, and *Al Na'ir III*, which had been close astern of her, now dropped out of sight. On this leg to Start Point the larger Class I yachts definitely had the best of it but later the leaders also hit a calm patch off the Lizard. *Gitana IV* was becalmed for six hours close inshore and did not pass England's most southerly point until dusk, followed later by *Caper*, *Figaro*, *Quiver IV* and *Zwerver*.

Then on the Sunday night the wind came in from the SE. At first the land breeze counteracted its effect, but soon spinnakers were hoisted for the first time in the race, and the fleet — with the exception of *Francesca* which somehow contrived to break her mast — at last began to make headway once more. *Noryema IV* was off the Lizard at 0447 on the Monday morning with *Griffin II* and *Bluejacket III* around it at about the same time. *Rabbit* passed it at 0700, still well up in the fleet, but by this time the leaders were out into the Irish Sea, *Zwerver*, *Shelmalier of Anglesey*, and *Vagabonde* passing the Scillies at 0115 on the Monday morning, followed by *Firebrand* at 0345. *Gitana IV*, still in the lead, had passed the Seven Stones at 0330 and with the wind piping up to force 5 on the port quarter she set her huge 5400 sq. foot spinnaker which began speeding her along at 13 knots. The distance between her and the next boats, *Caper*, *Giralda*, *Zwerver*, *Figaro* and *Quiver IV*, began to widen.

In the afternoon the wind increased to force 7 for the leaders and force 6 for the rest, and a nasty cross sea got up. But despite breaking both her spinnaker booms in quick succession *Gitana IV* pressed on at 10 knots with her quad genoa set, and rounded the Rock first at 2150 that night. Behind her, spinnakers began blowing out with great regularity and for a couple of boats there was bigger trouble in store. Near together when one squall swept in were *Vagabonde*, *Figaro*, *Caper*, *Outlaw*, *Quiver IV* and *Shelmalier of Anglesey*. George Fowler, a crew member on *Outlaw*, now owned by R.G. Fuller, was below chatting to the cook when the squall hit. 'What will happen if the mast goes?' the cook asked. 'It's never happened to me yet,' George replied. 'There's always a first time,' and at that precise moment, apparently, there was a large *crrrump* and *Outlaw*'s mast went over the side. While travelling at maximum hull speed the spinnaker guy had broken and the enormous compression caused by the spinnaker boom pressing against the forestay combined with the main boom hitting the lower shroud when the mainsheet was let go to prevent her broaching-to had been too much for the mast, and over it went.

*Vagabonde*, seeing what had happened to *Outlaw*, bore away towards the crippled yacht and, running by the lee, she was accidentally gybed and dipped her main boom deeply into the water and broke it. To compound her troubles she then broached-to, the spinnaker went out of control and its boom came adrift. It shot aft tearing a gaping hole in the mainsail and narrowly missed decapitating two of the crew. At this point *Fanfare* arrived on the scene and she doused her spinnaker and stood by the crippled *Outlaw* while *Vagabonde*'s crew set a trysail and headed back to Plymouth. Eventually, *Outlaw* limped into Crosshaven under power and *Fanfare* continued the race.

*Figaro* also had trouble in this squall, Bill Snaith losing one of his crew over the side when the spinnaker was being lowered. It took 17 minutes to get him back but this did not stop *Figaro* being fourth round the Rock and second in her class on corrected time.

*Gitana IV* had worked out such a lead that the next yacht, *Zwerver*, did not round until 0130 on the Tuesday morning, over three-and-a-half hours behind the huge French yawl. *Caper* was third round 25 minutes after the Dutchman, and 40 minutes after *Caper* came *Giralda*. Then came *Quiver IV* at 0400, followed by *Fanfare* at 0430 and by this time the wind had moderated considerably and veered SW. This meant the leaders could lay the course for the Bishop but as the day progressed the wind backed to to the south and became maddeningly variable. This change pushed *Quiver IV* NE of the rhumb line, a fate suffered by most on this leg at this time though *Noryema IV* managed to stay close-hauled on the starboard tack nearly all the way.

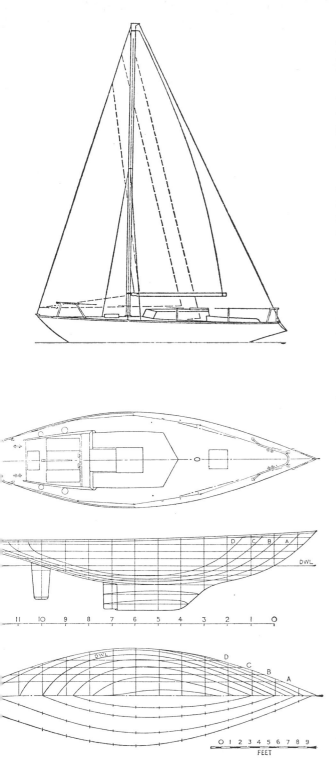

**65** The lines and sail plan of Dick Carter's phenomenally successful Class III sloop, *Rabbit*, which was the 1965 Fastnet winner.

For the smaller boats further back the wind backed even more – quite against what the weather forecast had predicted – and freshened to force 6 once more which meant a long flog back to the Bishop for most.

*Gitana IV*, however, was so far ahead on this leg that she practically had her own weather pattern and though she had to tack to clear the Bishop her speed never dropped below 10 knots. The Lizard was passed after dark but the crew did not even have to ask for *Gitana IV*'s position in the race for the message that was blinked to them was unequivocal: 'YOU ARE FIRST ONE BACK.' And indeed she was, by miles, and she finished at 0410 on the Wednesday morning, an incredible 17 hours ahead of the next boat, *Figaro*. Her elapsed time was 3 days, 9 hours, 40 minutes, easily breaking *Nordwind*'s 1939 record breaking run of 3 days, 16 hours, 28 minutes, and she had averaged 7.3 knots round the course and 8 knots from the Fastnet.

Hours after *Gitana IV* had finished, *Quiver IV*, *Caper* and *Zwerver* were all still struggling to round the Bishop in light airs. Once round, *Quiver IV* made the mistake of keeping too close inshore and *Caper*, having given both the Scillies and the Lizard a wide berth, finished this last leg of the course two hours ahead of the British boat. Peter Nicholson, on *Quiver IV*, said the move had cost them the race but they at least had the consolation of winning Class I and taking the Founder's Cup.

Most of Class II and III came in some time during the Thursday. *Rabbit* was one of these and on corrected time she pipped *Quiver IV* at the post by a mere 42 minutes to win the Fastnet Cup though she was only placed 17th on elapsed time. But midnight on Thursday still found some 50 boats at sea and though the weather had proved upside down in its behaviour it was not going to forsake the blow it always preserved for the tail-enders. But instead of blowing up from the west a force 6 or 7 came in from the east giving this last group a very unpleasant slog to the finish. Last over the line was *Gauntlet* having taken not far off seven days to complete the course.

That grand old man of ocean racing, John Illingworth, came third in Class II in *Monk of Malham* behind *Noryema IV* and *Tonnerre de Breskens*. Although smaller than *Myth of Malham*, *Monk of Malham* was the faster of the two, which Illingworth was able to prove during the race since *Myth* was being raced by her new owners, David and Bridget Livingston, as a member of the Irish Admiral's Cup team. Illingworth, however, did not regard it as a successful race. It made him, he wrote, realise that he was far past his peak as an ocean racing skipper. He had made errors and it was 'bad for the skipper to realise that he has made a lot of small mistakes and could have done better for the ship. I was already having to take five or six hours' sleep a day, instead of the usual two or three and the rest of the time on deck, or between the chart table and the deck. For ocean races are mostly won at night and the skipper should sleep by day and be up roughly all night.'

One wonders what the owners of the seven starters in the first Fastnet would have thought of that remark considering that in 1925 it would have been thought bad seamanship for a yacht not to shorten sail and slow down during the hours of darkness!

---

If the 1965 race belonged to Britain the 1967 one must be said to be Australia's. In the overall honours *Mercedes III* came third behind the phenomenally fast *Pen-Duick III* and *Figaro IV*, and took the Class II(a) prize; *Balandra* came third in Class I; and *Caprice of Huon* came second in Class II(a). Racing with such consistency won them the Admiral's Cup.

Although by 1967 the fin keel with the rudder fitted on a skeg was widely accepted as improving hull speed the three Australian boats had conventional configurations beneath their waterlines, the most radical of the trio being *Mercedes III* which had been built the previous year. 'When we went to England in 1967,' said her skipper Ted Kaufman some time afterwards, 'they regarded it as a stripped out boat, which it wasn't. A guy came up and asked how we tied the boat up as there were no cleats. I told him there were plenty of winches to tie something to, but that wasn't traditional. We were new and we did things that according to tradition we had no right to do.'

But though it was undoubtably Australia's year the most outstanding individual performance came from the Frenchman, Eric Tabarly, in *Pen-Duick III*. One of the first successful ocean racers to be built in aluminium, *Pen-Duick III* was the first boat home on elapsed as well as corrected time in the 1967 Fastnet, and she came to the line on 5 August with a string of wins already behind her: the Morgan Cup, the Channel Race, the Plymouth-La Rochelle Race, and class honours in the Round Gotland and La Rochelle-Benodet Races. She had been launched in June 1967 having been built specifically for the 1968 Single-Handed Trans-Atlantic Race, but this did not mean that Tabarly did not take full advantage of the RORC rule, for his boat was extremely favourably rated. Best described as a wishbone ketch – both mainmast and foremast were of identical height – a sail was set on a wishbone gaff between the two masts almost completely filling the gap. This wishbone sail was technically rated as a foresail and it carried no penalty and as the mainsail was small, and therefore accounted for a minimal percentage of the

66 The Dutch yacht, *Tonnerre de Breskens*, did well in 1965 to come second in Class II. She made the Dutch Admiral's Cup team that year and in 1967 and 1969.

67 Bill Snaith and his crew aboard *Figaro IV*, which came second overall and second in Class I in the 1967 Fastnet.

yacht's total sail area, about 25 per cent of the total sail area was free.

Competition was again hot for the British Admiral's Cup team with nine yachts competing for the three places, four of them – *Noryema V*, *Border Law*, *Musette* and *Breakaway of Parkstone* – being newly built. The first two were sisterships, built and designed by Camper and Nicholson with separate keels and rudders, while the second two, designed by Holman and Pye and Fred Parker respectively, had traditional keels. *Quiver IV*, *Firebrand* – now rebuilt with the new configuration of separate keel and skeg – *Clarion of Wight*, *Prospect of Whitby* and *Zest of Hamble* were the other contenders. *Quiver IV* and *Clarion of Wight* also had their underwater profile altered to the new fashion, but with *Quiver IV* it did not work particularly well. 'It was a mistake to alter her,' said Peter Nicholson. 'The Australian *Balandra*, which was an exact sistership, was unaltered and she went faster,' and certainly *Quiver IV* was unable to retain her berth in the British team. *Firebrand*, however, flourished with the new configuration though perhaps her performance was not wholly due to this alteration as her owner had made sure she was equipped with only the latest and best equipment and fittings, while her crew drove her, and themselves, to the limit. Up to that time it had been customary to have two watches, one on deck working the boat, the other below asleep or resting. Normally the crew off-watch would not be disturbed unless there was a dire emergency. Tradition had it that they were not to be called on deck unless the boat happened to be sinking. *Firebrand*'s crew changed all that, and when a sail change was needed everyone was on deck in a flash, day or night. It meant that when an alteration in the wind indicated a change of sails – there were around 19 headsails to choose from in top ocean racers at that time – no one waited to see if the change in wind direction or force was temporary or not. A new sail went up at once and if the wind speed or direction did alter, well it just meant another sail change. This attitude resulted in *Firebrand* being raced for 615 miles with the same intensity as if she were being raced round the buoys. It was an attitude that paid dividends and, inevitably perhaps, *Firebrand*, along with *Noryema V* and *Prospect of Whitby*, was chosen for the British team.

To avoid too many yachts starting at once the two smaller classes had been split up according to size so that the 139 entries were reasonably spaced out. However, this did not prevent a tangle when Class II(a) started with the Spanish yacht *Artako* being hit by *Norlethe*, and *Norlethe* being hit by *Cervantes II*. Class I started at 0945 in a near calm which later increased to a steady force 4 westerly. Because the tide was still foul this posed the old problem of whether to

tack up the eddy by Cowes Green or cross at the other end of the line, never quite as crowded, and make for the mainland shore to avoid the last of the flood. On this occasion opinions seemed to be divided as to what to do. *Pen-Duick III*, *Thunderbird*, *Moonduster*, *Noryema V*, *Chevalier* and *Kittiwake* decided to keep to the Island shore while the rest, headed by the Italian yacht, *Levantades*, went for the mainland shore. Surprisingly, considering her 90-foot length and deep draft, *Gitana IV* chose the Island side, but soon tired of rock-dodging and was the first to cross to the other shore.

*Levantades* led the fleet through the Needles Channel and once clear of the Solent the breeze hardened to around 20 knots or so. Most yachts took a long tack out into the Channel and those that did so were able to lay Start Point when the wind backed. However, some, including Dick Carter in *Rabbit II*, *Noryema V* and *Jouster*, chose to tack into Lyme Bay and were headed and forced to tack out. By this time *Gitana IV* had again worked out a big lead and she passed Start Point at 0145 some two-and-a-quarter hours ahead of *Pen-Duick III*, *Mercedes III*, *Figaro* and *Outlaw*.

In the afternoon the wind backed again and began to freshen. Spinnakers were hoisted after the Lizard and that night the fleet began to have a hair-raising ride in the steadily mounting wind and sea. By midnight off the Seven Stones it was blowing force 6 to 7 and steering was made difficult in the sharp cross seas. A crew member of *Tiderace* broke two ribs during this bumpy ride, *Thunderbird* broached-to, *Noryema V* blew out a spinnaker, *Clarionet* had trouble with a shackle, and *Firebrand* and *Balandra* broke their steering gear. Both carried on under emergency tillers. Other gear trouble included another member of the Australian Admiral's Cup team when *Mercedes III* broke her spinnaker jockey poles and 70 miles from the Rock the American yacht, *Tina*, ran into trouble when her spinnaker foreguy parted and she was forced to retire. In one of the most spectacular incidents the Belgian one-tonner, *De Schelde*, broke no less than three spinnaker halyards and the spinnaker managed to wrap itself *under* the boat. Until that happened she was making better than nine knots and the bow wave was reported to be 15 feet above the deck.

But potentially the most dangerous incident occurred when *Esprit de Rueil* gybed accidentally sweeping a member of the crew overboard. Luckily, he was not injured and was picked up within five minutes, which showed some fast thinking and excellent seamanship must have taken place.

Early on the Monday morning, *Gitana IV*, seven hours ahead of her time in the previous Fastnet, rounded the Rock in moderating winds having widened her lead on *Pen-Duick III* which did not round for another four hours, at 1020. *Rubin* rounded an hour after Tabarly with *Figaro IV* following just nine minutes later. Other leaders included *Outlaw*, which rounded at 1220, *Balandra* (1327), *Noryema V* (1513), and *Caprice of Huon* (1610), the first Class II boat to round.

As these boats began speeding back to the Bishop against a strong headwind, for those at the Rock it began to fade as the centre of a depression came to a halt right over the area. This cyclonic centre now began to play havoc with the fleet, the wind shifting from one quarter to another and sometimes dying altogether, though some experienced vicious rain squalls on the Monday night in between the calms. Some skippers decided to take the rhumb line course back to the Bishop while others held to the south in the hope that the wind, when it settled, would come from the south of west. Those that kept to the edge of the cyclonic centre did best, catching what wind there was and those who went as much as 20 miles south of the rhumb line produced two class winners to show how right their tactics had been. The American Class II (b) yacht, *Spirit*, made up over 12 hours by keeping south to win her class by over seven hours on corrected time from Dick Carter's *Rabbit II* and the class III(a) *Esprit de Rueil* also won her class by employing the same tactic though she had been 40 minutes behind the runner-up in this class, *Clarionet*, at the Rock.

Out ahead Erroll Bruce, in *Figaro IV*, had been meticulously collating and plotting all available meteorological information and this enabled the Americans to anticipate the sw breeze which eventually developed. Ahead of *Figaro IV*, *Pen-Duick III* had snatched the lead from *Gitana IV*, when the latter's mainsail headboard pulled out some 70 miles homeward bound from the Rock, and was heading for the Bishop which Tabarly fetched without trouble as did all those who kept to the south. But others, like *Noryema V*, *Outlaw*, *Mercedes III* and *Caprice of Huon* found themselves north of the rhumb line and had to tack, and by the time the rest of the fleet arrived at the Bishop during the afternoon of the Wednesday the wind had died again. However, *Pen-Duick III* managed to keep going and she crossed the finishing line at 0139 on the Wednesday morning.

After seven or eight long hours the wind filled in for the rest of the fleet and for the leaders it was quite a rough ride at times with the wind gusting to force 9 and the rain being interspersed with hail. *Gitana IV* was next home at 0249, followed by *Figaro* some three-and-a-half hours later. Then as abruptly as it had come the wind died once more, *Assegai II* taking 14 hours to cover the last 46 miles before finishing at

1322 on the Thursday afternoon, and with others being becalmed off Falmouth for several hours. The last boat in, *Susanna*, did not finish until nearly two and a half days after *Pen-Duick III* had crossed the line.

---

With their precious Admiral's Cup now in the hands of the Australians, with whom there was much friendly – and occasionally unfriendly – rivalry, the British responded with an all out effort to retrieve it in 1969. No less than 12 new yachts were built and there were 21 contenders for places in the British Admiral's Cup team though this was whittled down to 12 for the final inshore trials. 'The improvement in the general standard of the Admiral's Cup trialists,' wrote one British yachting journalist, 'was unmistakable and encouraging. Starts were something like class starts, spinnaker hoists and gybes would not suffer too much in comparison with America's Cup trials.' This showed that owners and crews were responding to the professionalism shown by the Australians and others – the Americans and *Firebrand*'s crew, for instance. Early training programmes became the rule not the exception and sail changing was practised with split-second precision. For the first time a non-sailing team manager was appointed and, also for the first time, the RORC accepted sponsorship for the Admiral's Cup series from Dunhills, the tobacco company, to ease the increasing financial burden of organizing what had become an international event more complicated even than an Olympic Regatta.

But it must not be forgotten that though the Admiral's Cup teams had by now grown to 11, the number of Admiral's Cup boats in the Fastnet were only a tiny fraction of the steadily growing number of yachts which entered from an amazing variety of nations. In 1969 there were 178 starters of which only 31 of these were Admiral's Cup boats (two nations, Bermuda and Spain, were allowed to field a team of only two yachts, the only year this was permitted). Many, perhaps most, were serious competitors, as keen as any member of an Admiral's Cup team to win points for the RORC class championships, and they campaigned modern boats equipped with the latest gear. But there were still a good number of people who went on the Fastnet for the fun of it and not because they had the remotest chance of coming anywhere near the top of their class. Private boat-for-boat battles went on well down in the fleet, the outcome of which was only ever known by those involved. And it wasn't just the Admiral's Cup boats whose halyards broke, whose masts went over the side, or who became becalmed near the finishing line, but the only news coverage the rest of the fleet got was what was

68 The Australian Class II Admiral's cupper, *Mercedes III*, which won her class in the 1967 Fastnet and helped Australia win the cup for the first time.

said to fellow yachtsmen after the race in the local pub or yacht club bar. So the Fastnet, despite the entrance of the Rt Hon. Edward Heath onto the scene in 1969, was still a race for ordinary yachtsmen who, provided their yacht was sound and they were fit and competent, could compete with the best. There are not many sports where this can happen, and it is one of the most appealing aspects of ocean racing.

It also happened that just as the number of starters began to increase so dramatically the Fastnet weather became less traditional. There were gale force winds in some of the races during the 1960s, and in 1971, but they were not severe by modern yachting standards and did not last for any length of time. There could therefore be some truth in the argument that at least part of the cause of the 1979 tragedy was that a new generation of yachtsmen, men and women who would take part in the RORC programme but who were not of international calibre, had never known a heavy-weather Fastnet. And if any of this new generation happened to read about the earlier Fastnets – only two finishing in 1927 or the loss of Col Hudson over the Labadie Bank in 1931 – they could be forgiven for thinking that that was in the old days, with modern

yachts and equipment that couldn't happen. But it can, and it did.

The 1969 Fastnet was an especially light weather one, too light for most of the starters. Bob Bavier was on board one of the American Admiral's cup boats, *Palawan*, and his comment was that it never blew over 20 knots or so, the sun shone every day, spray never came on deck and an Inland Lake scow could have completed the course without difficulty. But for all but the largest or fastest it was not a case of finishing without difficulty but of finishing at all, so feeble was the wind for most of the time for most of the fleet.

Having said that, a brisk breeze *was* blowing at the start on 9 August. It blew from the SE enabling spinnakers to be set shy, and when Class III started at 0900 heavy thunder clouds hung menacingly over the Solent. Class II followed 25 minutes later, then came Class I and finally, having a start to themselves for the first time, the Admiral's Cup teams. The storm clouds brought a short but quite vicious squall, accompanied by rain, thunder and lightning, but this cleared quickly, and by the time the fleet was at Portland the breeze had died right away.

Once out of the Needles Channel the fleet, as usual, split in two. Some, including the Australian Admiral's Cup team, *Ragamuffin*, *Koomooloo* and *Mercedes III*, and the larger American and Argentinian boats, kept offshore, while others, including the British team,

*Phantom*, *Prospect of Whitby* and *Casse Tete III*, kept in under the Bill. Dick Carter's *Red Rooster* did neither and passed the point about one-and-a-half miles offshore. John Illingworth, sailing his last full ocean racing season in the French yacht *Oryx*, which he partly owned, crept along against the tide very close inshore, but then the wind failed totally and he was forced to kedge while others only 200 yards ahead managed to squeeze into West Bay and keep sailing.

The 1969 Fastnet was to be a frustrating race from start to finish and those that did manage to dodge the tide at Portland then got held up at Start where the wind faded away again after a light NW had come in during the night. This enabled the smaller boats that had got caught at Portland to close up with the leaders, the first and last break they enjoyed. But during the morning a steady southerly came in which sent the ex-12-metre, *American Eagle*, skippered by newcomer Ted Turner, forging ahead towards the Lizard with the rest of the fleet following close on her heels. Those that stayed close to the shore fared the best on this leg and *Palawan*'s crew were disgusted to see Dick Carter's *Red Rooster*, a Class II boat and a member of the American Admiral's Cup team, come from inshore and tack across their bows with only *American Eagle*, *Crusade*, *Ragamuffin*, the huge *Kialoa II*, and the Argentinian Admiral's cupper, *Fortuna*, ahead of her. 'She had no business to be there,' said Bob Bavier, 'but there she was and she was flying.'

*Red Rooster* had already proved herself to be something of a phenomenon in the other Admiral's Cup races. She was really nothing much more than an enlarged dinghy, with a two-ton lifting lead keel and an outsider rudder which could also be lifted. Only Ron Amey's *Noryema VGX* – the initials stood for Variable Geometry Experiment – was as radical in design that year. And she had been designed, complete with lifting keel, by Carter as well, but was not so successful as *Red Rooster* and failed to win a berth in the British team.

Rounding the Lizard Carter proved the efficacy of having a lifting keel, for instead of giving the rocks that extend off the point a wide berth he skimmed by them and then headed for Land's End on a close reach. By this manoeuvre he saved many minutes on the other leaders, and as he won the race that year by only 68 seconds it was probably a winning one.

The front runners were able to carry their spinnakers for a while during the Sunday night. Out in front *American Eagle* reported making ten knots in the force 5 from the SSW, but by dawn it had veered to WSW and continued to veer so that most of the fleet met this heading wind as they rounded Land's End. With the veer the leaders, *American Eagle*, *Kialoa II*, *Palawan*, *Fortuna* and *Crusade*, went close hauled on

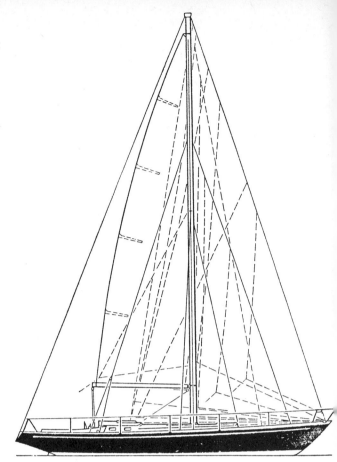

**69** The sail plan of *Prospect of Whitby*, another member of the British team in 1969. Designed by Sparkman and Stephens she came third in her class in the Fastnet that year. Her dimensions were: LOA: 42 ft 7 in, LWL: 32 ft 7 in, beam: 12 ft 2 in, draught: 7 ft 2 in.

**70** Geoff Pattinson's *Phantom* was a member of the British Admiral's Cup team in 1969, and in the Fastnet that year she came sixth in Class I. But the USA won the cup and Australia pushed Britain into third place.

the port tack for the Irish coast, but many of those following them, including *Red Rooster*, chose the other tack and approached the Rock from the south. The tactics on *Palawan* were to get under the lee of the Irish coast in the hope that the wind would veer northerly and this it did on the Monday night and *Palawan* was then able to head for the Rock at 9½ knots with slightly started sheets. Anticipating that the wind could head her she was held high so that when it did back at 0400 on the Tuesday morning she was still able to round a couple of hours later. She was fourth round behind *American Eagle* which had turned at 2230 the previous evening, *Kialoa II* (0030), and *Crusade* (0240). These first three managed to hang on to their spinnakers and the wind to the finish with the

white yawl *Kialoa II* steadily gaining ground on the smaller *American Eagle* so that at the finish only four minutes separated them. Ted Turner reckoned he had to use every trick in the book to keep ahead. He finished at 0248 on the Wednesday morning. Sir Max Aitken's *Crusade* finished third at 0915 and was well in the running to win not only Class I but overall honours as well, especially as the wind had begun to fail for the rest of the fleet.

Behind the first three boats to finish on the run back from the Rock were *Palawan*, *Fortuna*, *Red Rooster*, *Zeezot van Veere*, *Mersea Oyster*, *Sunmaid V*, *Angel*, *Voortrekker* and *Green Highlander*. Most of them gybed down wind to obtain maximum speed but Dick Carter simply raised his centreboard and sailed down the rhumb line, gaining ground on bigger boats such as *Crusade*. But by Tuesday afternoon the wind was beginning to fail, and though *Fortuna* and *Palawan*, which finished on the Wednesday at 1743 and 1810 respectively, managed to carry it to the line, and *Red Rooster* somehow managed to squeeze past the Bishop and into the English Channel, by noon on Wednesday most of the other front-runners were bunched together at the Bishop without a breath of wind while the rest of the fleet was beating into light headwinds. A few, however, managed to edge past the Scillies, and *Ragamuffin* was the next to finish at 2218, followed by

71  Dick Carter's phenomenally successful *Red Rooster*, the overall winner in the 1969 Fastnet.

72  Sir Max Aitken's Class I *Crusade* came within seconds of being the overall winner of the Fastnet in 1969.

*Runn*, *Coriolan* and *Carina* before midnight. Then in the early hours of Thursday came *Levantades*, *Pacha*, *Stormy*, *Phantom*, *Rubin* and *Red Rooster*, the last crossing at 0350. The calculation team went to work and came up with the result that *Red Rooster* had beaten *Crusade* by 68 seconds on corrected time. But the times for these two boats recorded by the official time-keepers were different from the times both put on their declaration sheets. The former gave *Red Rooster* the race while the latter made *Crusade* the winner. *Crusade* promptly lodged a protest.

For everyone else the finish was agonizingly slow and only a handful of boats, including the two remaining yachts in the British Admiral's Cup team, *Prospect of Whitby* and *Casse Tete III*, crossed the line on the Thursday. *Zeezot van Veere*, which had been well up amongst the leaders before the Bishop, struggled past the Lizard at 1748 on the Thursday but did not finish until 0745 on the Friday, and *Sunmaid V*

and *Green Highlander*, two other front-runners earlier, did not cross the line until lunchtime that day and both were forced to kedge before doing so. The last boat to finish, *Half Pint*, took 8½ days to cover the course. It was a sad anti-climax to what up to then had been a magnificent season's sailing. Up to the Bishop the Australians had had the Admiral's Cup in the bag but *Red Rooster*'s brilliant win – still to be confirmed – and ably backed by *Palawan* and *Carina II* ensured the Americans their second victory in the competition.

*Crusade*'s protest was heard on the Friday afternoon and after four hours' deliberation it was rejected on the grounds that the timekeepers' times were accurate and would therefore stand. But a number of competitors had questioned the timing and there was some concern whether the organisation of the race could keep pace with the increasing competitiveness of those who entered it. From 1971 onwards finishing times were recorded electronically.

---

By the time the next Fastnet came round Ted Heath had not only established himself as one of Britain's top racing yachtsmen, but he had become Prime Minister as well. This created conflicts for him but Heath seemed to be able to overcome most of them, and

having built a larger *Morning Cloud* he was chosen for the Admiral's Cup team and was also asked to captain it. This he did with such success that Britain won back the trophy from the Americans. This was a very creditable performance for not only Heath – who had to compete for a place in the British team against 27 other boats, 15 of which, including his own, were new – but for the team as a whole, for it had to face the stiffest international competition to date, with 11 countries competing, including first-timers Brazil and South Africa. Austria and New Zealand entered boats in the race for the first time, and the number of starters – now split into five classes – again increased, to 218, drawn from a total of 17 nations. And, for the first time, they were racing not under the RORC rule, which had been the mainstay of ocean racing in Britain for so many years, but under the new International Offshore Rating rule (IOR) which at long last removed longstanding anomalies between the RORC and CCA (Cruising Club of America) rules.

The vast fleet went over the line on Saturday, 7 August. The two smallest classes started first, At 1115, with the Admiral's Cup teams going last at 1200. The wind was fresh from just north of west, force 4 or 5, and with a strong tide under them the whole fleet, led by *American Eagle*, was clear of the Needles Channel before it changed. Portland presented the usual problem of whether to go out or stay in and some, as usual, made the right decision while others made the wrong one. *American Eagle* passed one mile south of the Bill at 1740, followed by *Crusade* and another Class I boat, *Apollo*, owned by Australian Alan Bond, while the two American Admiral's cuppers, *Bay Bea* and *Carina II*, went inside the race as did the eventual winners of Classes IV and V, *Pioneer X* and *Morbic III*.

The wind now became patchy and some of the smaller boats missed the tide. This split the fleet with the three smaller classes faring badly in the end results, not having one boat in the first 24 overall places. As the wind lightened the retirements started: the Class V sloop, *Polar Bear*, was the first to turn back, with mast trouble; then the Class V Belgian yacht, *Mordicus II*, was dismasted after her forestay had been sliced by a French yacht; and one of the two Swiss boats in the race, *Joran*, also lost her mast in the St Alban's Race.

*Prospect of Whitby*, one of the British Admiral's cup team again, saw *Joran*'s mast go overboard, and, having a doctor on board, Arthur Slater decided he'd better go and see if she needed help. She didn't, but it cost *Prospect* 8½ minutes of precious time, time she couldn't afford to lose as later she was becalmed for five hours (her time was subsequently adjusted by this amount). The Class I, *Border Viking*, was also ill served by the patchiness of the breeze and was becalmed for seven hours, and had the galling experience of seeing the small Class V boats drifting up to her. *Morning Cloud II* was bedevilled by headers and the crew later reckoned they lost any chance of winning in that first 24 hours. But *Ragamuffin* and the British Admiral's cupper, *Cervantes IV*, were two of the boats that found the strip of wind that seemed to be blowing between those well inshore and those right out. *Ragamuffin*, the eventual overall winner, had kept some six miles off from Portland Bill and was only 51 minutes behind *American Eagle*, the first yacht, at 1300, to pass the Lizard, with *Cervantes IV* passing at 1630, 16th overall but first on corrected time. Derek Boyer, in his new Class I *Carillion* cut the point too fine, hit a rock, and had to retire to Falmouth with his boat in sinking condition.

A depression coming in from the Atlantic eventually brought some wind with it which gave most of the leaders a good lift to the Longships. From there they could not quite lay the rhumb line to the Rock and went off on a long port tack, but then the wind began to veer for the rest of the fleet which were faced with a dead beat to the turning mark. This made it a strictly Class I race and while the first 36 boats in that class finished in under 100 hours elapsed time the only other yacht to do so was the eventual Class II winner, *Cervantes IV*, which completed the course in just under 98½ hours, a remarkable performance which enabled Britain to retrieve the Admiral's Cup from America.

*American Eagle* rounded the Rock first at 1440 on the Monday, followed by *Apollo*. But the leader on corrected time was still *Cervantes IV*, with *Ragamuffin* second, followed by *Nymphaea*, *Quailo III* and *Koomooloo*. The wind at the Fastnet was variable for nearly everyone but by Tuesday morning with the depression now off South Wales it began to increase, and conditions became squally and the seas sizeable. With her big spinnaker up, *Morning Cloud II* was difficult to control and at times two men were needed on the tiller. Ted Heath's instincts told him that his boat was being over-pressed and he ordered the spinnaker doused and the spanker set. The crew were not too happy about this change, and when the wind appeared to have lightened a bit up went the spinnaker again. But the British Prime Minister's instincts were soon proved correct for halfway back to the Bishop, while he was below, he heard a loud crack and the boat shuddered and then the motion of rolling from side to side eased. The owner went up on deck. 'I found,' he wrote later in his best-selling book, *Sailing: a Course of My Life*, 'that the cups holding the spinnaker poles had been torn out of their tracks on the mast and could not be repaired. This, I thought, can lose *Morning Cloud* a place and the British the

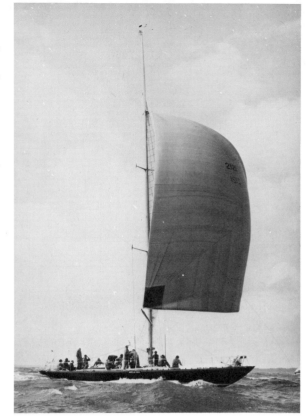

**73** Ted Turner's converted 12-metre *American Eagle* broke the course record in the 1971 Fastnet but could manage to finish only third overall.

**74** *Ragamuffin*, the overall winner of the 1971 Fastnet.

Admiral's Cup. Everyone was now on deck and the crew began to improvise. They quickly got a large headsail up and used a spinnaker pole hooked into an eye on the side of the mast to keep the sail well out. Then we began to think how we could rig a temporary arrangement to the spinnaker itself. The wind was getting lighter all the time and we knew that if we were to keep up any sort of speed at all we would have to fly the big spinnaker. Eventually, with a Heath-Robinson contraption, we hoisted the big spinnaker again with the pole similarly secured. The trouble was that the pole could hardly be adjusted at all. The outer end could be raised a little, but the inner end was securely fixed to the eye. When we had to gybe near the Scillies it took us nearly half an hour to move the pole from one side to the other.' Despite this handicap *Morning Cloud II* finished sixth in Class II on corrected time.

At one time it looked as if the Australians would take the Admiral's Cup with all three Australian boats

being well up amongst the leaders at the Rock. But then disaster struck for them when *Koomooloo*'s rudder broke not far from the Bishop and she was taken in tow by the St Mary's lifeboat. The force 7 winds also damaged the steering linkage of another Australian Admiral's cupper, *Salacia II*, but she was quickly able to resume racing under an emergency tiller.

Though the Admiral's Cup had now slipped beyond the Australians' grasp, the Fastnet Cup was still up for grabs and the crew of the third member of the Australian team, *Ragamuffin*, were working all out to get it. The wind was blowing around 40 knots as she sped back from the Rock under spinnaker. 'The water was shooting in a plume from the bow wave eight feet up the mast,' said *Ragamuffin*'s skipper, Syd Fischer, 'and I reckon the waves were 15 feet from trough to crest,' and once his boat performed what in the sport of surfing is known as 'doubling the wave' – she surfed down the face of one wave, then up the back of the wave ahead and then down its face, all at speeds in excess of 12 knots. Then five hours from the turning mark she was gybed all standing in the darkness and was knocked flat. The spinnaker was torn into shreds in seconds and water poured into the cabin through a submerged ventilator. Pinned by the force of the wind

the yacht could not right herself until the boom vang was released easing the pressure of the wind on the mainsail. Once this was done *Ragamuffin* came upright and a genoa jib was poled out while the crew cleared up the mess. The storm spinnaker was then put in stops by the watch below but thinking the wind was too strong for it to be hoisted they returned to their bunks. Fischer, however, would have none of it and insisted the storm spinnaker be hoisted. It was and *Ragamuffin* surged off into the night at breakneck speed. If ever a crew deserved a Fastnet victory, *Ragamuffin*'s did.

On that run back to the Bishop not many spinnakers or their halyards were equal to the strain. *American Eagle* lost her spinnaker before reaching the Lizard, which she passed at 1330 on the Tuesday. *Apollo*, which logged the fastest time between the Rock and the finish – she reduced *American Eagle*'s lead from nearly seven hours at the turning mark to just over two at Plymouth – blew out no less than three spinnakers, while *Quailo III* parted the same number of halyards. Both benefitted by this hard driving, *Apollo* finishing second behind Ted Turner, at 2110, elapsed time, and *Quailo III* coming second overall and second in Class I on corrected time.

But while most of the boats fought hard in the high

winds to prevent being broached-to others seemed to thrive in the conditions. The Class I boat, *Improbable*, known as a downwind marvel, picked up no less than 20 places on corrected time on the run from the Fastnet to the finish and gained fifth place overall as well as fifth in her class. A lot of boats gave up the unequal struggle with their spinnakers. The American Class III boat, *Witch*, for instance, hoisted a jib topsail with a spinnaker staysail beneath it and actually gained on larger boats carrying spinnakers, and did not prevent her from surfing at over 12 knots and finishing second in her class on elapsed time, fourth on corrected time.

But the speed performance for the 1971 Fastnet must go to Ted Turner's *American Eagle* which finished on the Tuesday evening at 1900, having taken just 79 hours, 11 minutes, 48 seconds to complete the course at an average speed of 8.5 knots, a time which broke *Gitana IV*'s 1965 record run by over two hours. *Apollo*, the second boat home, also broke the previous record, and Alan Bond reported that at times his boat had surfed at incredible speeds that approached 20 knots. *Crusade* was third in with *Ragamuffin* fourth, but on corrected time, *Ragamuffin* took overall honours as well as first place in her class, with *American Eagle* dropping to third place and *Apollo* sixth. Lapel buttons were all the rage at the time and supporters of the Australian winner wore theirs proudly. 'Rago's Arse beats Class,' the buttons proclaimed. How right they were.

Though the press splashed headlines like 'A Fast Fastnet' and their yachting columns were full of how well the Admiral's Cup teams in general, and the Prime Minister in particular, had fared, the ordinary yachtsmen from a variety of countries who made up the vast majority of entries did not necessarily find it either a glamorous race or a particularly fast one. Major Dennistoun, for instance, took over 7½ days to finish the course in his Class IV yacht, *Opus*, finishing a whole day after the rest of the fleet. And 20 failed to finish at all.

---

If the 1969 and 1971 Fastnets had their irritating calms neither were nearly as trying on the nerves as the 1973 race, and Ted Heath called it 'the most frustrating ocean race in which I have so far taken part,' and there wouldn't have been many of the 258 starters who'd have disagreed with him. The wind was so light on the morning of the race that the start had to be delayed half an hour, an unheard of occurrence.

Up to 1971, the sailing directions for the race had for many years simply instructed competitors to pass the Scillies on either hand and to do the same when rounding the Rock. But in 1973, to avoid some dangerous rock-dodging and to minimise the possibility of a collision at the turning mark, all competitors were instructed to 'leave the Isles of Scilly including all outlying islets and rocks, entirely to port or entirely to starboard' on the way to the Rock, and on the return leg to 'leave the Fastnet Rock, the Bishop Rock, the Isles of Scilly, including all islets or rocks, to port.'

The booming economies of the advanced countries and the worldwide publicity Ted Heath had given the sport resulted in a record entry for the 1973 race, and a record number of Admiral's Cup teams, 16, also took part. Among those competing for the first time was Portugal whose team included an old campaigner, *Foxhound*. Now rerigged by Olin Stephens, she was competing in a Fastnet for the first time since 1955.

The post-war affluence, which had been reflected by the growing number of entries during the 1960s, now enabled the sport to be injected with enormous amounts of money for developing and racing new machines – for that is what they really were now, not yachts – which would win honours for their owners and countries. To compare the Admiral's Cup series from 1973 onwards with the America's Cup races, in this respect, would not be absurd. And the Fastnet, with its award of triple points, was naturally the series' pinnacle, the race on which the final results always seemed to rest. The stakes became higher in the 1970s and those who could not, or would not, ante up fell by the wayside. The competition became too fierce to turn up in an out-of-date boat and an inexperienced crew.

The ordinary modern starter in the Fastnet might not be an Admiral's Cup contender but he, or she, is almost certainly aiming to gain as many points as possible for the RORC Championship table. There are now no tyros in the Fastnet fleet, it represents the cream of the ocean racing fraternity worldwide. It is not so much the course nowadays that draws this elite like a magnet – though, of course, it still had its fascinations and no navigator takes it lightly – but the fact that anyone entering it knows that he, or she, is competing with the best.

But in 1973 it was again the Admiral's Cup boats which drew all the interest. In *Ocean Racing Around the World* Paul Antrobus gives a vivid description of one of the new boats, *Frigate*, skippered by the British Admiral's Cup team captain, Robin Aisher, and the ever-increasing competitive spirit which drove her.

As far as Aisher was concerned, his only reason for taking up ocean racing was the challenge of winning a place in the Admiral's Cup team. That was the prime objective for the boat. If that objective was achieved, then helping the team to retain the Cup was the next. In building *Frigate*

75　The British Admiral's cupper, *Frigate*, ghosting towards the Bishop under reaching spinnaker during the 1973 Fastnet. She came first in Class II that year but the Admiral's Cup went to Germany.

which the crew often found themselves sleeping rather than in the bunks.

On a beat to windward, any crew below was woken up on each tack and moved to windward bunks. If on deck, they sat birds-on-a-branch style, facing outwards with their feet dangling over the weather side – although with their torsos in the strictly legal position *inside* the lifelines. There was no time to enjoy this business of sailing.

According to Antrobus, Aisher was also unimpressed by the starting methods of most of the racing skippers and saw no reason for not using the rules to beat an opponent over the line instead of letting him through. The last flicker of the traditional British sporting attitude died that year without one mourner.

But it was not only the increasing competitiveness of the crews which made the boats go faster that year. For 20 years or more the layouts of cockpits had more or less remained unaltered, but by 1973 new methods of sail handling had been developed and new mechanisms like linked winch systems manufactured, and these advances were reflected in new cockpit layouts. Slotted headstays and a return to cutter fore-triangles – so that a headsail could be temporarily hoisted while a change in genoas was taking place – enabled a yacht to maintain her speed; and spinnakers were now hoisted inside one another with the outer one being 'peeled' once the inner one had set. New in the early 1970s, these changes were standard by the middle and late 1970s, and anyone who took their racing seriously soon learned the new techniques involved and earned the increasingly large amounts of money to buy the necessary hardware.

Half an hour late the fleet started off on 11 August in the faintest of south-westerlies, with the 48-strong Admiral's Cup contingent starting last as usual. *Wa Wa Too*, *Matrero*, *Mabelle* and *Carolina*, were four Admiral's cuppers from a variety of nations which had to restart, and spent an agonizing hour painfully retracing their steps under spinnaker. The Italian yacht, *Mabelle*, was in fact not over the line at all and therefore needlessly threw away the race right at the beginning.

The French Class V boat, *Triel*, was through the Needles Channel first, followed by *Bes* and *Maraska*. The wind was still hardly more than a light air and *Morning Cloud III*, with the Prime Minister on board, was additionally slowed by the wakes of the many spectator boats milling around her. The Argentinian, *Recluta III*, led the Admiral's cuppers out towards Portland, followed by *Charisma*, *Jakaranda*, *Salty Goose*, *Saga* and *Quailo III*. Of all the Admiral's cuppers the Argentinian probably made the least mistakes in the fluky wind conditions and once

there was no consideration beyond this. She would be redundant after the series and there was no business investment involved. The designer, Dick Carter, was told to worry about nothing other than winning.

Crew selection, training and racing the boat were equally intense. On board life was spartan and extremely wet. Everything was planned to help the boat go faster. Before the race, sails were packed in tight bricks which were shifted around the boat to alter trim or add weight to windward. After they had been used, it was impossible to repack them into bricks on board, so, particularly in heavy weather, the inside of the boat was gradually filled up with a mass of wet sails, among through the Needles Channel she began to benefit from the stronger breeze which came up. 'Once out in the Channel,' Dick Kenny in his book, *To Win The Admiral's Cup*, quotes *Recluta III*'s navigator, Alan Morgan, as saying, 'we knew we had to average six knots to get around Portland with a fair tide. There was just no way we could manage that, so we tacked early, west of the Shingles, to Anvil Point (the headland stretching beyond Poole Bay). From there we rock-hopped against the tide almost to Lulworth Cove, putting in something like 200 tacks, literally in amongst the rocks. *Apollo*, *Battlecry*, *Saudade* and *Aura*, plus several others, all grounded. We just missed, but it was very close.'

Most of the fleet took the inside channel round Portland Bill and the Class I leader, *Sorcery*, along with *Salty Goose* and *Charisma*, just managed to carry the tide but many had the first of several sessions on the kedge anchor at this point. An easterly, which blew for most of the rest of the race — when there was anything blowing at all — now came in and spinnakers were hoisted for a fairly swift run to Land's End in poor visibility. *Sorcery*, having swopped the lead with *Salty Goose* at the Lizard, now took back the lead, followed by *Salty Goose*, *Charisma* and *Saga*. Then as dusk fell the fog came in all through Sunday night, and for much of Monday forenoon most yachts were sailing virtually blind. But the battle amongst the leaders did not slacken, with *Frigate* in particular going like a train. 'We passed 56 stern lights in four hours during the dusk of Sunday night,' reported a crew member of *Phantom*'s speed before the fog closed in. 'We were really flying along.'

In the bad visibility Arthur Slater's new *Prospect of Whitby* was having a close contest with the Australian Admiral's cupper, *Ginkgo*. 'We had a tremendous battle with them in the fog,' reported Slater, who, for the first time since 1965 had not won a berth in the British Admiral's cup team. 'We were never more than 200 yards from each other, until just before the rock. Then we ran into a 25-knot thunder squall from the north which pinned our spinnaker to the mast. She went around ahead, and we didn't catch her again until on the way back we passed her down to leeward doing a rate of knots.'

*Sorcery* was the first to round the Rock, at 1030 on the Monday, beating the previous record set by Ted Turner in *American Eagle* in the previous race by nearly five hours. At that moment it did not look as if it was going to be one of the slowest Fastnets on record. Next came *Charisma*, at 1145, and then *Saga*, at 1225. *Salty Goose*, well up with the leaders until quite near the turning mark, had an ETA of noon for the Rock, but things went badly wrong for her. Bob Bavier who was on board *Salty Goose* wrote:

Visibility was less than a mile. There is no radio beacon on the Fastnet, but there is one on a headland some nine miles beyond. By homing on that on a course of 310 degrees we should find the Fastnet. The rub was that a strong current was setting us to leeward and we did not sail quite high enough to maintain our bearing. At noon we suspected we may have passed it on the outside, dropped chute and went nearly hard on the wind at right angles to our original course. In the process we now know we passed just one mile to leeward of the Rock, but when we heard no sound signal (a gun is supposed to be fired every three minutes) we jumped to the conclusion that we must still be upwind of it and had not made the speed through the night that our speedometer had been telling us. Soundings, above and below the Rock on a direct course, were almost identical, but had we continued on a course of 020 degrees for another half-mile we would have discovered our miscalculation. Instead, much as I hate to admit it, we reset our spinnaker and tore off downwind for another five miles before forlornly beating back. When we picked up the Fastnet we had to loop it since we had passed outside of it originally. As a result we were within 100 yards of it for a full three minutes and no gun, cannon or any other sound signal was made. Maybe the British don't consider half-mile visibility as fog! Despite the absence of a fog signal, it was a monumental goof, made all the more incomprehensible by the fact that we had an excellent navigator with a distinguished record, navigating winners of the Bermuda, Newport-Annapolis, and SORC races. Could it have been overconfidence?

*Salty Goose* eventually rounded at 1417.

The first Class II boat to round just before midnight was the Canadian yacht, *C-Mirage*, while the first in the smallest class, V, *Maraska*, rounded at 0500 on the Tuesday which was good going especially as the wind was now beginning to fade. For the big boats, however, the wind held for their run back to the Bishop and there were thundery squalls which gusted to 30 knots. But for some it began to play tricks. 'Two-thirds of the way down the rhumb-line, the wind changed for us,' said the skipper of *Quailo III*, Don Parr. 'Boats behind us were able to fetch the Bishop under spinnaker whilst we couldn't even point at it, so the decision was made to tack south, leaving the Scillies well to the north, the theory being that the east wind would be just strong enough to kill any sea breezes that could have helped us close to the shore.'

The two leaders, *Charisma* and *Sorcery*, did not try this tactic but kept in close to the Bishop and, along

**76** One of the successful German Admiral's Cup team, *Saudade*, passes St Albans Head during the 1973 Fastnet.

with *Saga*, another of the front-runners, got caught by a dying freeze and a foul tide as did the group behind them consisting of *Safari*, *Salty Goose* and *Recluta III*. But the breeze behind the leaders held with the result that the gap between the leaders and the rest of the larger, faster boats began to close dramatically. By mid-afternoon on the Tuesday, *Charisma*, which at this point looked the clear winner, and *Sorcery*, along with *Saga* which was some way behind third, were struggling eastwards having barely covered the 16 miles to the Wolf Rock which marks the eastern limits of the Scillies. But by night-time the two leaders were beating past the Lizard with the expectation that the next fair tide would have them over the line. But it

was not to be. *Sorcery* took an agonizing ten hours to cover the last 25 miles, while *Charisma*, still the most likely winner, made her only gross error of the race. Unfortunately, in such conditions and especially during a Fastnet, one is usually all that's needed, and this indeed proved to be the case. Beating in close to land her navigator mistook a light eight miles west of Plymouth for the entrance to Plymouth Sound, and *Charisma* tacked in. As often happens the wind faded inshore and when the mistake was realised it was a long slow beat out again and at the end of it there was *Saga* a mile or so ahead instead of hull down astern which is how *Charisma*'s crew had last seen her. Near the finish the breeze faded almost entirely and *Sorcery* did not slip across the line with the help of a fair current until 0710 on the Wednesday morning and *Saga* crossed soon after at 0818.

At this point *Charisma* was still a mile astern of *Saga*, but with nearly half an hour of her time allowance still in hand she still had a good chance of winning. Slowly she crept up to the finishing line, reaching the breakwater at slack water. Then, with 300 yards to go, the wind died completely and she was forced to kedge, and wait. She waited and waited. And waited. It was, said Bob Bavier, 'the most agonizing anchor watch in ocean racing history,' and it went on for two hours before a mere zephyr pushed her across at 1031 to take a well deserved third in Class I on corrected time as well as being third overall.

*Salty Goose* was next over, finishing at 1142. Then came *Safari* and although she was only a boat's length behind *Salty Goose* when the latter had 300 yards to reach the finishing line she did not cross until 1212. Then came *Recluta III*, still very much in the running, and she crossed at 1337. The computer got to work and quickly calculated that *Saga* had beaten *Recluta III* on corrected time by 27 minutes. But if the wind came back it was still anybody's race. Instead it remained flat all day and the first Class II boat to finish, *Frigate*, did not cross until nearly a day after the overall winner *Saga*, and the smallest class, V, did not have its first boat home, *Maraska*, until another day after that. First home in Class III was *Hylas* which did not finish until 1845 on the Thursday, some $11\frac{1}{2}$ hours after *Frigate*, and the first in Class IV to cross was the French yacht, *Callbart*, which finished $8\frac{1}{2}$ hours behind *Hylas*. And these were the eventual winners of their respective classes on corrected time!

'Some tail-enders might still be out there,' wrote Bob Bavier in his report of the race for the readers of *Yachting*, 'unless they have died of frustration or scurvy.'

Though the Brazilian Admiral's cupper, *Saga*, was first overall, it was Germany that broke the English-speaking monopoly of Admiral's Cup victories by taking it back to Hamburg with them. Their team, *Saudade*, *Rubin*, and *Carina III*, came seventh, tenth and 11th in the Admiral's Cup Fastnet list, beating their nearest rivals, the Australians into second place, with Britain third and the United States fourth.

---

The 1975 Fastnet was a repeat of the 1973 one so far as the weather pattern was concerned, the light winds and contrary tides creating problems for the navigators and turning their calculations into little more than gambles. Lady Luck was either with you in 1975 or she wasn't. She was certainly a member of the crew of the overall winner, *Golden Delicious*, but, as always, you needed more than luck to win and *Golden Delicious* was sailed impeccably by the Bagnall twins, Richard and Harvey.

Hopes were temporarily raised that the weather would provide a proper blow for once when the start, on 9 August, was conducted in a fresh breeze from the wsw which was forecast to veer later. The huge fleet of 256 yachts, including 57 Admiral's cuppers from 19 nations, was split into six different starts, with the smallest, Class V, yachts going first at 1150 and the Admiral's Cup teams last at 1240. As usual, the direction of the wind and tide made most favour the Island side, but in fact the yachts at the other end of the line were soon doing better because of the fickleness of the force 4 breeze close inshore. The spring tide was ebbing strongly as the fleet made its way down the Solent and out through the Needles Channel, and the bigger boats had no trouble in clearing Portland before it began to flood. Even the Class IV *Golden Delicious*, designed by New Zealander Ron Holland, managed to squeeze through right under the Bill while others offshore were being hampered by the race and the beginnings of the new flood tide. She reached Portland at 1840, slipped into West Bay and then in a 20-knot wind from the ssw she sped towards Start which was reached at 0830 on Sunday. From Portland onwards the crew did not see one boat of a smaller rating than themselves ahead of them, and this early success in negotiating that first hurdle was certainly instrumental in making *Golden Delicious* overall winner that year.

At about the time *Golden Delicious* was approaching Start the crew of the Italian Admiral's cupper, *Vihuela*, discovered severe cracks in her mast below deck level, and this forced her withdrawal, one of the dozen or so retirements in the race that year.

*Irish Mist*, of the Irish team, was first of the Admiral's cuppers on corrected time at Portland, passing four miles off the headland before tacking into the Bay and passing *Yeoman XX* with whom she'd been duelling. Later, however, she went back out while most of the fleet stayed inshore. This gave her a better breeze and she was still first on corrected time when she passed the Lizard, followed by Ted Hood's *Robin*, a member of the American Admiral's Cup team, and two British Admiral's cuppers, *Noryema X* and *Battlecry*, and the New Zealand Admiral's cupper, *Inca*. All these were bunched together and rounded the Lizard between 1344 and 1435. Some of the bigger boats, like Ted Turner's *Tenacious* and *Charisma*, both of the American Admiral's Cup team, were also well placed at the Lizard, but it was the Australian team

**77** *Morning Cloud III* was built specially to win the 1973 Fastnet. But with her owner now Prime Minister and distracted by matters of State, she could not manage better than 15th place in her class. She sank, in tragic circumstances, the following year during a storm.

78 The 1973 winner *Saga*. She was one of the most remarkably consistent yachts to race in the Fastnet Races during the 1970s.

79 The start of the 1975 Fastnet. It was a slow race, but not as slow as 1977.

boat, *Bumblebee 3*, which actually passed the Lizard first, early Sunday morning.

One of the largest yachts in the race, Jim Kilroy's *Kialoa*, was also at the Lizard early on the Sunday morning by which time the wind had dropped to 15 knots and the visibility was down to two miles. For Kilroy, out to break Ted Turner's 1971 course record, the prospects didn't look too good, but the giant ketch was moving well and was reported to be half a knot faster than had been predicted in tank tests.

*Golden Delicious* was at the Lizard at 1855 that evening, and had the first of her lucky breaks when she hit a rock off the point and spun round, but was sailed off, and no damage was done. Later, after passing the Longships, her luck held again when one of crew who was working on the foredeck was bounced overboard. However, he managed to grab a lifeline as he went over and was quickly hauled in.

By the Sunday night the wind had veered as predicted and began to blow straight down the rhumb line course at force 3. Most tacked north to avoid the tide and when the wind began to back early on the Monday they were freed to head straight for the Rock under spinnaker. *Kialoa* was first to round, at 1444 on the Monday, followed by *Pen-Duick VI* (1703), *Saga* (1927), and *Gitana VI* (1940). By the time the last named was rounding the visibility had deteriorated badly and the first of the Admiral's cuppers to round, *Bumblebee 3*, did so in thickish fog at 2005. On corrected time though *Irish Mist* still led, followed by *Inca*, *Battlecry*, the German *Pinta*, *Noryema X*, another German Admiral's cupper, *Rubin*, *Tenacious* and the Argentinian *Red Rock III*. *Golden Delicious* rounded at 0942 on the Tuesday when the wind decreased, but then backed and filled giving the big boats a marvellous reach back in a 30-knot breeze but the smaller ones, still heading for the Rock, a rather unpleasant flog up to the turning mark.

Once round, the crew of *Golden Delicious* made another crucial decision, to head for a point well to the south of the Scillies so that maximum speed could be achieved, and this proved to be a winning move.

The increase in wind strength had come from a

**80**  In close company off the Lizard during the 1975 Fastnet.

**81**  Beating out past the Needles after the start of the 1975 Fastnet.

small local depression off southern Ireland which moved away NE and had not really been expected. It gave some of the bigger boats exceptional bursts of speed and a few hair-raising moments. *Yeoman XX*, for instance, broached-to, and her mast hit the water as she rounded up. Luckily for the British Admiral's Cup team, of which *Yeoman XX* was a member, no damage was done and the yacht, one of a long line which stretched back to Owen Aisher's 1951 winner, *Yeoman III*, ended the Admiral's Cup series joint second with the German yacht, *Pinta*.

By Tuesday evening the depression had moved away and the wind had veered and begun to fade. All that day the forecasters were predicting calms off the Scillies and for those who had chosen to take the rhumb line course back to the Bishop, or worse had kept to the north of it, the situation looked bleak. *Kialoa* was first to round the Bishop which she did some 12 miles ahead of *Pen-Duick VI*, with *Gitana VI* third, and by 2100 that evening *Bumblebee 3, Charisma, Sanumac, Tenacious, Noryema, Battlecry* and

*Rubin*, were all round and heading for the Lizard, while to the west of them *Golden Delicious* was flying along at 7½ knots under spinnaker.

Several of the leading boats, all Admiral's cuppers, now chose to stand out in the failing wind. The two Dutch boats, *Goodwin* and *Standfast*, the Hong Kong entry, *Trailblazer*, and the Spanish *Flamenco*, were among these and they gave the Bishop and the Lizard a 15-mile berth. As a result they sailed past the 50 or so boats that had kept inshore and became becalmed close to the Scillies. *Bumblebee 3* and *Charisma* were amongst this luckless bunch and though well up at that point on corrected time they eventually slumped to 36th and 15th places respectively in Class I, though *Charisma* was the first Admiral's cupper to finish, at 2113 on the Wednesday.

Conversely, those that kept south reaped the benefits. *Goodwin*, *Flamenco* and *Standfast* came first, second and third in Class II, and finished in that order on corrected time in the Admiral's Cup results list for the race. *Trailblazer* did almost as well coming fourth in the Admiral's Cup list and second in Class I behind the remarkable *Saga* – not, this year, in Brazil's team – which was third boat home behind *Kialoa*, which finished at 0555 on the Wednesday, and *Pen-Duick VI*. The first three home were the only yachts to complete the course in under 100 hours and Ted Turner's

record was safe for another two years.

Later, *Goodwin*'s navigator expressed surprise that the others had kept inshore for, as far as he was concerned, it was a golden rule of the course to stay out and away from what was by now a notorious calm patch. But, of course, those trapped inshore had no means of knowing there was wind further out and to sail all those extra miles on the off-chance that there was a breeze offshore could have proved to be a ghastly error. It proved to be for those that did it in 1977.

Some two-and-three-quarter hours after *Kialoa* had crossed the line as first boat home, the eventual overall winner, *Golden Delicious*, gybed and headed NE for the Bishop, but at 1000, after seeing as many as 57 yachts becalmed inshore, the crew changed course to keep out of the great calm patch which held so many competitors firmly in its grip. Later however *Golden Delicious* went right in and passed only one mile to the south of the Lizard. Here she came across the much bigger Australian Admiral's cupper, *Love and War*, and it was then that the crew began thinking they really had a chance of making it first on corrected time. Their efforts were redoubled to keep their boat moving at maximum speed, and in perfect sailing conditions, a broad reach, they made for home at six knots, crossing the line in an elapsed time of

115 hours, 2 minutes, 54 seconds, beating another Class IV yacht, the $\frac{3}{4}$-tonner, *Polar Bear*, to the Fastnet Cup by an hour and 16 minutes on corrected time.

*Trocar*, another Class IV yacht, was third overall. Having been built in 1969 she must have been one of the more elderly boats in the race but a new age allowance that had been introduced since the last Fastnet had given those who did not – or could not – buy a new boat regularly a much better chance of being amongst the prize-winners. But even a generous age allowance could not help the real old-timers, and *Latifa*, appearing in a Fastnet for the first time since 1951, could do no better than finish 73rd in Class I, one above another 1951 entry, *Iolaire*.

It was not a year for the big boats and no less than eight Class V boats, headed by *Maraska* repeating her 1973 success, finished ahead of the Class I yachts on corrected time as did the Class III winner, *Stress*.

The 1975 Fastnet and that year's Admiral's Cup series perhaps showed that Sparkman and Stephens was no longer the undisputed top yacht designing firm in the world. It had contributed so much over the last 35 years to yacht design and had produced so many out-and-out winners that it was surprising to see the names of other designers against some of the 1975 winners. But the German team, all S & S boats, did badly in the Fastnet and relinquished the Admiral's Cup to Britain whose sole S & S yacht, *Battlecry*, was the lowest scorer of the British trio. Even *Love and War*, fresh from her successes down-under, failed to show, as did another S & S Admiral's cupper, *Charisma*. By contrast, Ron Holland designed the overall winner, *Golden Delicious*, and the Argentinian, German Frers, became a front runner for the title of top designer with his highly successful *Noryema X* (third in Class I in the Fastnet and top of the Admiral's Cup points list) and the 1973 Argentinian Admiral's cupper, *Recluta III*, which had come second overall in the 1973 race. Or perhaps, as it so often is in the Fastnet, it was simply the luck of the draw.

---

By the time the 1977 Fastnet came round everyone was begging for a good blow. The run of light weather races was quite extraordinary – and unprecedented. Perhaps the 1933–1939 series of Fastnets were the nearest in weather pattern to the races that took place between 1971 and 1977. But none in the 1930s, taking an average of all the times, was quite as slow as the 1977 Fastnet. A good proportion, if not nearly all of the 57 retirements – 20 per cent of the fleet! – must have been caused by the tortoise-like pace of the race and not for any other reason. For some, businesses or families could not be neglected for so long, while for others –

ever mindful of unnecessary extra weight – it was a case of running low on food or water, or both.

Yet at the start it again looked as if the weather might produce some wind, for a good westerly breeze was blowing and the weather though fine was unsettled.

For the first time the really big yachts, the maxi-raters, were designated as Class O and were given a start of their own. As usual, the smallest class took the gun first, and was followed by the other five classes and then the Admiral's Cup teams, again 57 in number. However, so many Admiral's cuppers were over before the gun that there was a general recall and they started again 20 minutes late.

At first the ebbing tide and steady breeze carried the 286-strong fleet at a cracking pace through the Needles Channel and towards Portland. Though the smaller boats were held up when the tide changed the bigger ones got through all right and even boats like the Class IV *Simplicity* managed to creep over what was a very weak neap tide. Carrying the tide for longer than usual meant that the bigger boats reached the Lizard early on and there was optimism that it was going to be a fast Fastnet, maybe even a record one. This optimism was soon dashed, however, for it took these same boats most of the Sunday to cover the 20 miles to the Longships, by which time the smaller fry were all in sight again. The big creep had begun and though there were moments when the wind blew fair and steady it was an upside down race for most of the time with the smaller classes mixed up with the big boats and no one going anywhere very fast. The crew of Jeremy Rogers' Class I British Admiral's cupper, *Moonshine*, for instance, had thought they were doing well, but then were discouraged to see the much smaller Class II Holland designed American Admiral's cupper, *Imp*, almost alongside them; and the leading group of boats, which included *Imp* and *Moonshine* as well as two other Admiral's Cup boats, the Irish *Big Apple* and the Hong Kong entry *Vanguard*, were all in sight of one another not just for hour after hour but for day after day.

When the English Channel was left and the search for more wind began the sea produced neither waves nor swell, but just the occasional ripple. A lot of boats, including *Vanguard* and *Big Apple*, chose the starboard tack and stood out west of the rhumb line, but others, including *Bay Bea* and *Moonshine*, went north on the port tack. At the time it was probably anybody's guess which was the best move. The weather forecasts certainly weren't being much help with Peter Johnson, on *Simplicity*, afterwards remarking that 'a wind direction forecast at one bulletin disappears without trace or explanation in the next,' and all day Tuesday, in company with about 40 other

**82** Some of the old-timers still appeared at the line for a Fastnet. This is *Latifa*, which last raced in a Fastnet in 1951, seen returning from rounding the Rock during the 1975 race.

boats, *Simplicity* kept going westwards on the starboard tack being prevented from heading straight for the Rock by the light NW breeze. But on the Wednesday the wind switched right round to the SE and filled in nicely. Reported Johnson,

All morning and early afternoon, we rush towards the Fastnet − seven or eight knots at last − under tri-radial and shooter. First far out to the east, we see Class I and II boats moving back close hauled and we notice as we converge with their line that they cannot lay the Bishop Rock, first of the return marks. The fleet has been compressed by the earlier calms and we pass *Big Apple*, *Morning Cloud* and *Runaway* near the rock. We round its sunlit cragginess with the Japanese AC boat, *BB III*, and with *UFO* of our own class. But look, who is that? *Silver Jubilee* sailed by the 1975 Fastnet winner Richard Bagnall: surely she must be leading the fleet on corrected time at this stage.

The lack of wind which caused all this bunching − *Simplicity* rounded in sight of 56 other competitors amidst a blaze of multi-coloured spinnakers − was created by the area falling between two centres of high pressure, one over the Azores and one over the southern North Sea, and on the Tuesday some boats only made eight miles towards the Rock in a 12-hour period, with many of the fleet still being mixed together. Jack Knights and Malcolm McKeag in *Yachts and Yachting* reported:

The situation on *Tiderace III*, rating half-way up Class II, was typical. Pleased enough to be ahead of the Japanese Admiral's cuppers and alongside *Irish Mist II* [a slightly higher rated Class II boat]; in sight of *Synergy* [a Class I Norwegian Admiral's cupper] and having dumped a couple of Nich 55s; not so pleased to be slowly overhauling the One Tonner *Golden Apple* [a Class III entry]; amazed that a French Contessa 35, well and truly dumped before darkness fell the previous evening, should have crossed comfortably ahead early the next morning; and disgusted, though hardly surprised,

to see the Bagnalls and the Half Tonner *Silver Jubilee* (Class V) on the horizon astern.

The Italian maxi-rater, *Il Moro di Venezia*, was the first to round the Rock, followed by another maxi-rater, the 72-foot *Ballyhoo*, owned by Australian Jack Rooklyn, with *Moonshine* third at 0651 on the Wednesday. These three, and the others that followed them later that morning, were now headed by the SE wind that gave *Simplicity* and others such a good run to the turning mark. The weather in 1977 made sure no one got too far ahead and it was not until the Scillies that clear leaders began to appear.

While this south-easterly lasted – for the leading boats it blew for about six hours – it had those homeward bound on the starboard tack. Some chose to be close-hauled and to keep as close as possible to the rhumb line course for the Bishop, but others decided to sail freer – and faster – in the hope that the wind would free them at the Bishop to set a course straight for the Lizard. But the wind backed easterly on the Thursday morning and most of the leaders kept close inshore though *Imp* tacked early before the

**83** The 1977 Fastnet was the slowest ever – well, almost ever. This is the Class I *Black Fin* becalmed between Land's End and the Fastnet as seen from the Australian Admiral's cupper, *Iorana*.

**84** The overall winner of the 1977 Fastnet, *Imp*.

Bishop and kept going south. It did her no harm.

By midnight the breeze had dropped almost right away and while the leaders were passing the Lizard the group behind them were having to rock-hop round the Scillies in order to keep going. The Australian Class II *Vector* was one that got too close and bumped.

At the Lizard only the first 15 boats, which included *Saga*, on her way to yet another class win, got past the point before the tide turned foul. But some of those which managed to squeeze through before the tidal gate closed later came to grief by not keeping close inshore round the bay. It was here that *Ballyhoo* finally overtook *Il Moro di Venezia* by stealing between the Italian and the shore, and *Moonshine* lost

valuable time when she got a shade too far out and had to kedge for 20 minutes. Further back another of the British Admiral's Cup team, *Marionette*, just missed the tide at the Lizard and had to kedge for an hour and a half on the Thursday evening while the much smaller *Imp* began closing the gap between them. It was all nail-biting stuff which must have tried the strongest of nerves, and after the race some questioned whether something as important as the Admiral's Cup should be decided by a windless, six-day race. But as the two commentators reporting the race in *Yachts and Yachting* remarked: 'Ocean racing is not the artificial type of sailing which Olympic-style racing seems to espouse. Ocean racing involves surmounting natural obstacles: rocks, tidal streams and fickle weather. What other way is there to decide it?'

At last, some two days later than normal, the first boat to finish, *Ballyhoo*, crossed the line at 0024 on the Friday, followed by *Il Moro di Venezia*, over an hour later, with *Condor*, skippered by Robin Knox-Johnston, third, 48 minutes after that. *Gitana VI* was fifth in with *Bumblebee 3* sixth, and then came the

largest Admiral's Cup boat in the race, the Argentinian *Fortuna II*. *Moonshine* did exceptionally well to finish at 0746 but though she won her class she was pushed into second place overall by *Imp* which finished at 1112, giving her a better corrected time than the British boat by the small margin of 5 minutes, 38 seconds.

Hot on *Imp*'s heels came *Yeoman XX* to take second prize in Class II, and when *Marionette* turned up five hours after that it was obvious that Britain, with all her team home, had retained the trophy. But one of the most remarkable performances of the race came from a non-Admiral's Cup boat, *Saga*, now a maxi-rater, her owner Erling Lorentzen winning his class for the third Fastnet running, a record which has only been excelled post-war by the Nye family in their *Carina*s.

In many ways it had been a nightmare race, especially for those who had the extra strain and responsibility of representing their country. Dave Allen, for instance, who skippered the winning boat, *Imp*, reckoned he had not managed more than 15 hours sleep during the whole 6½ days *Imp* was at sea.

# Tragedy 1979

It was the roughest race in the history of ocean racing.
  Ted Turner, winning skipper of the 1979 Fastnet

The 1979 Fastnet started in much the same vein as the two earlier light-weather races, with a force 3 to 4 blowing from the west and a vast number of starters, this time a new record of 303. They were started in seven classes on 11 August with the smallest first at 1330 and the maxi-raters last at 1420. The Admiral's Cup teams, 54 yachts from 19 countries (three did not start), went over the line at 1410, with Ireland leading in the series, the United States second and Australia third. As usual the outcome of the series depended on the Fastnet results.

There had been some high winds during the previous Thursday of Cowes Week which had given many crews a taste of what was supposed to be traditional Fastnet weather and the BBC medium-range forecast had predicted a force 8 gale in the Fastnet area on the Monday. But there were no last-minute withdrawals because of this prediction, and as the fleet made its brisk way out through the Needles Channel, helped by a west-flowing tide, not one of the 2700 or so crew members aboard the armada of yachts could have had the least apprehension of what was to happen.

By the Needles the smallest, Class V, yachts were being passed by the larger boats and it soon became obvious that the strength of the wind was only going to allow the largest and the fastest of the fleet past Portland before the tide turned. And even some of these missed it, *Tenacious*, the overall winner, being one of those caught. Half opted to work inshore while most of the rest stayed out and by 2100 that first evening there were no less than 150 boats trying to round the Bill. It was a hopeless task, the sheer number of yachts in so small an area making it an impossibility to tack in the slack water under the Bill itself. Many were forced right inshore and literally bumped round, from rock to rock. *Impromptu* did it once too often and was forced to retire.

With the crowd so thick right inshore Jeremy Rogers took his British Admiral's cupper, *Eclipse*, out

in an effort to break through. But once out he found he was losing even more ground, and went back in again. *Imp*, the 1977 winner, was luckier and when she stood out to escape the congestion she found some wind and made good progress. Some, like *Ailish III*, went right out into the Channel, almost as far as Alderney, in order to pick up some wind and, eventually it was hoped, a favourable tide. When it did turn, after midnight, the huge fleet began to move steadily down channel.

Sunday brought fog and a veering wind. It also brought two early retirements because of rudder damage — a recurring problem throughout Cowes Week and the Admiral's Cup races, it was to be a feature of the Fastnet as well — but by 1500 *Acadia*, one of the Argentine's Admiral's Cup team, was off Falmouth in the van of all the other Admiral's cuppers. By dark most of Class I and Class II were round the Lizard, the smaller classes were still approaching it, and the maxi-raters were well on their way to the Rock. At that time visibility was poor and the winds variable.

At dawn on the Monday the wind dropped away altogether and many yachts were left drifting in circles, rolling their masts out in the swell that was coming in from the Atlantic. It was, literally, the lull before the storm, but by the late evening on the Monday all but the stragglers had cleared Land's End in the rapidly rising wind. All were able to take the rhumb line course for during the day the wind had swung NE and then south, and had increased steadily. At 1355 the shipping forecast for the area predicted a SW wind, force 4 to 5, later veering to the west and increasing to force 6 or 7. On *Toscana*, an American Class I boat, John Rousmaniere looked at the sky as *Toscana* creamed along in what was already a good force 5 and, as he relates in his book on the race, *Fastnet Force 10*, did not like what he saw. On the yacht's port bow, to the SW, were high white cirrus clouds, but to the NW were dark alto-cumulus, formed in ridges that are known to seamen as mackerel scales. Rousmaniere remembered the old warning, 'Mackerel scales, furl your sails,' and wondered whether the forecast was for once under-estimating the force of the wind to come.

However, way out ahead the maxi-raters, with spinnakers set shy, were revelling in these conditions and *Kialoa* was at the Rock in no time at all. She rounded at 1250 on the Monday having averaged an amazing 7.7 knots and was followed by *Condor of Bermuda* at 1357, *Siska* at 1511, *Il Moro di Venezia* at 1519, and *Mistress Quickly* at 1605 just about at the time that the small yachts, 200 miles behind, were beginning to round Land's End.

When *Condor* rounded the wind had dropped in the area to force 3 and even when *Tenacious* reached the turning mark, at 1830, it was only force 4 to 5, and blowing from just west of south.

It was the suddenness of the storm that was one of its most remarkable features. At 1505 the BBC had forecast that gales in the Fastnet area were imminent, i.e. would arrive within the next six hours. This was followed at 1750 by the shipping forecast which predicted only a veering wind, force 6, for Lundy, Fastnet and the Irish Sea, though this would increase locally to gale force 8. Nearly 50 miles NW of the Rock is the weather station at Valentia and this reported a barometric pressure of 1005 millibars, a relatively high reading. It was dropping, but only slowly.

On board *Toscana*, still 90 miles to the SE of the Rock, Rousmaniere tapped the ship's barometer. It had dropped only 10 millibars since the start of the race and now registered 1010 millibars, a very small drop when one considers a drop of 10 millibars in three hours is what is needed to predict a force 8 gale with certainty. It gave those on board *Toscana* no inkling of the force of the wind to come.

While the maxi-raters were starting their increasingly wild run back to the Bishop the rest of the fleet were still in the rhumb line course for the Rock and scattered over a fairly large area. Most, if not all, would have heard that 1750 shipping forecast and the crew must have started preparing for a hard night at sea. But few, if any, would have kept the radio tuned so that they heard the gale warning which was issued just ten minutes after the shipping forecast, for there are too many things to do on a yacht and batteries had to be conserved. Who, anyway, would expect a further gale warning just ten minutes after a shipping forecast? This further gale warning, based on Tiros N satellite pictures which had just become available, predicted that the wind would increase to force 9, and it was repeated twice, at 1830 and 1905. Then at 2300 a storm force 10 warning was forecast.

But by the time this last warning was broadcast the majority of the fleet were already experiencing force 10 conditions. Ambrose Greenway, the navigator on the Class I yacht, *Casse Tete V*, heard this last forecast. 'They've given out a force 10,' he shouted up to the skipper in the cockpit. 'You must be joking,' the skipper shouted back. 'We've already got 60 knots of wind up here.'

The staggering swiftness with which the storm had developed had caught the British forecasters napping and many people, who have never been ocean racing, thought that if the forecasters had given earlier warnings disaster would have been averted, for the race could have been abandoned and the yachts turned and sailed into safe ports. But the fact is that even if it had been possible to call off the race most of the yachts, if they had turned back, would have been caught by the storm on a lee shore and the resulting loss of life might have been very much higher than it was. At least in the open sea a vessel can lie a-hull or run before a storm, and this is indeed what the majority of yachts did.

As night approached on the Monday the wind increased as predicted to force 6 or 7 in the Fastnet area and to 5 or 6 around Land's End where most of smaller Class IV and Class V yachts were situated, and by midnight when the leaders of the Admiral's Cup teams were beginning to round the gale force winds had reached even the stragglers at the back. No sooner had one reef been taken in than another was needed, and the size of headsail was also steadily reduced. On John Ellis' Class V, *Kate*, about 70 miles clear of Land's End, the sail area was quickly decreased until by midnight she was sailing under a jib only.

At 2330 the first serious damage caused by the rising wind occurred when the French Admiral's cupper, *Accantio*, reported losing her rudder. At about the same time, the Dutch yacht, *Scaldis*, also reported losing hers, and what for a short time had been an exhilarating run for the bigger boats now became a struggle for survival for the whole fleet. Even the maxi-raters, well on their way back from the Rock, when the storm struck, had a hard time of it for a while. *Condor* was knocked flat once and later broached-to so violently that she came through 180 degrees and with her spinnaker pinned to her mast started making sternway. However, this did not deter the crew one bit for they were determined to beat their arch-rival, *Kialoa*, home, so *Condor* was swung round, the spinnaker filled and she began surfing again, sometimes at quite spectacular speeds which exceeded 27 knots. It was only when she put the whole of her foredeck right under that discretion became the better part of valour and the spinnaker was lowered. But this spectacular run won *Condor* the Erivale Cup for first boat home in the record breaking time of 71 hours,

25 minutes, 23 seconds, breaking *American Eagle*'s 1971 record by nearly eight hours. What's more she beat *Kialoa* – whose skipper Jim Kilroy had some ribs broken on the passage back – by six minutes on corrected time.

Rob James, who had crewed and skippered in two round-the-world races, was on board *Condor* and he said after the finish that the waves had been worse than any he had experienced around Cape Horn or in the southern oceans. Bob Bell, *Condor*'s owner, said that the wind was so strong that it was impossible to stand. 'We had to lie and crawl around the deck to sail the yacht,' he said. Ted Turner sailing *Tenacious*, which came in fifth behind *Siska* and *Mistress Quickly* but which won first place overall on corrected time, said he'd never encountered anything like it. 'It was the roughest race in the history of ocean racing,' he said afterwards. 'I've sailed over 100,000 miles off-shore in some of the toughest races around the world – the Sydney-Hobart, the Rio circuit, the '72 Bermuda Race, and a number of Trans-Atlantic races and I've never seen the likes of the conditions encountered in this Fastnet.'

The figures speak for themselves: out of 14 starters in Class O, 13 finished; out of 56 in Class I, 36 finished; out of 53 in Class II, 23 finished; out of 64 in Class III, only six finished; out of 57 starters in Class IV, only six finished; and out of 58 starters in Class V, only one, *Assent*, finished. In short, it was the same old story: the bigger, faster boats escaped the worst of the storm while the smaller, slower ones suffered the full force of it. And there's no doubt that the storm which low 'Y' created in the early hours of Tuesday 14 August was an extraordinary one, though not, apparently, unprecedented (a storm of similar proportions and ferocity had occurred in August 1970, a non-Fastnet year).

It has been generally accepted that the winds during that night were certainly force 10. That they gusted to force 11 is also widely accepted, though with the rider that the difference between the two forces for a small yacht must be somewhat academic. (It is interesting that no less than 31 per cent of the 235 starters in the race who filled in the RORC's questionnaire thought that the wind was *more* than force 11, 39 per cent thought it force 11, and only 20 per cent thought it force 10.) However, it was not so much the force of wind that caused the smaller boats a problem but the size and pattern of the waves. 'At daybreak the seas were spectacular,' said Cdr Peter Bruce, the navigator on *Eclipse*. 'They had become very large, very steep and broke awkwardly.'

*Windswept*, a Class III OOD-34, was one of the many yachts which was battered by these huge waves. Whilst lying a-hull at dawn on the Tuesday morning

85 Lifeboats towed or escorted to safety no less than 20 yachts during the 1979 Fastnet. Here *Casse Tete V* is being taken in tow.

86 The crew of the Class I *Casse Tete V* ride out the storm during the 1979 Fastnet. She was one of the yachts whose carbon-fibre rudders sheered and a jury rudder can be seen rigged over the pulpit.

she was rolled over. She righted herself quickly but not long afterwards a wave got under her bow and she was knocked completely upside down and stayed there long enough for the crew trapped in the inverted cabin to get seriously worried as to whether she would ever right herself. She eventually did but the skipper George Tinley had suffered a broken nose and wrist, and had been knocked unconscious. 'There were seas coming at one angle with breakers on them,' Rousmaniere quotes Tinley in his book, 'but there were seas coming at another angle also with breakers, and then there were the most fearsome things where the two met in the middle.' Major Maclean on the army yacht *Fluter* also gave Rousmaniere a vivid description of the viciousness of the seas that night, his account

being verified by dozens of similar ones from highly experienced yachtsmen.

All around were white horses with their spray flurrying horizontally and slashing against us with the added impetus of the occasional rain squalls. But these white horses were just the top of some monster waves which hunched up, their tops flaring with spume, and marched on leaving us high at one minute so we could glimpse around, and then bringing us some fifty feet down into their troughs so we could appreciate the enormity of the next wave following. Some waves had boiling foam all over them where they were moving through the break of a previous wave, or, when the foam had fizzled away, they were deep green from the disturbance of the water. Otherwise the sea was black.

*Windswept*'s experience of being knocked down and then completely overturned was not unique and at least she eventually returned to harbour safely and, incredibly, did not lose her mast. But of the 235 replies to the questionnaire sent out by the RORC and which formed the basis of their inquiry on the disaster in conjunction with the Royal Yachting Association, no less than 48 per cent, 112 yachts, replied 'yes' to the question 'Did you experience a knockdown to horizontal or almost horizontal?' while 33 per cent, 77 yachts, suffered a knockdown beyond the horizontal and of these 11 lost their masts. Given that it is simply not practical to rig a yacht so that her mast can always withstand a knockdown beyond the horizontal it is remarkable that only one-seventh of the yachts involved in a knockdown of this severity were dismasted. This statistic, combined with the fact that very little structural damage was caused to any of the hulls, must be of great credit to the designers and builders concerned.

The same, however, cannot be said of those yachts which lost their rudders, a structural failure which crippled a number of entries and caused several to be abandoned. Out of the 235 who answered the question 'Was there any significant damage to the steering gear?' 14 out of the 25 who answered 'yes' put the failure down to the breakage of their rudder. A significant proportion of these failures were with the new light-weight carbon fibre rudders and it was the only form of damage to which the larger boats seemed more susceptible. 'Designers who specified carbon fibre rudders for boats sailing in this race,' said the RORC/RYA report, 'are acutely aware of their high failure rate and are already taking positive steps to establish the exact cause of the failures in order to prevent a recurrence.'

There was also criticism that in the search for speed designers had minimized the wetted surface of their designs by reducing to a dangerous extent the lateral plane of both rudder and keel, thereby making yachts less seaworthy. But while the International Offshore Rule (IOR) as interpreted by designers had led to increasingly light displacement boats, and in 1978 the Offshore Racing Council (ORC) which administered the rule brought in penalties for excessively light displacement designs, the RORC/RYA report pointed out that the rule does not control the underwater profile. Nor, the report added, was there any proof that the underwater configuration of a modern racing yacht was inherently less seaworthy than one with the traditional long keel. To the layman it does seem however that the OOD-34s in the race seemed especially vulnerable to the conditions. The RORC/RYA report was careful to say there was insufficient statistical evidence to prove unseaworthiness or otherwise but the fact that nine out of the 11 OOD-34s taking part in the race suffered knockdowns beyond the horizontal does give pause for thought. Two of the five yachts – *Charioteer* and *Griffin* – which sunk were OOD-34s.

One of the main problems encountered during the storm – and this did not apply just to the OOD-34s – was that the washboards protecting the cabin from water coming below dropped out when a yacht was driven well beyond the horizontal allowing the sea unimpeded passage to the cabin. Loose batteries and cookers were another danger. The majority of boats that were abandoned – 24 in all – were left because of these problems and because the crews thought they would be safer in the yacht's liferaft than in the yacht itself in a sinking condition.

Some of the 15 who died were thrown overboard when their yachts were knocked down. Their lifelines broke and they were swept away and drowned. Others died when their liferafts either capsized or disintegrated, and some became victims of hypothermia. Typical of what happened at the height of the storm was what occurred on board *Festina Tertia*, a Class III yacht which had already abandoned the race. Sean Thrower, a crew member, said:

I was asleep at 1:30pm, after having been on deck all morning when the boat suddenly swung round. The main boom had already been broken in the night. I came up and saw the huge waves, about 40 feet high, with the wind gusting at the top of

**87** The St Mary's lifeboat punching her way through the seas during the rescue operations.

**88** Midshipman Harrison flying in a Sea King of 819 Squadron out of Prestwick in Scotland prepares to double lift the last crew member from the Class V yacht, *Grimalkin*. One of the crew was already dead and the others were in the yacht's liferaft.

the waves. At one time the sun was shining, which made the whole thing look even more frightening; we were about 50 miles from the Fastnet Rock when Roger, one of my crewmates, was washed overboard. This was when the boat swung round violently. We turned the boat round but we could not stop and we passed him in the water. I jumped into the water with a line but somebody shouted, 'It's no good, he's dead.'

As soon as the extent of the disaster became known a major rescue operation was launched. This involved 13 lifeboats; helicopters from the Royal Naval Air Station at Culdrose, Cornwall; Nimrod reconnaissance aircraft from Kinloss and St Mawgan, and several other fixed-wing aircraft; *Overijssel*, the Royal Netherlands Navy warship which was acting as guardship; *Morningtown*, a motor/sailer which was acting as a radio relay vessel for the Admiral's Cup teams; and HMS *Anglesey*, a fishery protection vessel. Between them the lifeboats towed or escorted 20 yachts to

safety while the helicopters and rescue ships plucked crews that had abandoned their yachts from the water. Michael Campbell, the skipper of an OOD-34, *Allamanda*, was one of those who decided that it was safer for himself and his crew to be picked up by a helicopter than stay with his yacht. In an interview in *The Observer* he said:

We were going very nicely, broad reaching in 50 knots of wind with a small headsail and two reefs in the main. Then the wind increased very rapidly and we were not quick enough getting canvas down. At half past midnight the mast broke at coachroof level and fell on the leeward bow. It took us three-quarters of an hour to cut it free and get rid of it. There hadn't been much sea before, but now it got up rapidly. We let off some flares and were approached by the yacht *Trophy* [she was later dismasted and abandoned] and then *Morningtown*.

We got our engine going and under minimum power and keeping the seas on the port quarter, we went along like that for two hours. Then there came a peculiar wave, out of direction with the rest of the sea and infinitely higher than all the waves before. In no time we had gone right over and we were all out in the water. The boat had gone through 180 degrees and back again. Of course we were all clipped on and as she came up

we were strung along the side like a row of fenders. The crew from below came up and hauled us in and we found washboards had come out and the cabin was full of water to the level of the saloon table. The liferaft had inflated itself and was flying about like a toy balloon. We tried to secure it but the wind was so strong that by the morning it had gone. We had also lost all our flares. To complicate matters, the cooker had come off its gimballs and crashed through a window.

We spent the rest of the night pumping in watches; strapped in, of course. Then at 6:30pm on Tuesday a helicopter appeared from nowhere and I assessed the situation. No mast, no engine, no liferaft, no flares: I decided to hitch the lift.

Many of the helicopter crews at RNAS Culdrose were on leave when the storm blew up. But those on duty responded immediately to the flood of distress signals, and those on leave returned at once to help in the rescue operations. These were extensive and went on for several days – the last yacht, *Kalisana*, was not accounted for until 1400 on the Thursday – and their intensity can be judged by a single page from the ten page summary of them. Three types of helicopter were used, the Wessex (WX), the Sea King (SK) and the Lynx, and 75 yachtsmen were airlifted by them out of the disaster area.

Weather in the search area SW severe gale 9 to storm 10, showers, good visibility.

R20 (WX) returned to Culdrose to refuel, reporting, nothing sighted at the Scillies.

R21 (WX) tasked to *Grimalkin* in position 30 miles NW of Land's End.

SitRep at 0615Z:-

1. R01 (Nimrod) and Dutch Frigate *Overijssel* investigating four men in a life raft 50.40N 08.10W.
2. *Tarantula* in position 50.30N 07.10W, no assistance available at this time.
3. *Red Flares* sighted by Nimrod in position 51.00N 07.10W, no action being taken, other than being kept under observation.
4. *Maligaway* dismasted in position 50.50N 07.30W. R97 (SK) tasked to assist.
5. *Magic* rudderless in position 50.30N 07.00W R77 (SK) tasked to assist.
6. *Grimalkin* capsized in position 30 miles NW Land's End R21 (WX) tasked to assist.

From R21 (WX) at 0730Z am not in communication with anyone, returning to Culdrose.

R20 (WX) at 0745Z tasked to position 50.50N 06.50W to pick up the crew of *Grimalkin*.

Three survivors sighted at 0746Z in position 50.50N 06.50W. R20 (wx) will transit this position en route to *Grimalkin* and from R77 (sk) at the same time, have double lifted one casualty from *Tarantula* remaining *Tarantula*'s crew remaining onboard.

0750Z A further seaking crew recalled from leave.

R77 (sk) end of endurance returned to Culdrose at 0820Z.

R21 (wx) also reports returned Culdrose 0830Z.

At 0835Z R77 (sk) R79 (sk) and R21 (wx) returned to scene of search.

From R20 (wx) returning to Culdrose with five survivors from *Magic*. All crew members accounted for.

R21 (wx) returned 0930Z refuelled and returned scene of search 0935Z. R97 (sk) picked up two survivors from *Grimalkin* in position 50.00N 07.30W and three from *Trophy* at 0939Z, reporting there are three plus one dead in a dinghy who will be picked up by the Dutch frigate.

HNLMS *Overijssel* rescued three crews, two from their liferaft and one directly from a yacht being abandoned. HMS *Anglesey* rescued another crew which transferred to her from their yacht by liferaft. The coaster *Nanna* picked up two members of another crew after their liferaft overturned, but three other members were lost as they did not have the strength to get up the pilot ladder which had been lowered. Two more crew were taken off their yachts by fishing vessels and one crew was rescued by an oil rig supply vessel.

Three crews who had taken to their liferafts were rescued by other crews competing in the race. The French Class IV yacht, *Lorelei*, was some 40 miles SE of the Rock in the early hours of the Tuesday morning when her crew saw flares and shortly afterwards they spotted a liferaft. After some brilliant manoeuvring in mountainous seas and pitch darkness the French skipper, Alain Catherineau, managed, with the help of his engine, to get alongside the liferaft and rescue those in it who were from *Griffin* the RORC's club boat. The rescue took almost two hours to accomplish and Catherineau was later awarded equal second place in his class by the RORC. He was subsequently made Yachtsman of the Year in Britain, a popular choice.

A Class III yacht, *Moonstone*, rescued the crew of a French yacht, *Alvena*, from their liferaft, and the crew of *Dasher* rescued the crew of another French yacht, *Maligawa III*. *Alvena* was later recovered but *Maligawa III* sank. Other yachts attempted to go to the aid of those in distress but either got into trouble themselves or simply could not manoeuvre sufficiently to be of any help.

The storm raged during the hours of darkness on Tuesday morning and through the forenoon. It was at its height for most of the competitors between 0200 and 0600, and by afternoon it had moderated to gale force 8. By Tuesday midnight the first five boats had finished but it was not until the following afternoon and evening that the bulk of the Class I boats began to arrive. A non-Admiral's Cup boat, *Sleuth*, was first home in Class I, followed by *Acadia* and *Red Rock IV*. *Morning Cloud*, which had been incorrectly reported as losing her rudder, crossed the line at 1745, 20th on corrected time. 'No one,' said Ted Heath, who was again captaining the British Admiral's Cup team, 'who has been through an experience of that kind would wish to go through it again. We got knocked down very badly two hours after we had gone round the Fastnet Rock. It was blowing force 10, gusting 11, when a massive wave knocked us on our side.'

First home in Class II was the Australian Admiral's cupper, *Police Car*, which arrived at 1246 on the Wednesday, followed by the French Admiral's cupper, *Jubilee VI*, at 1258, but on corrected time *Eclipse* won Class II with *Jubilee VI* second, and the two Australian Admiral's cuppers, *Impetuous* and *Police Car*, third and fourth respectively. With *Ragamuffin* eighth on corrected time in Class I, the Australians took home the Admiral's Cup with them for the second time.

Only one Class III boat finished on the Wednesday, *Revolution* coming in at 1741 to win class honours on corrected as well as elapsed time. In Class IV the French yacht *Samsara* crossed first at 1151 on the Thursday but was beaten into second place on corrected time by the RAF's yacht, *Black Arrow*, which had ridden out the storm off the Irish coast before rounding the Rock. *Assent*, the one yacht to finish in Class V, crossed the line at 0142 on the Friday. Out of 303 starters, 85 finished.

The unusual severity of the storm, the rapidity with which it developed, and the steepness and irregularity of the wave formations, caused some puzzlement. 'There are things about the weather of the Fastnet storm,' wrote meteorological expert Alan Watts in *Yachting World* immediately after the race, 'that are in many ways mysterious, things we do not yet know and things we may never know,' and he mentioned that there could possibly have been a storm within a storm, and that the sudden veer in the wind from SW to NW was certainly an important factor in causing the extremely confused seas.

Soon afterwards an article appeared in the Colour magazine of *The Observer* headed 'How Thirty-Four Fathoms Doomed the Fastnet.' This put the blame for the steep confused seas on the Labadie Bank but without presenting any scientific evidence to support

**89** A Wessex V helicopter of 771 Squadron hovers over a winchman preparing to lift a survivor from the Class V yacht, *Camargue*.

this claim. The Labadie Bank is 34 fathoms at its most shallow, some 200 feet shallower than the surrounding shelf. This, according to Lawrence Draper of the Institute of Oceanographic Sciences, whom Bob Fisher quotes in his book, *Fastnet and After*, is too deep to have much affect on shortening the wave formations, no more than a reduction of 4 per cent he calculated.

Nearly a year after the disaster Alan Watts wrote another article in *Yachting World* and contributed to an update of Adlard Coles' *Heavy Weather Sailing*. In these he put forward a theory, based on meticulously collating the barograph readings of 21 yachts which encountered the storm and plotting them on a chart in relation to the yachts' distances from the Rock. His conclusion, a controversial one not accepted by some experts, was that there were indeed storms within the general storm pattern and that the wind in certain very localised areas blew very much harder for a sustained period – they could in no sense be called gusts – and that these channels of wind whipped up great walls of waves for a short distance

laterally, while on either side the same wave was not nearly so precipitous. Wrote Watts:

When it goes rapidly from being 50–60kt in one place to being half that speed within say a mile or less, then the waves in the middle of the corridor may be great and sausage-like but they have on their extremities to change to much slighter waves. The result is fast-moving patches of chaos that most sailors will never have seen before except when they have survived the similar conditions in hurricanes between the low wind speeds in the eye and the shrieking blast that signals the passage of the eye. I believe there were linear hurricanes in Fastnet that night and this accounts for the observations and the survival conditions experienced by some yachts, but mercifully not all.

It is interesting that 50 years ago, W.B. Luard, the skipper of *Maitenes II*, commented on how amazingly local the 1931 storm seemed to be. The fact that he was also over the Labadie Bank at the time that Colonel Hudson was lost overboard must, however, be put down to coincidence.

When the extent of the disaster became known the

**90** A Wessex V helicopter hovering over the English yacht *Camargue*. The other members of the crew have already jumped into the sea and have been rescued, but the remaining man stayed aboard her. *Camargue* was later taken in tow by a French trawler which was prevented from taking her into Milford Haven to claim salvage by the crew of the British yacht, *Animal*, which survived the storm with only minor damage. 'We have all been through a very emotional situation,' said the skipper of *Animal* later. 'We nearly lost our lives. Others lost theirs and we figured this French trawler was out to make money from the tragedy.' The matter was later settled amicably.

RORC came in for a good deal of ill-informed criticism, but there were others, Ted Heath among them, who suggested improvements could be made. Subsequently, the RORC/RYA report made certain recommendations which involved the organisation of the race, yacht construction, sails and equipment including safety equipment, and the identification of yachts. It also responded to the pressure to make transmitter sets and reporting schedules compulsory by pointing out that 65 per cent of the Fastnet fleet carried VHF anyway; that the failure rate of these sets, 15 per cent, was higher than the percentage of crews who abandoned their yachts (8 per cent); and that in any weather the radio failure rate is likely to exceed the number of yachts in distress by that number. It also made the point that it is only too easy to miss a reporting schedule and that failure to report on time could cause the authorities to believe a yacht was missing when it was not. But the report did not dismiss the idea of compulsory VHF sets – a VHF or SSB radio is in fact compulsory now – and it urged that the possible relaxation of the rigorous installation standards imposed by the British authorities on MF sets should be fully explored as the latter were of more practical use because of their greater range.

A number of changes have been implemented since the Inquiry and in November 1980 the secretary of the RORC, Alan Green, detailed the main ones.

First of all, extensive research into stability continued particularly at ORC level. The RORC itself carried out further technical work between the publication of the Report in December 1979 and the special ORC meetings in April 1980. The isolation of undesirable characteristics proved to be a difficult task and time and again formulae which appeared to solve the problem with exaggerated cases would also pick out other vessels whose stability was not really in question. However, some limits have been brought into effect this month having been advertised in advance in April. Apart from putting numbers to the problems, the study of it in the Inquiry Report had undoubtedly brought it into focus with virtually all yacht designers and must now form part of their basic thinking. A number of small changes in special regulations were introduced dealing with matters like loose companionway shutters, and (in RORC

regulations) the separation of bilge pump outlets from cockpit drains, and so on. Trisails were introduced as mandatory equipment. The next Fastnet will require each yacht to be fitted with VHF and SSB radio, and more importantly will call for crew and boat offshore experience before an entry is considered. Electronic aids have been debated hard and long but the RORC has decided that for 1981 there should be no change in the list of restrictions. Of course, as with the engine, they may have the equipment on board and if they believe it is essential to use it for safety reasons they may do so but will not be able to continue racing. Finally, the long awaited 'scantlings rule', which was being worked on by the ORC and ABS (American Bureau of Shipping) before the last Fastnet, has just been completed, but at present is still an advisory document.

The report concluded its findings thus: 'The Fastnet is a supreme challenge to ocean racing yachtsmen in British waters. In the 1979 race the sea showed that it can be a deadly enemy and those who go to sea for pleasure must do so in the full knowledge that they may encounter dangers of the highest order. However, provided that the lessons so harshly taught in this race are well learnt we feel that yachts should continue to race over the Fastnet course.'

Let it be hoped they do just that for many years to come, and that their crews get as much pleasure and excitement out of the race as their predecessors enjoyed during the previous 56 years.

# Yachts, Owners, Elapsed Time and Corrected Time     1925–79

DNF – did not finish

TNR – time not recorded

## 1925 (15 AUGUST)

| YACHT | OWNER (SAILED BY) | ELAPSED TIME | | | | CORRECTED TIME | | | | |
|---|---|---|---|---|---|---|---|---|---|---|
| | | *days* | *hr.* | *mn.* | *sc.* | *days* | *hr.* | *mn.* | *sc.* | |
| 1 *Jolie Brise* | Mr E.G. Martin | 21 | 14 | 45 | 30 | 21 | 14 | 45 | 30 | (*scratch boat*) |
| 2 *Fulmar* | Royal Engineer Yacht Club | 22 | 10 | 48 | 05 | 21 | 22 | 28 | 05 | |
| 3 *Gull* | Mr H.P.F. Donegan | 22 | 11 | 35 | 15 | 22 | 02 | 35 | 15 | |
| 4 *Saladin* | Mr Ingo Simon | 22 | 18 | 54 | 30 | 22 | 12 | 54 | 30 | |
| 5 *Banba IV* | Mr H.R. Barrett | 23 | 00 | 56 | 30 | not known | | | | |
| *Jessie L* | Mr M.C.J. Hussey | DNF | | | | | | | | |
| *North Star* | Capt. M. Tennant | DNF | | | | | | | | |

## 1926 (14 AUGUST)

| YACHT | OWNER | ELAPSED TIME | | | | CORRECTED TIME | | | | |
|---|---|---|---|---|---|---|---|---|---|---|
| 1 *Ilex* | Royal Engineer Yacht Club | 18 | 21 | 21 | 22 | 18 | 03 | 14 | 52 | |
| 2 *Primrose IV* | Mr F.L. Ames | 19 | 07 | 48 | 30 | 18 | 03 | 28 | 00 | |
| 3 *Hallowe'en* | Col. J.F.N. Baxendale | 18 | 09 | 05 | 30 | 18 | 09 | 05 | 30 | (*scratch boat*) |
| 4 *Saladin* | Mr Ingo Simon | 19 | 09 | 57 | 50 | 18 | 10 | 33 | 36 | |
| 5 *Jolie Brise* | Mr E.G. Martin | 19 | 04 | 04 | 19 | 18 | 12 | 41 | 49 | |
| 6 *Banba IV* | Mr H.R. Barrett | 20 | 02 | 32 | 02 | 18 | 17 | 03 | 02 | |
| 7 *Penboch* | Mr R. Somerset | 20 | 08 | 07 | 39 | 18 | 17 | 51 | 39 | |
| *Altair* | Mrs Aitken Dick | DNF | | | | | | | | |
| *Gull* | Mr H.P.F. Donegan | DNF | | | | | | | | |

## 1927 (13 AUGUST)

| YACHT | OWNER | ELAPSED TIME | | | | CORRECTED TIME | | | | |
|---|---|---|---|---|---|---|---|---|---|---|
| 1 *Tally Ho!* | Lord Stalbridge | 19 | 02 | 31 | 47 | 18 | 17 | 38 | 47 | |
| 2 *La Goleta* | Mr R. Peverley | 19 | 01 | 49 | 35 | 18 | 21 | 54 | 10 | |
| *Jolie Brise* | Dr Brownlow Smith | DNF | | | | | | | | (*scratch boat*) |
| *Nicanor* | Mr Daniel Simonds and Mr Warner Ferrier | DNF | | | | | | | | |
| *Morwenna* | Mr W. Curtis Green | DNF | | | | | | | | |
| *Spica* | Mrs A.M. Hunt and Mr J.T. Hunt | DNF | | | | | | | | |
| *Ilex* | Royal Engineer Yacht Club | DNF | | | | | | | | |
| *Saoirse* | Mr Conor O'Brien | DNF | | | | | | | | |
| *Content* | Mr R. D'Oyly-Carte | DNF | | | | | | | | |
| *Thalassa* | Mr Edward Ponsonby | DNF | | | | | | | | |
| *Altair* | Mrs Aitken Dick | DNF | | | | | | | | |
| *Maitenes* | Lt W.B. Luard | DNF | | | | | | | | |
| *Nelly* | Mr M.S. Solly and Mr H.C. Tetley | DNF | | | | | | | | |
| *Penboch* | Mr R. Somerset | DNF | | | | | | | | |

## 1928 (15 AUGUST)

| | YACHT | OWNER (SAILED BY) | ELAPSED TIME days hr. mn. sc. | | | | CORRECTED TIME days hr. mn. sc. | | | | |
|---|---|---|---|---|---|---|---|---|---|---|---|
| 1 | *Nina* | Mr Paul Hammond | 20 | 00 | 18 | 20 | 19 | 17 | 28 | 20 | |
| 2 | *Jolie Brise* | Mr W.L. Ferrier and Dr B. Smith | 20 | 13 | 05 | 05 | 19 | 22 | 54 | 20 | |
| 3 | *Mohawk* | Mr Dudley F. Wolfe | 20 | 09 | 51 | 45 | 20 | 00 | 58 | 45 | |
| 4 | *Neptune* | Lt Col. G.L. Chambers | 20 | 12 | 27 | 30 | 20 | 03 | 55 | 00 | |
| 5 | *Ilex* | Royal Engineer Yacht Club | 20 | 22 | 31 | 45 | 20 | 05 | 37 | 00 | |
| 6 | *Lassie* | Mr R.A. Thomas | 20 | 23 | 05 | 25 | 20 | 08 | 54 | 40 | |
| 7 | *Magnet* | Mr W. Frothingham Roach | 21 | 19 | 27 | 00 | 20 | 17 | 17 | 15 | |
| 8 | *Amaryllis* | Royal Naval College, Dartmouth | 21 | 07 | 14 | 05 | 20 | 20 | 37 | 05 | |
| | *Viking* | Lt R. Lindsay Fisher | DNF | | | | | | | | |
| | *Mamango* | Capt. F. Stevens | DNF | | | | | | | | |
| | *L'Oiseau Bleu* | Mon. Leon Diot | DNF | | | | | | | | |
| | *Noreen* | Mr H.M. Cranshaw | DNF | | | | | | | | *(scratch boat)* |

## 1929 (14 AUGUST)

| | YACHT | OWNER (SAILED BY) | ELAPSED TIME days hr. mn. sc. | | | | CORRECTED TIME days hr. mn. sc. | | | | |
|---|---|---|---|---|---|---|---|---|---|---|---|
| 1 | *Jolie Brise* | Mr R. Somerset | 19 | 18 | 35 | 36 | 19 | 08 | 50 | 06 | |
| 2 | *Saladin* | Mr Ingo Simon | 20 | 20 | 09 | 00 | 20 | 02 | 53 | 45 | |
| 3 | *Ilex* | Royal Engineer Yacht Club | 20 | 15 | 52 | 30 | 20 | 05 | 17 | 00 | |
| 4 | *Maitenes II* | Lt W.B. Luard | 20 | 21 | 10 | 15 | 20 | 05 | 47 | 45 | |
| 5 | *Grey Fox* | Mr H. Newglass | 20 | 22 | 18 | 30 | 20 | 16 | 40 | 15 | |
| 6 | *Amaryllis* | Royal Naval College, Dartmouth | 21 | 06 | 20 | 20 | 21 | 02 | 34 | 30 | |
| 7 | *Guerveur* | Baron de Neufville | 21 | 1200 | approx. | | not officially | | | | *(scratch boat)* |
| 8 | *Neptune* | Col. G.L. Chambers | DNF | | | | timed | | | | |
| | *Vega* | Mon. G. Baldenweck | DNF | | | | | | | | |
| | *Cariad* | Cmdr H.F. Nash | DNF | | | | | | | | |

## 1930 (12 AUGUST)

| | YACHT | OWNER (SAILED BY) | ELAPSED TIME days hr. mn. sc. | | | | CORRECTED TIME days hr. mn. sc. | | | | |
|---|---|---|---|---|---|---|---|---|---|---|---|
| 1 | *Jolie Brise* | Mr R. Somerset | 18 | 18 | 17 | 17 | 18 | 12 | 28 | 47 | |
| 2 | *Maitenes II* | Lt W.B. Luard | 19 | 08 | 51 | 56 | 18 | 18 | 29 | 56 | |
| 3 | *Ilex* | Royal Engineer Yacht Club | 19 | 06 | 10 | 16 | 18 | 22 | 49 | 31 | |
| 4 | *Amaryllis* | Royal Naval College, Dartmouth | 19 | 12 | 46 | 37 | 19 | 12 | 46 | 37 | *(scratch boat)* |
| | *Neptune* | Lt Col. G.L. Chambers | DNF | | | | | | | | *(scratch boat)* |
| | *Lelanta* | Mr R. Peverley | DNF | | | | | | | | |
| | *Ariel* | Mon. G. Baldenweck | DNF | | | | | | | | |
| | *Viking* | Lt R. Lindsay Fisher | DNF | | | | | | | | |
| | *Magnet* | Dr W. Frothingham Roach | DNF | | | | | | | | |

## 1931 (11 AUGUST)

| | YACHT | OWNER (SAILED BY) | ELAPSED TIME days hr. mn. sc. | | | | CORRECTED TIME days hr. mn. sc. | | | | |
|---|---|---|---|---|---|---|---|---|---|---|---|
| 1 | *Dorade* | Messrs Rod and Olin Stephens | 15 | 17 | 17 | 18 | 14 | 21 | 38 | 33 | |
| 2 | *Water Gypsey* | Mr W. McMillan | 15 | 16 | 35 | 18 | 15 | 05 | 39 | 18 | |
| 3 | *Mistress* | Mr G.E. Roosevelt | 15 | 17 | 41 | 25 | 15 | 10 | 00 | 10 | |
| 4 | *Highland Light* | Mr Dudley F. Wolfe | 15 | 16 | 14 | 18 | 15 | 14 | 11 | 18 | |
| 5 | *Lexia* | Maj. T.P. Rose-Richards | 15 | 19 | 23 | 57 | 15 | 15 | 58 | 57 | |
| 6 | *Patience* | Mr H.E. West | 15 | 16 | 13 | 00 | 15 | 16 | 13 | 00 | *(scratch boat)* |
| 7 | *Jolie Brise* | Mr R. Somerset | 16 | 08 | 17 | 43 | 15 | 23 | 24 | 43 | |
| 8 | *Ilex* | Royal Engineer Yacht Club | 16 | 20 | 17 | 06 | 16 | 09 | 21 | 06 | |
| 9 | *Brise Vent* | Mon. G. Fortin | 16 | 21 | 45 | 06 | 16 | 12 | 22 | 06 | |
| 10 | *Amaryllis* | Royal Naval College, Dartmouth | 16 | 17 | 39 | 53 | 16 | 13 | 23 | 38 | |
| 11 | *Neptune* | Lt Col. G.L. Chambers | 16 | 21 | 54 | 12 | 16 | 18 | 39 | 27 | |
| 12 | *Skal* | Mr R.F. Lawrence | 17 | 17 | 44 | 42 | 17 | 05 | 47 | 12 | |
| 13 | *Amberjack II* | Mr Paul Rust | 19 | 10 | 02 | 31 | 18 | 02 | 46 | 46 | |
| 14 | *Ariel* | Mon. G. Baldenweck | 19 | 08 | 27 | 28 | 18 | 23 | 13 | 58 | |
| 15 | *Viking* | Lt R. Lindsay Fisher | 20 | 19 | 12 | 36 | 19 | 22 | 11 | 51 | |
| | *Noreen* | Mr M.A. Bellville | DNF | | | | | | | | |
| | *Maitenes II* | Lt W.B. Luard and Col Hudson | DNF | | | | | | | | |

## 1933 (22 JULY)

| | YACHT | OWNER (SAILED BY) | ELAPSED TIME | | | | CORRECTED TIME | | | | |
|---|---|---|---|---|---|---|---|---|---|---|---|
| | | | days | hr. | mn. | sc. | days | hr. | mn. | sc. | |
| 1 | Dorade | Messrs Rod and Olin Stephens | 28 | 11 | 23 | 15 | 27 | 15 | 59 | 15 | |
| 2 | Grenadier | Messrs Henry A. and Sherman Morss | 28 | 12 | 14 | 37 | 27 | 23 | 14 | 37 | |
| 3 | Flame | Mr Charles E. Nicholson | 28 | 05 | 15 | 06 | 28 | 02 | 51 | 06 | (scratch boat) |
| 4 | Brilliant | Mr W.T. Barnum | 28 | 12 | 12 | 23 | 28 | 03 | 48 | 23 | |
| 5 | Ilex | Royal Engineer Yacht Club | 29 | 01 | 44 | 00 | 28 | 13 | 44 | 00 | |
| | Lexia | Maj. T.P. Rose-Richards | DNF | | | | | | | | |

## 1935 (7 AUGUST)

| | YACHT | OWNER (SAILED BY) | ELAPSED TIME | | | | CORRECTED TIME | | | | |
|---|---|---|---|---|---|---|---|---|---|---|---|
| 1 | Stormy Weather | Mr P. Le Boutillier | 12 | 03 | 44 | 15 | 11 | 11 | 40 | 57 | |
| 2 | Trenchemer | Mr W.D.M. Bell | 12 | 03 | 31 | 58 | 11 | 18 | 09 | 23 | |
| 3 | Ilex | Royal Engineer Yacht Club | 12 | 17 | 07 | 24 | 11 | 22 | 07 | 25 | |
| 4 | Foxhound | Mr Isaac Bell | 12 | 13 | 32 | 51 | 12 | 01 | 59 | 37 | |
| 5 | Kismet III | Mr J. Colin Newman | 12 | 02 | 01 | 54 | 12 | 02 | 01 | 54 | (scratch boat) |
| 6 | Thalassa | Mr G. Napier Martin | 13 | 01 | 38 | 11 | 12 | 02 | 32 | 33 | |
| 7 | Isis | Mon. G. Baldenweck | 13 | 01 | 49 | 48 | 12 | 02 | 42 | 22 | |
| 8 | Carmela | Mr G.E.W. Potter | 12 | 20 | 33 | 03 | 12 | 07 | 41 | 04 | |
| 9 | Emmeline | Royal Air Force Yacht Club | 12 | 18 | 14 | 18 | 12 | 09 | 04 | 24 | |
| 10 | MacNab | Mr J.J. Joass | 13 | 11 | 58 | 46 | 12 | 09 | 08 | 24 | |
| 11 | Rose | Mr C.F. King | 12 | 15 | 54 | 59 | 12 | 09 | 10 | 21 | |
| 12 | Hygie | Mon. Adrien Verliac | 12 | 18 | 40 | 20 | 12 | 09 | 43 | 06 | |
| 13 | Tai-Mo-Shan | The Admiralty | 13 | 11 | 59 | 01 | 12 | 11 | 27 | 46 | |
| 14 | Brise Vent | Mon. G. Fortin | 13 | 13 | 28 | 31 | 13 | 20 | 45 | 14 | |
| 15 | Amy | Sub. Lt I.R.M. McGeoch | TNR | | | | | | | | |
| | Maud | Group Capt. B.A. Playne | DNF | | | | | | | | |
| | Banba | Mr A. Rosling | DNF | | | | | | | | |

## 1937 (7 AUGUST)

| | YACHT | OWNER (SAILED BY) | ELAPSED TIME | | | | CORRECTED TIME | | | | |
|---|---|---|---|---|---|---|---|---|---|---|---|
| 1 | Zeearend | K. Bruynzeel | 11 | 17 | 32 | 00 | | | 85 | 29 | |
| 2 | Stiarna | Lt J.F.B. Gage | 11 | 14 | 17 | 00 | | | 87 | 46 | |
| 3 | Maid of Malham | Lt Cmdr J. Illingworth and N. Jones | 12 | 07 | 06 | 00 | | | 89 | 46 | |
| 4 | Bloodhound | Mr Isaac Bell | 11 | 17 | 33 | 00 | | | 89 | 54 | |
| 5 | Elizabeth McCaw | Mr R.J. Reynolds | 11 | 13 | 24 | 00 | | | 90 | 09 | |
| 6 | Ortac | Mr C.F. King | 12 | 07 | 53 | 00 | | | 91 | 93 | |
| 7 | Latifa | Mr M.H. Mason | 11 | 14 | 03 | 00 | | | 92 | 40 | |
| 8 | Hamburg | Hamburger Verein Seefahrt | 12 | 09 | 09 | 00 | | | 98 | 54 | |
| 9 | Firebird | Mr Ralph Hawkes | 12 | 00 | 30 | 00 | | | 100 | 56 | |
| 10 | Banba | Mr A. Rosling | 12 | 07 | 15 | 00 | | | 101 | 01 | |
| 11 | Ilex | Royal Engineer Yacht Club | 12 | 18 | 03 | 00 | | | 101 | 55 | |
| 12 | Aile Noire | Mon. G. Baldenweck | 12 | 16 | 57 | 00 | | | 101 | 58 | |
| 13 | Neith | Maj. G. Henderson | 12 | 11 | 21 | 00 | | | 102 | 57 | |
| 14 | Trenchemer | Mr W.D.M. Bel | 12 | 09 | 36 | 00 | | | 106 | 35 | |
| 15 | Rose | Royal Artillery Yacht Club | 12 | 09 | 17 | 00 | | | 108 | 00 | |
| 16 | MacNab | Mr J.J. Joass | 13 | 18 | 44 | 00 | | | 112 | 49 | |
| 17 | Asta | Marine Regatta Verein | 11 | 20 | 14 | 00 | | | 113 | 08 | |
| 18 | Roland von Bremen | Segelkameradschaft das Wappen von Bremen | 13 | 03 | 31 | 00 | | | 115 | 41 | |
| 19 | Phryne | Mr R.A. Bevan and Mr H.W. Paton | 13 | 19 | 53 | 00 | | | 116 | 12 | |
| 20 | Nanette | Mr N. King | 14 | 26 | 31 | 00 | | | 121 | 20 | |
| 21 | Zoraida | Capt. Franklin Ratsey | 13 | 18 | 58 | 00 | | | 121 | 59 | |
| 22 | Senta | Herr H. Schmidt | 13 | 18 | 37 | 00 | | | 123 | 21 | |
| 23 | Chough | Mr W.A. Wetherby-Mein | 14 | 12 | 48 | 00 | | | 124 | 48 | |
| 24 | Saladin | Highland Brigade Club | 14 | 11 | 15 | 00 | | | 130 | 02 | |
| 25 | Arktur | U.Deutschlander | 14 | 08 | 11 | 00 | | | 131 | 32 | |
| 26 | Peter von Danzig | A.S.V. Danzig | 14 | 05 | 47 | 00 | | | 133 | 41 | |
| 27 | Ettsi IV | W.V. Alter Corpsstudenten, EV | 14 | 18 | 28 | 00 | | | 140 | 42 | |
| 28 | Pam | Lt E.A. Woodward | 13 | 22 | 54 | 00 | | | 167 | 08 | |
| | Tai-Mo-Shan | The Admiralty | DNF | | | | | | | | |

# 1939 (5 AUGUST)

| | YACHT | OWNER (SAILED BY) | ELAPSED TIME days hr. mn. sc. | | | | CORRECTED TIME hr. mn. sc. | | |
|---|---|---|---|---|---|---|---|---|---|
| 1 | Bloodhound | Mr Isaac Bell | 9 | 07 | 39 | 02 | 79 | 04 | 02 |
| 2 | Zeearend | Mr K. Bruynzeel | 9 | 13 | 50 | 06 | 80 | 09 | 22 |
| 3 | Roland von Bremen | Segelkameradschaft das Wappen von Bremen | 9 | 20 | 26 | 37 | 80 | 18 | 24 |
| 4 | Latifa | Mr M.H. Mason | 9 | 05 | 01 | 21 | 80 | 56 | 22 |
| 5 | Benbow | Mr E. Gore-Lloyd | 9 | 07 | 19 | 12 | 82 | 15 | 40 |
| 6 | Olivier van Noort | Mr A.W. Goudriaan | 9 | 19 | 25 | 20 | 82 | 44 | 51 |
| 7 | Erivale | Mr J.H. Rawlings | 9 | 19 | 23 | 40 | 83 | 07 | 45 |
| 8 | Lara | Mr Kenneth Poland | 9 | 15 | 46 | 33 | 83 | 33 | 09 |
| 9 | Evenlode | Mr T.C. Ratsey | 9 | 22 | 56 | 00 | 84 | 40 | 50 |
| 10 | Nordwind | Kriegsmarine | 9 | 04 | 28 | 20 | 85 | 02 | 54 |
| 11 | Aile Noire | Mon. G. Baldenweck | 9 | 22 | 58 | 56 | 85 | 03 | 41 |
| 12 | Maid of Malham | Royal Naval Sailing Association | 10 | 03 | 16 | 20 | 85 | 39 | 46 |
| 13 | Morva | Mr P.M. Holman | 9 | 22 | 31 | 55 | 87 | 45 | 01 |
| 14 | Walkure | Kriegsmarine | 10 | 00 | 36 | 20 | 88 | 24 | 17 |
| 15 | Phryne | Mr R.A. Bevan and Mr H.W. Paton | 10 | 11 | 19 | 31 | 89 | 13 | 54 |
| 16 | Mary Bower | Maj. R. Bryson | 10 | 08 | 25 | 30 | 89 | 57 | 45 |
| 17 | Rose | Royal Artillery Yacht Club | 9 | 22 | 17 | 20 | 92 | 02 | 47 |
| 18 | Stiarna | Lt J.B.F. Gage | 9 | 23 | 25 | 00 | 92 | 40 | 06 |
| 19 | Ilex | Royal Engineer Yacht Club | 10 | 12 | 56 | 46 | 95 | 32 | 51 |
| 20 | Golden Dragon | Mr H.S. Rouse | 10 | 20 | 46 | 07 | 97 | 36 | 23 |
| 21 | Thalassa | Mr A.B. Baker | 11 | 03 | 33 | 33 | 102 | 55 | 48 |
| 22 | Griffin | H.E. West and E.G. Martin | 11 | 19 | 08 | 22 | 111 | 03 | 15 |
| 23 | Zoraida | Capt. F. Ratsey | 11 | 13 | 14 | 28 | 115 | 36 | 42 |
| | Joyrena | Mr J.F.R. Mitchell | DNF | | | | | | |
| | Iyruna | Dr N.F. Adeney | DNF | | | | | | |
| | Forban | C.I. and A.C. Perkins | DNF | | | | | | |

# 1947 (8 AUGUST)

*Class I*

| | YACHT | OWNER (SAILED BY) | | | | | | | |
|---|---|---|---|---|---|---|---|---|---|
| 1 | Latifa | Mr M.H. Mason | 127 | 24 | 30 | | 118 | 08 | 08 |
| 2 | Bloodhound | Mr M.D.N. Wyatt | 142 | 08 | 37 | | 122 | 36 | 29 |
| 3 | Zeearend | Mr K. Bruynzeel | 153 | 28 | 15 | | 125 | 44 | 21 |
| 4 | Benbow | Mr E. Gore-Lloyd | 153 | 22 | 45 | | 138 | 09 | 51 |
| 5 | Lara | Mr K. Poland | 169 | 25 | 45 | | 141 | 32 | 52 |
| 6 | Theodora | Maj. J.H. Parsons, Maj. R.G.F. Schofield and Lt Col. J. French | 200 | 49 | 00 | | 165 | 44 | 02 |
| 7 | Neith | Maj. G. Henderson | 200 | 10 | 00 | | 166 | 18 | 19 |
| 8 | Orion | Royal Naval Sailing Association (Clyde) | 204 | 14 | 00 | | 210 | 50 | 03 |
| | Rulewater | Maj. A.W. Rainey | DNF | | | | | | |

*Class II*

| | YACHT | OWNER (SAILED BY) | | | | | | | |
|---|---|---|---|---|---|---|---|---|---|
| 1 | Myth of Malham | Capt. J.H. Illingworth | 154 | 17 | 29 | | 112 | 13 | 54 (1st overall) |
| 2 | Phryne | R.A. Bevan and F.A. Haworth | 164 | 10 | 10 | | 123 | 41 | 07 |
| 3 | Erivale | E.G. Greville | 160 | 30 | 10 | | 129 | 12 | 17 |
| 4 | Corabia II | Mr J. Kars | 171 | 21 | 15 | | 129 | 48 | 03 |
| 5 | Aideen | Mr Arthur W. Mooney | 205 | 02 | 00 | | 149 | 06 | 01 |
| 6 | Peter | Mr J.M. Turner | 198 | 05 | 00 | | 150 | 19 | 32 |
| 7 | Maid of Malham | Mr N.F. Adeney | 199 | 00 | 00 | | 151 | 30 | 00 |
| 8 | Marama | Mr H. Osterberg | 201 | 05 | 00 | | 154 | 16 | 16 |
| 9 | Thalassa | Mr A.D. Baker | 206 | 59 | 00 | | 157 | 08 | 31 |
| 10 | Olivier van Noort | Mr A.W. Goudriaan | 198 | 17 | 00 | | 158 | 37 | 36 |
| 11 | Griffin | Royal Ocean Racing Club | 225 | 49 | 00 | | 165 | 58 | 31 |
| 12 | Gauntlet | Royal Naval Engineering College, Manadon | 238 | 51 | 40 | | 173 | 01 | 51 |
| | Seamew | Royal Engineer Yacht Club | DNF | | | | | | |
| | Concara | Maj. H.G. Moore | DNF | | | | | | |
| | Goodewind | Mr D. Rylandes Smith | DNF | | | | | | |
| | MacNab | Mr J.J. Joass | DNF | | | | | | |

# 1949 (6 AUGUST)

| YACHT | OWNER (SAILED BY) | ELAPSED TIME | | | CORRECTED TIME | | | |
|---|---|---|---|---|---|---|---|---|
| | | hr. | mn. | sc. | hr. | mn. | sc. | |
| **Class I** | | | | | | | | |
| 1 *Bloodhound* | M.D.N. Wyatt | 108 | 40 | 40 | 93 | 44 | 43 | |
| 2 *Latifa* | Mr M. Mason | 103 | 13 | 03 | 94 | 58 | 15 | |
| 3 *Theodora* | RACYC | 236 | 37 | 00 | 192 | 10 | 26 | |
| 4 *Avalanche of Aldershot* | Royal Engineer Yacht Club | 264 | 04 | 00 | 216 | 59 | 01 | |
| *Erivale* | Dr E. Greville | DNF | | | | | | |
| *Eostra* | Mr Hugh W. Astor | DNF | | | | | | |
| *Helgoland* | Royal Navy Barracks, Portsmouth | DNF | | | | | | |
| *Mariella* | R.M. Teacher | DNF | | | | | | |
| *Gulvain* | J.H. Rawlings | DNF | | | | | | |
| **Class II** | | | | | | | | |
| 1 *Myth of Malham* | Capt. J.H. Illingworth | 114 | 32 | 36 | 85 | 30 | 23 | (*1st overall*) |
| 2 *St Barbara* | Royal Artillery Yacht Club | 129 | 11 | 40 | 102 | 08 | 01 | |
| 3 *Joanne* | Rene Salem | 139 | 18 | 15 | 107 | 37 | 35 | |
| 4 *Sea Otter* | HMS *Vernon* | 163 | 17 | 50 | 122 | 10 | 54 | |
| 5 *Griffin* | Royal Ocean Racing Club | 242 | 32 | 00 | 177 | 37 | 33 | |
| *Galahad* | Royal Naval Engineering College, Plymouth | DNF | | | | | | |
| *Olivier van Noort* | A.W. Goudriaan | DNF | | | | | | |
| *Pleiades of Rhu* | M. Clayton | DNF | | | | | | |
| *Fandango* | Maj. G. Potter | DNF | | | | | | |
| *Sea Saga* | F.W. Morgan | DNF | | | | | | |
| *Ortac* | I.S.C. Henderson and Dr R.D. Scott | DNF | | | | | | |
| *Farewell* | Mon. Jean Marin | DNF | | | | | | |
| *Corabia II* | Dr J. Kars | DNF | | | | | | |
| *Phryne* | F.A. Haworth | DNF | | | | | | |
| *Sea Wraith* | HMS *Excellent* | DNF | | | | | | |
| *Golden Dragon* | H.S. Rouse | DNF | | | | | | |
| *Sea Feather* | HMS *Dolphin* | DNF | | | | | | |
| *Leopard* | Royal Naval College, Dartmouth | DNF | | | | | | |
| *Harpy* | Royal Naval College, Dartmouth | DNF | | | | | | |
| *Karin III* | G.C.L. Payne | DNF | | | | | | |

# 1951 (11 AUGUST)

| YACHT | OWNER (SAILED BY) | days | hr. | mn. | sc. | hr. | mn. | sc. | |
|---|---|---|---|---|---|---|---|---|---|
| **Class I** | | | | | | | | | |
| 1 *Jocasta* | G.P. Pattinson | 5 | 08 | 23 | 45 | 104 | 33 | 56 | |
| 2 *Circe* | C. Hardeberg | 5 | 07 | 31 | 30 | 105 | 28 | 32 | |
| 3 *Olivier van Noort* | A.W. Goudriaan | 5 | 17 | 21 | 05 | 109 | 55 | 20 | |
| 4 *Bloodhound* | M.D.N. Wyatt | 5 | 07 | 42 | 45 | 109 | 59 | 10 | |
| 5 *Marabu* | HMS *Hornet* | 5 | 15 | 03 | 00 | 112 | 23 | 18 | |
| 6 *Lara* | K.G. Poland | 5 | 16 | 13 | 30 | 113 | 35 | 53 | |
| 7 *Foxhound* | Hon. Mrs Pitt-Rivers | 5 | 15 | 25 | 30 | 115 | 01 | 49 | |
| 8 *Kranich* | Royal Air Force | 6 | 04 | 47 | 45 | 124 | 24 | 41 | |
| 9 *Overlord* | Royal Engineer Yacht Club | 6 | 05 | 13 | 05 | 125 | 11 | 39 | |
| *Aegir X* | British Kiel Yacht club | DNF | | | | | | | |
| *Latifa* | M. Mason | DNF | | | | | | | |
| *Lively* | British Kiel Yacht Club | DNF | | | | | | | |
| *Erivale* | Dr E.G. Greville | DNF | | | | | | | |
| **Class II** | | | | | | | | | |
| 1 *Yeoman* | O.A. Aisher | 5 | 10 | 26 | 05 | 99 | 07 | 02 | (*1st overall*) |
| 2 *Zeevalk* | K. Bruynzeel | 5 | 12 | 47 | 45 | 100 | 30 | 47 | |
| 3 *St Barbara* | Royal Artillery Yacht Club | 5 | 11 | 29 | 00 | 104 | 04 | 56 | |
| 4 *Iolaire* | R. Somerset | 6 | 14 | 53 | 00 | 114 | 19 | 57 | |
| 5 *Waltzing Matilda* | P.R. Davenport | 6 | 20 | 23 | 56 | 117 | 18 | 04 | |
| 6 *Maid of Malham* | H. Dick Broom | 6 | 15 | 40 | 40 | 121 | 17 | 29 | |

| YACHT | OWNER (SAILED BY) | ELAPSED TIME days hr. mn. sc. | | | | CORRECTED TIME hr. mn. sc. | | | |
|---|---|---|---|---|---|---|---|---|---|
| 7 Thalassa | A.B. Baker | 6 | 23 | 09 | 50 | 122 | 54 | 56 | |
| Fandango | Maj. G.E. Potter | DNF | | | | | | | |
| Malabar XIII | K. Jewett | DNF | | | | | | | |
| Farewell | J. Marin | DNF | | | | | | | |
| Huff of Arklow | R.D. Heard | DNF | | | | | | | |
| Lucrezia | Dr B.H.C. Matthews | DNF | | | | | | | |
| Griffin | Royal Ocean Racing Club | DNF | | | | | | | |
| Phizz | F.P.L. Jackson | DNF | | | | | | | |
| Rebel Maid | Lt Cmdr L. Peyton-Jones and others | DNF | | | | | | | |
| Tilly Twin | W.F. Cartwright | DNF | | | | | | | |

# 1953 (8 AUGUST)

*Class I*

| | | | | | | | | | |
|---|---|---|---|---|---|---|---|---|---|
| 1 Lutine | Lloyd's Yacht Club | 5 | 07 | 27 | 10 | 103 | 54 | 45 | |
| 2 Jocasta | G.P. Pattinson | 5 | 08 | 05 | 10 | 104 | 11 | 07 | |
| 3 Olivier van Noort | A.W. Goudriaan | 5 | 10 | 22 | 15 | 104 | 19 | 22 | |
| 4 Gesture | A. Howard Fuller | 5 | 08 | 05 | 15 | 104 | 48 | 51 | |
| 5 Erivale | Dr E.G. Greville | 5 | 10 | 52 | 00 | 104 | 51 | 01 | |
| 6 Janabel | J. Barbou | 5 | 09 | 50 | 20 | 107 | 19 | 28 | |
| 7 Foxhound | Hon. Mrs Pitt-Rivers | 5 | 07 | 56 | 20 | 108 | 40 | 17 | |
| 8 Marabu | HMS Hornet | 5 | 11 | 16 | 45 | 110 | 14 | 06 | |
| 9 Bloodhound | M.D.N. Wyatt | 5 | 07 | 09 | 41 | 110 | 50 | 47 | |
| 10 Kailua | Lord Avebury | 6 | 00 | 40 | 28 | 119 | 15 | 18 | |
| 11 Overlord | Royal Engineer Yacht Club | 6 | 01 | 36 | 27 | 121 | 45 | 25 | |
| Nordwind | H.W. Astor | DNF | | | | | | | |

*Class II*

| | | | | | | | | | |
|---|---|---|---|---|---|---|---|---|---|
| 1 Uomie | S.B. Slater | 5 | 12 | 03 | 32 | 97 | 18 | 03 | |
| 2 Carina | R. Nye | 5 | 12 | 28 | 54 | 98 | 37 | 58 | |
| 3 St Barbara | Royal Artillery Yacht Club | 5 | 09 | 49 | 00 | 102 | 45 | 46 | |
| 4 Phizz | F.P.L. Jackson | 5 | 22 | 48 | 58 | 103 | 04 | 13 | |
| 5 Joliette | F.W. Morgan | 6 | 00 | 51 | 48 | 104 | 14 | 37 | |
| 6 Zeevalk | K. Bruynzeel | 5 | 15 | 05 | 47 | 104 | 18 | 28 | |
| 7 Schlussel von Bremen | Segelkameradschaft das *Wappen von Bremen* | 5 | 22 | 44 | 00 | 104 | 47 | 41 | |
| 8 Disdaine | HMS Drake | 6 | 00 | 29 | 18 | 106 | 55 | 17 | |
| 9 Glance | F.C. Hopkirk | 6 | 00 | 16 | 13 | 107 | 28 | 53 | |
| 10 Water Music | A.V. Sainsbury and others | 6 | 00 | 46 | 00 | 107 | 35 | 26 | |
| 11 Wyvern II | W.R. Murdoch | 5 | 22 | 17 | 20 | 108 | 34 | 00 | |
| 12 Griffin | Royal Ocean Racing Club | 6 | 07 | 51 | 11 | 110 | 55 | 43 | |
| 13 Evenlode | T.C. Ratsey | 5 | 21 | 56 | 02 | 111 | 20 | 50 | |
| 14 Fandango | Lt Col. R.G.F. Scholfield | 5 | 22 | 47 | 02 | 111 | 34 | 17 | |
| 15 Thalassa | A.B. Baker | 6 | 07 | 56 | 10 | 113 | 31 | 30 | |
| 16 Morva | P.M. Holman | 6 | 00 | 44 | 04 | 114 | 06 | 31 | |
| 17 Zadig | S.N. Marris | 6 | 07 | 29 | 55 | 115 | 30 | 09 | |
| 18 Fedoa | J.R.D. James | 6 | 06 | 39 | 30 | 117 | 44 | 22 | |
| Kay | S. Frisell | DNF | | | | | | | |

*Class III*

| | | | | | | | | | |
|---|---|---|---|---|---|---|---|---|---|
| 1 Favona | Sir Michael Newton | 6 | 01 | 51 | 13 | 96 | 11 | 26 | (*1st overall*) |
| 2 Lothian | F.R. Woodroffe | 6 | 01 | 28 | 24 | 97 | 00 | 06 | |
| 3 Loki | Dr Gifford Pinchot | 5 | 20 | 21 | 06 | 97 | 37 | 43 | |
| 4 Cohoe II | K. Adlard Coles | 6 | 03 | 46 | 28 | 97 | 54 | 55 | |
| 5 Alexandra of Itchenor | J.P. Whitehead | 6 | 05 | 58 | 27 | 98 | 33 | 47 | |
| 6 Rum Runner | R.T. Lowein | 6 | 05 | 43 | 02 | 99 | 36 | 25 | |
| 7 Right Royal | Royal Engineer Yacht Club | 6 | 00 | 23 | 08 | 102 | 38 | 38 | |
| 8 Ann Speed | John Lewis Partnership's Sailing Club | 6 | 22 | 40 | 00 | 110 | 42 | 00 | |
| 9 Larph | Lt Col. R. Blewitt | 6 | 18 | 55 | 01 | 116 | 59 | 54 | |

# 1955 (6 AUGUST)

| YACHT | OWNER (SAILED BY) | ELAPSED TIME | | | | CORRECTED TIME | | | |
|-------|-------------------|------|------|------|------|------|------|------|------|
| | | days | hr. | mn. | sc. | hr. | mn. | sc. | |

**Class I**

| | | | | | | | | | |
|---|---|---|---|---|---|---|---|---|---|
| 1 *Lutine* | Lloyd's Yacht Club | 4 | 07 | 55 | 53 | 84 | 23 | 32 | |
| 2 *Foxhound* | Hon. Mrs R. Pitt-Rivers | 4 | 04 | 33 | 58 | 85 | 25 | 14 | |
| 3 *Mare Nostrum* | Capt. Enrique Urrutia | 3 | 22 | 48 | 34 | 86 | 01 | 48 | |
| 4 *Jocasta* | G.P. Pattinson | 4 | 09 | 59 | 10 | 86 | 06 | 11 | |
| 5 *Circe* | Carl Hovgard | 4 | 09 | 51 | 33 | 87 | 33 | 22 | |
| 6 *Bloodhound* | M.D.N. Wyatt | 4 | 08 | 31 | 17 | 88 | 16 | 42 | |
| 7 *Olivier van Noort* | A.W. Goudriaan | 4 | 17 | 17 | 51 | 90 | 39 | 39 | |
| 8 *Marabu* | Royal Naval Volunteer Reserve Sailing Club | 4 | 12 | 31 | 56 | 91 | 08 | 04 | |
| 9 *Gladeye* | Household Brigade Yacht Club Syndicate | 4 | 20 | 45 | 05 | 95 | 32 | 58 | |
| 10 *Farewell II* | Jean Marin | 4 | 15 | 13 | 15 | 96 | 41 | 04 | |
| 11 *Lumberjack* | Hon. Max Aitken | 5 | 07 | 23 | 01 | 101 | 55 | 57 | |
| 12 *Flamingo* | 2nd TAF Sailing Association | 5 | 10 | 12 | 29 | 107 | 12 | 31 | |

**Class II**

| | | | | | | | | | |
|---|---|---|---|---|---|---|---|---|---|
| 1 *Carina* | Richard S. Nye | 4 | 08 | 28 | 55 | 81 | 43 | 32 | *(1st overall)* |
| 2 *Ondine* | S.A. Long | 4 | 10 | 02 | 21 | 82 | 31 | 11 | |
| 3 *Cyane* | Henry B. du Pont | 4 | 16 | 42 | 18 | 88 | 43 | 58 | |
| 4 *Uomie* | S.B. Slater | 5 | 00 | 39 | 01 | 88 | 53 | 42 | |
| 5 *St Barbara* | Royal Artillery Yacht Club | 4 | 20 | 34 | 46 | 91 | 36 | 29 | |
| 6 *Zeezwaluw* | G. Sikkema | 5 | 02 | 27 | 32 | 91 | 50 | 39 | |
| 7 *Vrouwe Emilia* | H.C.M. Merkx | 5 | 04 | 42 | 20 | 93 | 08 | 33 | |
| 8 *Fandango* | Lt Col. R.G.F. Scholfield | 5 | 01 | 55 | 31 | 95 | 24 | 23 | |
| 9 *Griffin* | Royal Ocean Racing Club | 5 | 18 | 37 | 04 | 101 | 15 | 37 | |
| 10 *Glance* | F.C. Hopkirk | 5 | 17 | 34 | 08 | 101 | 29 | 20 | |
| 11 *Maid of Pligh* | R.E. Smith | 5 | 18 | 23 | 05 | 103 | 56 | 26 | |
| 12 *Thalassa* | A.B. Baker | 6 | 01 | 00 | 28 | 108 | 07 | 57 | |
| *Theta* | B.A. Passmore | DNF | | | | | | | |

**Class III**

| | | | | | | | | | |
|---|---|---|---|---|---|---|---|---|---|
| 1 *Mouse of Malham* | Capt. (E) J.H. Illingworth and Peter Green | 5 | 18 | 37 | 02 | 88 | 38 | 45 | |
| 2 *Rondinella* | J.M. Tomlinson | 5 | 18 | 35 | 29 | 89 | 36 | 47 | |
| 3 *Honey* | H. Myren | 5 | 12 | 27 | 53 | 89 | 46 | 18 | |
| 4 *Maze* | C. van Stolk | 5 | 20 | 57 | 48 | 90 | 09 | 35 | |
| 5 *Favona* | Sir Michael Newton | 5 | 18 | 22 | 04 | 91 | 04 | 26 | |
| 6 *Alexandra* | J.P. Whitehead | 5 | 18 | 34 | 33 | 91 | 07 | 39 | |
| 7 *Annasona* | Royal Engineer Yacht Club | 5 | 18 | 30 | 37 | 91 | 26 | 40 | |
| 8 *Lothian* | F.R. Woodroffe | 5 | 16 | 34 | 44 | 93 | 02 | 14 | |
| 9 *Casella* | Y. Cassel | 5 | 16 | 00 | 42 | 93 | 14 | 10 | |
| 10 *Eloise* | F. Hervé and M. Lelievre | 5 | 16 | 09 | 07 | 94 | 57 | 09 | |
| 11 *Cohoe II* | K. Adlard Coles | 5 | 24 | 40 | 26 | 95 | 16 | 04 | |
| 12 *Lapwing* | H.M. Willcox | 5 | 19 | 37 | 43 | 95 | 18 | 26 | |
| 13 *Planet* | HMS *Fisgard* | 5 | 18 | 09 | 15 | 96 | 25 | 53 | |
| 14 *Gipsy Moth* | Francis Chichester | 6 | 07 | 59 | 31 | 96 | 45 | 29 | |
| 15 *Right Royal* | Royal Engineer Yacht Club | 5 | 16 | 22 | 55 | 96 | 57 | 14 | |
| 16 *Jose* | Dr R.J. Melhuish | 6 | 05 | 45 | 31 | 97 | 52 | 02 | |
| 17 *Ratch* | H. Venditti | 6 | 05 | 08 | 06 | 97 | 57 | 07 | |
| 18 *Gauntlet* | HMS *Thunderer* | 6 | 08 | 10 | 09 | 101 | 17 | 56 | |
| 19 *Syrinx* | D.P.S. Fox | 6 | 04 | 41 | 28 | 104 | 11 | 17 | |
| 20 *Prelude* | Maj. Gen. Sir Millis Jefferis | 6 | 05 | 02 | 23 | 104 | 40 | 14 | |
| *Evora* | D. Barnes | DNF | | | | | | | |
| *Harrier* | Raymond C. Hunt | DNF | | | | | | | |

# 1957 (10 AUGUST)

| YACHT | OWNER (SAILED BY) | ELAPSED TIME days hr. mn. sc. | | | | CORRECTED TIME hr. mn. sc. | | | |
|---|---|---|---|---|---|---|---|---|---|

Class I

| | | | | | | | | | |
|---|---|---|---|---|---|---|---|---|---|
| 1 Carina | R.S. Nye | 4 | 10 | 32 | 24 | 82 | 55 | 50 | (1st overall) |
| 2 Kay | S. Frisell | 4 | 13 | 35 | 37 | 85 | 52 | 39 | |
| 3 Jocasta | G.P. Pattinson | 4 | 13 | 39 | 05 | 89 | 09 | 26 | |
| 4 Lutine | Lloyd's Yacht Club (F.A. Haworth) | 4 | 20 | 16 | 13 | 94 | 48 | 25 | |
| 5 Bloodhound | M.D.N. Wyatt | 4 | 18 | 53 | 27 | 96 | 27 | 45 | |
| Aile Noire | Union Nationale des Croiseurs | DNF | | | | | | | |
| Drumbeat | Hon. Max Aitken | DNF | | | | | | | |
| Evenlode | T.C. Ratsey (F.R. Woodroffe) | DNF | | | | | | | |
| Gladeye | Household Brigade Yacht Club Syndicate | DNF | | | | | | | |
| Hamburg VI | Hamburgischer Verein Seefahrt | DNF | | | | | | | |
| Kormoran | W. Bruns (K. Hegewisch) | DNF | | | | | | | |
| Marabu | HMS Hornet | DNF | | | | | | | |
| Overlord | Royal Army Service Corps Yacht Club | DNF | | | | | | | |
| St Barbara | Royal Artillery Yacht Club | DNF | | | | | | | |
| Vanity | M.P.R. Boyle | DNF | | | | | | | |

Class II

| | | | | | | | | | |
|---|---|---|---|---|---|---|---|---|---|
| 1 Myth of Malham | Capt. J.H. Illingworth and Peter Green | 4 | 21 | 21 | 25 | 88 | 04 | 35 | |
| 2 White Mist | G.W. Blunt White | 4 | 22 | 52 | 02 | 90 | 08 | 12 | |
| 3 Figaro | W. Snaith | 4 | 23 | 43 | 26 | 90 | 09 | 50 | |
| 4 Griffin II | Royal Ocean Racing Club | 4 | 23 | 46 | 44 | 91 | 22 | 03 | |
| 5 Bluejacket | D.J. Maw | 5 | 21 | 35 | 42 | 102 | 57 | 13 | |
| Astrea II | Kon-Mar. Yacht Club (Lt Cmdr R. van Wely) | DNF | | | | | | | |
| Black Soo | M.H.R. Pruett | DNF | | | | | | | |
| Corabia | Dr J. Kars | DNF | | | | | | | |
| Disdaine | Royal Naval Barracks, Devonport | DNF | | | | | | | |
| Inschallah | W. Andreae | DNF | | | | | | | |
| Right Royal | Royal Engineer Yacht Club | DNF | | | | | | | |
| Santander | Richard Greene | DNF | | | | | | | |
| See Hexe | Home Air Command Sailing Association | DNF | | | | | | | |
| Tilly Whim | B.V. Richardson | DNF | | | | | | | |
| Uomie | S.B. Slater | DNF | | | | | | | |
| Water Music | A.V. Sainsbury | DNF | | | | | | | |

Class III

| | | | | | | | | | |
|---|---|---|---|---|---|---|---|---|---|
| 1 Cohoe III | K. Adlard Coles | 5 | 15 | 15 | 10 | 90 | 20 | 56 | |
| 2 Elseli IV | G. Plym | 5 | 15 | 49 | 25 | 94 | 30 | 22 | |
| Calliope VIII | G.C. Thompson (R.G. Pitcher) | DNF | | | | | | | |
| Casquet | E. Ellsworth Jones | DNF | | | | | | | |
| Faem | C.P. Humphris | DNF | | | | | | | |
| Galloper | A. Myer and S. Yelloly | DNF | | | | | | | |
| Gauntlet | Royal Naval Engineering College | DNF | | | | | | | |
| Jancis | D.P. Norton | DNF | | | | | | | |
| Maze | A.P. van Stolk and C. van Rietschoten | DNF | | | | | | | |
| Ratch | H. Venditti | DNF | | | | | | | |

# 1959 (8 AUGUST)

Class I

| | | | | | | | | | |
|---|---|---|---|---|---|---|---|---|---|
| 1 Carina | R.S. Nye | 5 | 07 | 48 | 14 | 99 | 33 | 33 | |
| 2 Olivier van Noort | A.W. Goudriaan | 5 | 07 | 21 | 00 | 101 | 36 | 46 | |
| 3 Ramrod | S.B. Slater and R. McLoughlin | 5 | 11 | 38 | 30 | 101 | 38 | 26 | |
| 4 Zwerver | W.N.H. van der Vorm (O.J. van der Vorm) | 5 | 07 | 02 | 12 | 102 | 50 | 11 | |
| 5 Lutine | Lloyd's Yacht Club (B.A. Stewart) | 5 | 07 | 31 | 20 | 103 | 58 | 55 | |
| 6 Anna Marina | K.E. Hedborg | 5 | 01 | 46 | 38 | 105 | 35 | 34 | |
| 7 Mait II | Comm. I. Monzino | 5 | 11 | 57 | 20 | 111 | 04 | 47 | |
| 8 St Barbara | Royal Artillery Yacht Club | 6 | 05 | 31 | 40 | 116 | 07 | 24 | |
| 9 Zeevalk | K. Bruynzeel | 6 | 06 | 08 | 00 | 116 | 14 | 54 | |
| 10 Evenlode | Capt. F. Ratsey, RN (ret.), (M.H.R. Pruett) | 6 | 06 | 37 | 00 | 117 | 22 | 32 | |

| YACHT | OWNER (SAILED BY) | ELAPSED TIME days hr. mn. sc. | | | | CORRECTED TIME hr. mn. sc. | | | |
|---|---|---|---|---|---|---|---|---|---|
| 11 *Marabu* | C.-in-C. Portsmouth (Lt Cmdr J. Fairbank) | 5 | 23 | 58 | 09 | 118 | 01 | 31 | |
| 12 *Wyvern II* | W.R. Murdoch | 6 | 08 | 59 | 26 | 118 | 44 | 09 | |
| 13 *Drumbeat* | Hon. Max Aitken | 6 | 05 | 42 | 05 | 119 | 01 | 39 | |
| 14 *Vadura* | J. Howden Hume | 6 | 09 | 05 | 34 | 144 | 36 | 41 | |
| *Bloodhound* | M.D.N. Wyatt | DNF | | | | | | | |
| *Capella* | Britannia Royal Naval College | DNF | | | | | | | |
| *Seabill* | Sir Arthur V. Harvey | DNF | | | | | | | |

## Class II

| YACHT | OWNER (SAILED BY) | ELAPSED TIME days hr. mn. sc. | | | | CORRECTED TIME hr. mn. sc. | | | |
|---|---|---|---|---|---|---|---|---|---|
| 1 *Anitra* | S. Hansen | 5 | 08 | 39 | 35 | 97 | 02 | 52 | (*1st overall*) |
| 2 *Griffin II* | Royal Ocean Racing Club (Maj. G. Potter) | 5 | 08 | 08 | 06 | 97 | 46 | 01 | |
| 3 *Clair de Lune* | A.E. Bird (G.P. Pattinson) | 6 | 07 | 24 | 18 | 107 | 04 | 24 | |
| 4 *Myth of Malham* | Capt. J.H. Illingworth and Peter Green | 5 | 22 | 34 | 00 | 107 | 18 | 37 | |
| 5 *Moonlight II* | T.D. Mitchell | 6 | 10 | 55 | 58 | 109 | 25 | 44 | |
| 6 *Bluejacket* | David J. Maw | 6 | 08 | 07 | 56 | 110 | 04 | 03 | |
| 7 *Right Royal* | Royal Engineer Yacht Club (Col. E.F. Parker) | 6 | 11 | 59 | 00 | 110 | 54 | 15 | |
| 8 *Quiver II* | S.H.R. Clarke | 6 | 09 | 33 | 00 | 112 | 13 | 47 | |
| 9 *Water Music* | A.V. Sainsbury | 6 | 09 | 53 | 00 | 112 | 39 | 28 | |
| 10 *Tilly Whim* | B.V. Richardson | 6 | 19 | 11 | 10 | 115 | 06 | 43 | |
| 11 *Silvio* | Hon. Robert Boscawen | 6 | 20 | 18 | 05 | 119 | 30 | 46 | |
| 12 *Fair Judgment II (A)* | P.F. Carter-Ruck | 7 | 01 | 35 | 35 | 121 | 26 | 44 | |
| 13 *Rapparee* | Baltic Exchange Yachting Association (H.A. Rapp) | 7 | 08 | 40 | 00 | 125 | 56 | 45 | |
| *Amokura* | G. Millar | DNF | | | | | | | |
| *Eloise II* | F. Hervé | DNF | | | | | | | |
| *Jen* | Carl Koch | DNF | | | | | | | |
| *Kiff* | Eric Barker | DNF | | | | | | | |
| *Marie-Christine III* | J.-C. Menu | DNF | | | | | | | |
| *St Francois* | G. Craipeau | DNF | | | | | | | |
| *Sea Wraith* | HMS *Excellent* | DNF | | | | | | | |
| *Solace II* | Robert Lochner | DNF | | | | | | | |
| *Thalassa* | Alan B. Baker (E.P. de Guingand) | DNF | | | | | | | |

## Class III

| YACHT | OWNER (SAILED BY) | ELAPSED TIME days hr. mn. sc. | | | | CORRECTED TIME hr. mn. sc. | | | |
|---|---|---|---|---|---|---|---|---|---|
| 1 *Danegeld* | R.T. Lowein | 6 | 10 | 25 | 39 | 101 | 51 | 36 | |
| 2 *Faem* | C.P. Humphris and R.C. Farnham | 6 | 15 | 04 | 02 | 102 | 32 | 05 | |
| 3 *Pym* | D.J. Boyer | 6 | 05 | 02 | 14 | 103 | 56 | 18 | |
| 4 *Cohoe III* | K. Adlard Coles | 6 | 12 | 01 | 06 | 104 | 06 | 39 | |
| 5 *Meon Maid II* | HMS *Mercury* | 6 | 09 | 55 | 06 | 105 | 01 | 05 | |
| 6 *Swan Lake* | Maj. D.P. Kayll | 6 | 16 | 40 | 00 | 106 | 17 | 49 | |
| 7 *Gauntlet* | HMS *Thunderer* | 6 | 14 | 29 | 29 | 106 | 43 | 41 | |
| 8 *Vashti* | J.M. Laing | 6 | 13 | 51 | 05 | 107 | 09 | 56 | |
| 9 *Lora* | D. Edwards and D.M. Cuthbert | 6 | 20 | 43 | 05 | 109 | 22 | 22 | |
| 10 *Petasus* | Royal Signals Yacht Club (Maj. L.D. Line) | 6 | 21 | 29 | 55 | 110 | 20 | 17 | |
| 11 *Ros Beiaard* | R. Das | 7 | 00 | 18 | 00 | 111 | 24 | 53 | |
| 12 *Jabula* | J. Boardman | 6 | 21 | 25 | 28 | 112 | 19 | 24 | |
| 13 *Stardrift* | W.B. Howell | 7 | 06 | 31 | 30 | 113 | 20 | 11 | |
| 14 *Rondinella* | M. Tomlinson | 7 | 07 | 52 | 15 | 114 | 49 | 34 | |
| 15 *Nantucket* | A.J.M. Miller | 7 | 10 | 03 | 34 | 123 | 16 | 14 | |
| 16 *Rummer* | C.R. Holman | 8 | 04 | 37 | 30 | 128 | 35 | 33 | |
| *Belmore* | T.W.M. Steele (Lt Cmdr L.E.D. Wise, RN) | DNF | | | | | | | |
| *Maze* | C. van Rietschoten and A.P. van Stolk | DNF | | | | | | | |
| *New Dawn* | D.C. Corry | DNF | | | | | | | |
| *Sabrina Fair* | W. Johnston | DNF | | | | | | | |

# 1961 (5 AUGUST)

| YACHT | OWNER (SAILED BY) | ELAPSED TIME | | | | CORRECTED TIME | | | |
|---|---|---|---|---|---|---|---|---|---|
| | | days | hr. | mn. | sc. | hr. | mn. | sc. | |

**Class I**

| | YACHT | OWNER (SAILED BY) | days | hr. | mn. | sc. | hr. | mn. | sc. | |
|---|---|---|---|---|---|---|---|---|---|---|
| 1 | Zwerver | W.N.H. van der Vorm (O.J. van der Vorm) | 4 | 04 | 43 | 20 | 81 | 32 | 03 | (1st overall) |
| 2 | Anitra | S. Hansen | 4 | 18 | 21 | 33 | 86 | 15 | 40 | |
| 3 | Figaro | William Snaith | 4 | 17 | 41 | 28 | 86 | 29 | 05 | |
| 4 | Myth of Malham | Capt. J. Illingworth and Peter J.F. Green | 4 | 20 | 07 | 36 | 87 | 24 | 31 | |
| 5 | Springtime | A.E. Bird | 4 | 21 | 33 | 09 | 88 | 46 | 33 | |
| 6 | Stormvogel | K. Bruynzeel | 3 | 20 | 58 | 13 | 89 | 40 | 45 | |
| 7 | Griffin II | Royal Ocean Racing Club (Maj. G. Potter) | 4 | 22 | 35 | 44 | 90 | 29 | 19 | |
| 8 | Constellation | Mrs S.A. Langmuir | 4 | 04 | 02 | 00 | 90 | 31 | 49 | |
| 9 | Cyane | H.B. du Pont | 4 | 20 | 56 | 03 | 90 | 33 | 56 | |
| 10 | Lutine | Lloyd's Yacht Club (F.A. Haworth) | 4 | 17 | 47 | 44 | 92 | 44 | 36 | |
| 11 | Olivier van Noort | A.W. Goudriaan | 4 | 20 | 18 | 10 | 92 | 47 | 54 | |
| 12 | Dione | O. Wettergren | 4 | 23 | 18 | 34 | 92 | 47 | 56 | |
| 13 | Drumbeat | Hon. Max Aitken | 5 | 05 | 01 | 10 | 99 | 18 | 11 | |
| 14 | Marabu | Admiralty (C.-in-C. Portsmouth) | 5 | 04 | 24 | 10 | 101 | 59 | 08 | |
| 15 | Ortac | Hamburg Sailing Club (R.H. Siemssen) | 5 | 19 | 28 | 00 | 108 | 42 | 11 | |
| 16 | Striana | Dr J. Auclair and M. Chasagny | 5 | 15 | 21 | 07 | 112 | 18 | 05 | |
| | Flame | C.M. Carpenter | DNF | | | | | | | |
| | Hamburg VI | Hamburg Sailing Club (H. Stichert) | DNF | | | | | | | |
| | Lydie | Dr R. Brignol | DNF | | | | | | | |
| | Pen-Duick | E. Tabarly | DNF | | | | | | | |
| | St Barbara | Royal Artillery Yacht Club (Maj.-Gen. J. Morris) | DNF | | | | | | | |
| | Ramrod | F.W. Morgan and U. Stephenson | DNF | | | | | | | |
| | Theodora | C. St J. Ellis | DNF | | | | | | | |
| | Zulu | B.A. Stewart | DNF | | | | | | | |

**Class II**

| | YACHT | OWNER (SAILED BY) | days | hr. | mn. | sc. | hr. | mn. | sc. | |
|---|---|---|---|---|---|---|---|---|---|---|
| 1 | Quiver III | S.H.R. Clarke | 4 | 20 | 07 | 03 | 84 | 32 | 01 | |
| 2 | Windrose | J. Isbrandtsen | 4 | 20 | 10 | 00 | 86 | 07 | 34 | |
| 3 | Assegai | W.M. Vernon | 5 | 05 | 24 | 13 | 87 | 40 | 56 | |
| 4 | Pym | D.J. Boyer | 5 | 05 | 28 | 42 | 87 | 49 | 20 | |
| 5 | Staika III | S. Roden | 5 | 06 | 00 | 09 | 88 | 05 | 18 | |
| 6 | Zarabanda | G.P. Pattinson | 5 | 06 | 50 | 04 | 88 | 53 | 08 | |
| 7 | Silvio | Hon. R. Boscawen | 5 | 04 | 37 | 35 | 90 | 39 | 12 | |
| 8 | Whirlwind | R.S. Wilkins | 5 | 07 | 23 | 21 | 90 | 50 | 29 | |
| 9 | Marie Christine III | J.-C. Menu | 5 | 05 | 28 | 17 | 93 | 18 | 02 | |
| 10 | Eloise II | J. Lelèivre and F. Hervé | 5 | 05 | 34 | 49 | 93 | 22 | 08 | |
| 11 | Rapparee | H.A. Rapp | 5 | 11 | 44 | 05 | 93 | 30 | 18 | |
| 12 | Bluejacket | David J. Maw | 5 | 12 | 28 | 58 | 93 | 33 | 34 | |
| 13 | Taiseer V | J.F. Holman | 5 | 10 | 36 | 30 | 93 | 46 | 36 | |
| 14 | Matambu | D.E.P. Norton | 5 | 13 | 35 | 00 | 94 | 58 | 39 | |
| 15 | Corabia | Dr J. Kars (H.F. Zuiderbaan) | 5 | 11 | 19 | 50 | 95 | 48 | 20 | |
| 16 | Water Music II | Mr and Mrs A.V. Sainsbury | 5 | 11 | 54 | 08 | 96 | 24 | 27 | |
| 17 | Martlet | Britannia Royal Naval College | 5 | 16 | 41 | 34 | 98 | 57 | 07 | |
| 18 | Salamander | A.W.G. and G. Lockyer | 6 | 00 | 43 | 15 | 100 | 35 | 43 | |
| 19 | Pegasus | Britannia Royal Naval College | 5 | 21 | 55 | 00 | 102 | 44 | 01 | |
| 20 | Noryema | R.W. Amey | 6 | 04 | 39 | 40 | 103 | 09 | 21 | |
| 21 | Tumbelina | D. le S. Campbell and W.F. Cartwright | 6 | 04 | 14 | 08 | 104 | 18 | 48 | |
| 22 | New Dawn | D.C. Corry (R. Corry) | 6 | 03 | 47 | 48 | 104 | 52 | 35 | |
| 23 | Four Square | Brian Smart | 6 | 07 | 11 | 00 | 105 | 27 | 55 | |
| 24 | Wish Stream | Royal Military Academy Sailing Club (Lt Col. J.C. Calver) | 6 | 09 | 37 | 10 | 109 | 00 | 30 | |
| 25 | Ar Men II | J.M. and A. Auclair | 6 | 09 | 49 | 24 | 109 | 59 | 01 | |
| 26 | Pundit | E. Ellsworth Jones | 6 | 19 | 58 | 00 | 115 | 48 | 35 | |
| 27 | Corinna | N. Richards (H. King Spark) | 7 | 06 | 14 | 05 | 125 | 56 | 12 | |
| | Gryphis | Britannia Royal Naval College | DNF | | | | | | | |
| | Jabadao | M. Trebaol | DNF | | | | | | | |
| | Leopard | Britannia Royal Naval College | DNF | | | | | | | |
| | Nantucket | A.J. Miller (RNSA—Cmdr R.B.L. Foster) | DNF | | | | | | | |

|  | *Naseby* | R.T. Paget | DNF | | | | | | |
|  | *Right Royal* | Royal Engineer Yacht Club | DNF | | | | | | |
|  | *Sundew* | R.A.H. Perkins | DNF | | | | | | |
|  | *Tandala* | B.V. Richardson | DNF | | | | | | |
|  | *Tryad* | Mr and Mrs R.H.G. Lee | DNF | | | | | | |
|  | *Whanesheen* | Mr and Mrs M.M. Brown | DNF | | | | | | |
|  | *Witte Raaf* | Th. P. Tromp | DNF | | | | | | |
|  | *Wyvern* | Britannia Royal Naval College | DNF | | | | | | |

*Class III*

| 1 | *Belmore* | T.W.M. Steele | 5 | 06 | 44 | 45 | 86 | 27 | 58 |
| 2 | *Galloper* | V. Powell | 5 | 09 | 23 | 07 | 88 | 55 | 35 |
| 3 | *Vashti* | J.M. Laing | 5 | 11 | 44 | 30 | 89 | 38 | 13 |
| 4 | *Cohoe III* | K. Adlard Coles | 5 | 13 | 10 | 34 | 90 | 47 | 10 |
| 5 | *Mister Cube* | Sir Adrian Jarvis | 5 | 15 | 23 | 44 | 91 | 08 | 05 |
| 6 | *Alcina* | Lt Cmdr J.A.F. Lawson | 5 | 20 | 38 | 00 | 93 | 58 | 17 |
| 7 | *Maica* | H. Rouault | 5 | 23 | 19 | 07 | 94 | 22 | 30 |
| 8 | *Micronair* | F. Britten and N.D. Norman | 5 | 18 | 19 | 50 | 94 | 44 | 33 |
| 9 | *Arabel II* | Dr R. Le Couteur | 6 | 05 | 03 | 30 | 97 | 08 | 29 |
| 10 | *Viking of Mersea* | Rodney Hill | 6 | 04 | 41 | 55 | 97 | 32 | 46 |
| 11 | *Contango* | Dr I. Kinross | 6 | 04 | 43 | 25 | 99 | 58 | 19 |
| 12 | *Damian B* | D.P. Miller | 6 | 03 | 57 | 02 | 100 | 00 | 00 |
| 13 | *Electron* | HMS *Collingwood* | 6 | 04 | 18 | 20 | 100 | 55 | 19 |
| 14 | *Jose* | Dr R.J. Melhuish | 6 | 13 | 36 | 29 | 102 | 18 | 12 |
| 15 | *Aile Bleue* | E.C.C. (E. Desvignes) | 6 | 10 | 52 | 04 | 102 | 20 | 12 |
| 16 | *Annasona* | Royal Engineer Yacht Club | 6 | 13 | 48 | 49 | 104 | 24 | 34 |
| 17 | *Maze* | Dr R. Binning and G. Paterson | 7 | 03 | 09 | 04 | 114 | 57 | 25 |
| 18 | *Navara* | H.W. Turner (Sqn Ldr R. Edwards) | 7 | 11 | 34 | 00 | 117 | 02 | 29 |
| 19 | *Sounion* | C.M.G. Butterfield | 7 | 10 | 11 | 27 | 118 | 09 | 29 |
|  | *Harmony* | Dr R.H. O'Hanlon | DNF | | | | | | |
|  | *Ben's Choice* | N.H. Jones (D.M. Jones) | DNF | | | | | | |
|  | *Capreolus* | Sir John Power | DNF | | | | | | |
|  | *Faem* | C.P. Humphris and R. Farnham | DNF | | | | | | |
|  | *El Vigo* | R. Lochner | DNF | | | | | | |
|  | *Gauntlet* | HMS *Thunderer* | DNF | | | | | | |
|  | *Islay Mist* | T. Wilks | DNF | | | | | | |
|  | *Jabula* | J. Boardman and W. Gough Cooper | DNF | | | | | | |
|  | *Jethou* | Royal Air Force Sailing Association | DNF | | | | | | |
|  | *Mako of Burnham* | L.B. Dyball | DNF | | | | | | |
|  | *Orthops* | H. Orr | DNF | | | | | | |
|  | *Pellegrina* | J.M. Tomlinson | DNF | | | | | | |
|  | *Petasus* | Royal Signals Yacht Club | DNF | | | | | | |

# 1963 (10 AUGUST)

*Class I*

| 1 | *Figaro* | W.T. Snaith | 4 | 20 | 51 | 30 | 88 | 24 | 54 |
| 2 | *Carina* | R.S. Nye (R.B. Nye) | 4 | 18 | 25 | 32 | 89 | 24 | 44 |
| 3 | *Rubin* | H.O. Schumann | 4 | 17 | 15 | 24 | 89 | 46 | 43 |
| 4 | *Baccarat* | G. Coumantaros (E.M. Mitchell) | 4 | 18 | 50 | 25 | 90 | 36 | 32 |
| 5 | *Dyna* | Clayton Ewing | 4 | 13 | 25 | 38 | 90 | 40 | 16 |
| 6 | *Outlaw* | Hon. Max Aitken and R. Lowein | 4 | 20 | 40 | 30 | 91 | 02 | 30 |
| 7 | *Vagabonde* | G.A. Lindberg | 4 | 17 | 52 | 42 | 91 | 04 | 07 |
| 8 | *Myth of Malham* | B. and D. Livingston | 5 | 01 | 43 | 50 | 91 | 17 | 09 |
| 9 | *Griffin II* | Royal Ocean Racing Club (J.W. Roome) | 5 | 01 | 30 | 30 | 92 | 22 | 14 |
| 10 | *Eloise II* | F. Hervé | 5 | 02 | 40 | 15 | 92 | 22 | 16 |
| 11 | *Ramrod* | F.W. Morgan and U. Stephenson | 5 | 01 | 23 | 30 | 92 | 43 | 52 |
| 12 | *Cyane* | H.B. du Pont | 5 | 01 | 12 | 55 | 93 | 37 | 36 |
| 13 | *Dione* | O. Wettergren | 5 | 01 | 17 | 49 | 94 | 22 | 15 |
| 14 | *Glenan* | Centre Nautique des Glénans (T. Sandot) | 5 | 03 | 05 | 25 | 94 | 33 | 37 |
| 15 | *Zulu* | B.A. Stewart | 5 | 04 | 50 | 20 | 94 | 48 | 54 |
| 16 | *Helen of Howth* | P.H. Greer | 5 | 04 | 58 | 00 | 96 | 31 | 27 |

| YACHT | OWNER (SAILED BY) | ELAPSED TIME days hr. mn. sc. | | | | CORRECTED TIME hr. mn. sc. | | |
|---|---|---|---|---|---|---|---|---|
| 17 Capricia | E. Hansen (S. Hansen) | 4 | 08 | 51 | 06 | 96 | 32 | 50 |
| 18 Diana II | H.S. Thomas | 4 | 23 | 15 | 00 | 96 | 34 | 50 |
| 19 Ondine | S.A. Long | 4 | 23 | 10 | 45 | 97 | 09 | 18 |
| 20 Bolero | Mrs S.A. Langmuir | 4 | 10 | 19 | 15 | 97 | 34 | 53 |
| 21 St Barbara | Royal Artillery Yacht Club (Capt. J. Myatt) | 5 | 05 | 48 | 35 | 97 | 54 | 19 |
| 22 Kay | S. Frisell | 5 | 06 | 28 | 50 | 98 | 20 | 19 |
| 23 Merlin | Home Air Command Sailing Association | 5 | 02 | 43 | 50 | 98 | 22 | 07 |
| 24 Inschallah | W. Andreae | 5 | 05 | 43 | 00 | 98 | 42 | 00 |
| 25 Ile de Feu | A. Viant and M. Normand | 5 | 06 | 06 | 10 | 99 | 09 | 17 |
| 26 Lutine | Lloyd's Yacht Club (F.A. Haworth) | 5 | 01 | 48 | 25 | 99 | 39 | 01 |
| 27 Striana | Dr J. Auclair | 5 | 03 | 30 | 35 | 101 | 35 | 56 |
| 28 Marabu | Coastal Forces Sailing Association (Lt J. Trinder, RN) | 5 | 03 | 33 | 25 | 101 | 36 | 03 |
| 29 Stormvogel | K. Bruynzeel | 4 | 09 | 38 | 44 | 102 | 24 | 08 |
| 30 Evenlode | H.V.L. Hall (Lt Cmdr B. Baxter, RNR) | 5 | 14 | 12 | 00 | 104 | 32 | 31 |
| 31 Avrion | D.W. Morphy (Lt Col. L. Line) | 5 | 14 | 14 | 00 | 105 | 19 | 10 |
| 32 Corsaro II | Italian Navy | 5 | 01 | 59 | 15 | 108 | 18 | 02 |
| Aloha | Capt. F. Kemmis Betty, RNR | DNF | | | | | | |
| Giralda | HRH The Count of Barcelona | DNF | | | | | | |
| Starfire | J. Boardman and W. Gough Cooper | DNF | | | | | | |

Class II

| YACHT | OWNER (SAILED BY) | ELAPSED TIME days hr. mn. sc. | | | | CORRECTED TIME hr. mn. sc. | | | |
|---|---|---|---|---|---|---|---|---|---|
| 1 Clarion of Wight | D. Boyer and D. Miller | 5 | 01 | 10 | 30 | 86 | 34 | 13 | (1st overall) |
| 2 Camelot | D.R. Anstey | 5 | 06 | 48 | 40 | 87 | 29 | 13 | |
| 3 Tulla | S. de Wit | 5 | 05 | 54 | 25 | 88 | 08 | 51 | |
| 4 Gerfaut | C. and P. Renot | 5 | 07 | 29 | 50 | 88 | 15 | 12 | |
| 5 Whirlaway | R.S. Wilkins (C.R. Holman) | 5 | 05 | 30 | 00 | 88 | 45 | 13 | |
| 6 Slokop | A. le Comte | 5 | 08 | 55 | 00 | 89 | 11 | 51 | |
| 7 Quiver III | S.H.R. Clarke | 5 | 02 | 29 | 45 | 89 | 12 | 06 | |
| 8 Varna | F. Fournier | 5 | 09 | 14 | 20 | 89 | 16 | 42 | |
| 9 Brigantine | B. Moreau and P. Mulot | 5 | 08 | 45 | 30 | 89 | 25 | 59 | |
| 10 Guinevere | G. Moffett | 5 | 06 | 47 | 35 | 89 | 54 | 32 | |
| 11 Hephzibah | J.M. Laing | 5 | 06 | 55 | 10 | 89 | 59 | 54 | |
| 12 Staika III | S. Roden | 5 | 11 | 21 | 10 | 90 | 45 | 54 | |
| 13 Musketeer | Peter Green | 5 | 02 | 09 | 45 | 90 | 47 | 29 | |
| 14 Force Seven | Warren A. Brown and T. Watson, Jr | 5 | 07 | 44 | 24 | 91 | 00 | 07 | |
| 15 Noryema III | R.W. Amey | 5 | 05 | 13 | 25 | 91 | 16 | 32 | |
| 16 Sitzmark IV | Dr W. Neumann | 5 | 06 | 01 | 35 | 91 | 28 | 57 | |
| 17 Querida | D.N. Doyle | 5 | 09 | 49 | 30 | 91 | 30 | 49 | |
| 18 Dambuster | Royal Air Force Sailing Association | 5 | 08 | 35 | 35 | 91 | 52 | 01 | |
| 19 Marie-Christine III | J.-C. Menu | 5 | 04 | 32 | 15 | 92 | 36 | 22 | |
| 20 Najade | Kon-Mar Yacht Club (Capt. R. van Wely, RNN) | 5 | 04 | 22 | 45 | 92 | 44 | 14 | |
| 21 Primevere | E.M. Osborne | 5 | 04 | 28 | 35 | 92 | 45 | 51 | |
| 22 Windrose | J. Isbrandtsen | 5 | 06 | 34 | 05 | 94 | 21 | 24 | |
| 23 Matambu | D.E.P. Norton | 5 | 12 | 55 | 00 | 94 | 30 | 14 | |
| 24 Whanesheene | Mr and Mrs M.M. Brown | 5 | 10 | 40 | 00 | 94 | 51 | 51 | |
| 25 Greylag of Arklow | Lt Cmdr T. Sheppard | 5 | 15 | 07 | 00 | 95 | 02 | 28 | |
| 26 Deseret | T.W. Howard (Royal Air Force Sailing Association) | 5 | 14 | 26 | 10 | 95 | 32 | 38 | |
| 27 Water Music II | J.C. Foot | 5 | 13 | 06 | 30 | 97 | 17 | 20 | |
| 28 Martlet | Britannia Royal Naval College | 5 | 13 | 52 | 00 | 97 | 27 | 17 | |
| 29 Rainy Day III | Raglan Squire | 5 | 14 | 34 | 00 | 98 | 14 | 01 | |
| 30 Bianca II | E. Bjerede | 5 | 23 | 17 | 15 | 99 | 07 | 34 | |
| 31 Christina | Dr P.F. Chambonnet | 5 | 14 | 26 | 45 | 99 | 18 | 05 | |
| 32 Pas Seul | Miss A.G. and T.I., R.A. and D.C. Perkins | 5 | 22 | 09 | 13 | 99 | 21 | 04 | |
| 33 Gryphis | Britannia Royal Naval College | 5 | 18 | 15 | 00 | 100 | 33 | 47 | |
| 34 Eloe | Dr J. Descamps | 5 | 17 | 27 | 20 | 100 | 48 | 36 | |
| 35 Leopard | Britannia Royal Naval College (R/Admiral H.R. Law) | 5 | 21 | 56 | 00 | 103 | 10 | 17 | |
| 36 Felise | J.W.C. Robinson (J. Greenfield) | 6 | 05 | 08 | 04 | 107 | 20 | 49 | |
| 37 Rampage | The Lord Burnham | 6 | 09 | 06 | 03 | 110 | 23 | 09 | |

| YACHT | OWNER (SAILED BY) | ELAPSED TIME days hr. mn. sc. | | | | CORRECTED TIME hr. mn. sc. | | |
|---|---|---|---|---|---|---|---|---|
| *Assegai* | W.M. Vernon | DNF | | | | | | |
| *Bonaventura II* | L.J.V. Lejeune | DNF | | | | | | |
| *Cockade* | J.D. Boswell | DNF | | | | | | |
| *Corabia* | Mrs J. Kars (H. Zuiderbaan) | DNF | | | | | | |
| *En Rapport* | R.W. Sheppard (C. Oliver) | DNF | | | | | | |
| *Eos* | B. Malmberg | DNF | | | | | | |
| *Gayrock* | B.V. Richardson | DNF | | | | | | |
| *Gimcrack* | D.S. Cottell | DNF | | | | | | |
| *Saboo* | Arthur Slater | DNF | | | | | | |
| *Tumbelina* | D. le S. Campbell | DNF | | | | | | |
| *Wish Stream* | Royal Military Academy Sailing Club | DNF | | | | | | |
| *Witte Raaf* | Th. P. Tromp. | DNF | | | | | | |

*Class III*

| | YACHT | OWNER (SAILED BY) | days | hr. | mn. | sc. | hr. | mn. | sc. |
|---|---|---|---|---|---|---|---|---|---|
| 1 | *Cohoe IV* | K. Adlard Coles | 5 | 07 | 46 | 25 | 86 | 40 | 08 |
| 2 | *Pen Ar Bed* | P. Lemaire | 5 | 14 | 15 | 05 | 87 | 17 | 26 |
| 3 | *Belmore II* | T.W.M. Steele | 5 | 06 | 48 | 05 | 87 | 19 | 42 |
| 4 | *Astrolabe* | B.C.M.E. Imbert | 5 | 14 | 10 | 45 | 88 | 00 | 29 |
| 5 | *Pionier* | E.G. van de Stadt | 5 | 15 | 51 | 50 | 88 | 13 | 49 |
| 6 | *Sportlust VI* | P.W. Vroon | 5 | 14 | 18 | 12 | 88 | 25 | 31 |
| 7 | *Golden Samphire* | J.A. Sampson | 5 | 17 | 17 | 30 | 89 | 16 | 02 |
| 8 | *Penelope* | Chantier Jouet et Cie | 5 | 18 | 02 | 00 | 89 | 17 | 38 |
| 9 | *Pellegrina* | J.M. Tomlinson | 5 | 10 | 12 | 55 | 89 | 20 | 27 |
| 10 | *Blue Charm* | Royal Air Force Sailing Association | 5 | 16 | 10 | 05 | 89 | 35 | 55 |
| 11 | *Grenade* | Col. and Mrs K. Wylie and Lt Col. M. Tickell | 5 | 13 | 36 | 10 | 89 | 47 | 43 |
| 12 | *Maica* | H. Rouault | 5 | 18 | 45 | 02 | 91 | 09 | 33 |
| 13 | *Rockaby* | C.P. Murch | 5 | 17 | 31 | 00 | 91 | 37 | 39 |
| 14 | *Temeraire* | Britannia Royal Naval College | 5 | 14 | 41 | 00 | 91 | 46 | 24 |
| 15 | *Can-Can II* | E. Kindberg | 5 | 15 | 36 | 55 | 92 | 05 | 46 |
| 16 | *Misty* | F. Ratsey-Woodroffe | 5 | 18 | 57 | 00 | 92 | 22 | 26 |
| 17 | *Chamois* | H.D. and A.D. Drake | 5 | 18 | 31 | 41 | 92 | 49 | 40 |
| 18 | *Shangri-La* | A. Costa | 5 | 19 | 38 | 28 | 93 | 15 | 09 |
| 19 | *Heyli* | H.O.J.C. Jonas | 5 | 18 | 13 | 04 | 93 | 40 | 12 |
| 20 | *Ben's Choice* | N. Jones and D.M. Jones | 5 | 19 | 04 | 04 | 93 | 43 | 04 |
| 21 | *Braganza* | HMS *Excellent* (Lt Cmdr J. Crisp) | 5 | 21 | 39 | 52 | 94 | 01 | 21 |
| 22 | *Trident* | Club Nautique Marine, Brest | 5 | 17 | 52 | 25 | 94 | 09 | 14 |
| 23 | *Margilic V* | Costantini-Tabarly | 5 | 20 | 55 | 02 | 95 | 40 | 08 |
| 24 | *Janessa* | Hon. Mrs R. Pitt-Rivers and M. Pitt-Rivers | 6 | 00 | 27 | 50 | 98 | 14 | 08 |
| 25 | *Faem* | C. Humphris and R. Farnham | 6 | 10 | 14 | 06 | 99 | 23 | 20 |
| 26 | *El Vigo* | Robert Lochner | 6 | 08 | 33 | 06 | 100 | 56 | 36 |
| 27 | *Capreolus* | Sir John Power | 6 | 09 | 14 | 00 | 102 | 42 | 45 |
| 28 | *Islay Mist* | T.M. Wilks | 6 | 09 | 36 | 22 | 102 | 54 | 03 |
| 29 | *Ilex II* | Royal Engineer Yacht Club (Brig. E.F. Parker) | 6 | 12 | 55 | 56 | 103 | 49 | 35 |
| 30 | *Zeehond* | W.B. Waterfall | 6 | 18 | 33 | 30 | 105 | 26 | 57 |
| 31 | *Aktaion* | J.N. Karreman | 6 | 20 | 06 | 30 | 107 | 34 | 23 |
| 32 | *Callisto* | R.E., J.C. and Mrs M. Davidson and C.T. Miller | 6 | 18 | 40 | 25 | 107 | 57 | 00 |
| 33 | *Annasona* | Royal Engineer Yacht Club (Maj. P. Brazier) | 6 | 22 | 03 | 00 | 109 | 38 | 35 |
| 34 | *Lundy Lady* | L.H. Alexander | 6 | 21 | 10 | 40 | 111 | 40 | 36 |
| | *Alcina* | Belge d'Equipages Course-Croisière (Dr R. Etienne) | DNF | | | | | | |
| | *Gunfleet* | L.B. Dyball | DNF | | | | | | |
| | *Meon Maid II* | Portsmouth Command | DNF | | | | | | |
| | *Micronette* | F. Britten and N. Norman | DNF | | | | | | |
| | *Mister Cube* | J.P.L. Glover | DNF | | | | | | |
| | *Moon River* | N.A. Fulton | DNF | | | | | | |
| | *Oberon* | Maj. G. Potter and G. Plum | DNF | | | | | | |
| | *Pequod* | A. Bruinsma | DNF | | | | | | |
| | *Rondinella* | V.A. Hounsell | DNF | | | | | | |

# 1965 (7 AUGUST)

| YACHT | OWNER (SAILED BY) | ELAPSED TIME days hr. mn. sc. | | | | CORRECTED TIME hr. mn. sc. | | |
|---|---|---|---|---|---|---|---|---|
| *Class I* | | | | | | | | |
| 1 *Quiver IV* | S.H.R. Clarke | 4 | 04 | 58 | 40 | 86 | 43 | 47 |
| 2 *Figaro* | William Snaith | 4 | 02 | 59 | 21 | 87 | 15 | 33 |
| 3 *Fanfare* | G.P. Pattinson | 4 | 09 | 04 | 40 | 89 | 41 | 40 |
| 4 *Al Na'ir III* | Dr A. Pierobon | 4 | 09 | 16 | 30 | 90 | 15 | 46 |
| 5 *Caper* | H. Irving Pratt | 4 | 03 | 08 | 13 | 90 | 20 | 01 |
| 6 *Gitana IV* | Baron E. de Rothschild | 3 | 09 | 40 | 00 | 90 | 42 | 55 |
| 7 *Zwerver* | O.L. van der Vorm | 4 | 04 | 53 | 33 | 91 | 45 | 41 |
| 8 *Giralda* | HRH The Count of Barcelona | 4 | 09 | 02 | 15 | 92 | 29 | 08 |
| 10 *Glénan* | Centre Nautique des Glénans | 4 | 12 | 58 | 16 | 93 | 48 | 47 |
| 11 *Anahita* | O. Berger | 4 | 10 | 23 | 35 | 94 | 51 | 37 |
| 12 *Musketeer* | Peter Green | 4 | 14 | 54 | 55 | 94 | 53 | 17 |
| 13 *Najade* | Kon-Mar. Yacht Club (Capt. R. van Wely, RNN) | 4 | 16 | 26 | 31 | 95 | 19 | 02 |
| 14 *Eloise II* | F. Hervé | 4 | 17 | 01 | 00 | 96 | 24 | 12 |
| 15 *Stiren* | D. Berthelin (A. Viant) | 4 | 15 | 38 | 10 | 96 | 34 | 35 |
| 16 *Shelmalier of Anglesey* | K.A. Wilby | 4 | 10 | 39 | 52 | 96 | 52 | 22 |
| 17 *Moonduster* | D.N. Doyle | 4 | 16 | 36 | 38 | 96 | 55 | 25 |
| 18 *Myth of Malham* | B. and D. Livingston | 4 | 18 | 17 | 45 | 97 | 08 | 24 |
| 19 *Sonata* | H.P. Goodbody | 4 | 16 | 20 | 10 | 97 | 12 | 56 |
| 20 *Witte Raaf* | Th. P. Tromp | 4 | 18 | 19 | 15 | 97 | 53 | 35 |
| 21 *Ortac* | Hamburg Sailing Club (D. Rost) | 4 | 17 | 58 | 35 | 98 | 23 | 03 |
| 22 *Griffin II* | Royal Ocean Racing Club (Lt Cmdr K.N. Hoare) | 4 | 18 | 24 | 28 | 98 | 24 | 29 |
| 23 *Evenlode* | H.V.L. Hall (Cmdr B. Baxter RNR) | 4 | 17 | 01 | 07 | 99 | 20 | 37 |
| 24 *Zulu* | B.A. Stewart | 4 | 19 | 50 | 06 | 99 | 23 | 11 |
| 25 *St Barbara* | Royal Artillery Yacht Club (Maj. J.E. Myatt) | 4 | 17 | 32 | 39 | 99 | 44 | 14 |
| 26 *China Clipper* | A.J.M. Miller | 4 | 20 | 07 | 13 | 100 | 16 | 11 |
| 26 *Lutine* | Lloyd's Yacht Club (K.H. Gross) | 4 | 13 | 33 | 22 | 100 | 35 | 00 |
| 27 *Drumbeat* | Sir Max Aitken | 4 | 17 | 15 | 11 | 101 | 23 | 03 |
| 28 *Springtime* | N.G. Watson | 4 | 23 | 36 | 06 | 101 | 52 | 37 |
| 29 *Marabu* | C.-in-C. Portsmouth (Cmdr J.H.L. Spill) | 4 | 17 | 16 | 31 | 104 | 28 | 26 |
| 30 *Ile de Feu* | A.F. Viant (Y. Guillerot) | 5 | 00 | 52 | 51 | 107 | 03 | 08 |
| *Aloha* | Capt. F. Kemmis Betty, RNR | DNF | | | | | | |
| *Outlaw* | G.R. Fuller | DNF | | | | | | |
| *Vagabonde* | G.A. Lindberg | DNF | | | | | | |
| *Class II* | | | | | | | | |
| 1 *Noryema IV* | R.W. Amey | 4 | 09 | 15 | 40 | 88 | 25 | 48 |
| 2 *Tonnerre de Breskens* | P.W. Vroon | 4 | 16 | 20 | 28 | 88 | 44 | 18 |
| 3 *Monk of Malham* | Capt. J. Illingworth and R. Degain | 4 | 16 | 19 | 13 | 90 | 10 | 55 |
| 4 *Prospect of Whitby* | Arthur Slater | 4 | 14 | 11 | 59 | 90 | 31 | 46 |
| 5 *Caprice of Huon* | G.W. Ingate | 4 | 13 | 51 | 56 | 90 | 44 | 08 |
| 6 *Whistler of Paget* | de Forest Trimingham | 4 | 18 | 10 | 37 | 90 | 59 | 16 |
| 7 *Tulla* | S. de Wit | 4 | 17 | 48 | 38 | 91 | 03 | 35 |
| 8 *Firebrand* | D.P. Miller | 4 | 16 | 10 | 20 | 91 | 12 | 26 |
| 9 *Honey* | H. Myrén | 4 | 17 | 42 | 22 | 91 | 14 | 16 |
| 10 *Bluejacket III* | David J. Maw | 4 | 16 | 08 | 05 | 91 | 23 | 23 |
| 11 *Freya* | T. and M. Halvorsen | 4 | 18 | 15 | 35 | 91 | 27 | 12 |
| 12 *Clarion* | Derek Boyer | 4 | 17 | 02 | 24 | 91 | 31 | 02 |
| 13 *Dambuster* | Royal Air Force Sailing Association | 4 | 17 | 11 | 33 | 91 | 39 | 07 |
| 14 *Casella* | Y. Cassel | 4 | 16 | 58 | 49 | 91 | 51 | 52 |
| 15 *Varna II* | F. Fournier | 4 | 17 | 20 | 20 | 92 | 01 | 53 |
| 16 *Yanica* | Dr J. Descamps | 4 | 18 | 22 | 02 | 92 | 06 | 41 |
| 17 *Armide* | Groupement des Equipages de Haute Mer | 4 | 20 | 35 | 24 | 92 | 21 | 45 |
| 18 *Rebel* | Frank King | 4 | 17 | 49 | 40 | 92 | 26 | 22 |
| 19 *Assegai II* | W.M. Vernon | 4 | 18 | 18 | 17 | 92 | 37 | 16 |
| 20 *Border Law* | J. Boardman | 4 | 15 | 49 | 54 | 92 | 38 | 28 |
| 21 *Fair Judgment III* | P.F. Carter-Ruck and Viscount Caldecote | 4 | 17 | 55 | 26 | 93 | 22 | 19 |
| 22 *Pen-Duick II* | E. Tabarly | 4 | 15 | 55 | 53 | 93 | 28 | 26 |

| YACHT | OWNER (SAILED BY) | ELAPSED TIME days hr. mn. sc. | | | | CORRECTED TIME hr. mn. sc. | | | |
|---|---|---|---|---|---|---|---|---|---|
| 23 Cervantes II | R.C. Watson | 4 | 20 | 32 | 37 | 93 | 57 | 27 | |
| 24 Matambu | D.E.P. Norton | 4 | 21 | 48 | 25 | 94 | 22 | 30 | |
| 25 Norlethe | L.B. Dyball | 4 | 18 | 41 | 59 | 94 | 44 | 31 | |
| 26 Margilic VI | M. Costantini | 4 | 21 | 00 | 41 | 95 | 02 | 53 | |
| 27 Windrose | J. Isbrandtsen | 4 | 16 | 39 | 25 | 95 | 11 | 42 | |
| 28 Parting Shot | Sir John Power and J.P. Whitehead | 4 | 22 | 22 | 23 | 95 | 42 | 59 | |
| 29 La Sybille | J.C. Simon | 4 | 21 | 09 | 17 | 95 | 44 | 19 | |
| 30 Bonaventura II | L.J.V. Lejeune | 4 | 20 | 56 | 54 | 96 | 02 | 16 | |
| 31 Hephzibah | Sir Maurice Laing | 4 | 22 | 22 | 21 | 96 | 24 | 52 | |
| 32 Staika IV | S. Rodén | 4 | 22 | 39 | 49 | 96 | 40 | 30 | |
| 33 Salamander of Parkstone | A.W.G. and G. Lockyer | 5 | 01 | 50 | 46 | 96 | 54 | 15 | |
| 34 Oisin | S. O'Mara | 5 | 02 | 51 | 15 | 97 | 02 | 33 | |
| 35 Cockade | J.D. Boswell | 4 | 19 | 30 | 16 | 97 | 15 | 18 | |
| 36 Corina | J. Chomé | 5 | 04 | 33 | 59 | 98 | 54 | 21 | |
| 37 Rampage | Lt Col. The Lord Burnham | 5 | 03 | 47 | 31 | 101 | 38 | 44 | |
| 38 Ar-Men II | Dr A. Auclair | 5 | 09 | 27 | 27 | 103 | 11 | 20 | |
| 39 Gawaine | Royal Naval Engineering College (S/Lt I.E. Craig) | 5 | 04 | 55 | 58 | 103 | 14 | 40 | |
| 40 Galahad | Royal Naval Engineering College (Lt Cmdr W.B. Stawell) | 5 | 05 | 04 | 57 | 103 | 25 | 06 | |
| 41 Pas Seul | T.I., R.A.D.C. and Miss A.G. Perkins | 5 | 09 | 33 | 32 | 103 | 30 | 16 | |
| 42 Firedancer | D.S. Cottell | 5 | 10 | 39 | 59 | 105 | 25 | 17 | |
| 43 Alchemy of Wight | B.V. Richardson | 5 | 19 | 34 | 23 | 111 | 19 | 24 | |
| 44 Ariadne | H. Vogeler (K. Oldenburg) | 5 | 20 | 19 | 21 | 111 | 30 | 51 | |
| 45 Thea | B.A. Passmore | 5 | 18 | 35 | 50 | 112 | 02 | 32 | |
| 46 Sundew | A.E. Goodfellow | 6 | 01 | 10 | 43 | 115 | 13 | 12 | |
| 47 Bootlegger | David Bowen | 6 | 10 | 52 | 30 | 123 | 49 | 21 | |
| 48 Popinjay | Capt. the Lord Teynham RN | 6 | 17 | 59 | 34 | 135 | 12 | 55 | |

Class III

| YACHT | OWNER (SAILED BY) | ELAPSED TIME days hr. mn. sc. | | | | CORRECTED TIME hr. mn. sc. | | | |
|---|---|---|---|---|---|---|---|---|---|
| 1 Rabbit | R.E. Carter | 4 | 18 | 33 | 12 | 86 | 01 | 46 | (1st overall) |
| 2 Camille of Seaforth | R. Swanson | 4 | 17 | 25 | 56 | 89 | 31 | 45 | |
| 3 Green Highlander | T.C. Chadwick | 5 | 00 | 54 | 18 | 90 | 27 | 40 | |
| 4 Lorita Maria | Norman Rydge | 4 | 19 | 46 | 06 | 90 | 40 | 11 | |
| 5 Alcatraz | Guy Dewavrin (A. Gliksman) | 4 | 22 | 35 | 09 | 91 | 11 | 34 | |
| 6 Daïquiri | J.G. Edmiston (N.P. Edmiston) | 4 | 21 | 03 | 30 | 91 | 28 | 10 | |
| 7 Belmore II | T.W.M. Steele | 4 | 19 | 54 | 12 | 91 | 30 | 20 | |
| 8 Monsunen III | A. Eliasson | 4 | 21 | 16 | 16 | 91 | 33 | 12 | |
| 9 Belmore | S. Königson | 4 | 21 | 31 | 13 | 91 | 37 | 49 | |
| 10 Pristis II | Dr J. Clavreul | 4 | 21 | 00 | 27 | 91 | 41 | 55 | |
| 11 Fervent | L. Vanek | 5 | 00 | 43 | 34 | 91 | 50 | 55 | |
| 12 Brigantine | B. Moureau and P. Mulot | 4 | 20 | 50 | 18 | 91 | 51 | 29 | |
| 13 Pen Ar Bed II | P. Lemaire | 5 | 03 | 01 | 02 | 92 | 09 | 07 | |
| 14 Cohoe III | K. Adlard Coles | 5 | 00 | 18 | 36 | 92 | 29 | 40 | |
| 15 Griselidis | J.M.P. Challe | 5 | 00 | 03 | 50 | 93 | 48 | 22 | |
| 16 Andorran | D. Edwards and Lord Chelmer | 5 | 06 | 20 | 30 | 93 | 48 | 31 | |
| 17 Fabius | Tom Smith | 5 | 03 | 27 | 40 | 94 | 18 | 43 | |
| 18 Gerfaut | C. and P. Renot | 4 | 23 | 30 | 46 | 94 | 22 | 45 | |
| 19 Aladdin | E.G. van de Stadt | 5 | 04 | 59 | 57 | 94 | 32 | 58 | |
| 20 Blue Saluki | Royal Naval Sailing Association (S/Lt J. Williams) | 5 | 05 | 02 | 00 | 96 | 34 | 33 | |
| 21 Marelle | Mrs H.E. Spink | 5 | 04 | 05 | 57 | 96 | 38 | 10 | |
| 22 Electron of Portsea | HMS Collingwood | 5 | 05 | 04 | 36 | 97 | 01 | 19 | |
| 23 Aimee | J.F. and K.G. Richardson | 5 | 05 | 31 | 17 | 97 | 56 | 40 | |
| 24 Summertime | P.C.P. Johnson | 5 | 10 | 33 | 51 | 98 | 34 | 33 | |
| 25 Tjaldur | Dr R.H. O'Hanlon | 5 | 06 | 39 | 05 | 99 | 04 | 00 | |
| 26 Heyli | H.O.J.C. Jonas | 5 | 07 | 46 | 27 | 99 | 22 | 13 | |
| 27 Oberon | W.B. Waterfall | 5 | 07 | 41 | 25 | 99 | 50 | 28 | |
| 28 Guarantee | Dr I. Kinross | 5 | 08 | 55 | 23 | 100 | 08 | 04 | |
| 29 Winwilloe of Portlemouth | N.W. Jephcott | 5 | 14 | 20 | 53 | 101 | 41 | 17 | |
| 30 Sweet Reason | R.G. Hill | 5 | 18 | 00 | 55 | 102 | 31 | 54 | |
| 31 Jouster | J.A.W. Bush and H.B. Walford | 5 | 15 | 33 | 50 | 103 | 12 | 18 | |
| 32 Vashti | L. Doble | 5 | 13 | 00 | 00 | 103 | 39 | 37 | |

| YACHT | OWNER (SAILED BY) | ELAPSED TIME days hr. mn. sc. | | | | CORRECTED TIME hr. mn. sc. | | |
|---|---|---|---|---|---|---|---|---|
| 33 *Mowgli* | D.M. and Q.J. Jones | 5 | 15 | 47 | 06 | 103 | 41 | 56 |
| 34 *Caper B* | R.J. Ogle | 5 | 19 | 24 | 27 | 105 | 26 | 53 |
| 35 *Edelweiss* | Dr P. Arnaud | 5 | 19 | 53 | 08 | 105 | 31 | 46 |
| 36 *Goblet* | Col. and Mrs K. Wylie and Brig. E.F. Parker | 5 | 19 | 27 | 16 | 105 | 41 | 34 |
| 37 *Taranto* | Naval Air Command Sailing Association | 5 | 19 | 04 | 51 | 105 | 52 | 05 |
| 38 *Pen Dir* | ECC-TA | 5 | 19 | 52 | 05 | 106 | 00 | 22 |
| 39 *Chin Blu II* | J. Tible | 5 | 20 | 04 | 27 | 106 | 30 | 45 |
| 40 *Zeenar* | T.H. Bevan | 5 | 22 | 36 | 52 | 106 | 46 | 31 |
| 41 *Liz of Lymington* | Mr and Mrs P.J.B. Webster | 5 | 19 | 55 | 10 | 106 | 49 | 43 |
| 42 *Rockaby* | C.P. Murch | 5 | 19 | 35 | 00 | 106 | 56 | 55 |
| 43 *Zita VII* | J. Broberg | 5 | 19 | 46 | 54 | 107 | 02 | 42 |
| 44 *Trident* | Marine Nationale | 5 | 17 | 44 | 58 | 107 | 09 | 20 |
| 45 *Sandettie* | James N. White | 5 | 19 | 57 | 10 | 107 | 34 | 03 |
| 46 *Mistress* | V. de Goede | 5 | 19 | 55 | 40 | 107 | 35 | 26 |
| 47 *Islay Mist* | T.M. Wilks | 5 | 19 | 27 | 11 | 107 | 36 | 07 |
| 48 *Ilex II* | Royal Engineer Yacht Club (Maj. J.B. Hackford) | 5 | 20 | 01 | 18 | 107 | 39 | 46 |
| 49 *Forerunner* | G.E.N. Mason Elliott | 5 | 21 | 45 | 05 | 107 | 41 | 18 |
| 50 *Wayfarer of Emsworth* | P.G. Crompton (G. Greenfield) | 5 | 17 | 45 | 30 | 107 | 44 | 26 |
| 51 *Callisto* | R.E.J.C., M.C. Davidson and C. Miller | 5 | 22 | 51 | 35 | 107 | 46 | 24 |
| 52 *Pen Ar Bed* | F. Theuveny | 6 | 01 | 33 | 37 | 107 | 55 | 58 |
| 53 *Temeraire* | Britannia Royal Naval College | 5 | 18 | 09 | 10 | 107 | 58 | 00 |
| 54 *Blue Charm* | D.E. Cook and J.M. Barr | 6 | 00 | 21 | 15 | 108 | 47 | 07 |
| 55 *Greenfly* | J.W. Roome and H.B. Bicket | 5 | 19 | 54 | 31 | 108 | 55 | 58 |
| 56 *Foggy Dew* | M.J. Gilkes | 5 | 21 | 51 | 55 | 110 | 04 | 24 |
| 57 *Lundy Lady* | L.H. Alexander | 5 | 23 | 45 | 40 | 110 | 06 | 24 |
| 58 *Lugo* | E.W. Dorrell | 6 | 03 | 35 | 15 | 110 | 14 | 00 |
| 59 *Sarie Marais* | Royal Marines Sailing Club | 6 | 01 | 17 | 30 | 110 | 47 | 06 |
| 60 *Akka* | H. Asselbergs | 6 | 04 | 45 | 45 | 111 | 33 | 25 |
| 61 *Lancer of Mersea* | R.R. Clifford | 6 | 05 | 19 | 15 | 113 | 28 | 08 |
| 62 *St George of England* | Royal Corps of Transport Yacht Club | 6 | 05 | 03 | 57 | 113 | 42 | 27 |
| 63 *Colbart* | M.A. Boitard | 6 | 05 | 55 | 25 | 114 | 03 | 43 |
| 64 *Sereine* | Centre Nautique des Glénans | 6 | 03 | 13 | 05 | 115 | 33 | 58 |
| 65 *Alcina* | ABEC | 6 | 08 | 16 | 34 | 115 | 45 | 38 |
| 66 *Katic II* | P. le Guillermic | 6 | 06 | 27 | 20 | 116 | 53 | 20 |
| 67 *King's Ransom* | C.J. Oliver | 6 | 12 | 06 | 05 | 120 | 02 | 31 |
| 68 *Gauntlet* | Royal Naval Engineering College, Manadon | 6 | 18 | 27 | 03 | 125 | 50 | 03 |
| *Francesca* | Cmdr C.J.W. Simpson | DNF | | | | | | |
| *Midship-Ca* | Club Nautique de l'Ecole Navale | DNF | | | | | | |

# 1967 (5 AUGUST)

## Class I

| | YACHT | OWNER | ELAPSED TIME | | | CORRECTED TIME | | | |
|---|---|---|---|---|---|---|---|---|---|
| 1 | *Pen-Duick III* | E. Tabarly | 87 | 54 | 10 | 78 | 39 | 19 | (*1st overall*) |
| 2 | *Figaro IV* | William Snaith | 92 | 38 | 05 | 81 | 04 | 16 | |
| 3 | *Balandra* | R. Crichton-Brown | 97 | 32 | 55 | 83 | 07 | 51 | |
| 4 | *Outlaw* | G.R. Fuller | 94 | 47 | 56 | 83 | 15 | 43 | |
| 5 | *Rubin* | H.-O. Schumann | 96 | 20 | 55 | 83 | 25 | 07 | |
| 6 | *Oryx* | F. Bouygues | 96 | 28 | 30 | 83 | 46 | 01 | |
| 7 | *Carina* | R.S. Nye | 95 | 49 | 10 | 84 | 00 | 52 | |
| 8 | *Levantades* | G. Diano | 96 | 18 | 55 | 85 | 02 | 47 | |
| 9 | *Thunderbird* | T.V. Learson | 101 | 19 | 41 | 85 | 05 | 43 | |
| 10 | *Noryema V* | R.A. Amey | 102 | 10 | 40 | 85 | 46 | 42 | |
| 11 | *Quiver IV* | S.H.R. Clarke | 101 | 03 | 38 | 85 | 54 | 05 | |
| 12 | *Bohemia* | L. Milton | 102 | 52 | 15 | 88 | 02 | 13 | |
| 13 | *Diana II* | D. Monheim | 100 | 44 | 55 | 91 | 39 | 04 | |
| 14 | *Glenan* | Centre Nautique des Glénans | 108 | 26 | 10 | 92 | 45 | 22 | |
| 15 | *Moonduster* | D.N. Doyle | 109 | 19 | 45 | 93 | 10 | 52 | |
| 16 | *Gitana IV* | Baron E. de Rothschild | 89 | 05 | 10 | 96 | 42 | 43 | |
| 17 | *Kittiwake* | H.B. Simson | 124 | 34 | 13 | 105 | 31 | 25 | |
| 18 | *Jan Pott III* | N. Lorck-Schierning | 123 | 02 | 00 | 106 | 39 | 27 | |

| YACHT | OWNER (SAILED BY) | ELAPSED TIME | | | CORRECTED TIME | | |
|---|---|---|---|---|---|---|---|
| | | hr. | mn. | sc. | hr. | mn. | sc. |
| 19 Zulu | B.A. Stewart | 125 | 23 | 22 | 107 | 10 | 13 |
| 20 Marie-Christine III | J.-C. Menu | 129 | 54 | 10 | 109 | 17 | 14 |
| 21 Elske | A.J. Wullschleger | 130 | 08 | 45 | 110 | 35 | 06 |
| 22 Chevalier | E.G. Marshall | 131 | 43 | 00 | 112 | 07 | 49 |
| 23 Zest of Hamble | E.J. Haddon | 134 | 03 | 29 | 112 | 32 | 30 |
| 24 Najade | Kon-Mar Yacht Club (Cmdr H.M. Juta) | 134 | 39 | 02 | 113 | 34 | 40 |
| 25 Hamburg VII | N.R.V. (H.F. Stichert) | 129 | 53 | 55 | 113 | 48 | 15 |
| 26 Wappen von Bremen | Segelkameradschaft das Wappen von Bremen | 129 | 48 | 51 | 114 | 03 | 17 |
| 27 Witte Raaf | Th. P. Tromp | 133 | 51 | 30 | 114 | 11 | 49 |
| 28 Avrion | R. Cassou | 129 | 51 | 08 | 115 | 40 | 20 |
| 29 Atao | G. Bertho | 137 | 50 | 06 | 115 | 45 | 14 |
| 30 Lutine | Lloyd's Yacht Club (K.H. Cross) | 129 | 46 | 21 | 118 | 49 | 58 |
| 31 Fanfare | Royal Ocean Racing Club (Capt. P. Dane) | 132 | 59 | 02 | 119 | 24 | 00 |
| Stiren | D. Berthelin | DNF | | | | | |
| Striana | Dr J. Auclair | DNF | | | | | |

### Class II(a)

| YACHT | OWNER (SAILED BY) | ELAPSED TIME | | | CORRECTED TIME | | |
|---|---|---|---|---|---|---|---|
| 1 Mercedes III | H.T. Kaufman | 102 | 08 | 40 | 82 | 04 | 23 |
| 2 Caprice of Huon | G. Reynolds | 102 | 28 | 45 | 84 | 35 | 11 |
| 3 Firebrand | D.P. Miller | 104 | 58 | 20 | 84 | 49 | 41 |
| 4 Can-Can III | E. Kindberg (B. Willenius) | 122 | 15 | 40 | 98 | 28 | 53 |
| 5 Lygaia | P. Herlin | 122 | 30 | 44 | 99 | 30 | 16 |
| 6 Assegai II | W.M. Vernon | 123 | 22 | 24 | 99 | 45 | 35 |
| 7 Gerfaut II | C. and P. Renot | 123 | 46 | 29 | 100 | 29 | 34 |
| 8 Zinganee | E.S. Moore III | 123 | 24 | 40 | 101 | 27 | 23 |
| 9 Prospect of Whitby | Arthur Slater | 125 | 36 | 25 | 101 | 41 | 29 |
| 10 Border Law | J. Boardman | 125 | 14 | 20 | 103 | 37 | 22 |
| 11 Bluejacket III | David J. Maw | 129 | 17 | 32 | 103 | 53 | 11 |
| 12 Tulla | S. de Wit | 130 | 26 | 46 | 104 | 21 | 25 |
| 13 Eva II | A. Lindqvist | 129 | 45 | 54 | 104 | 37 | 46 |
| 14 Artako | J.M. de Gamboa | 129 | 15 | 33 | 104 | 45 | 06 |
| 15 Jaynor | I. Selig | 125 | 06 | 27 | 104 | 51 | 09 |
| 16 Christina II | Dr P.F. Chambonnet | 129 | 32 | 23 | 105 | 15 | 50 |
| 17 Clarion of Wight | Sir Maurice Laing | 130 | 27 | 49 | 106 | 09 | 30 |
| 18 Fionnuala | Ross Courtney | 130 | 26 | 20 | 106 | 24 | 43 |
| 19 Tamure | G. Chaillet and R.McG. Nell | 130 | 49 | 06 | 107 | 00 | 34 |
| 20 St Barbara II | Royal Artillery Yacht Club | 132 | 22 | 07 | 107 | 29 | 48 |
| 21 St David's Light | S. Gates | 134 | 39 | 51 | 107 | 43 | 53 |
| 22 Gentilhomme de Fortune | D.M.H. Moureau | 134 | 21 | 10 | 107 | 53 | 55 |
| 23 Dambuster | Royal Air Force Sailing Association (Fl. Lt A.I. Morgan) | 134 | 16 | 25 | 108 | 43 | 17 |
| 24 Cervantes | R.C. Watson | 135 | 28 | 02 | 109 | 12 | 49 |
| 25 Bonaventura II | L. Lejeune | 135 | 16 | 10 | 110 | 25 | 16 |
| 26 Norlethe | L.B. Dyball | 133 | 59 | 27 | 110 | 49 | 26 |
| 27 Wish Stream | Royal Military Academy Sailing Club | 138 | 48 | 00 | 111 | 40 | 43 |
| 28 Pierrette III | W.P.J.M. Pierrot | 129 | 55 | 30 | 112 | 59 | 52 |
| 29 Tyressa | A.E. Goodfellow | 139 | 12 | 55 | 113 | 28 | 28 |
| 30 Gawaine | Royal Naval Engineering College (S/Lt K. Humphries RN) | 137 | 35 | 11 | 113 | 42 | 05 |
| 31 Galahad | Royal Naval Engineering College (S/Lt N. Mallard, RN) | 139 | 32 | 35 | 116 | 35 | 51 |
| Margaret Lindsay | B. Bullough | DNF | | | | | |
| Margilic VI | M. Costantini | DNF | | | | | |
| Monk of Malham | Capt. J. Illingworth and R. Degain | DNF | | | | | |
| Musette | L.J. Last | DNF | | | | | |

| YACHT | OWNER (SAILED BY) | ELAPSED TIME | | | CORRECTED TIME | | |
|---|---|---|---|---|---|---|---|
| | | hr. | mn. | sc. | hr. | mn. | sc. |

*Class II(b)*

| YACHT | OWNER (SAILED BY) | hr. | mn. | sc. | hr. | mn. | sc. |
|---|---|---|---|---|---|---|---|
| 1 *Spirit* | G.C. Kidkaddon | 110 | 56 | 48 | 88 | 18 | 49 |
| 2 *Rabbit II* | R.E. Carter | 119 | 32 | 35 | 95 | 17 | 16 |
| 3 *Tonnerre de Breskens* | P.W. Vroon | 130 | 24 | 42 | 101 | 01 | 01 |
| 4 *Deb* | E. Barker | 130 | 06 | 10 | 103 | 21 | 13 |
| 5 *Zeezot van Veere* | P.W. Deerns (W.F.P. Deerns) | 139 | 34 | 00 | 103 | 32 | 12 |
| 6 *Cohoe III* | K. Adlard Coles | 134 | 10 | 45 | 103 | 59 | 20 |
| 7 *Heyli* | H.O.J.C. Jonas | 135 | 19 | 42 | 105 | 14 | 41 |
| 8 *Blue Saluki* | D.D. Matthews and P. Bathurst | 135 | 18 | 26 | 105 | 19 | 23 |
| 9 *Vamp of Hamble* | Maj. D. Walter and Capt. D. Carey | 135 | 29 | 20 | 105 | 36 | 00 |
| 10 *Armide* | Société GEHM | 135 | 01 | 02 | 105 | 40 | 41 |
| 11 *Unda-Maris* | Dr E. Westendorf | 134 | 47 | 10 | 105 | 54 | 54 |
| 12 *Camelot of Wessex* | R.W. Lawes | 134 | 34 | 10 | 106 | 12 | 56 |
| 13 *Wayfarer of Emsworth* | P.G. Crompton (G.G. Greenfield) | 135 | 51 | 24 | 106 | 15 | 13 |
| 14 *Tiderace* | D.E.P. Norton | 135 | 00 | 08 | 106 | 26 | 09 |
| 15 *Oberon* | W.B. Waterfall | 137 | 07 | 41 | 106 | 34 | 33 |
| 16 *Fram* | Maj. Sir Derrick Gunston | 137 | 17 | 52 | 106 | 51 | 32 |
| 17 *Guinevere* | Royal Naval Engineering College (Lt Cmdr J. Crisp, RN) | 137 | 22 | 37 | 107 | 05 | 07 |
| 18 *Arauna* | A. Pelletier | 137 | 58 | 56 | 107 | 05 | 17 |
| 19 *Guarantee* | Dr I. Kinross | 138 | 18 | 22 | 107 | 07 | 55 |
| 20 *Stargazer* | R. Dreschfield | 136 | 48 | 58 | 107 | 52 | 46 |
| 21 *Temeraire* | Britannia Royal Naval College | 138 | 12 | 02 | 107 | 58 | 34 |
| 22 *Tyrovic* | Royal Naval Barracks, Portsmouth | 139 | 15 | 50 | 108 | 03 | 17 |
| 23 *Zeenar II* | T.H. Bevan | 137 | 59 | 45 | 108 | 08 | 01 |
| 24 *Griffon* | E.C.C.-T.A. | 135 | 49 | 54 | 108 | 37 | 29 |
| 25 *Similou II* | R. Feldmann | 136 | 46 | 12 | 109 | 19 | 13 |
| 26 *Karmatan II* | J. Balleste | 137 | 57 | 42 | 109 | 51 | 32 |
| 27 *Flarepath* | E.P.J. Scanlan | 142 | 21 | 00 | 111 | 20 | 46 |
| *Whistler of Paget* | deForest W. Trimingham | DNF | | | | | |

*Class III(a)*

| YACHT | OWNER (SAILED BY) | hr. | mn. | sc. | hr. | mn. | sc. |
|---|---|---|---|---|---|---|---|
| 1 *Esprit de Rueil* | A. Viant and E. Jaupart | 122 | 38 | 12 | 94 | 11 | 06 |
| 2 *Clarionet* | D.J. Boyer | 123 | 08 | 14 | 94 | 39 | 20 |
| 3 *De Schelde II* | Royal YC de Belgique | 123 | 28 | 50 | 94 | 55 | 55 |
| 4 *Roundabout* | Sir Max Aitken and R.T. Lowein | 124 | 59 | 08 | 96 | 00 | 05 |
| 5 *Joran* | J. Berger | 128 | 49 | 21 | 99 | 01 | 33 |
| 6 *Wathara II* | Bruce E. Cameron | 128 | 55 | 11 | 99 | 07 | 35 |
| 7 *L'Orgueil IV* | G. des Moutis | 130 | 15 | 09 | 100 | 05 | 57 |
| 8 *Breeze of Yorkshire* | K.G. Richardson | 132 | 31 | 05 | 101 | 47 | 14 |
| 9 *Fairwain* | J. Schutter | 134 | 07 | 11 | 102 | 28 | 03 |
| 10 *Chamois* | A.D. and H.D. Drake | 137 | 03 | 26 | 104 | 01 | 35 |
| 11 *Jouster* | J.A. Bush and H.B. Walford | 136 | 56 | 27 | 104 | 15 | 11 |
| 12 *Electron of Portsea* | HMS *Collingwood* (Lt D. Stracey Clitherow) | 135 | 22 | 52 | 104 | 22 | 44 |
| 13 *Ilex II* | Royal Engineer Yacht Club | 137 | 38 | 03 | 104 | 22 | 54 |
| 14 *Trident* | Club Nautique de la Marine, Brest | 136 | 36 | 31 | 104 | 43 | 30 |
| 15 *Forerunner II* | G.E.N. Mason Elliott | 136 | 59 | 42 | 105 | 05 | 20 |
| 16 *Mowgli* | D.M. and Q.J. Jones | 138 | 02 | 43 | 105 | 25 | 31 |
| 17 *Freemerle* | Brig. P.O.G. Wakeham | 138 | 42 | 05 | 105 | 35 | 36 |
| 18 *Reder-Mor VI* | P. Lavollée | 138 | 02 | 56 | 106 | 07 | 55 |
| 19 *St George of England* | Royal Corps of Transport Yacht Club | 139 | 21 | 59 | 106 | 15 | 11 |
| 20 *Matchless* | Lt Cmdr T.P.G. Poland | 138 | 26 | 37 | 106 | 20 | 19 |
| 21 *Midship-Ca* | C.N. de Ecole Navale | 138 | 31 | 24 | 106 | 41 | 26 |
| 22 *Gioconda* | M.A. Gaze | 140 | 55 | 45 | 108 | 17 | 24 |
| 23 *Vain-Lady* | L.G. Goodfellow | 142 | 36 | 55 | 108 | 29 | 15 |
| 24 *Susanna* | D.M. Sterans | 146 | 54 | 10 | 112 | 14 | 54 |
| *Tikerak* | ABEC (G. van der Hofstadt) | DNF | | | | | |
| *Tina* | E.R. Stettinius | DNF | | | | | |

*Class III(b)*

| YACHT | OWNER (SAILED BY) | hr. | mn. | sc. | hr. | mn. | sc. |
|---|---|---|---|---|---|---|---|
| 1 *Rustler of Wessex* | D. Parker (M.R. Baxter) | 134 | 51 | 28 | 101 | 00 | 31 |
| 2 *Coquelicot* | Groupe Internationale des Croiseurs | 133 | 54 | 34 | 101 | 08 | 30 |
| 3 *Andorran* | D. Edwards and Lord Chelmer | 136 | 33 | 41 | 101 | 23 | 49 |

| YACHT | OWNER (SAILED BY) | ELAPSED TIME _hr. mn. sc._ | | | CORRECTED TIME _hr. mn. sc._ | | |
|---|---|---|---|---|---|---|---|
| 4 *Winwilloe of Portlemouth* | N.W. Jephcott | 134 | 21 | 35 | 101 | 33 | 45 |
| 5 *Belita's Rabbit* | J.S. Bouman | 135 | 23 | 54 | 101 | 41 | 03 |
| 6 *Contrail* | Royal Air Force Sailing Association | 135 | 24 | 05 | 101 | 50 | 07 |
| 7 *Green Highlander* | T.C. Chadwick | 137 | 15 | 24 | 102 | 31 | 51 |
| 8 *Vaudair* | P.J. Clowes | 140 | 30 | 02 | 103 | 59 | 55 |
| 9 *Summertime* | P.C.P. Johnson | 138 | 55 | 33 | 104 | 04 | 10 |
| 10 *Baloo* | J.C. Haeffner | 138 | 49 | 02 | 104 | 15 | 56 |
| 11 *Midnight* | R.H. Brann | 138 | 16 | 50 | 104 | 29 | 55 |
| 12 *Annasona* | Royal Engineer Yacht Club | 138 | 43 | 15 | 104 | 35 | 44 |
| 13 *Strider* | Russell Anstey | 138 | 35 | 50 | 105 | 00 | 05 |
| 14 *Blaze* | W. Jackson | 140 | 56 | 30 | 106 | 08 | 35 |
| 15 *Sarie Marais* | Royal Marines Sailing Club (Lt H.J. Wiltshire, RM) | 141 | 57 | 00 | 107 | 28 | 13 |
| *Aquilon* | Dr P. Bouyssou | DNF | | | | | |
| *Pen Dir* | ECC-TA | DNF | | | | | |

# 1969 (9 AUGUST)

*Class I*

| YACHT | OWNER (SAILED BY) | ELAPSED TIME | | | CORRECTED TIME | | |
|---|---|---|---|---|---|---|---|
| 1 *Crusade* | Sir Max Aitken and R.T. Lowein | 95 | 25 | 20 | 91 | 39 | 45 |
| 2 *Ragamuffin* | S. Fischer | 108 | 03 | 25 | 92 | 54 | 26 |
| 3 *American Eagle* | R.E. Turner III | 88 | 58 | 00 | 93 | 16 | 22 |
| 4 *Kialoa II* | John B. Kilroy | 89 | 02 | 10 | 94 | 21 | 38 |
| 5 *Carina* | Richard S. Nye | 108 | 41 | 20 | 94 | 36 | 49 |
| 6 *Phantom* | G.P. Pattinson | 112 | 51 | 15 | 95 | 19 | 40 |
| 7 *Levantades* | G. Diano | 110 | 31 | 10 | 96 | 16 | 25 |
| 8 *Noryema VII* | R.W. Amey | 109 | 57 | 10 | 96 | 22 | 25 |
| 9 *Coriolan* | C. de Galéa | 108 | 35 | 10 | 97 | 44 | 18 |
| 10 *Palawan* | T.J. Watson, Jr | 103 | 55 | 35 | 97 | 56 | 25 |
| 11 *Fortuna* | Argentine Naval Academy (Capt. A. Heredia) | 103 | 28 | 25 | 97 | 59 | 59 |
| 12 *Rubin* | H.-O. Schümann | 113 | 30 | 10 | 98 | 18 | 58 |
| 13 *Pacha* | F. Bouygues | 111 | 02 | 00 | 98 | 49 | 11 |
| 14 *Stormy* | K. Bruynzeel | 112 | 20 | 00 | 102 | 33 | 37 |
| 15 *Quiver V* | S.H.R. Clarke | 121 | 22 | 20 | 102 | 35 | 45 |
| 16 *Diana II* | D. Monheim | 113 | 34 | 30 | 102 | 43 | 43 |
| 17 *Moonduster* | D.N. Doyle | 134 | 41 | 25 | 114 | 47 | 47 |
| 18 *Kuenda* | A.F.A. Acevedo | 134 | 49 | 00 | 119 | 28 | 28 |
| 19 *Glenan* | C.N. des Glénans | 145 | 47 | 55 | 121 | 01 | 39 |
| 20 *Blithe Spirit* | Forbes Morse | 144 | 21 | 45 | 122 | 02 | 39 |
| 21 *Oryx* | Société ORYX | 145 | 47 | 16 | 123 | 23 | 41 |
| 22 *Voortrekker* | South African Ocean Racing Trust | 137 | 07 | 10 | 123 | 40 | 05 |
| 23 *Kittiwake* | H.B. Simson | 147 | 12 | 35 | 124 | 31 | 29 |
| 24 *Elske* | A.J. Wullschleger | 147 | 29 | 21 | 124 | 52 | 45 |
| 25 *Musketeer* | P.J.F. Green | 146 | 54 | 41 | 125 | 14 | 31 |
| 26 *Griffin III* | Royal Ocean Racing Club (Maj. H. Bruce, RM) | 147 | 49 | 52 | 126 | 16 | 38 |
| 27 *Shearwater* | Dr. G.H.A. Clowes, Jr | 147 | 20 | 16 | 126 | 39 | 06 |
| 28 *Jaynor* | Ivan I. Selig | 151 | 46 | 01 | 127 | 19 | 57 |
| 29 *Najade* | Kon-Mar. Yacht Club (Lt T.R. Deelder, RNN) | 152 | 47 | 44 | 127 | 51 | 33 |
| 30 *Adele* | R.M. Burnes | 151 | 23 | 17 | 128 | 09 | 00 |
| 31 *Foolscap* | A.B. Hanson | 151 | 22 | 47 | 128 | 18 | 34 |
| 32 *Gabrielle III* | P.R. Sandwell | 147 | 18 | 52 | 128 | 33 | 41 |
| 33 *Zulu* | B.A. Stewart | 152 | 46 | 52 | 128 | 36 | 40 |
| 34 *Hamburg VII* | NRV (U. Ernst) | 148 | 56 | 30 | 129 | 25 | 49 |
| 35 *Myth of Malham* | N.T.J. Bevan | 153 | 40 | 48 | 129 | 45 | 07 |
| 36 *Outlaw* | Brig. P.O.G. Wakeham | 147 | 51 | 54 | 130 | 27 | 41 |
| 37 *Griffin II* | Maj. J. Masterman and partners | 154 | 09 | 10 | 130 | 52 | 32 |
| 38 *Gallant* | F. King and K. Geddes | 148 | 52 | 18 | 131 | 13 | 49 |
| 39 *Spirit of Cutty Sark* | Lt J.R.L. Williams, RN (RNSA) | 150 | 52 | 30 | 132 | 43 | 29 |
| 40 *Xanadu II* | E. Bates McKee | 152 | 02 | 37 | 133 | 30 | 34 |
| 41 *Alaunt of Corfe* | R.C. Sharples, MP | 151 | 58 | 31 | 134 | 43 | 34 |

| YACHT | OWNER (SAILED BY) | ELAPSED TIME | | | CORRECTED TIME | | | |
|---|---|---|---|---|---|---|---|---|
| | | hr. | mn. | sc. | hr. | mn. | sc. | |
| 42 Shelmalier of Anglesey | G.R. Fuller | 151 | 13 | 10 | 136 | 25 | 48 | |
| 43 Aglaia | A.E. Edwards | 154 | 27 | 48 | 136 | 33 | 40 | |
| 44 Evenlode | H.V.L. Hall (D.J.L. Hall) | 157 | 51 | 43 | 137 | 02 | 24 | |
| 45 Sauvage III | J.R. Goiot | 151 | 33 | 37 | 139 | 58 | 52 | |
| 46 Sir Thomas Lipton | G.J. Williams | 150 | 24 | 51 | 140 | 58 | 59 | |
| Drumbeat | Maj. D. Walter | DNF | | | | | | |
| Stella Polare | Italian Navy | DNF | | | | | | |

Class II(a)

| YACHT | OWNER (SAILED BY) | ELAPSED TIME | | | CORRECTED TIME | | | |
|---|---|---|---|---|---|---|---|---|
| 1 Red Rooster | R.E. Carter | 113 | 35 | 20 | 91 | 38 | 37 | (1st overall) |
| 2 Mabelle | S. Zaffagni | 115 | 29 | 00 | 95 | 51 | 46 | |
| 3 Prospect of Whitby | Arthur Slater | 122 | 39 | 40 | 98 | 25 | 24 | |
| 4 Runn | M. Berner | 132 | 30 | 01 | 108 | 55 | 42 | |
| 5 Casse Tete III | | | | | | | | |
| 6 Mersea Oyster | D.M. Powell | 137 | 19 | 45 | 109 | 52 | 37 | |
| 7 Gabriella | A. Lindqvist | 134 | 00 | 10 | 111 | 24 | 36 | |
| 8 Wizard of Paget | De Forest Trimingham | 142 | 22 | 44 | 114 | 45 | 27 | |
| 9 Zeezot van Veere | P.W. Deerns (W.F.P. Deerns) | 141 | 48 | 42 | 115 | 24 | 23 | |
| 10 Brambers | A.W. Barr | 141 | 13 | 10 | 115 | 51 | 23 | |
| 11 La Meloria | Mrs M. Pera | 141 | 21 | 06 | 116 | 02 | 08 | |
| 12 Mercedes III | H.T. Kaufman | 145 | 11 | 52 | 116 | 09 | 30 | |
| 13 Koomooloo | D. O'Neil | 145 | 11 | 13 | 116 | 50 | 47 | |
| 14 Longbow II | D. Macaulay | 146 | 00 | 22 | 116 | 58 | 48 | |
| 15 Suca | W. Kuhrt | 146 | 29 | 01 | 117 | 12 | 05 | |
| 16 Klaar Kimming | P.H. Entz-V-Zerssen | 146 | 37 | 32 | 117 | 36 | 30 | |
| 17 Quest of Paget | K. Fenton Trimingham | 146 | 59 | 48 | 118 | 26 | 07 | |
| 18 Stampede | Mr and Mrs Alan Drake | 145 | 58 | 19 | 118 | 53 | 39 | |
| 19 Flame | Camper and Nicholson (N. Rydge) | 146 | 04 | 42 | 118 | 57 | 58 | |
| 20 Hawk | Capt. A.W. Joppe (D. Joppe) | 149 | 18 | 29 | 120 | 16 | 57 | |
| 21 Yeoman XVI | Owen A. Aisher | 148 | 32 | 50 | 120 | 27 | 25 | |
| 22 Tonnerre de Breskens | P.W. Vroon | 150 | 18 | 55 | 120 | 41 | 17 | |
| 23 Assegai II | W.M. Vernon | 149 | 31 | 52 | 120 | 54 | 39 | |
| 24 Gerfaut II | Pol Renot | 149 | 35 | 17 | 121 | 27 | 02 | |
| 25 Fjord V | G. Frers | 146 | 45 | 34 | 121 | 27 | 29 | |
| 26 Artako | J.M. de Gamboa | 150 | 19 | 11 | 121 | 49 | 09 | |
| 27 Lygaia | P. Herlin (K. Petäjä) | 150 | 00 | 08 | 121 | 49 | 54 | |
| 28 El Monje | Capt. J. Balleste | 152 | 23 | 27 | 122 | 07 | 34 | |
| 29 Nonchalent | S. Ahlquist | 152 | 24 | 24 | 122 | 13 | 48 | |
| 30 Musette | L.J. Last | 151 | 39 | 46 | 122 | 14 | 25 | |
| 31 Clarion of Wight | Sir Maurice Laing | 152 | 06 | 27 | 122 | 28 | 37 | |
| 32 Bluejacket III | D.J. Maw | 152 | 47 | 35 | 122 | 46 | 09 | |
| 33 Ravelin | Royal Engineer Yacht Club (Lt Col. J. Hamilton) | 151 | 48 | 28 | 123 | 04 | 14 | |
| 34 Wish Stream II | Royal Military Academy (Capt. A.N. Carlier) | 152 | 19 | 07 | 124 | 03 | 49 | |
| 35 Fair Judgment III | P.F. Carter-Ruck | 154 | 44 | 23 | 124 | 42 | 17 | |
| 36 Norlethe | L.B. Dyball | 152 | 23 | 11 | 124 | 44 | 37 | |
| 37 Parting Shot | Sir John Power | 154 | 10 | 36 | 124 | 44 | 40 | |
| 38 Tyressa | A.E. Goodfellow | 155 | 54 | 33 | 124 | 53 | 56 | |
| 39 Pierrette III | W.P.J.M. Pierrot | 152 | 18 | 07 | 124 | 59 | 39 | |
| 40 St Barbara II | Royal Artillery Yacht Club (Maj. J.P. Barden) | 154 | 58 | 31 | 125 | 15 | 04 | |
| 41 Silene | P.W. Messel | 151 | 45 | 20 | 125 | 21 | 00 | |
| 42 Caroline | C. Brochmann | 153 | 30 | 59 | 125 | 27 | 13 | |
| 43 Border Law | P.J. Compton (G.G. Greenfield) | 153 | 54 | 18 | 127 | 20 | 27 | |
| 44 Griffon | ECC-TA | 158 | 34 | 23 | 127 | 29 | 34 | |
| 45 Shareen | S.J. Cole | 159 | 45 | 54 | 128 | 48 | 09 | |
| 46 Sheenaloa | D.L. Campbell and C. Davies | 158 | 26 | 10 | 129 | 12 | 16 | |
| 47 Mutineer | J.M.A. Paterson | 159 | 58 | 10 | 129 | 12 | 26 | |
| 48 Atao | G. Bertho | 158 | 18 | 35 | 131 | 23 | 49 | |
| 49 Gawaine | Royal Naval Engineering College, Manadon | 189 | 26 | 48 | 152 | 04 | 08 | |
| 50 Firecrest | D.M. Stearns | 191 | 00 | 40 | 159 | 27 | 22 | |

| YACHT | OWNER (SAILED BY) | ELAPSED TIME | | | CORRECTED TIME | | |
|---|---|---|---|---|---|---|---|
| | | hr. | mn. | sc. | hr. | mn. | sc. |

*Class II(b)*

| | YACHT | OWNER (SAILED BY) | hr. | mn. | sc. | hr. | mn. | sc. |
|---|---|---|---|---|---|---|---|---|
| 1 | *Clarionet* | D.J. Boyer | 146 | 49 | 10 | 113 | 42 | 42 |
| 2 | *Gazela* | A.W. Goudriaan | 150 | 00 | 42 | 116 | 23 | 39 |
| 3 | *Marionette II* | C.A.F. Dunning | 152 | 11 | 35 | 117 | 52 | 25 |
| 4 | *Carte Blanche* | J. Britten, D. Norman and C. Kaula | 152 | 13 | 54 | 118 | 04 | 15 |
| 5 | *Coscoroba* | T.H. Bevan | 152 | 22 | 28 | 118 | 20 | 57 |
| 6 | *Tiderace* | D.E.P. Norton | 149 | 34 | 31 | 118 | 38 | 35 |
| 7 | *Drot* | K. Nielsen | 152 | 17 | 05 | 118 | 38 | 42 |
| 8 | *Kalisana* | R. Dreschfield | 152 | 36 | 41 | 119 | 48 | 55 |
| 9 | *Pellegrina* | J.M. Tomlinson | 158 | 21 | 44 | 123 | 04 | 45 |
| 10 | *Palamedes* | A.J. Sheldon | 158 | 28 | 01 | 123 | 37 | 11 |
| 11 | *Xuxu* | D.C. Barham | 159 | 59 | 35 | 123 | 54 | 53 |
| 12 | *Belmore II* | T.W.M. Steele | 157 | 19 | 15 | 124 | 50 | 03 |
| 13 | *Pellinore* | Mrs N.K. and C.J.W. Godfrey | 159 | 56 | 27 | 124 | 56 | 45 |
| 14 | *Maid of Mourne* | F.D. Tughan | 162 | 27 | 45 | 128 | 10 | 00 |
| 15 | *Temeraire* | Britannia Royal Naval College | 182 | 20 | 20 | 140 | 20 | 47 |
| 16 | *Ann Speed II* | John Lewis Partnership's Sailing Club | 204 | 23 | 43 | 157 | 42 | 40 |
| | *Blue Saluki* | Dr D. Matthews and P. Bathurst | DNF | | | | | |
| | *Camelot of Wessex* | R.W. Lawes | DNF | | | | | |

*Class III(a)*

| | YACHT | OWNER (SAILED BY) | hr. | mn. | sc. | hr. | mn. | sc. |
|---|---|---|---|---|---|---|---|---|
| 1 | *Rainbow II* | C. Bouzaid | 140 | 12 | 55 | 107 | 49 | 32 |
| 2 | *The Hawk* | Ideal Partnership | 143 | 10 | 40 | 110 | 06 | 13 |
| 3 | *Belita VI* | J.S. Bouman | 146 | 34 | 26 | 112 | 42 | 55 |
| 4 | *Tina* | E.R. Stettinius | 146 | 56 | 55 | 112 | 45 | 13 |
| 5 | *Sunmaid V* | G.B. Bowles (Dr R. Coles) | 147 | 29 | 06 | 113 | 23 | 11 |
| 6 | *Esprit de Rueil* | A. Viant and E. Jaupart | 148 | 00 | 47 | 113 | 44 | 00 |
| 7 | *Green Highlander II* | T.C. Chadwick | 148 | 07 | 27 | 113 | 54 | 27 |
| 8 | *Hestia* | H.A. van Beuningen | 149 | 28 | 22 | 113 | 58 | 23 |
| 9 | *Morningtown* | M. Winfield | 148 | 36 | 53 | 114 | 13 | 31 |
| 10 | *Oberon II* | W.B. Waterfall | 152 | 44 | 27 | 115 | 51 | 14 |
| 11 | *Cavalier Seul* | D. Paul-Cavallier | 152 | 33 | 42 | 117 | 02 | 43 |
| 12 | *L'Orgueil IV* | G. des Moutis | 152 | 51 | 43 | 117 | 18 | 22 |
| 13 | *Sarnia* | J.G. Sisk | 152 | 36 | 01 | 117 | 26 | 28 |
| 14 | *Trident* | C.N.M. Brest | 155 | 26 | 05 | 117 | 37 | 03 |
| 15 | *Callirhoe III* | Dr P. Bouyssou and D. Lamarche | 153 | 03 | 07 | 117 | 57 | 26 |
| 16 | *Schuttevaer* | J.C.W. van Dam | 153 | 56 | 51 | 118 | 21 | 17 |
| 17 | *Sylvia II* | P. Paris | 156 | 36 | 00 | 119 | 16 | 56 |
| 18 | *Jouster* | J.A.W. Bush | 159 | 19 | 13 | 120 | 49 | 43 |
| 19 | *Forerunner II* | G.E.N. Mason Elliott | 159 | 08 | 07 | 121 | 57 | 41 |
| 20 | *Tyrovic* | Royal Naval Barracks, Portsmouth (J.C. Mardel) | 159 | 46 | 18 | 122 | 09 | 41 |
| 21 | *Mayro of Skerries* | R.A. Wayte | 158 | 57 | 56 | 122 | 39 | 28 |
| 22 | *Matchless* | Lt Cmdr T.P.G. Poland | 159 | 47 | 49 | 122 | 44 | 24 |
| 23 | *Electron of Portsea* | PCSA Collingwood Sailing Club (C. Wigston) | 160 | 49 | 52 | 122 | 45 | 44 |
| 24 | *St George of England* | Royal Corps of Transport Yacht Club (Lt Col. G. Worsley) | 165 | 45 | 35 | 125 | 50 | 41 |
| 25 | *Pen Ar Vir* | Ecole Navale | 167 | 30 | 15 | 125 | 58 | 47 |
| 26 | *Domeilla of Saamsui* | T.R. Winser | 165 | 42 | 45 | 126 | 19 | 21 |
| 27 | *Guinevere* | Royal Naval Engineering College, Manadon | 165 | 33 | 30 | 126 | 21 | 15 |
| | *Arabel III* | Dr R. Le Couteur | DNF | | | | | |
| | *Enif* | K. Jaworski | DNF | | | | | |
| | *Midship-Ca* | Ecole Navale | DNF | | | | | |

*Class III(b)*

| | YACHT | OWNER (SAILED BY) | hr. | mn. | sc. | hr. | mn. | sc. |
|---|---|---|---|---|---|---|---|---|
| 1 | *Morning After* | R.G. Hill | 150 | 27 | 32 | 113 | 27 | 33 |
| 2 | *Starspinner* | M. Henderson and J. Hetherington | 154 | 09 | 53 | 113 | 27 | 55 |
| 3 | *Angel* | D. Edwards | 152 | 07 | 23 | 113 | 58 | 14 |
| 4 | *Sootica* | J.A. Sampsom | 155 | 13 | 30 | 114 | 27 | 46 |
| 5 | *Slipstream of Cowley* | Royal Air Force Sailing Association (Sqn Ldr A. Morgan) | 152 | 32 | 41 | 115 | 03 | 52 |
| 6 | *Malaise* | N. Speidel | 153 | 28 | 12 | 115 | 33 | 46 |
| 7 | *Morning Cloud* | Rt Hon. Edward Heath, MP | 153 | 13 | 04 | 115 | 36 | 10 |

| YACHT | OWNER (SAILED BY) | ELAPSED TIME | | | CORRECTED TIME | | |
|---|---|---|---|---|---|---|---|
| | | hr. | mn. | sc. | hr. | mn. | sc. |
| 8 Prolific | H. Formgren | 153 | 37 | 43 | 115 | 41 | 52 |
| 9 Nickel Coin | W.B. Stawell | 157 | 41 | 10 | 116 | 02 | 28 |
| 10 Arauna II | A. Pelletier | 156 | 39 | 00 | 116 | 27 | 13 |
| 11 Ternesse | A. Moggré | 154 | 15 | 28 | 116 | 30 | 39 |
| 12 Poinciana | The. E.W. Vinke | 156 | 06 | 01 | 116 | 37 | 21 |
| 13 Andorran | Mr and Mrs H.O.J.C. Jonas | 159 | 53 | 07 | 118 | 29 | 27 |
| 14 Sauvagine | H. Quiviger | 159 | 51 | 53 | 118 | 49 | 39 |
| 15 Trocar | Drs N.R. and E.G. Grenville | 160 | 58 | 10 | 119 | 16 | 42 |
| 16 Midnight | R.H. Brann | 160 | 01 | 28 | 119 | 17 | 53 |
| 17 Mowgli | D.M. and Q.J. Jones | 160 | 01 | 40 | 119 | 46 | 51 |
| 18 Walde | H. Renaut | 163 | 34 | 25 | 120 | 18 | 30 |
| 19 Sea Wraith | Portsmouth Command Sailing Association | 161 | 10 | 24 | 120 | 20 | 53 |
| 20 Ballerina of Torbay | S.R.G. Jeffery | 161 | 52 | 48 | 120 | 27 | 18 |
| 21 Duellant | B.-O. Holmberg | 159 | 25 | 00 | 120 | 36 | 53 |
| 22 Winwilloe of Portlemouth | N.W. Jephcott | 162 | 56 | 42 | 121 | 53 | 57 |
| 23 Goblet | Col. and Mrs K.N. Wylie | 160 | 56 | 52 | 121 | 57 | 00 |
| 24 Dingbat | J.L. Ranscombe and J. Stringer | 163 | 28 | 15 | 122 | 16 | 34 |
| 25 Misty | G. Kavanagh | 167 | 20 | 16 | 123 | 49 | 48 |
| 26 Contrail | Royal Air Force Sailing Association (F/Sgt B. Leamon) | 165 | 01 | 03 | 123 | 59 | 39 |
| 27 Marula | J.C. McConnell | 164 | 21 | 46 | 124 | 31 | 16 |
| 28 Wavelacer | J.W. Dennis | 190 | 08 | 35 | 143 | 58 | 35 |
| 29 Sarie Marais | Royal Marines Sailing Club (Capt. H. Wiltshire, RM) | 197 | 42 | 18 | 148 | 10 | 47 |
| 30 Half Pint | S.E.L. de Casembroot | 204 | 12 | 15 | 152 | 16 | 30 |
| Coquelicot | G.I.C. (P. Bernadin) | DNF | | | | | |
| Aktaion | J.N. Karreman | DNF | | | | | |
| Xelahu II | Royal Artillery Yacht Club (Maj. M.J.R. May) | DNF | | | | | |

# 1971 (7 AUGUST)

Class I

| | | | | | | | | |
|---|---|---|---|---|---|---|---|---|
| 1 Ragamuffin | S. Fischer | 85 | 51 | 14 | 76 | 08 | 38 | (1st overall) |
| 2 Quailo III | T.D. Parr | 87 | 26 | 17 | 78 | 31 | 10 | |
| 3 American Eagle | R.E. Turner III | 79 | 11 | 48 | 79 | 31 | 45 | |
| 4 Yankee Girl | D.D. Steere | 89 | 49 | 11 | 79 | 37 | 25 | |
| 5 Improbable | D.W. Allen | 91 | 23 | 25 | 79 | 52 | 30 | |
| 6 Apollo | A. Bond | 81 | 18 | 58 | 80 | 23 | 50 | |
| 7 Bay Bea | P.E. Haggerty | 90 | 25 | 09 | 80 | 28 | 56 | |
| 8 Jakaranda | T. Bester (B. Dalling) | 87 | 11 | 06 | 80 | 41 | 54 | |
| 9 Noryema VG | R.W. Amey | 90 | 25 | 14 | 81 | 03 | 11 | |
| 10 Salacia II | A.W. Byrne | 98 | 11 | 35 | 81 | 56 | 32 | |
| 11 Standfast | Standfast Syndicate (P. Vroon and F. Maas) | 98 | 11 | 35 | 81 | 56 | 32 | |
| 12 Shinda | A.F. Acevedo | 95 | 23 | 02 | 82 | 06 | 23 | |
| 13 Aura | W.J. Stenhouse, Jr | 95 | 23 | 02 | 82 | 06 | 23 | |
| 14 Prospect of Whitby | A. Slater | 98 | 11 | 47 | 82 | 06 | 43 | |
| 15 Carina | R.S. Nye | 93 | 36 | 23 | 82 | 25 | 13 | |
| 16 Zephyros | J.L. Baringer | 91 | 26 | 37 | 82 | 28 | 23 | |
| 17 Actaeon | T. Playle and D. Johnson | 91 | 58 | 49 | 82 | 53 | 00 | |
| 18 Levantades | G. Diano | 93 | 40 | 47 | 82 | 56 | 05 | |
| 19 Pacha | R. Crichton-Brown | 90 | 36 | 21 | 82 | 58 | 04 | |
| 20 Lutine | Lloyd's Yacht Club (M. Baxter) | 93 | 34 | 36 | 83 | 34 | 58 | |
| 21 Matrero | E. Kocourek | 94 | 14 | 37 | 83 | 35 | 05 | |
| 22 Kohinoor | Delta Reederei | 92 | 56 | 46 | 83 | 40 | 46 | |
| 23 Crusade | Sir Max Aitken and R.T. Lowein | 85 | 34 | 53 | 83 | 43 | 27 | |
| 24 Rubin | H.-O. Schümann | 94 | 40 | 38 | 83 | 49 | 04 | |
| 25 Tarantella | A. Raffaelli | 90 | 59 | 16 | 83 | 52 | 21 | |
| 26 Gitana V | Baron E. de Rothschild | 88 | 41 | 57 | 83 | 56 | 10 | |
| 27 Pluft | I. Klabin | 93 | 47 | 04 | 84 | 35 | 03 | |
| 28 Inschallah | W. Andreae | 90 | 02 | 09 | 84 | 40 | 11 | |

| YACHT | OWNER (SAILED BY) | ELAPSED TIME | | | CORRECTED TIME | | |
|---|---|---|---|---|---|---|---|
| | | hr. | mn. | sc. | hr. | mn. | sc. |
| 29 *Mabelle* | Miss S. Zaffagni | 99 | 15 | 17 | 84 | 46 | 24 |
| 30 *Phantom* | A. Moorkens | 100 | 00 | 53 | 85 | 00 | 09 |
| 31 *Sassenach* | J.A. Boyden | 95 | 14 | 41 | 85 | 04 | 21 |
| 32 *Hippokampos* | Sir John Power | 102 | 22 | 56 | 85 | 36 | 43 |
| 33 *Iorana* | W.W. Denzel | 89 | 11 | 29 | 86 | 00 | 26 |
| 34 *Border Viking* | J. Boardman | 103 | 31 | 37 | 87 | 43 | 43 |
| 35 *Diana II* | D. Monheim | 96 | 55 | 02 | 88 | 31 | 27 |
| 36 *Salty Tiger* | J.L. Powell | 99 | 50 | 17 | 88 | 32 | 48 |
| 37 *Moonduster* | D.N. Doyle | 107 | 24 | 40 | 89 | 09 | 43 |
| 38 *Stella Polare* | Italian Navy | 94 | 44 | 18 | 91 | 37 | 17 |
| 39 *Striana* | J.-M. Auclair | 101 | 15 | 45 | 93 | 05 | 26 |
| 40 *Pierrette III* | W.P.J.M. Pierrot | 112 | 50 | 42 | 93 | 30 | 53 |
| 41 *Ortac* | Hamburg Verein Seefahrt (M. Lutz) | 109 | 50 | 53 | 94 | 14 | 19 |
| 42 *Griffin III* | Royal Ocean Racing Club (Cmdr D. Seth-Smith) | 112 | 17 | 44 | 94 | 35 | 12 |
| 43 *Silene* | P. van Messel | 113 | 34 | 39 | 94 | 48 | 11 |
| 44 *Gazelle V* | H.W. Meyer, Jr | 114 | 23 | 42 | 95 | 27 | 45 |
| 45 *Najade* | Kon-Mar. Yacht Club | 112 | 34 | 13 | 95 | 28 | 15 |
| 46 *Musketeer* | N. Pattison | 113 | 22 | 54 | 96 | 31 | 59 |
| 47 *Ramrod* | U. Stephenson | 112 | 47 | 02 | 97 | 19 | 16 |
| 48 *Disparate* | Count de Zubiria | 113 | 04 | 27 | 99 | 39 | 08 |
| 49 *Pristis III* | Dr J. Clavreul | 115 | 22 | 38 | 101 | 37 | 02 |
| 50 *Norlethe* | L.B. Dyball | 123 | 06 | 27 | 101 | 54 | 30 |
| 51 *Gallivanter* | J.M.A. Paterson | 112 | 55 | 35 | 102 | 01 | 04 |
| 52 *Sardonyx IV* | Mr and Mrs A. Foucard | 124 | 57 | 49 | 103 | 33 | 26 |
| 53 *Zulu* | B.A. Stewart | 121 | 09 | 42 | 103 | 39 | 57 |
| 54 *Wappen von Bremen* | Segelkameradschaft das *Wappen von Bremen* (H. Seyde) | 119 | 23 | 14 | 105 | 01 | 30 |
| 55 *Bloodhound* | P.E. Dobbs | 113 | 21 | 30 | 105 | 12 | 28 |
| 56 *Griffin II* | F. St. M. Brierly and others | 137 | 38 | 14 | 118 | 46 | 02 |
| *Alaunt of Corfe* | Maj. R.C. Sharples | DNF | | | | | |
| *Carillion* | D. Boyer | DNF | | | | | |
| *Kyla* | L.L. Warry | DNF | | | | | |
| *Nymphaea* | A.W. Goudriaan | DNF | | | | | |
| *Outlaw* | Brig. P.O.G. Wakeham | DNF | | | | | |

*Class II*

| | | | | | | | |
|---|---|---|---|---|---|---|---|
| 1 *Cervantes IV* | R.C. Watson | 98 | 22 | 49 | 79 | 00 | 33 |
| 2 *Belita VII* | J.S. Bouman | 101 | 08 | 01 | 80 | 45 | 19 |
| 3 *Mersea Oyster* | D.M. Powell | 101 | 31 | 19 | 81 | 26 | 27 |
| 4 *Wizard of Paget* | de Forest Trimingham | 101 | 37 | 06 | 82 | 04 | 38 |
| 5 *Tritsch-Tratsch* | Dr O. Glaser | 101 | 31 | 37 | 82 | 11 | 10 |
| 6 *Morning Cloud* | Rt Hon. Edward Heath, MP | 101 | 03 | 09 | 82 | 16 | 01 |
| 7 *Firebrand II* | D.P. Miller | 100 | 08 | 31 | 83 | 02 | 16 |
| 8 *Recluta II* | C.A. Corna | 100 | 01 | 23 | 83 | 07 | 09 |
| 9 *Marionette III* | C.A.F. Dunning | 101 | 47 | 06 | 83 | 40 | 39 |
| 10 *Staron* | Dr W.M. Oosterwyke | 104 | 39 | 03 | 83 | 45 | 37 |
| 11 *Sawadi* | H. Formgren | 105 | 26 | 51 | 84 | 53 | 07 |
| 12 *Tiderace II* | D.E.P. Norton | 103 | 41 | 45 | 85 | 14 | 54 |
| 13 *Winsome* | D.O. May | 103 | 56 | 06 | 85 | 26 | 42 |
| 14 *Omuramba* | H. Berker | 103 | 17 | 37 | 85 | 28 | 32 |
| 15 *Izenah* | M. Holley | 104 | 43 | 04 | 85 | 43 | 19 |
| 16 *Wa-Wa-Too* | F.L.N. de Abreu | 103 | 02 | 47 | 85 | 53 | 58 |
| 17 *Poinciana* | Th. W. Vinke | 105 | 48 | 21 | 85 | 56 | 46 |
| 18 *Bolero* | J.J. Hozee | 106 | 11 | 48 | 86 | 27 | 17 |
| 19 *Mercury* | G. Neill | 105 | 30 | 40 | 87 | 35 | 05 |
| 20 *Milene* | A. Mirlesse | 105 | 50 | 51 | 87 | 40 | 24 |
| 21 *Avilion II* | H.C.R. Ballam | 106 | 27 | 07 | 87 | 48 | 06 |
| 22 *Thumper* | P. Crompton (Cmdr G.G. Greenfield) | 106 | 16 | 11 | 88 | 12 | 52 |
| 23 *Klaar Kimming* | J.H. Anthon | 110 | 17 | 03 | 89 | 35 | 02 |
| 24 *Ree* | H. and K. Redlefsen | 110 | 44 | 41 | 89 | 53 | 07 |
| 25 *Clarion of Wight* | Dr R. O'Hanlon | 112 | 08 | 53 | 90 | 34 | 55 |
| 26 *Philippides* | Bembridge Ocean Racing Syndicate (J. Britten) | 112 | 42 | 43 | 90 | 50 | 04 |

| YACHT | OWNER (SAILED BY) | ELAPSED TIME hr. mn. sc. | | | CORRECTED TIME hr. mn. sc. | | |
|---|---|---|---|---|---|---|---|
| 27 St Barbara III | Royal Artillery Yacht Club | 112 | 16 | 59 | 91 | 06 | 23 |
| 28 Cedrene | W. Brown and G. Jones | 112 | 52 | 41 | 91 | 22 | 29 |
| 29 Port Rex | B.P.H. Curran | 110 | 24 | 20 | 91 | 32 | 54 |
| 30 Sasha | Sir Maurice Laing | 112 | 40 | 13 | 91 | 37 | 24 |
| 31 Scarlett O'Hara | H. Wolfs | 114 | 53 | 53 | 91 | 44 | 46 |
| 32 Flame | H.V.L. Hall (D.J.L. Hall) | 113 | 42 | 48 | 91 | 50 | 47 |
| 33 Lancer of Hamble | G.R. Fuller | 113 | 04 | 26 | 91 | 51 | 00 |
| 34 Stampede of Arne | Alan D. Drake | 112 | 37 | 00 | 91 | 53 | 02 |
| 35 Sea Jouster | Lord Amherst of Hackney | 114 | 28 | 30 | 92 | 02 | 58 |
| 36 Bluejacket III | D.J. Maw | 114 | 43 | 11 | 92 | 03 | 04 |
| 37 Carina III | B. Nylen | 111 | 30 | 27 | 92 | 21 | 42 |
| 38 Callirhoe | A.F. Pauwels | 111 | 27 | 47 | 92 | 25 | 30 |
| 39 Matchless | Lt Cmdr T.P. Poland | 112 | 26 | 13 | 93 | 13 | 58 |
| 40 Tchaïka | J.P. Augendre | 114 | 38 | 00 | 93 | 30 | 23 |
| 41 Flaharn | Guillerot and Borde | 112 | 31 | 47 | 93 | 38 | 09 |
| 42 Orana | J.D. Pearson | 116 | 08 | 58 | 94 | 01 | 23 |
| 43 Water Music III | J.C. Foot | 115 | 51 | 46 | 94 | 06 | 55 |
| 44 Villegagnon | Lt Cmdr O.M.M. Forte | 113 | 42 | 04 | 94 | 23 | 00 |
| 45 Wishstream II | Royal Military Academy | 117 | 49 | 33 | 94 | 50 | 59 |
| 46 Madame II | B. Hogbom | 118 | 46 | 58 | 95 | 37 | 12 |
| 47 Ravelin | Royal Engineer Yacht Club and Sailing Association | 119 | 55 | 19 | 96 | 38 | 42 |
| 48 Jandavina II | R.G. Moody | 116 | 33 | 23 | 97 | 09 | 41 |
| 49 Border Law | A.E. Goodfellow | 119 | 32 | 44 | 97 | 30 | 48 |
| 50 Breakaway of Parkstone | L.C. Smith | 121 | 53 | 49 | 97 | 53 | 44 |
| 51 Griffon | ECC-TA | 123 | 33 | 57 | 100 | 01 | 36 |
| 52 Sakr El Bahr | A.J. Methuen (Maj. M. Miller) | 125 | 10 | 32 | 101 | 06 | 15 |
| 53 Galahad | Royal Navy | 139 | 18 | 52 | 112 | 02 | 12 |
| Gawaine | Royal Navy | DNF | | | | | |
| Koomooloo | N.B. Rydge | DNF | | | | | |
| Schuylkill | A.J. Wilson | DNF | | | | | |

Class III

| YACHT | OWNER (SAILED BY) | ELAPSED TIME hr. mn. sc. | | | CORRECTED TIME hr. mn. sc. | | |
|---|---|---|---|---|---|---|---|
| 1 Morningtown | R.G. Hill | 106 | 31 | 51 | 83 | 45 | 55 |
| 2 L'Orgueil IV | G. des Moutis | 112 | 38 | 06 | 86 | 16 | 42 |
| 3 Mosquito | B. Söderstam | 112 | 32 | 59 | 86 | 52 | 38 |
| 4 Witch | Nutmeg Syndicate (R. Bavier, Jr) | 111 | 58 | 22 | 87 | 11 | 35 |
| 5 Polka-Dos | W.H. Kesteloo | 114 | 02 | 14 | 87 | 28 | 00 |
| 6 Kealoha | Mr and Mrs L.J. Holliday | 112 | 00 | 41 | 87 | 44 | 59 |
| 7 Zeehaas | M.J. Vroon | 113 | 15 | 08 | 88 | 43 | 18 |
| 8 Ruffian | W.P., R.P. and T. Brown | 112 | 34 | 55 | 88 | 44 | 13 |
| 9 Gale | Col. and Mrs K.N. Wylie | 114 | 17 | 16 | 88 | 59 | 45 |
| 10 Teleri | C. Green | 114 | 19 | 28 | 89 | 01 | 28 |
| 11 Bandersnatch | R. Courtney | 114 | 07 | 22 | 89 | 44 | 05 |
| 12 Ojala | Alpha Shipping (A.C. Holland) | 114 | 57 | 07 | 89 | 50 | 06 |
| 13 Salidi of Lytham | J. Ellis | 115 | 13 | 29 | 89 | 56 | 40 |
| 14 Speedwell | A. le Comte and J. Whittemore | 115 | 57 | 12 | 89 | 57 | 24 |
| 15 Cavallier Seul | D. Paul-Cavallier | 116 | 32 | 25 | 90 | 17 | 43 |
| 16 Coscoroba | T.H. Bevan | 116 | 46 | 13 | 90 | 35 | 25 |
| 17 Ailish II | B. Foulger | 119 | 46 | 40 | 91 | 58 | 38 |
| 18 Flood Tide | W.P. Vinten | 119 | 14 | 33 | 92 | 30 | 30 |
| 19 Sinbad of Abersoch | G.I. Bye | 120 | 10 | 49 | 92 | 31 | 36 |
| 20 Hastings | D. Leguillon | 125 | 12 | 31 | 96 | 09 | 37 |
| 21 Portcullis II | National Westminster Bank Sailing Club | 128 | 51 | 15 | 99 | 20 | 01 |
| 22 Sainte Anne VII | Centre Nautique des Glénans | 127 | 45 | 12 | 100 | 10 | 17 |
| 23 Camelot of Wessex | R.W. Lawes | 130 | 46 | 58 | 101 | 11 | 12 |
| 24 Marelle | Dr N. Beaton | 134 | 27 | 42 | 102 | 52 | 36 |
| 25 Ann Speed II | John Lewis Partnership's Sailing Club | 138 | 46 | 09 | 105 | 06 | 14 |
| 26 Electron of Portsea | Lt Cmdr P.F. Whelan, RN | 138 | 30 | 25 | 105 | 34 | 12 |
| 27 Lady of Hamford | G.W. Thake | 136 | 49 | 27 | 105 | 44 | 16 |
| 28 Domeila of Saamsui | T.R. Winser | 143 | 15 | 27 | 109 | 02 | 51 |
| 29 Isabella | O. Schroeder | 143 | 08 | 57 | 109 | 30 | 33 |
| 30 Prinses Margriet | Kon-Mar. Yacht Club | 151 | 07 | 08 | 117 | 14 | 17 |
| Blue Saluki | Dr D. Matthews | DNF | | | | | |
| Croesus | H. Comberg | DNF | | | | | |
| Joran | J.C. Berger | DNF | | | | | |

| YACHT | OWNER (SAILED BY) | ELAPSED TIME hr. mn. sc. | | | CORRECTED TIME hr. mn. sc. | | |
|---|---|---|---|---|---|---|---|
| Ocean wave of Albany | Royal Marines Sailing Club | DNF | | | | | |
| Victoria | G. Lundberg | DNF | | | | | |

## Class IV

| | YACHT | OWNER (SAILED BY) | | | | | | |
|---|---|---|---|---|---|---|---|---|
| 1 | Pionier 10 | F. King (A. Bourdon) | 114 | 07 | 37 | 85 | 28 | 11 |
| 2 | Setanta of Skerries | R.A. Wayte | 113 | 39 | 41 | 85 | 55 | 41 |
| 3 | Olbia IV | J. Archer | 113 | 42 | 12 | 86 | 11 | 14 |
| 4 | Gay Gannet IV | Cmdr F.W.B. Edwards | 115 | 11 | 14 | 86 | 57 | 59 |
| 5 | Trocar | Dr N.R. Greville | 116 | 24 | 11 | 87 | 03 | 28 |
| 6 | Striva | Y. Cudennec | 114 | 56 | 56 | 87 | 07 | 52 |
| 7 | Midas of Mersea | B.R. Pearson | 115 | 38 | 51 | 87 | 11 | 54 |
| 8 | Artaban | M. and R. Letortu | 115 | 13 | 23 | 87 | 20 | 21 |
| 9 | Ossian III | P. Ratzel | 115 | 34 | 03 | 87 | 22 | 08 |
| 10 | Pagan | J.C. Clothier (D. Edwards) | 115 | 56 | 11 | 87 | 31 | 55 |
| 11 | Terpsichore | C.L. Sandblom | 115 | 30 | 53 | 87 | 47 | 28 |
| 12 | Quickstep II of Wessex | D.M. Watkinson | 115 | 52 | 04 | 88 | 03 | 34 |
| 13 | Slipstream of Cowley | Royal Air Force Sailing Association | 116 | 09 | 24 | 88 | 09 | 46 |
| 14 | Korsar | J.A. Mackeown (J. Bourke) | 115 | 54 | 17 | 88 | 26 | 07 |
| 15 | Morning Melody | Group Capt. D.E. Gillam | 116 | 38 | 19 | 88 | 45 | 43 |
| 16 | Ancasta | M.J. Brade and C.C. Lowe | 117 | 07 | 29 | 88 | 46 | 50 |
| 17 | Ballerina IV | S.R.G. Jeffery | 118 | 18 | 36 | 89 | 12 | 21 |
| 18 | Malaise | N. Spiedel | 118 | 15 | 11 | 89 | 52 | 20 |
| 19 | Sea Wraith III | Portsmouth Branch Royal Naval Sailing Association | 121 | 29 | 59 | 91 | 43 | 56 |
| 20 | Greenfly | J.W. Roome | 122 | 33 | 58 | 92 | 20 | 29 |
| 21 | Belmore | S. Königson | 123 | 22 | 12 | 93 | 19 | 01 |
| 22 | Red Velvet | P.M.F. Babbe | 123 | 27 | 02 | 93 | 27 | 07 |
| 23 | Tirade | C.J. and Mrs N. Godfrey | 124 | 15 | 13 | 93 | 56 | 09 |
| 24 | Breeze of Yorkshire | M.J.W. Hall | 125 | 36 | 18 | 95 | 12 | 31 |
| 25 | Mar del Norte | Capt. R.S. Aspinall | 130 | 23 | 28 | 95 | 36 | 10 |
| 26 | Jouster | J.A.W. Bush | 131 | 22 | 47 | 97 | 07 | 44 |
| 27 | Craft IV | J. Dentraygues | 128 | 22 | 08 | 97 | 10 | 31 |
| 28 | Guinevere | Royal Navy | 131 | 15 | 05 | 98 | 22 | 22 |
| 29 | Mowgli | D.M. and Q.J. Jones | 134 | 12 | 33 | 100 | 02 | 22 |
| 30 | Sarie Marais | Lt Cmdr D.D. Gay, RN | 138 | 05 | 34 | 102 | 47 | 46 |
| 31 | Meon Mist | J.A. Wilks | 140 | 14 | 34 | 104 | 17 | 55 |
| 32 | Taranto | Naval Air Command Sailing Association | 143 | 00 | 45 | 105 | 43 | 45 |
| 33 | Golden Samphire | F.K. Beazley | 144 | 30 | 48 | 106 | 15 | 39 |
| 34 | Daiquiri | A. Fabre (K.H. Gross) | 141 | 57 | 40 | 106 | 23 | 08 |
| 35 | Coquelicot | Centre Nautique des Glénans | 141 | 40 | 58 | 107 | 23 | 44 |
| 36 | Volunteer | Royal Naval Volunteer Reserve Sailing Club | 142 | 34 | 04 | 108 | 38 | 12 |
| 37 | Casino | H.V. Gordon | 149 | 07 | 55 | 109 | 20 | 36 |
| 38 | Tudor Rose | E.H. Crisp | 148 | 25 | 00 | 110 | 28 | 53 |
| 39 | Judicious | Dr W.E. Lavelle | 156 | 27 | 00 | 115 | 30 | 26 |
| 40 | Opus | Maj. J. Dennistoun | 185 | 18 | 13 | 137 | 10 | 55 |
| | Temeraire | Britannia Royal Naval College | DNF | | | | | |

## Class V

| | YACHT | OWNER (SAILED BY) | | | | | | |
|---|---|---|---|---|---|---|---|---|
| 1 | Morbic III | H. Elies | 114 | 41 | 49 | 83 | 14 | 49 |
| 2 | Maraska | M. Girard | 114 | 47 | 24 | 83 | 18 | 52 |
| 3 | Araok-Atao II | P. LeBaud (G. LeBaud) | 116 | 21 | 19 | 83 | 57 | 01 |
| 4 | Shetoo | D. Fitzgerald (D. Colquhoun) | 115 | 57 | 30 | 84 | 02 | 48 |
| 5 | El Pepito | Dr P. Moné | 116 | 35 | 50 | 84 | 52 | 58 |
| 6 | Callypige | L. Cordelle | 116 | 28 | 11 | 84 | 54 | 23 |
| 7 | Ricochet | J. Harrison (R. Matthews) | 120 | 52 | 54 | 86 | 49 | 45 |
| 8 | Crocodile | J.A. Carter | 120 | 16 | 42 | 87 | 02 | 43 |
| 9 | Z | M. Petrelius | 121 | 24 | 38 | 87 | 51 | 53 |
| 10 | Archibald | M. Dufour | 122 | 14 | 09 | 88 | 43 | 07 |
| 11 | Gwalarn | Centre Nautique des Glénans | 123 | 26 | 35 | 90 | 15 | 42 |
| 12 | Windsprite of Hamble | B. Banks | 125 | 25 | 13 | 90 | 37 | 43 |
| 13 | Galiote | Voilerie Le Rose (A. Griot) | 130 | 48 | 50 | 93 | 57 | 49 |
| 14 | Dynamo | J. Rix | 130 | 52 | 27 | 94 | 00 | 25 |
| 15 | Scuba | R.G. Jordan | 139 | 21 | 32 | 100 | 06 | 05 |
| 16 | Lauric | Mr and Mrs R.W. Elliott | 137 | 07 | 19 | 100 | 41 | 19 |

| YACHT | OWNER (SAILED BY) | ELAPSED TIME | | | CORRECTED TIME | | |
|---|---|---|---|---|---|---|---|
| | | hr. | mn. | sc. | hr. | mn. | sc. |
| 17 Precedent | Civil Service Sailing Association | 145 | 03 | 40 | 104 | 20 | 32 |
| 18 Tumblehome | A. Smith | 145 | 22 | 34 | 106 | 08 | 20 |
| 19 Salidi | R. Yates | 148 | 21 | 22 | 108 | 27 | 47 |
| 20 Starspinner | C.H. Towers | 147 | 45 | 50 | 108 | 58 | 33 |
| Bucentaure | Baronne de Turkheim | DNF | | | | | |
| Debonair II | G. Fonda | DNF | | | | | |
| Esprit | A. Viant and others | DNF | | | | | |
| Great Bear | W.M. Henderson | DNF | | | | | |
| Lara of Chichester | W.W.A. Lee | DNF | | | | | |
| Mordicus II | C. Volters | DNF | | | | | |

# 1973 (11 AUGUST)

### Class I

| YACHT | OWNER (SAILED BY) | ELAPSED TIME | | | CORRECTED TIME | | | |
|---|---|---|---|---|---|---|---|---|
| 1 Saga | E. Lorentzen | 93 | 33 | 00 | 105 | 11 | 00 | (1st overall) |
| 2 Recluta III | C.A. Corna | 98 | 52 | 08 | 105 | 38 | 24 | |
| 3 Charisma | J. Philips | 95 | 46 | 26 | 106 | 49 | 03 | |
| 4 Salty Goose | W. Frank and R. Derecktor | 96 | 57 | 40 | 108 | 08 | 43 | |
| 5 Safari | P.W. Adams | 97 | 27 | 30 | 108 | 46 | 52 | |
| 6 Sorcery | J.F. Baldwin | 92 | 45 | 40 | 108 | 58 | 16 | |
| 7 Aura | W.J. Stenhouse | 102 | 04 | 37 | 109 | 28 | 57 | |
| 8 Prospect of Whitby | A. Slater | 106 | 24 | 59 | 111 | 22 | 48 | |
| 9 Quailo III | T.D. Parr | 103 | 40 | 47 | 112 | 23 | 32 | |
| 10 Saudade | A. Bull | 111 | 16 | 08 | 115 | 27 | 57 | |
| 11 Apollo | J. Rookeyn | 102 | 25 | 32 | 115 | 46 | 13 | |
| 12 Wa-Wa-Too III | F. Nabuco de Abreu | 110 | 14 | 57 | 119 | 03 | 44 | |
| 13 Carillion | D. Boyer | 115 | 54 | 23 | 119 | 09 | 52 | |
| 14 Pen-Duick VI | E. Tabarly | 103 | 02 | 46 | 119 | 25 | 52 | |
| 15 Carina III | D. Monheim | 116 | 36 | 26 | 119 | 59 | 17 | |
| 16 Stuart Little | C.D. Williamson | 116 | 21 | 11 | 120 | 25 | 35 | |
| 17 Rubin | H.O. Schumann | 115 | 14 | 47 | 120 | 44 | 45 | |
| 18 Battlecry | J. Prentice | 117 | 00 | 15 | 120 | 55 | 05 | |
| 19 Antigua V | N. Richter (M. Hurrell) | 117 | 20 | 44 | 121 | 10 | 28 | |
| 20 Chastenet | N.A. Brick | 117 | 39 | 57 | 121 | 13 | 00 | |
| 21 Ginkgo | G. Bogard | 115 | 49 | 22 | 121 | 14 | 27 | |
| 22 Whirlwind III | N. Lister and D. Searle | 115 | 50 | 11 | 121 | 35 | 48 | |
| 23 Jakaranda | O.R.I. (B. Bongers) | 113 | 15 | 17 | 122 | 00 | 28 | |
| 24 Spirit of Delft | W. Oosterwijk (U. de Vries) | 117 | 25 | 50 | 122 | 20 | 37 | |
| 25 Milene II | A. Mirlesse | 116 | 45 | 32 | 122 | 24 | 59 | |
| 26 Apollo II | A. Bond | 117 | 10 | 46 | 122 | 34 | 39 | |
| 27 Ragamuffin | S. Fischer | 116 | 19 | 02 | 122 | 43 | 29 | |
| 28 Carolina | T. Koristo | 119 | 16 | 25 | 123 | 13 | 56 | |
| 29 Duva II | Dr H.H. Lubinus | 120 | 49 | 27 | 123 | 55 | 42 | |
| 30 Jan Pot | N. Lorck-Schierning | 117 | 15 | 15 | 124 | 16 | 18 | |
| 31 Firebrand III | D. Miller | 116 | 42 | 52 | 124 | 30 | 08 | |
| 32 Adventure | Royal Navy (Cmdr J. Bryans) | 117 | 27 | 04 | 124 | 51 | 18 | |
| 33 War Baby | Warren and A. Brown | 119 | 44 | 27 | 125 | 14 | 06 | |
| 34 Kiss III | P. Teichert | 115 | 50 | 04 | 125 | 40 | 44 | |
| 35 Oyster | D.M. Powell and R.H. Martin | 121 | 09 | 18 | 126 | 14 | 08 | |
| 36 Sayula II | R. Carlin | 112 | 16 | 15 | 128 | 14 | 19 | |
| 37 Inschallah | W. Andreae | 119 | 51 | 10 | 129 | 15 | 24 | |
| 38 Superstar | A. Graham and D.H. Johnson | 126 | 06 | 27 | 129 | 25 | 19 | |
| 39 Zumbido | W.A.J. Hibberd | 126 | 41 | 14 | 129 | 36 | 28 | |
| 40 Matchmaker | R.A.B. Grigg and L. Smith | 126 | 36 | 34 | 129 | 47 | 05 | |
| 41 Kealoha | Mr and Mrs L. Holliday | 127 | 21 | 06 | 130 | 22 | 52 | |
| 42 Noryema IX | R.W. Amey | 123 | 44 | 52 | 130 | 36 | 03 | |
| 43 Tritsch-Tratsch II | Dr O. Glaser | 126 | 25 | 59 | 130 | 54 | 54 | |
| 44 Formosa | W.H. Hawkins | 127 | 52 | 43 | 131 | 00 | 39 | |
| 45 Windliese XII | P.H. Entz-v-Zerssen | 126 | 35 | 21 | 131 | 07 | 10 | |
| 46 Weald II | F.G. Cummiskey | 126 | 08 | 13 | 131 | 19 | 39 | |
| 47 Phantom II | A. Moorkens | 126 | 22 | 50 | 131 | 21 | 06 | |
| 48 Windrush II | F.C. Magnan | 127 | 47 | 24 | 131 | 35 | 20 | |
| 49 Matrero | E. Kocourek | 125 | 41 | 47 | 132 | 05 | 24 | |

| YACHT | OWNER (SAILED BY) | ELAPSED TIME hr. mn. sc. | | | CORRECTED TIME hr. mn. sc. | | |
|---|---|---|---|---|---|---|---|
| 50 *Four Winds* | R. Cassou (M. Cassou) | 129 | 00 | 55 | 132 | 06 | 32 |
| 51 *Dagon* | P.J. Orban | 126 | 25 | 36 | 132 | 54 | 40 |
| 52 *Lutine* | Lloyd's Yacht Club | 126 | 29 | 56 | 133 | 20 | 02 |
| 53 *Solution* | T. Ramsing | 128 | 40 | 09 | 133 | 21 | 49 |
| 54 *Cangaceiro* | D. Barreto | 128 | 53 | 19 | 133 | 40 | 19 |
| 55 *Jet* | J.E. Thomsen | 129 | 25 | 17 | 134 | 13 | 52 |
| 56 *Moonduster* | D.N. Doyle | 130 | 16 | 17 | 135 | 08 | 05 |
| 57 *Naif* | R. Gardini | 125 | 57 | 05 | 135 | 10 | 16 |
| 58 *Stortebeker* | HVS (U. Ernst) | 129 | 28 | 03 | 135 | 17 | 19 |
| 59 *Chasseur* | F.V. Snyder | 126 | 27 | 08 | 136 | 12 | 10 |
| 60 *Guia* | G. Falck | 126 | 51 | 20 | 136 | 32 | 56 |
| 61 *Grand-Louis* | A. Viant | 129 | 43 | 14 | 137 | 53 | 27 |
| 62 *Supercilious* | N.C.S. Rawlings | 129 | 31 | 26 | 138 | 44 | 48 |
| 63 *Pierrette III* | W.P.J.M. Pierrot | 138 | 59 | 03 | 138 | 49 | 38 |
| 64 *Zulu* | B.A. Stewart | 140 | 42 | 23 | 139 | 26 | 35 |
| 65 *Second Life* | M.R. Ainslie | 128 | 44 | 42 | 140 | 11 | 18 |
| 66 *Foxhound* | Antonio X.B.M. Nogueira | 123 | 43 | 10 | 141 | 48 | 17 |
| 67 *Bengali* | J. Le Couteur | 139 | 28 | 22 | 141 | 59 | 36 |
| 68 *Silene* | P. van Messel | 143 | 22 | 05 | 143 | 18 | 25 |
| 69 *Alaunt of Corfe* | Hon. C. Sharples (RORC) | 141 | 38 | 13 | 146 | 38 | 11 |
| *Sabre* | MOD, JSSC | DNF | | | | | |
| *Gallivanter* | J.M.A. Paterson | DNF | | | | | |
| *Kohinoor* | D. Reederei | DNF | | | | | |
| *Mad Carew* | D.A.D. Munro | DNF | | | | | |
| *British Soldier* | C. Blyth (Maj. Carlier) | DNF | | | | | |
| *Synergy* | D.W.H. McCowan | DNF | | | | | |

*Class II*

| YACHT | OWNER (SAILED BY) | ELAPSED TIME hr. mn. sc. | | | CORRECTED TIME hr. mn. sc. | | |
|---|---|---|---|---|---|---|---|
| 1 *Frigate* | J.A. Boyden and R. Aisher | 116 | 30 | 15 | 117 | 28 | 37 |
| 2 *Pinta* | W. Illbruck | 117 | 45 | 10 | 118 | 37 | 56 |
| 3 *Marionette IV* | C.A.F. Dunning | 117 | 40 | 11 | 118 | 53 | 15 |
| 4 *Lightnin'* | R.E. Turner | 122 | 48 | 15 | 122 | 48 | 15 |
| 5 *C-Mirage* | G.W. Moog | 120 | 56 | 27 | 123 | 50 | 00 |
| 6 *Sagittarius* | G. Carriero | 124 | 11 | 40 | 125 | 33 | 52 |
| 7 *Tai Fat* | J.H. Anderson | 126 | 35 | 43 | 126 | 35 | 43 |
| 8 *Nymphaea* | Th. E.W. Vinke and R. Morelisse | 123 | 55 | 02 | 126 | 43 | 22 |
| 9 *Can-Can IV* | E. Kindberg | 126 | 54 | 02 | 127 | 46 | 32 |
| 10 *Standfast II* | F. Maas and P.W. Vroon | 126 | 10 | 39 | 127 | 53 | 06 |
| 11 *Atrevido* | A. Grandi | 126 | 20 | 47 | 128 | 32 | 50 |
| 12 *Procelaria* | F.P. Duarte | 126 | 13 | 50 | 128 | 33 | 55 |
| 13 *Rajada* | V. Polisaitis | 126 | 36 | 54 | 128 | 40 | 10 |
| 14 *Revolution* | J.L. Fabry and M. Hennebert | 128 | 20 | 31 | 128 | 54 | 04 |
| 15 *Morning Cloud* | Rt Hon. Edward Heath, MP | 126 | 07 | 43 | 128 | 56 | 07 |
| 16 *Wizard of Paget* | The Hon. de F. Trimingham | 128 | 15 | 34 | 128 | 58 | 30 |
| 17 *Gunfleet of Hamble* | R. Jones | 128 | 57 | 15 | 129 | 07 | 05 |
| 18 *Tam O'Shanter* | J.M. Park | 129 | 16 | 55 | 129 | 16 | 55 |
| 19 *Polka Mara* | W. Kesteloo | 129 | 23 | 03 | 129 | 23 | 03 |
| 20 *Bumblebee II* | J.D. Kahlbetzer | 126 | 38 | 43 | 129 | 30 | 07 |
| 21 *Fantasque* | P. Chormarat | 120 | 01 | 56 | 129 | 30 | 19 |
| 22 *Samphire* | J.A. Sampson | 128 | 52 | 53 | 129 | 30 | 36 |
| 23 *L'Orgueil V* | G. des Moutis | 129 | 15 | 47 | 129 | 39 | 44 |
| 24 *Green Highlander* | T.C. Chadwick | 127 | 54 | 40 | 130 | 00 | 05 |
| 25 *Colombe III* | P. d'Andrimont | 129 | 27 | 56 | 130 | 01 | 06 |
| 26 *Mabelle* | Signorina S. Zaffagni | 129 | 13 | 17 | 130 | 09 | 23 |
| 27 *Chandanna* | C.H. Fenn | 128 | 53 | 44 | 130 | 16 | 16 |
| 28 *Morningtown* | R. Hill | 128 | 58 | 40 | 130 | 25 | 30 |
| 29 *Easy Glider* | H. Wolfs | 129 | 15 | 57 | 130 | 29 | 27 |
| 30 *Tiderace III* | D.E.P. Norton | 128 | 13 | 16 | 130 | 30 | 23 |
| 31 *Arend* | Y. van der Plasse | 128 | 55 | 01 | 130 | 47 | 03 |
| 32 *Omuramba* | H.J. Berker | 128 | 51 | 12 | 130 | 47 | 08 |
| 33 *Postulat* | F. Moureau and F. Pringuet | 129 | 15 | 55 | 130 | 55 | 00 |
| 34 *Loujaine* | Sir Maurice Laing | 128 | 39 | 45 | 131 | 04 | 26 |
| 35 *Spanker* | J. Fitzjohn and A. Bourdon | 128 | 35 | 47 | 131 | 15 | 55 |
| 36 *Avilion III* | H.C.R. Ballam | 128 | 45 | 15 | 131 | 25 | 07 |
| 37 *Belita VII* | J.S. Bouman | 130 | 54 | 26 | 131 | 36 | 08 |
| 38 *Flame* | H.V.L. Hall (D.J.L. Hall) | 130 | 59 | 53 | 131 | 36 | 44 |

| YACHT | OWNER (SAILED BY) | ELAPSED TIME hr. mn. sc. | | | CORRECTED TIME hr. mn. sc. | | |
|---|---|---|---|---|---|---|---|
| 39 Bolero | J.J. Hozee | 130 | 24 | 39 | 131 | 50 | 07 |
| 40 Outburst | W.C. O'Reilly | 130 | 06 | 50 | 132 | 17 | 21 |
| 41 Matchless | T.P.G. Poland | 131 | 15 | 11 | 133 | 39 | 29 |
| 42 Nemesis | P. Crompton (Cmdr Greenfield) | 132 | 03 | 59 | 133 | 47 | 55 |
| 43 Kyria | Baron M. von Schroder | 135 | 59 | 35 | 135 | 59 | 35 |
| 44 Volle Maen | L. Aardenburg | 135 | 58 | 00 | 136 | 58 | 00 |
| 45 Stampede of Arne | A.D. Drake | 136 | 00 | 40 | 137 | 12 | 44 |
| 46 Border Ally | J. Boardman | 136 | 01 | 00 | 138 | 31 | 40 |
| 47 Tritsch-Tratsch | J. McLaren | 139 | 16 | 06 | 140 | 01 | 38 |
| 48 Philippides | Bembridge Ocean Racing Syndicate (F. Britten) | 139 | 44 | 52 | 140 | 09 | 54 |
| 49 Dark Horse | Lloyd's Bank Yacht Club (B. Ray) | 140 | 27 | 13 | 140 | 56 | 20 |
| 50 Paprika | J.J. Flood III | 140 | 45 | 21 | 140 | 57 | 42 |
| 51 Ravelin | Royal Engineer Yacht Club | 141 | 03 | 08 | 141 | 40 | 05 |
| 52 St Barbara III | Royal Artillery Yacht Club | 140 | 56 | 59 | 141 | 41 | 34 |
| 53 Solivan III | P. Lamotte | 141 | 28 | 33 | 141 | 57 | 17 |
| 54 Sea Jouster | Lord Amherst of Hackney | 141 | 40 | 56 | 141 | 57 | 23 |
| 55 Rapier | D.L. Campbell and C. Davies | 141 | 01 | 50 | 142 | 25 | 51 |
| 56 Sasha | A. Barnard and Miss D. Seldon | 141 | 42 | 00 | 142 | 34 | 09 |
| 57 Saschinka of Cowes | S. Spannenburg | 141 | 01 | 54 | 142 | 46 | 08 |
| 58 Flaharn | Messrs Guillerot and Borde | 141 | 32 | 35 | 143 | 56 | 38 |
| 59 Gawaine | Royal Naval Engineering College | 149 | 49 | 34 | 147 | 34 | 56 |
| 60 Green Chartreuse | F.R. Ducker | 141 | 30 | 24 | 149 | 59 | 20 |
| Becca | Hon. Vere Harmsworth | DNF | | | | | |
| Griffon | ECCTA | DNF | | | | | |
| Starchaser | J. Harrington | DNF | | | | | |

Class III

| YACHT | OWNER (SAILED BY) | ELAPSED TIME hr. mn. sc. | | | CORRECTED TIME hr. mn. sc. | | |
|---|---|---|---|---|---|---|---|
| 1 Hylas | D. Edwards | 127 | 52 | 36 | 126 | 56 | 12 |
| 2 Thunder | J.C. and Dr J.D. Rogers and D. Pitt-Pitts | 129 | 23 | 51 | 128 | 07 | 12 |
| 3 Variag | M. Henrion | 131 | 04 | 58 | 128 | 07 | 51 |
| 4 Olivia-Anne V | Mr and Mrs M.B. Swain | 130 | 39 | 45 | 128 | 17 | 42 |
| 5 Croix du Cygne | K. van Exter | 129 | 22 | 52 | 128 | 27 | 24 |
| 6 Tiburon | P.H. de Koster | 130 | 53 | 53 | 128 | 49 | 10 |
| 7 Stress | B. Blumenthal | 131 | 27 | 22 | 129 | 06 | 35 |
| 8 Bon Chance | Mr and Mrs J.A. Rade II | 129 | 58 | 24 | 129 | 13 | 34 |
| 9 Machichaco | J. Olabarri and J. Churruca | 130 | 15 | 16 | 129 | 15 | 30 |
| 10 Northwind | Bruce B. Banks | 129 | 36 | 07 | 129 | 31 | 14 |
| 11 Liz of Lymington | Mr and Mrs P.J.B. Webster | 130 | 56 | 30 | 129 | 41 | 29 |
| 12 Flying Chance | Royal Air Force Sailing Association | 130 | 00 | 06 | 129 | 45 | 31 |
| 13 Cascadeur | M.A. Gaze (R. Gardiner) | 132 | 22 | 10 | 131 | 13 | 07 |
| 14 Altricia | B.M. Baird | 136 | 21 | 53 | 132 | 35 | 33 |
| 15 Sylvia II | P. Paris | 141 | 16 | 13 | 136 | 00 | 52 |
| 16 Gillane III | G.H. Bottomley | 137 | 58 | 54 | 136 | 04 | 14 |
| 17 Avilion | A.M. Smith | 141 | 30 | 13 | 136 | 20 | 22 |
| 18 Palamedes | A.J. Sheldon | 141 | 37 | 10 | 136 | 22 | 01 |
| 19 Ruffian | D.J. Kemsett | 138 | 03 | 40 | 136 | 34 | 41 |
| 20 Sabina IV | H. Noack | 138 | 09 | 45 | 136 | 50 | 42 |
| 21 Hoodwinker | J.A. and I.S. Wilks | 139 | 55 | 34 | 137 | 05 | 00 |
| 22 Vuurvlieg II | H. Klaus (D.M.G. Joppe) | 140 | 13 | 42 | 137 | 34 | 48 |
| 23 Schulykill | A.J. Wilson | 138 | 36 | 53 | 138 | 01 | 14 |
| 24 Surf Scoter | O.A. Burge and W. Davis | 139 | 18 | 19 | 138 | 10 | 03 |
| 25 Zeehaas | M.J.F. Vroon | 139 | 57 | 43 | 138 | 20 | 42 |
| 26 Coscoroba | T.H. Bevan | 140 | 54 | 01 | 138 | 43 | 02 |
| 27 Duette | C.F. Journeaux | 139 | 52 | 11 | 138 | 54 | 00 |
| 28 Northern Swan | C.F. Smith | 141 | 14 | 41 | 139 | 04 | 16 |
| 29 Schuttevaer | Dr J.C.W. van Dam | 140 | 17 | 17 | 139 | 24 | 12 |
| 30 Escapade | A. Stewart | 141 | 36 | 48 | 139 | 47 | 13 |
| 31 Clarionet | Midland Bank Sailing Club | 142 | 56 | 25 | 140 | 38 | 38 |
| 32 Subversion | M. Joubert | 140 | 58 | 51 | 140 | 41 | 47 |
| 33 Snow Maiden II | Dr J.H. Hale | 141 | 36 | 21 | 141 | 02 | 01 |
| 34 Tessanda | E.J.M. Dent and A. Lambert | 143 | 06 | 07 | 142 | 01 | 03 |
| 35 Billycan | B. Mackay | 137 | 16 | 54 | 142 | 03 | 08 |
| 36 Scoundrel | G. Downham | 146 | 46 | 01 | 144 | 24 | 58 |
| 37 Dalcassian | J.A. Ryan | 141 | 15 | 09 | 145 | 51 | 23 |
| 38 Berenice II | P.G. Stanton | 140 | 43 | 05 | 146 | 35 | 27 |

| YACHT | OWNER (SAILED BY) | ELAPSED TIME | | | CORRECTED TIME | | |
|---|---|---|---|---|---|---|---|
| | | hr. | mn. | sc. | hr. | mn. | sc. |
| 39 *Cyn III* | L.B. Ercolani | 150 | 28 | 42 | 148 | 10 | 13 |
| 40 *Suka* | H.D. Suhrborg | 150 | 00 | 20 | 148 | 17 | 51 |
| 41 *Ocean Wave* | Royal Marines Sailing Club | 151 | 18 | 25 | 149 | 20 | 07 |
| 42 *Prinses Margriet* | KMJC (F. van Werver) | 153 | 47 | 03 | 156 | 45 | 55 |

*Class IV*

| | | | | | | | |
|---|---|---|---|---|---|---|---|
| 1 *Colbart III* | Mm Boitard, Vadet and Landegren | 136 | 28 | 58 | 131 | 58 | 22 |
| 2 *Olbia IV* | J.F. Archer | 138 | 11 | 14 | 133 | 52 | 32 |
| 3 *Ballerina IV* | S.R.G. Jeffery | 140 | 09 | 38 | 135 | 44 | 43 |
| 4 *Reiver of Mersea* | P.W. Wells | 143 | 51 | 06 | 135 | 48 | 01 |
| 5 *Trocar* | Dr N.R. Greville | 141 | 13 | 34 | 136 | 26 | 40 |
| 6 *Striva* | Y. Cudennec | 140 | 39 | 28 | 136 | 28 | 35 |
| 7 *Ceilidh* | I.R.R. Gillespie | 141 | 18 | 22 | 136 | 38 | 22 |
| 8 *Sleuth Hound* | C.S. Drummond | 142 | 08 | 25 | 137 | 05 | 14 |
| 9 *Pagan* | J.C. Clothier | 141 | 07 | 59 | 137 | 10 | 54 |
| 10 *Jantine* | D. Koopmans | 140 | 07 | 39 | 137 | 11 | 46 |
| 11 *Oberon* | W.B. Waterfall | 140 | 42 | 44 | 137 | 14 | 22 |
| 12 *Gay Gannet IV* | Cmdr F.W.B. Edwards | 141 | 27 | 12 | 137 | 31 | 05 |
| 13 *Sea Wraith III* | Royal Naval Sailing Association (Portsmouth) | 141 | 33 | 08 | 137 | 31 | 12 |
| 14 *Romanee* | H. Quiviger | 140 | 55 | 30 | 138 | 01 | 22 |
| 15 *Gay Gannett III* | A. O'Leary | 141 | 49 | 21 | 138 | 06 | 04 |
| 16 *Setanta of Howth* | J.F. McGuire | 142 | 02 | 32 | 138 | 08 | 11 |
| 17 *My Hope* | G.W. Thake | 142 | 18 | 05 | 138 | 36 | 10 |
| 18 *Broadside* | R.S. Foster | 143 | 02 | 26 | 139 | 22 | 38 |
| 19 *Ena Bee II* | D.C. Cox | 143 | 23 | 09 | 139 | 32 | 51 |
| 20 *Mowgli* | D. and Q. Jones (H. Jonas) | 146 | 47 | 08 | 139 | 56 | 08 |
| 21 *Fiddler Too* | D. Cassidy | 144 | 01 | 29 | 140 | 13 | 06 |
| 22 *Divette II* | P.L. Dorey | 144 | 16 | 07 | 141 | 02 | 33 |
| 23 *Cavalcade* | Mr and Mrs M. Pocock | 145 | 48 | 43 | 141 | 59 | 55 |
| 24 *Summer Lightning* | N.H. Case | 150 | 47 | 49 | 144 | 31 | 24 |
| 25 *Judicious* | Dr W.E. Lavelle | 149 | 30 | 04 | 144 | 55 | 33 |
| 26 *Braganza* | HMS *Excellent* (Cmdr Thomas) | 151 | 50 | 39 | 145 | 19 | 59 |
| 27 *Solent Saracen* | J.S. McCarthy | 141 | 49 | 06 | 145 | 20 | 51 |
| 28 *Spread Eagle* | Barclays Bank Ltd (M. Waight) | 150 | 42 | 31 | 147 | 08 | 49 |
| 29 *Guinevere* | Royal Naval Engineering College | 153 | 49 | 17 | 147 | 26 | 54 |
| 30 *Slipstream of Cowley* | Royal Air Force Sailing Association | 150 | 55 | 51 | 147 | 38 | 36 |
| 31 *Daiquiri* | A. Faure | 156 | 31 | 00 | 150 | 12 | 55 |
| 32 *Temeraire* | Britannia Royal Naval College | 157 | 35 | 00 | 151 | 47 | 45 |
| 33 *Volunteer* | Royal Naval Volunteer Reserve Sailing Club | 155 | 19 | 16 | 152 | 33 | 57 |
| 34 *St George of England* | Royal Corps of Transport Yacht Club (Maj. K. Rollinson) | 159 | 39 | 00 | 152 | 42 | 00 |
| 35 *Morning Melody* | Group Capt. D.E. Gillam | 157 | 17 | 50 | 154 | 23 | 38 |
| *Guenole* | N.W. Jephcott | DNF | | | | | |

*Class V*

| | | | | | | | |
|---|---|---|---|---|---|---|---|
| 1 *Maraska* | M. Girard | 140 | 42 | 08 | 133 | 37 | 44 |
| 2 *Cassiterite* | J. Tanon | 141 | 59 | 15 | 134 | 13 | 59 |
| 3 *Triel II* | Yacht Club de Triel | 141 | 37 | 52 | 134 | 30 | 26 |
| 4 *El Pepito* | P. Moné | 141 | 41 | 48 | 134 | 34 | 44 |
| 5 *Il* | P. Le Faou | 141 | 45 | 01 | 134 | 46 | 13 |
| 6 *Morbic III* | H. Elies | 141 | 44 | 55 | 134 | 53 | 37 |
| 7 *Aquila of Arne* | J.N. Leach and B.C. Robertson | 141 | 59 | 27 | 134 | 53 | 59 |
| 8 *Targaz* | P. Martinie | 141 | 45 | 28 | 134 | 54 | 13 |
| 9 *Tikocco* | M. Caillere | 141 | 55 | 42 | 134 | 57 | 51 |
| 10 *Blue Dragoon* | Lt Col. and Maj. Barne | 141 | 58 | 50 | 135 | 01 | 16 |
| 11 *Alouette de Mer* | H.P. Coveney | 141 | 38 | 24 | 135 | 09 | 06 |
| 12 *White Knight* | Royal Armoured Corps Yacht Club (Capt. P. Schofield) | 143 | 44 | 36 | 135 | 09 | 58 |
| 13 *Aquila* | Dr D.S. Park | 141 | 53 | 43 | 135 | 10 | 42 |
| 14 *Kimoa II* | M. Tribut | 142 | 10 | 03 | 135 | 13 | 29 |
| 15 *Aigle des Mers* | S. Linsale | 142 | 07 | 00 | 135 | 17 | 38 |
| 16 *Chough of Parkstone* | L. Dyball and B. Cooke | 142 | 38 | 48 | 135 | 21 | 36 |

| YACHT | OWNER (SAILED BY) | ELAPSED TIME | | | CORRECTED TIME | | |
|---|---|---|---|---|---|---|---|
| | | hr. | mn. | sc. | hr. | mn. | sc. |
| 17 *Iromiguy VI* | G. Brunet | 142 | 44 | 21 | 135 | 35 | 33 |
| 18 *Askel-Gwenn* | Dr M. Nedelee | 142 | 44 | 41 | 135 | 43 | 20 |
| 19 *Shere Khan* | Mm du Plessix, Lepage and Parent | 141 | 57 | 45 | 136 | 20 | 09 |
| 20 *Bes* | E. Duchemin | 143 | 36 | 36 | 136 | 39 | 58 |
| 21 *Arctic Skua* | M.C. Richardson | 144 | 10 | 54 | 137 | 10 | 06 |
| 22 *Barada II* | Col. K.N. Wylie | 146 | 37 | 06 | 137 | 14 | 42 |
| 23 *Parthia* | P.G. Fairlie-Clarke | 143 | 30 | 01 | 137 | 24 | 12 |
| 24 *Gwalarn* | G.I.C. des Glénans | 144 | 31 | 26 | 138 | 51 | 20 |
| 25 *Shesha* | Dr and Mrs Warr | 147 | 04 | 20 | 140 | 34 | 01 |
| 26 *Tamasin* | R.T. Bishop | 147 | 29 | 22 | 141 | 01 | 17 |
| 27 *Golden Samphire* | F.K. Beazley | 150 | 22 | 15 | 142 | 14 | 07 |
| 28 *Contessa Catherine* | Royal Engineer Yacht Club | 147 | 54 | 37 | 142 | 16 | 48 |
| 29 *Waarschip of Poole* | G.A. Warner | 150 | 18 | 00 | 143 | 51 | 10 |
| 30 *Ambush* | P.J. Thrower | 150 | 57 | 57 | 144 | 06 | 14 |
| 31 *Columba III* | J. Pouchet | 150 | 51 | 00 | 144 | 13 | 07 |
| 32 *Korimako* | B. Woodhouse | 151 | 23 | 51 | 145 | 03 | 06 |
| 33 *Tigo III* | G.J. Davis | 150 | 20 | 42 | 145 | 06 | 50 |
| 34 *Baubriant-Levesque* | A. Dhallenne | 150 | 47 | 45 | 145 | 16 | 49 |
| 35 *Bombard* | Royal Artillery Yacht Club (Maj. R.E.A. James) | 151 | 58 | 51 | 145 | 47 | 52 |
| 36 *La Daurade* | P.S. Dubosky | 151 | 08 | 04 | 145 | 57 | 45 |
| 37 *Snowbird of Hamble* | N.W. Neal | 152 | 01 | 15 | 146 | 03 | 56 |
| 38 *Cilla* | J.M. Dean | 153 | 43 | 00 | 147 | 07 | 41 |
| 39 *La Bamba of Mersea* | J.B. Holtom | 153 | 37 | 07 | 148 | 26 | 03 |
| 40 *Spunyarn* | A.W. Firebrace and G.P. Ridsdill-Smith | 153 | 58 | 10 | 149 | 00 | 38 |
| 41 *Lara of Chichester* | W.W.A. Lee | 158 | 36 | 10 | 153 | 48 | 27 |
| *Zeerob* | E.G. Jacques | DNF | | | | | |

# 1975 (9 AUGUST)

*Class I*

| | | | | | | | |
|---|---|---|---|---|---|---|---|
| 1 *Saga* | E.S. Lorentzen | 96 | 39 | 43 | 112 | 59 | 52 |
| 2 *Trailblazer* | J.P. Adams (W. Jeffrey) | 108 | 17 | 27 | 114 | 38 | 51 |
| 3 *Noryema* | R.W. Amey | 106 | 25 | 45 | 114 | 53 | 25 |
| 4 *Rubin* | H.O. Schumann | 106 | 31 | 43 | 115 | 21 | 35 |
| 5 *Pinta* | W. Illbruck | 106 | 32 | 52 | 115 | 22 | 50 |
| 6 *Battlecry* | J.O. Prentice | 106 | 35 | 29 | 115 | 54 | 27 |
| 7 *Jan Pott* | N. Lorck-Schierning | 106 | 43 | 31 | 116 | 03 | 11 |
| 8 *Tenacious* | R.E. Turner | 105 | 15 | 28 | 116 | 05 | 20 |
| 9 *Tritsch-Tratsch II* | Dr O. Glaser | 108 | 15 | 02 | 116 | 07 | 13 |
| 10 *Gerontius* | G. Eder | 107 | 48 | 24 | 116 | 08 | 24 |
| 11 *Mandrake* | Dr G. Carriero | 105 | 57 | 59 | 116 | 17 | 15 |
| 12 *Weald II* | F.J. Cummiskey | 107 | 10 | 34 | 116 | 37 | 44 |
| 13 *Red Rock III* | B. Mandelbaum | 108 | 17 | 48 | 117 | 38 | 33 |
| 14 *Duva* | P. Lubinus | 108 | 52 | 52 | 117 | 54 | 26 |
| 15 *Charisma* | J. Philips | 104 | 38 | 21 | 118 | 10 | 46 |
| 16 *Easy Rider* | J. Martens | 113 | 34 | 18 | 118 | 21 | 51 |
| 17 *Loujaine* | Sir Maurice Laing and L.J. Holliday | 113 | 49 | 31 | 118 | 37 | 43 |
| 18 *British Soldier* | JSSC (Lt Col. J. Myatt) | 106 | 31 | 24 | 119 | 32 | 25 |
| 19 *Carina III* | D. Monheim | 113 | 33 | 12 | 119 | 40 | 26 |
| 20 *Assiduous* | Clayton Love Jnr | 112 | 55 | 22 | 119 | 41 | 12 |
| 21 *Ariel* | G. Wilhelmsen | 113 | 26 | 13 | 119 | 41 | 14 |
| 22 *Spanker II* | A. Bourdon and Partners | 113 | 50 | 37 | 119 | 50 | 35 |
| 23 *Illusion* | P. Fahning | 113 | 52 | 34 | 119 | 52 | 38 |
| 24 *Morning Cloud* | Rt Hon. Edward Heath, MP | 113 | 05 | 06 | 119 | 58 | 59 |
| 25 *Prospect of Whitby* | A. Slater | 113 | 57 | 44 | 120 | 06 | 16 |
| 26 *Sanumac* | J. Camunas | 106 | 22 | 04 | 120 | 14 | 55 |
| 27 *Izenah IV* | M. Holley | 113 | 46 | 02 | 120 | 18 | 32 |
| 28 *Sea Streaker* | R.W. Hitchings | 114 | 48 | 08 | 120 | 34 | 36 |
| 29 *Liz* | J. Godager | 113 | 39 | 08 | 120 | 35 | 06 |
| 30 *Humbug XIX* | P. Pettersson | 112 | 49 | 52 | 120 | 38 | 20 |
| 31 *Tantara* | L.E. Birdzell | 113 | 29 | 08 | 120 | 40 | 49 |
| 32 *Struntje V* | Dr G. Havemann | 113 | 49 | 51 | 120 | 46 | 28 |
| 23 *Brother Cup* | E.G. Juer | 113 | 09 | 47 | 120 | 52 | 09 |
| 34 *Sarabande* | J.J. Hozee | 114 | 31 | 36 | 120 | 58 | 28 |

| YACHT | OWNER (SAILED BY) | ELAPSED TIME hr. mn. sc. | | | CORRECTED TIME hr. mn. sc. | | |
|---|---|---|---|---|---|---|---|
| 35 Wa Wa Too II | F.L. Nabuco de Abreu | 106 | 04 | 59 | 121 | 13 | 15 |
| 36 Bumblebee 3 | J.D. Kahlbetzer | 106 | 02 | 14 | 121 | 23 | 29 |
| 37 Kialoa | J.B. Kilroy | 89 | 25 | 56 | 121 | 26 | 24 |
| 38 Love & War | P. Kurts | 112 | 54 | 05 | 121 | 29 | 35 |
| 39 More Opposition | A.W.C. Morgan (B. Guttinger) | 112 | 52 | 20 | 121 | 35 | 50 |
| 40 Moonduster | D.N. Doyle | 113 | 11 | 53 | 121 | 41 | 16 |
| 41 Phantom | A. Moorkens | 112 | 57 | 09 | 121 | 58 | 39 |
| 42 Dynamo | G.W. Foog | 113 | 19 | 32 | 122 | 05 | 08 |
| 43 Ceil V | B. Turnbull | 112 | 59 | 55 | 122 | 07 | 03 |
| 44 Guia III | Ing. G. Falck | 112 | 59 | 37 | 122 | 08 | 46 |
| 45 Carina | R.S. Nye | 112 | 54 | 46 | 122 | 09 | 38 |
| 46 Congere | B.D. Koeppel | 106 | 22 | 03 | 122 | 12 | 58 |
| 47 Kealoha | Mr and Mrs L. Holliday (W. Mitchinson) | 117 | 02 | 13 | 122 | 39 | 59 |
| 48 Diva | B.A. Sully | 112 | 59 | 02 | 122 | 51 | 31 |
| 49 Spirit of Delft | Dr W.M. Oosterwijk | 113 | 02 | 26 | 123 | 18 | 17 |
| 50 Atair | A. Sutsch | 112 | 51 | 23 | 123 | 43 | 28 |
| 51 Synergy | B. McCowen | 113 | 04 | 50 | 123 | 58 | 13 |
| 52 Matrero | E. Kocourek | 112 | 58 | 17 | 124 | 11 | 22 |
| 53 Rana II | Col. J.B. Daubard | 114 | 10 | 12 | 124 | 32 | 12 |
| 54 Dagon | P. Ortan | 113 | 00 | 11 | 125 | 03 | 37 |
| 55 Puffin | E.R. Greef | 120 | 29 | 58 | 126 | 07 | 36 |
| 56 Blauwe Dolfyn II | C. Wargnies | 120 | 31 | 47 | 126 | 17 | 28 |
| 57 Standfast | G.H. and J. Sisk | 121 | 36 | 57 | 126 | 27 | 22 |
| 58 Carillion | Christian Sailing Centre (D. Hester) | 121 | 11 | 53 | 126 | 27 | 29 |
| 59 Pen Duick VI | E. Tabarly | 96 | 44 | 44 | 126 | 34 | 54 |
| 60 Adventure | JSSC (C. Hazeldine) | 113 | 27 | 11 | 126 | 58 | 36 |
| 61 Coriolan II | C. de Gallea | 113 | 23 | 03 | 127 | 27 | 59 |
| 62 Adele | R.M. Burnes | 120 | 53 | 45 | 127 | 29 | 48 |
| 63 Fanfare of Essex | Murray R. Prior | 123 | 01 | 48 | 127 | 35 | 40 |
| 64 Dasher | JSSC (R. Mullender) | 113 | 21 | 31 | 128 | 43 | 48 |
| 65 Gitana VI | Baron Edmund de Rothschild | 105 | 23 | 01 | 129 | 34 | 09 |
| 66 Musketeer | H. Williams | 125 | 00 | 16 | 129 | 38 | 32 |
| 67 Perseverance | Sir Max Aitken and R.T. Lowein | 113 | 12 | 02 | 129 | 49 | 06 |
| 68 Lord Trenchard | D.W.B. Farrar | 115 | 16 | 46 | 130 | 19 | 24 |
| 69 Inschallah | W. Andreae | 112 | 58 | 45 | 131 | 00 | 38 |
| 70 Tornado | Y.K.M. Kotwica | 114 | 52 | 38 | 134 | 13 | 21 |
| 71 La Goleta | C. Lawrence | 134 | 37 | 31 | 141 | 52 | 53 |
| 72 Gallivanter | J.M.A. Paterson | 127 | 16 | 30 | 143 | 13 | 21 |
| 73 Latifa | L. Dovey | 113 | 50 | 48 | 144 | 39 | 44 |
| 74 Iolaire | D. Street | 147 | 43 | 32 | 149 | 04 | 11 |
| Antigua VII | N. Richter | DNF | | | | | |
| Saudade | A. Buell | DNF | | | | | |
| Stortebeker | HVS | DNF | | | | | |
| Vihuela | F. Violati | DNF | | | | | |
| Inca | E. Julian | Disqualified | | | | | |

*Class II*

| | | | | | | | |
|---|---|---|---|---|---|---|---|
| 1 Goodwin | J. van Drongelan | 107 | 27 | 25 | 109 | 49 | 15 |
| 2 Flamenco | G. Cryns | 108 | 02 | 20 | 110 | 08 | 05 |
| 3 Standfast II | P.W. Vroon and F. Maas | 106 | 47 | 47 | 110 | 28 | 51 |
| 4 Arc en Ciel | H. Hamon | 109 | 30 | 49 | 111 | 46 | 50 |
| 5 Revolution | J.L. Fabry | 113 | 30 | 09 | 113 | 32 | 52 |
| 6 Nymphea | Th. E.W. Vinke (M. Simoes) | 110 | 04 | 04 | 113 | 55 | 52 |
| 7 Frigate | CASA (B. Bongers) | 113 | 32 | 10 | 115 | 09 | 35 |
| 8 Casse Tete | D.H. Johnson (H.H. Ross) | 115 | 22 | 13 | 115 | 33 | 18 |
| 9 Olbia V | J.F. Archer | 114 | 10 | 47 | 115 | 39 | 50 |
| 10 Yeoman XX | R.A. and A. Aisher | 111 | 37 | 09 | 115 | 44 | 56 |
| 11 Charlatan | R.W. Appelbee | 113 | 42 | 29 | 115 | 54 | 50 |
| 12 Mabelle | Federacion Espanola de Vela | 115 | 11 | 52 | 116 | 04 | 24 |
| 13 Robin | T. Hood | 112 | 08 | 02 | 116 | 16 | 58 |
| 14 Attaque | C. Rydqvist | 114 | 56 | 51 | 116 | 44 | 26 |
| 15 Omuramba | H. Berker | 114 | 26 | 58 | 116 | 55 | 58 |
| 16 Katsou | A. Viant and D. Paul-Cavallier | 113 | 08 | 29 | 117 | 02 | 41 |
| 17 Irish Mist | A. O'Leary | 113 | 12 | 30 | 117 | 06 | 50 |
| 18 Barnacle Bill | R. Jarden (R. Haslar) | 113 | 25 | 17 | 117 | 20 | 04 |
| 19 Fair Judgement IV | P.F. Carter-Ruck | 116 | 25 | 20 | 117 | 20 | 31 |

| YACHT | OWNER (SAILED BY) | ELAPSED TIME | | | CORRECTED TIME | | |
|---|---|---|---|---|---|---|---|
| | | hr. | mn. | sc. | hr. | mn. | sc. |
| 20 *On Dit* | H. Ringeisen | 115 | 11 | 18 | 117 | 34 | 22 |
| 21 *Don Alberto* | G. Frers | 113 | 15 | 30 | 117 | 35 | 05 |
| 22 *Deception I* | V. Mandelli | 113 | 09 | 00 | 117 | 45 | 19 |
| 23 *Mercedes IV* | H.T. Kaufman | 113 | 10 | 12 | 117 | 46 | 34 |
| 24 *Colombe* | P. d'Andrimont | 113 | 34 | 18 | 116 | 43 | 44 |
| 25 *Samphire* | J.A. Sampson | 116 | 02 | 18 | 117 | 50 | 55 |
| 26 *Marionette V* | C.A.F. Dunning | 113 | 15 | 51 | 117 | 52 | 26 |
| 27 *Golden Fleece* | G.J. Neill | 115 | 01 | 59 | 118 | 42 | 51 |
| 28 *Amiral de Siam* | C. Poirier | 114 | 31 | 49 | 118 | 46 | 05 |
| 29 *Scamander* | S.T. Nauta | 121 | 34 | 15 | 119 | 17 | 51 |
| 30 *Procelaria* | F.J. Pimentel Duarte | 116 | 38 | 11 | 119 | 47 | 08 |
| 31 *Red Lancer* | R. Fuller | 116 | 46 | 14 | 120 | 01 | 00 |
| 32 *Belita VII* | J.S. Bouman | 121 | 19 | 36 | 121 | 31 | 15 |
| 33 *Gunfleet of Hamble* | R. Jones | 120 | 39 | 42 | 121 | 46 | 18 |
| 34 *Dorothea* | W.C. Petersen | 116 | 12 | 51 | 121 | 46 | 51 |
| 35 *Sasha* | W. Slee | 121 | 26 | 33 | 122 | 15 | 22 |
| 36 *Sawadi Song* | H. Formgren | 120 | 24 | 55 | 122 | 17 | 37 |
| 37 *Kyria* | Baron Manfred van Schroder | 123 | 29 | 27 | 122 | 44 | 15 |
| 38 *Sagamore* | F. Grape (P. Lorange) | 121 | 01 | 18 | 123 | 04 | 01 |
| 39 *High Noon* | F.D. Tughan | 121 | 19 | 35 | 123 | 32 | 04 |
| 40 *Niob V* | F. Bigotte | 121 | 04 | 34 | 123 | 42 | 12 |
| 41 *St Barbara III* | Royal Artillery Yacht Club | 125 | 53 | 59 | 124 | 58 | 05 |
| 42 *Avilion III* | H.C.R. Ballam | 120 | 39 | 11 | 125 | 10 | 39 |
| 43 *Savoire Faire* | R.P. Riesco | 123 | 44 | 50 | 125 | 12 | 27 |
| 44 *Kanata* | Vladimir Plavsic | 121 | 13 | 47 | 125 | 51 | 38 |
| 45 *Sunburst* | J.H. Barker | 131 | 26 | 34 | 130 | 10 | 04 |
| 46 *Brynoth* | H. Sherrard | 134 | 28 | 20 | 131 | 02 | 35 |
| 47 *Wishtream 2* | Royal Military Academy Sailing Club (Maj. M. Miller) | 134 | 25 | 15 | 132 | 25 | 53 |
| 48 *Nefertiti* | B. Hancock | 130 | 49 | 34 | 133 | 21 | 50 |
| 49 *Griffon* | ECCTA (Gen. Archamreaud) | 134 | 28 | 15 | 134 | 10 | 30 |
| 50 *Rave III* | Royal Engineer Yacht Club and Sailing Association | 142 | 53 | 58 | 141 | 41 | 05 |
| *Derring-do* | P.S. du Posky | DNF | | | | | |
| *Nemesis* | Capt. G. Greenfield | DNF | | | | | |
| *Tina-I-Punkt* | G. Friese | DNF | | | | | |

*Class III*

| YACHT | OWNER (SAILED BY) | ELAPSED TIME | | | CORRECTED TIME | | |
|---|---|---|---|---|---|---|---|
| 1 *Stress* | B. Blumenthal | 115 | 42 | 14 | 111 | 05 | 55 |
| 2 *Machichaco* | J. Clabarri and J. Churruca | 114 | 54 | 50 | 111 | 27 | 59 |
| 3 *Schuttevaer* | Dr J.C.W. van Dam | 114 | 43 | 31 | 112 | 14 | 50 |
| 4 *Windsprite* | B.B. Banks | 117 | 11 | 21 | 112 | 21 | 39 |
| 5 *Chartreuse II* | F.R. Ducker | 115 | 10 | 03 | 112 | 50 | 28 |
| 6 *Akela B* | G.S.C. Clarabut | 115 | 35 | 12 | 113 | 15 | 06 |
| 7 *Dulle Griet* | L. Cappuyns | 116 | 46 | 53 | 113 | 56 | 37 |
| 8 *Golden Apple* | J. Ewart | 116 | 20 | 21 | 113 | 59 | 20 |
| 9 *Crazy Wolf* | J.A. Harrison and B.R. Pearson | 117 | 30 | 38 | 114 | 19 | 34 |
| 10 *Dictator* | D. and J. Irwin | 117 | 24 | 11 | 114 | 52 | 02 |
| 11 *Impala* | B.E. Ruys | 116 | 50 | 26 | 114 | 57 | 34 |
| 12 *Zeehaas* | M.J.F. Vroon | 120 | 45 | 22 | 114 | 58 | 45 |
| 13 *Bootlicker* | J.C. and Dr J.D. Rogers and D. Pitt-Pitts | 117 | 21 | 05 | 114 | 58 | 51 |
| 14 *Pordin-Nancq* | Dr J. Lamouric | 117 | 55 | 52 | 115 | 52 | 02 |
| 15 *Betula* | B.C. Ryan | 123 | 36 | 17 | 116 | 39 | 29 |
| 16 *Tiburon* | P.H. de Koster | 121 | 43 | 20 | 117 | 34 | 17 |
| 17 *Combat* | G.H. Bottomley and D. Gillam | 120 | 58 | 42 | 117 | 52 | 09 |
| 18 *Flying Yorkshireman* | J.M. Murray | 122 | 51 | 14 | 118 | 08 | 10 |
| 19 *Flycatcher* | J.W. Roome | 120 | 54 | 16 | 118 | 17 | 34 |
| 20 *Schuylkill* | A.J. Wilson | 121 | 21 | 23 | 118 | 22 | 16 |
| 21 *Golden Griffin* | Midland Bank Sailing Club (S. Dack) | 120 | 41 | 18 | 118 | 25 | 09 |
| 22 *Electron II* | Royal Naval Sailing Association | 123 | 21 | 21 | 118 | 26 | 46 |
| 23 *Super Tension* | A.M. Smith | 121 | 57 | 23 | 118 | 49 | 20 |
| 24 *Xara* | D.C. Barham | 120 | 53 | 34 | 118 | 56 | 47 |
| 25 *Jubile* | H. Hamon | 121 | 36 | 05 | 119 | 08 | 42 |
| 26 *Pen-Ar-Vir IV* | P. Bonnet | 121 | 58 | 10 | 119 | 20 | 06 |
| 27 *Crackerjack* | J.M. Miller | 124 | 06 | 31 | 119 | 20 | 34 |

| YACHT | OWNER (SAILED BY) | ELAPSED TIME | | | CORRECTED TIME | | | |
|---|---|---|---|---|---|---|---|---|
| | | hr. | mn. | sc. | hr. | mn. | sc. | |
| 28 *Croix du Cygne* | K. van Exter | 123 | 29 | 15 | 119 | 26 | 58 | |
| 29 *Tam O'Shanter* | J.C. Butler | 121 | 22 | 43 | 119 | 31 | 17 | |
| 30 *Tessanda II* | E.J.M. Dent and A.G. Lambert | 122 | 03 | 33 | 119 | 35 | 37 | |
| 31 *Brigante* | H. Watson | 122 | 37 | 44 | 119 | 49 | 14 | |
| 32 *Pepsi* | A. Milton | 122 | 45 | 53 | 119 | 57 | 12 | |
| 33 *Hylas* | D. Edwards | 122 | 37 | 57 | 119 | 59 | 01 | |
| 34 *Thunder* | B. Tanghe | 122 | 58 | 45 | 120 | 29 | 42 | |
| 35 *Billycan* | B. Mackay | 123 | 09 | 27 | 120 | 29 | 50 | |
| 36 *Pizco* | Y. Debat | 123 | 33 | 38 | 121 | 03 | 53 | |
| 37 *Altricia* | B.M. Baird | 128 | 12 | 04 | 122 | 11 | 18 | |
| 38 *Maligawa* | G. Foures | 125 | 32 | 40 | 123 | 00 | 30 | |
| 39 *Paprika* | J.J. Flood (J. Soutar) | 124 | 10 | 07 | 123 | 50 | 45 | |
| 40 *Betelgueze* | S. van Hagen | 134 | 35 | 08 | 129 | 59 | 46 | |
| 41 *Timona* | S.E. Bjerser | 122 | 20 | 23 | 120 | 02 | 23 | |
| 42 *Bilou-Belle* | D. Malbraud | 127 | 41 | 47 | 121 | 41 | 40 | |
| *Griffin IV* | Royal Ocean Racing Club | DNF | | | | | | |
| *Palamedes* | A.J. Sheldon | DNF | | | | | | |
| *Pilgrim* | Y. Boucher | DNF | | | | | | |
| *Surf Scoter* | W.J. Davies | DNF | | | | | | |

*Class IV*

| YACHT | OWNER (SAILED BY) | ELAPSED TIME | | | CORRECTED TIME | | | |
|---|---|---|---|---|---|---|---|---|
| 1 *Golden Delicious* | P. Nicholson (R. Bagnall) | 115 | 02 | 54 | 107 | 16 | 16 | (*1st overall*) |
| 2 *Polar Bear* | J.C. Clothier | 115 | 48 | 19 | 108 | 29 | 52 | |
| 3 *Trocar* | Dr N.R. Greville | 121 | 17 | 39 | 109 | 33 | 54 | |
| 4 *Gay Gannet V* | Cmdr F.W.B. Edwards | 121 | 55 | 47 | 113 | 52 | 12 | |
| 5 *Malaise* | G.S. Golder | 124 | 13 | 52 | 114 | 03 | 23 | |
| 6 *Flamenca* | L. Chaves | 121 | 59 | 52 | 114 | 17 | 59 | |
| 7 *Ossian* | P. Ratzel | 122 | 15 | 15 | 114 | 21 | 23 | |
| 8 *Carronade of Mersea* | Mr and Mrs P. Clements | 123 | 29 | 11 | 114 | 32 | 01 | |
| 9 *Maridadi* | R. Dreschfield | 124 | 24 | 58 | 115 | 03 | 38 | |
| 10 *Samurai* | R.G. Jordan | 121 | 52 | 37 | 115 | 16 | 16 | |
| 11 *Oberon II* | G.C. Skelley | 125 | 56 | 16 | 115 | 26 | 50 | |
| 12 *Champagne Magnum* | W.K. and R. Stead | 123 | 48 | 30 | 115 | 48 | 37 | |
| 13 *Oriana* | Mr and Mrs K. Geddes | 126 | 43 | 35 | 116 | 24 | 39 | |
| 14 *Va Hini III* | M. Faque | 125 | 58 | 09 | 116 | 50 | 11 | |
| 15 *Hindostan* | Britannia Royal Naval College (S.K. Armistead) | 125 | 29 | 58 | 117 | 12 | 14 | |
| 16 *Striva* | Y. Cudennec | 126 | 39 | 31 | 117 | 17 | 09 | |
| 17 *Fleur de Cactus* | G. Griot | 123 | 34 | 32 | 114 | 39 | 12 | |
| 18 *Thunderflash* | Royal Naval Engineering College (Lt N. Williams) | 125 | 35 | 22 | 117 | 17 | 16 | |
| 19 *UFO* | R. Matthews | 125 | 45 | 34 | 117 | 49 | 26 | |
| 20 *Tyfoon V* | G. Versluys | 126 | 39 | 01 | 117 | 50 | 07 | |
| 21 *Le Jovial Tiburon* | M. Lefevre | 124 | 02 | 05 | 117 | 50 | 43 | |
| 22 *Slipstream* | Royal Air Force Sailing Association | 129 | 50 | 30 | 117 | 52 | 13 | |
| 23 *Lorelei* | M. Catherineau | 124 | 51 | 29 | 117 | 54 | 12 | |
| 24 *Spirit of Victoria* | D. Koopmans | 125 | 05 | 14 | 118 | 18 | 27 | |
| 25 *Romanee* | H. Quiviger and H. Le Quesne | 125 | 24 | 34 | 118 | 58 | 33 | |
| 26 *Minoc* | G. Craipeau | 132 | 18 | 48 | 120 | 32 | 15 | |
| 27 *Flashlight* | Royal Naval Engineering College (Col. P. Wyatt) | 129 | 02 | 31 | 120 | 53 | 57 | |
| 28 *Velleda* | The French Navy (Asp. Douchy) | 130 | 58 | 04 | 121 | 28 | 21 | |
| 29 *Broadside* | R.S. Foster | 132 | 02 | 17 | 122 | 27 | 56 | |
| 30 *Volunteer* | Royal Naval Volunteer Reserve Sailing Club | 134 | 51 | 26 | 123 | 48 | 45 | |
| 31 *Ancaster* | C. Lowe | 135 | 57 | 31 | 125 | 53 | 51 | |
| 32 *Gerhemi* | G. Amelineau | 133 | 57 | 12 | 127 | 16 | 08 | |
| 33 *Roi Arthur* | Ecole Nationale de Voile | 139 | 56 | 45 | 127 | 42 | 02 | |
| 34 *Red Arrow* | G.H. Crawford | 139 | 43 | 12 | 131 | 43 | 41 | |
| 35 *Pryderi* | Dr G.B. Hollings | 143 | 19 | 58 | 132 | 06 | 30 | |
| 36 *Reiver of Mersea* | P.W. Wells | 147 | 21 | 05 | 133 | 06 | 03 | |
| 37 *Sarie Marais* | Cmdr D.D.E. Gay | 147 | 33 | 58 | 133 | 27 | 31 | |
| 38 *Kashamara* | M.E. Blan | 144 | 52 | 40 | 134 | 52 | 00 | |
| 39 *Fleur de Mer* | R.J. Bubear | 147 | 47 | 05 | 135 | 04 | 31 | |
| 40 *Spread Eagle* | Barclays Bank Sailing Club (M. Waight) | 149 | 16 | 15 | 137 | 46 | 37 | |
| 41 *Judicious* | Dr W.E. Lavelle | 150 | 35 | 21 | 138 | 05 | 25 | |

| YACHT | OWNER (SAILED BY) | ELAPSED TIME | | | CORRECTED TIME | | |
|---|---|---|---|---|---|---|---|
| | | hr. | mn. | sc. | hr. | mn. | sc. |

*Class V*

| | | | | | | | |
|---|---|---|---|---|---|---|---|
| 1 *Maraska* | M. and F. Girard | 123 | 18 | 50 | 110 | 08 | 38 |
| 2 *Zett* | Mr and Mrs B. Saffery Cooper | 123 | 55 | 50 | 110 | 41 | 41 |
| 3 *Quasar* | R. Locke | 127 | 46 | 43 | 111 | 44 | 32 |
| 4 *Cathys Clown* | Mr and Mrs A. Gill | 125 | 54 | 08 | 111 | 50 | 20 |
| 5 *Spirale* | M. Mallet | 125 | 55 | 38 | 111 | 51 | 40 |
| 6 *Fragola* | G.I.C. des Glénans | 127 | 44 | 15 | 111 | 55 | 24 |
| 7 *Morbic 3* | H. Elies | 126 | 39 | 48 | 111 | 59 | 37 |
| 8 *Tamasin II* | R.T. Bishop | 126 | 21 | 15 | 112 | 51 | 34 |
| 9 *Valross* | T.H. Bevan | 127 | 39 | 06 | 114 | 01 | 06 |
| 10 *Callibistris* | M. Hennebert | 127 | 49 | 04 | 114 | 10 | 00 |
| 11 *Blue Dragoon* | Lt Col. A.M. and Maj. C. Barne | 129 | 19 | 43 | 115 | 18 | 33 |
| 12 *Racer Bruin* | R. Manning | 130 | 02 | 10 | 116 | 08 | 54 |
| 13 *Windy of Hamble* | R. Ewart Smith | 131 | 23 | 13 | 116 | 11 | 07 |
| 14 *Aquila of Arne* | J.N. Leach | 131 | 02 | 09 | 116 | 37 | 18 |
| 15 *D'Arcy Spice* | L. Baker and J. Pugh | 131 | 01 | 30 | 117 | 01 | 53 |
| 16 *Callisto* | R.E. Davidson and J. Miller | 136 | 31 | 55 | 118 | 20 | 45 |
| 17 *Barada II* | Col. and Mrs K.N. Wylie | 134 | 58 | 32 | 118 | 35 | 22 |
| 18 *Flamingo II* | B. Charman | 135 | 01 | 01 | 118 | 44 | 02 |
| 19 *Hurricantoo* | B. Simms | 134 | 17 | 11 | 119 | 56 | 41 |
| 20 *Gwalarn* | G.I.C. des Glénans | 136 | 33 | 06 | 120 | 45 | 09 |
| 21 *Grinde* | M. Miller | 137 | 18 | 30 | 122 | 25 | 27 |
| 22 *Buluba II* | J.F. Watton | 140 | 17 | 39 | 122 | 41 | 14 |
| 23 *Flicka V* | T. Nielsen | 136 | 03 | 31 | 123 | 43 | 05 |
| 24 *Sandpiper* | R.P. Billinghurst | 137 | 13 | 01 | 124 | 06 | 45 |
| 25 *Fildelyn* | D.R. Matthews | 142 | 42 | 41 | 126 | 11 | 59 |
| 26 *Pinguino* | G.M. Dorey | 145 | 34 | 00 | 126 | 49 | 26 |
| 27 *Contessa Catherine* | Royal Engineer Yacht Club | 143 | 25 | 06 | 128 | 12 | 06 |
| 28 *Gelinotte* | J. Le Guen | 143 | 20 | 29 | 128 | 30 | 20 |
| 29 *Chough* | L. Dyball and B. Cooke | 147 | 14 | 28 | 128 | 31 | 36 |
| 30 *Mar del Norte* | Capt. R.S. Aspinall | 147 | 30 | 45 | 130 | 32 | 55 |
| 31 *Kinabalu II* | Mrs J.T. Graves | 148 | 54 | 17 | 133 | 34 | 03 |
| 32 *Longay II* | I.M.C. Scott | 152 | 46 | 00 | 138 | 25 | 18 |
| *Bombard* | Royal Artillery Yacht Club | DNF | | | | | |
| *Dael* | Y. Limoges | DNF | | | | | |
| *Golden Shotok* | G. Dupuy | DNF | | | | | |
| *Gollywogs* | J. Lewthwaite and P. Mayes | DNF | | | | | |
| *Roulette* | Mr and Mrs R. Barton | DNF | | | | | |

# 1977 (6 AUGUST)

*Class Zero*

| | | | | | | | |
|---|---|---|---|---|---|---|---|
| 1 *Saga* | Erling S. Lorentzen | 136 | 23 | 35 | 158 | 44 | 03 |
| 2 *Gitana VI* | E. de Rothschild | 130 | 24 | 45 | 158 | 52 | 07 |
| 3 *Demon* | A.J. Gilson | 140 | 20 | 18 | 161 | 40 | 11 |
| 4 *Il Moro di Venezia* | R. Gardini | 128 | 10 | 02 | 166 | 13 | 58 |
| 5 *Inshallah* | W. Andree | 144 | 38 | 07 | 169 | 48 | 59 |
| 6 *Flyer* | C. van Rietschoten | 141 | 56 | 55 | 171 | 39 | 30 |
| 7 *Ballyhoo* | J. Rooklyn | 127 | 04 | 41 | 172 | 33 | 33 |
| 8 *Condor* | R. Knox-Johnston and L. Williams | 128 | 58 | 45 | 177 | 19 | 14 |
| 9 *Black Fin* | A.F. Jefferson | 137 | 01 | 04 | 182 | 09 | 05 |
| *Japy Hames* | J.M. Viant | DNF | | | | | |
| *Neptune* | B. de Guy | DNF | | | | | |
| *War Baby* | Warren A. Brown | DNF | | | | | |
| *Kings Legend* | N.O. Ratcliff | DNF | | | | | |
| *That Boat* | Miss C. Francis | DNF | | | | | |
| *Great Britain* | C. Blyth | DNF | | | | | |
| *Disque Dor* | P.P. Fehlman | DNF | | | | | |

| YACHT | OWNER (SAILED BY) | ELAPSED TIME hr. mn. sc. | | | CORRECTED TIME hr. mn. sc. | | |
|---|---|---|---|---|---|---|---|

*Class I*

| | YACHT | OWNER (SAILED BY) | hr. | mn. | sc. | hr. | mn. | sc. |
|---|---|---|---|---|---|---|---|---|
| 1 | Moonshine | J.C. Rogers and W. Green | 134 | 27 | 22 | 141 | 32 | 31 |
| 2 | Bay Bea | P.E. Haggerty | 135 | 16 | 44 | 145 | 06 | 49 |
| 3 | Assiduous | M. Berger | 141 | 16 | 49 | 146 | 36 | 23 |
| 4 | Marionette | C.A.F. Dunning | 137 | 39 | 33 | 146 | 42 | 12 |
| 5 | Red Rock III | Dr O. Glaser | 137 | 57 | 04 | 148 | 26 | 57 |
| 6 | Emeraude | J. Dewailly | 133 | 05 | 06 | 148 | 29 | 46 |
| 7 | Mandrake | G. Carriero | 140 | 17 | 22 | 149 | 30 | 23 |
| 8 | Ragamuffin | S. Fischer | 138 | 27 | 00 | 150 | 43 | 00 |
| 9 | Bumblebee 3 | J.D. Kahlbetzer | 132 | 14 | 55 | 151 | 05 | 39 |
| 10 | Scaramouche | C. Kirsch | 137 | 59 | 25 | 151 | 16 | 43 |
| 11 | Fortuna II | Armada Argentina | 132 | 19 | 34 | 151 | 20 | 29 |
| 12 | Victoria | E. Kocourek | 139 | 40 | 14 | 152 | 02 | 43 |
| 13 | Moonduster | D.N. Doyle | 140 | 46 | 20 | 152 | 09 | 38 |
| 14 | Scaldis | S.T. Nauta | 139 | 04 | 49 | 153 | 12 | 39 |
| 15 | Recluta IV | C.A. Corna | 139 | 45 | 29 | 153 | 13 | 00 |
| 16 | Vanina | V. Mandelli | 144 | 58 | 29 | 153 | 39 | 31 |
| 17 | Big Apple | Messrs Coveney, Fielding and Love | 146 | 13 | 37 | 155 | 40 | 24 |
| 18 | Azahara | Duke of Arion | 142 | 49 | 54 | 155 | 48 | 02 |
| 19 | Spirit of Delft | Dr W.M. Oosterwijk | 141 | 47 | 50 | 156 | 59 | 52 |
| 20 | Chaser | JSSC (C. Forrest) | 141 | 47 | 13 | 157 | 54 | 29 |
| 21 | Brandywine | W.R. Slee | 153 | 26 | 21 | 161 | 10 | 21 |
| 22 | Loujaine | Sir Maurice Laing | 156 | 16 | 18 | 161 | 42 | 35 |
| 23 | Sunbird V | T. Yamasaki | 145 | 47 | 33 | 163 | 26 | 52 |
| 24 | Odiseus | Sr L. Garcia Meca | 152 | 11 | 18 | 163 | 36 | 09 |
| 25 | Alexandre | M. Marchais | 155 | 37 | 31 | 164 | 00 | 48 |
| 26 | Blauwe Dolfyn II | C. Wargnies | 159 | 21 | 15 | 164 | 50 | 09 |
| 27 | Noryema | R.W. Amey | 153 | 42 | 07 | 166 | 06 | 20 |
| 28 | Dorothea | W.C. Petersen | 157 | 59 | 09 | 166 | 07 | 19 |
| 29 | Mersea Pearl | W. Newman | 158 | 35 | 42 | 166 | 20 | 04 |
| 30 | White Quailo | T.D. Parr | 154 | 42 | 30 | 166 | 28 | 54 |
| 31 | Morning Cloud | Rt Hon. Edward Heath, MP | 157 | 50 | 50 | 166 | 32 | 40 |
| 32 | Carina III | D. Monheim | 158 | 51 | 14 | 166 | 43 | 59 |
| 33 | Phantom II | A. Moorkens | 158 | 36 | 05 | 166 | 57 | 34 |
| 34 | Blue Jennifer | N.C.S. Rawlings | 158 | 40 | 32 | 167 | 13 | 41 |
| 35 | Synergy | E. Koefoed | 154 | 02 | 55 | 169 | 03 | 10 |
| 36 | Kennebec | G.K. Smith | 159 | 03 | 05 | 169 | 09 | 39 |
| 37 | Rubin | Osterreichischer S-V | 157 | 46 | 53 | 170 | 00 | 34 |
| 38 | Superstar | K. Farfor | 157 | 22 | 42 | 170 | 04 | 44 |
| 39 | Duva | Dr R. Lubinus | 157 | 36 | 49 | 170 | 08 | 38 |
| 40 | Volle Maen | L. Aardenburg | 156 | 39 | 17 | 170 | 42 | 24 |
| 41 | Milene III | A. Mirlesse | 158 | 27 | 19 | 170 | 52 | 41 |
| 42 | Atair | A. Sutsch | 157 | 12 | 19 | 170 | 56 | 42 |
| 43 | Jan Pott | L. Hubert | 158 | 50 | 29 | 171 | 50 | 04 |
| 44 | Lord Trenchard | JSSC (D. Farrar) | 156 | 06 | 00 | 173 | 02 | 07 |
| 45 | British Soldier | Lt Col. J. Myatt | 158 | 55 | 59 | 176 | 24 | 56 |
| 46 | Lord Portal | JSSC (A. Lethem) | 159 | 05 | 11 | 177 | 20 | 58 |
| 47 | Mad Carew | D.A.D. Munro | 166 | 17 | 07 | 179 | 45 | 15 |
| | Clodagh | L. Godinot | DNF | | | | | |
| | Traite de Rome | Sail for Europe | DNF | | | | | |
| | Rubin | Hans-Otto Schumann | DNF | | | | | |
| | Aquis Granus | I. Sauer | DNF | | | | | |
| | Struntje V | Dr G. Havemann | DNF | | | | | |
| | Miyakadori III | H. Okasaki | DNF | | | | | |
| | Brother Cup | Osterreichischer S-V | DNF | | | | | |
| | Racer | Lt Cmdr Richardson | DNF | | | | | |
| | Battlecry | J.O. Prentice | DNF | | | | | |
| | Outlaw | Mr and Mrs Fewtrell | DNF | | | | | |
| | Carillion of Wight | Christian Sailing Centre | DNF | | | | | |
| | Sarabande | J.J. Hozee | DNF | | | | | |
| | Sea Streaker | R.W. Hitchings | DNF | | | | | |

| YACHT | OWNER (SAILED BY) | ELAPSED TIME hr. mn. sc. | | | CORRECTED TIME hr. mn. sc. | | | |
|---|---|---|---|---|---|---|---|---|
| **Class II** | | | | | | | | |
| 1 *Imp* | D. Allen | 137 | 53 | 26 | 141 | 26 | 53 | (*1st overall*) |
| 2 *Yeoman XX* | R.A. and A. Aisher | 138 | 02 | 43 | 141 | 36 | 25 | |
| 3 *Pinta* | W. Illbruck | 138 | 11 | 40 | 143 | 28 | 24 | |
| 4 *Yachtman* | Sindicato AC77 | 140 | 27 | 06 | 145 | 27 | 57 | |
| 5 *Liz of Hankø* | J.B. Godager | 140 | 15 | 14 | 145 | 36 | 41 | |
| 6 *Vineta* | F. Scheder-Bieschin | 140 | 25 | 00 | 145 | 46 | 50 | |
| 7 *Knockout* | Sir Max Aitken and R. Lowein | 141 | 11 | 52 | 145 | 53 | 59 | |
| 8 *Iorana III* | W.W. Denzel | 142 | 04 | 12 | 146 | 15 | 39 | |
| 9 *La Pantera* | E. de Lasala and P. Ostenfeld | 140 | 59 | 56 | 147 | 45 | 09 | |
| 10 *Champagne* | P. Westphal-Langloh | 143 | 41 | 11 | 149 | 10 | 30 | |
| 11 *Standfast* | P.W. Vroon and F.L. Maas | 143 | 46 | 28 | 149 | 47 | 53 | |
| 12 *Moby Dick* | L.F. Bortolotti | 153 | 42 | 36 | 157 | 51 | 36 | |
| 13 *Brynoth* | H. Sherrard | 166 | 30 | 33 | 157 | 55 | 02 | |
| 14 *Revolution* | J.L. Fabry | 158 | 35 | 25 | 158 | 16 | 23 | |
| 15 *White Rabbit* | J. Ma | 153 | 01 | 37 | 158 | 18 | 22 | |
| 16 *Katsou* | A. Viant and P. Facque | 153 | 41 | 55 | 159 | 00 | 04 | |
| 17 *Schuttevaer* | Dr J.C.W. van Dam | 157 | 41 | 53 | 159 | 44 | 53 | |
| 18 *Tigre* | F.P. Duarte | 154 | 08 | 23 | 159 | 50 | 34 | |
| 19 *Raveling* | L. van den Bossche | 159 | 09 | 59 | 160 | 15 | 53 | |
| 20 *Impromptu* | J. Ewart | 154 | 57 | 47 | 160 | 41 | 48 | |
| 21 *Vanguard* | D. Lieu | 157 | 19 | 20 | 162 | 10 | 04 | |
| 22 *Morningtown* | R.G. Hill | 161 | 40 | 12 | 162 | 18 | 02 | |
| 23 *Runaway* | J. Hardy | 157 | 29 | 05 | 162 | 31 | 27 | |
| 24 *Olbia V* | J. Archer | 159 | 51 | 15 | 162 | 38 | 08 | |
| 25 *Nymphaea* | A. Goudriaan and Th. E. Vinkel | 158 | 40 | 22 | 162 | 49 | 48 | |
| 26 *Vector* | J. Diamond | 159 | 31 | 46 | 162 | 49 | 54 | |
| 27 *Yena* | S. Doni | 158 | 22 | 24 | 163 | 02 | 43 | |
| 28 *Uin Na Mara III* | Mr and Mrs H. Ross | 158 | 21 | 09 | 163 | 13 | 47 | |
| 29 *Findabar of Howth* | J.P. Jameson | 165 | 40 | 32 | 163 | 22 | 22 | |
| 30 *Orion III* | E. Barth | 157 | 38 | 10 | 163 | 28 | 07 | |
| 31 *Victoria* | G. Lundberg | 158 | 13 | 50 | 163 | 41 | 22 | |
| 32 *Golden Leigh* | N. Cordiner | 158 | 52 | 25 | 163 | 46 | 00 | |
| 33 *Tiderace III* | D.E.P. Norton | 159 | 24 | 17 | 163 | 51 | 07 | |
| 34 *Kamaiura* | E. Falkenberg | 158 | 53 | 19 | 164 | 10 | 46 | |
| 35 *Irish Mist II* | A. O'Leary | 158 | 42 | 33 | 164 | 11 | 04 | |
| 36 *Soizic* | J. Dobbelaere | 158 | 42 | 36 | 164 | 46 | 21 | |
| 37 *Chastanet* | N.A. Brick | 158 | 11 | 04 | 164 | 48 | 44 | |
| 38 *Goodwill* | H. Formgren | 158 | 22 | 26 | 164 | 49 | 11 | |
| 39 *Hajduk* | E. Hoffmann | 159 | 43 | 48 | 165 | 02 | 56 | |
| 40 *Relance* | Syndicat Relance | 159 | 16 | 20 | 165 | 21 | 23 | |
| 41 *Goodwin* | J. van Drongelen | 157 | 58 | 49 | 165 | 21 | 28 | |
| 42 *B B III* | Y. Sawano | 163 | 10 | 23 | 165 | 30 | 23 | |
| 43 *Nick-Nack* | N. Langley-Pope | 163 | 40 | 54 | 165 | 36 | 47 | |
| 44 *Bumerang* | Jacht Klub Stal | 160 | 10 | 16 | 165 | 41 | 49 | |
| 45 *Nemesis* | Capt. G.G. Greenfield | 164 | 23 | 43 | 165 | 57 | 25 | |
| 46 *St Barbara III* | Royal Artillery | 169 | 08 | 50 | 166 | 05 | 35 | |
| 47 *Susette* | C.W. Edstroem | 159 | 13 | 52 | 166 | 17 | 06 | |
| *Hamburg* | Hamburg V.S. | DNF | | | | | | |
| *Savoir Faire* | R.P. Riesco | DNF | | | | | | |
| *Derring-Do* | P.S. Du Bosky | DNF | | | | | | |
| *Philippides* | Philippides Ocean Charter | DNF | | | | | | |
| *Spaniel* | Jacht Klub Pasat | DNF | | | | | | |
| *Griffon* | AECCTA (G. Jolly) | DNF | | | | | | |
| **Class III** | | | | | | | | |
| 1 *Variag* | M. Henrion | 160 | 25 | 20 | 150 | 31 | 27 | |
| 2 *Blue Bird* | A. Gerard | 160 | 43 | 14 | 151 | 42 | 15 | |
| 3 *Croix du Cygne* | K. van Exter | 159 | 52 | 22 | 153 | 10 | 27 | |
| 4 *Clarionet* | G. and N. Playfair | 164 | 54 | 15 | 153 | 51 | 20 | |
| 5 *Teleri* | C. Green | 164 | 53 | 30 | 154 | 14 | 23 | |
| 6 *Drakkar* | M. Bretche | 159 | 38 | 44 | 154 | 14 | 58 | |
| 7 *Callirhoe III* | Dr P. Bouyssou | 164 | 04 | 23 | 154 | 34 | 24 | |
| 8 *Saracen* | J.S. McCarthy | 158 | 07 | 16 | 154 | 55 | 37 | |
| 9 *Lancer* | G.R. Fuller | 159 | 08 | 47 | 155 | 16 | 45 | |

| YACHT | OWNER (SAILED BY) | ELAPSED TIME | | | CORRECTED TIME | | |
|---|---|---|---|---|---|---|---|
| | | hr. | mn. | sc. | hr. | mn. | sc. |
| 10 *Golden Apple* | H.L. McKelvie | 158 | 54 | 55 | 155 | 24 | 12 |
| 11 *Zeehaas* | M.J.F. Vroon | 164 | 20 | 29 | 155 | 27 | 02 |
| 12 *Schuylkill* | A.J. Wilson | 158 | 55 | 31 | 155 | 29 | 33 |
| 13 *Stress* | B. Blumenthal and G. Winberg | 159 | 01 | 28 | 155 | 35 | 22 |
| 14 *Pordin Nancq* | Dr J. Lamouric | 159 | 33 | 01 | 156 | 13 | 54 |
| 15 *Proton* | T.P. Daniels | 159 | 39 | 45 | 156 | 14 | 45 |
| 16 *Hylas* | D. Edwards | 160 | 12 | 43 | 156 | 21 | 03 |
| 17 *Delnic* | L. Rousselin | 159 | 36 | 40 | 156 | 23 | 13 |
| 18 *Super Tension* | T. Smith | 159 | 37 | 23 | 156 | 23 | 55 |
| 19 *Irish Mist* | D. Kalis and R. Johnson | 160 | 19 | 15 | 156 | 27 | 26 |
| 20 *Prospect of Puffin* | U.C. Taylor | 159 | 03 | 28 | 156 | 29 | 49 |
| 21 *Maligawa II* | A. Hagnere and G. Foures | 159 | 54 | 03 | 156 | 34 | 30 |
| 22 *Lady of Solent* | O. Moussey | 160 | 22 | 39 | 156 | 35 | 33 |
| 23 *Tam O'Shanter* | J.C. Butler | 160 | 47 | 06 | 156 | 48 | 40 |
| 24 *45° South II* | C. Cooper | 159 | 18 | 41 | 156 | 58 | 10 |
| 25 *Impala* | B.E. Ruys | 160 | 15 | 58 | 157 | 01 | 43 |
| 26 *Assassin* | N.G. Watson | 159 | 56 | 02 | 157 | 29 | 13 |
| 27 *Cavale II* | P. Baud | 160 | 38 | 35 | 157 | 30 | 38 |
| 28 *Jantine* | D. Koopmans | 164 | 24 | 41 | 157 | 38 | 15 |
| 29 *Good in Tension* | C.W. Billington | 160 | 46 | 45 | 157 | 57 | 56 |
| 30 *Cyclone* | D. Boyer | 161 | 36 | 54 | 158 | 02 | 36 |
| 31 *40 Carats* | A. Tournis | 161 | 51 | 23 | 158 | 09 | 00 |
| 32 *Tenacity* | P. Lavollee | 161 | 48 | 57 | 158 | 14 | 23 |
| 33 *Crazy Wolf* | B.R. Pearson | 163 | 46 | 20 | 159 | 01 | 22 |
| 34 *Pepsi* | J.J. Smith | 164 | 03 | 23 | 159 | 58 | 17 |
| 35 *Xara* | D.C. Barham | 164 | 37 | 32 | 160 | 59 | 14 |
| 36 *Ballydonna* | B.J. Hodgson | 164 | 08 | 20 | 161 | 29 | 46 |
| 37 *Sarnia* | R.S. Dix | 176 | 55 | 40 | 165 | 04 | 30 |
| 38 *Borodino* | J.R. Woods | 169 | 56 | 12 | 166 | 10 | 40 |
| 39 *Tai-Luk* | P.C. Frankcom | 179 | 25 | 00 | 169 | 35 | 04 |
| *Cavalier Seul* | P. Lunven | DNF | | | | | |
| *Sextus* | Dr G. Vermynck | DNF | | | | | |
| *Hunza* | J. Burnford | DNF | | | | | |
| *Flycatcher* | J.W. Roome | DNF | | | | | |
| *Billycan* | B. Mackay and A. Milton | DNF | | | | | |
| *Ailish III* | B. Foulger | DNF | | | | | |
| *Jiminy Cricket* | Group Capt. R. Wardman | DNF | | | | | |
| *Kalisana* | Royal Naval Sailing Association, Portsmouth | DNF | | | | | |
| *Dai Mouse III* | D.W.T. Hague | DNF | | | | | |

Class IV

| | | | | | | | |
|---|---|---|---|---|---|---|---|
| 1 *Bertheaume* | P. Lucas | 161 | 19 | 30 | 148 | 41 | 36 |
| 2 *Bally* | P. Bruninx and M. Desimpelaere | 160 | 22 | 08 | 148 | 47 | 25 |
| 3 *Baradozic* | G. Ganachaud | 159 | 49 | 33 | 149 | 30 | 04 |
| 4 *Kalik* | M. Lambrechts and A. Wilmet | 159 | 36 | 10 | 149 | 31 | 55 |
| 5 *Alvena* | Dr Le Bozec | 159 | 59 | 22 | 149 | 39 | 15 |
| 6 *Mallemok* | I. Rommens | 159 | 56 | 11 | 149 | 50 | 40 |
| 7 *Iromiguy* | G. Brunet | 160 | 00 | 40 | 149 | 54 | 52 |
| 8 *Prolific* | M. Matell | 165 | 21 | 28 | 150 | 05 | 43 |
| 9 *Greeneye* | R.W. Noble | 160 | 21 | 31 | 150 | 14 | 24 |
| 10 *Korsar* | R. Mollard | 165 | 46 | 48 | 150 | 27 | 43 |
| 11 *UFO IV* | R. Matthews | 160 | 56 | 10 | 150 | 32 | 23 |
| 12 *Velleda* | Ecole Navale Française | 164 | 23 | 05 | 150 | 48 | 24 |
| 13 *Moonlighter* | D. Ide | 159 | 46 | 29 | 150 | 52 | 31 |
| 14 *Thunderflash* | Royal Naval Engineering College (Lt A. Stephenson) | 163 | 38 | 21 | 151 | 05 | 17 |
| 15 *Flashlight* | Royal Naval Engineering College | 163 | 39 | 11 | 151 | 17 | 50 |
| 16 *Ultimatum* | J. Chorley and P. Dyball | 161 | 31 | 14 | 152 | 02 | 21 |
| 17 *Tessanda III* | E.J.M. Dent and A.G. Lambert | 162 | 21 | 14 | 152 | 06 | 34 |
| 18 *Sandettie* | J. Knijgsman | 162 | 25 | 32 | 152 | 10 | 35 |
| 19 *Jinjy* | P. Visick | 162 | 44 | 16 | 152 | 13 | 30 |
| 20 *Panache* | R. Smith | 163 | 40 | 05 | 152 | 36 | 15 |
| 21 *Goniocoque* | P. Lardy | 163 | 33 | 42 | 152 | 45 | 00 |
| 22 *Fragola II* | G.I.C. des Glénans | 163 | 37 | 44 | 153 | 18 | 14 |

| YACHT | OWNER (SAILED BY) | ELAPSED TIME hr. mn. sc. | | | CORRECTED TIME hr. mn. sc. | | |
|---|---|---|---|---|---|---|---|
| 23 *Uforia* | L.E. Rodgers | 163 | 44 | 33 | 153 | 24 | 37 |
| 24 *Kamisado* | M.J.W. Green | 163 | 45 | 30 | 153 | 25 | 31 |
| 25 *Taurus* | S. Carter | 164 | 02 | 51 | 153 | 27 | 00 |
| 26 *Myfoe* | A.W. Bartlett | 164 | 03 | 57 | 153 | 28 | 02 |
| 27 *Ordalie* | M. Bodin | 164 | 44 | 50 | 153 | 32 | 40 |
| 28 *Clair de Lune* | B. Labey | 166 | 23 | 44 | 153 | 33 | 59 |
| 29 *Golden Phoenix* | J.R.H. Williams | 167 | 13 | 40 | 153 | 42 | 57 |
| 30 *Polar Bear* | J.C. Clothier | 164 | 17 | 02 | 153 | 55 | 03 |
| 31 *Shetwin XI* | S. Linsale | 164 | 08 | 42 | 154 | 02 | 01 |
| 32 *Spineck III* | M. Riché | 164 | 25 | 54 | 154 | 03 | 22 |
| 33 *Jaws* | N.D. Svendsen | 164 | 30 | 29 | 154 | 03 | 50 |
| 34 *Ariadne* | E. Nitoslawska | 165 | 04 | 06 | 154 | 24 | 18 |
| 35 *Cassiopee* | R. Hubert | 164 | 22 | 23 | 154 | 28 | 40 |
| 36 *Darling Jill* | V. de Goede | 167 | 04 | 14 | 154 | 37 | 31 |
| 37 *Midnight Rambler* | J. Everitt | 167 | 14 | 56 | 154 | 55 | 22 |
| 38 *Simplicity* | R.R. King | 165 | 38 | 59 | 155 | 11 | 50 |
| 39 *Gregal 7* | J.P. Peche | 165 | 41 | 21 | 155 | 14 | 03 |
| 40 *Le Jovial Tiburon* | B.G.E. Lefevre | 166 | 00 | 07 | 155 | 16 | 42 |
| 41 *Rochelle* | R. Ould | 171 | 18 | 30 | 155 | 41 | 06 |
| 42 *Astraka* | N. Ioday | 166 | 30 | 51 | 156 | 00 | 26 |
| 43 *Nephthys* | Y. Bodin | 167 | 08 | 12 | 156 | 05 | 20 |
| 44 *Griffin* | Royal Ocean Racing Club (Dr Vadasz) | 167 | 36 | 59 | 157 | 02 | 23 |
| 45 *Braganza* | HMS *Excellent* (Lt Cmdr W. Thomas) | 177 | 39 | 30 | 157 | 53 | 06 |
| 46 *Saint Amour* | Dr P.J.A. Viel | 170 | 30 | 10 | 158 | 23 | 49 |
| 47 *Reiver of Mersea* | P.W. Wells | 177 | 57 | 50 | 159 | 15 | 36 |
| 48 *Morning Rose* | Bank of England (B. Timbrell) | 174 | 36 | 29 | 159 | 51 | 13 |
| 49 *Czardas* | J.U. de Boer | 170 | 39 | 17 | 160 | 22 | 52 |
| 50 *Icebreaker* | Mr and Mrs R. Hawkes | 175 | 22 | 32 | 160 | 43 | 54 |
| 51 *Sarie Marais* | Cmdr D.D.E. Gay | 181 | 47 | 26 | 161 | 13 | 48 |
| 52 *Hindostan* | Britannia Royal Naval College | 175 | 02 | 15 | 161 | 36 | 44 |
| 53 *Copernicus* | A. Morton and B. Jackson | 176 | 34 | 00 | 162 | 50 | 50 |
| 54 *Diable Jaune* | P. Gassy | 177 | 38 | 12 | 166 | 25 | 40 |
| *Gay Gannet V* | Cmdr F.W.B. Edwards | DNF | | | | | |
| *Slipstream* | Royal Air Force Sailing Association | DNF | | | | | |
| *Ann Speed II* | John Lewis Partnership | DNF | | | | | |
| *Volunteer* | Royal Naval Volunteer Reserve Sailing Club | DNF | | | | | |
| *Romanee* | B. Junck | DNF | | | | | |
| *Cavalcade* | J. Gaynor | DNF | | | | | |
| *Ginsky* | Dr B.M. Woodward | DNF | | | | | |
| *Jubilee B* | R. Brann and O. Burge | DNF | | | | | |
| *Papillon Bleu* | C.J. Evans | DNF | | | | | |
| *Limelight* | S. Gittins | DNF | | | | | |
| *Stripper* | C.S. Heaton | DNF | | | | | |
| *Samurai* | R. Jordan | DNF | | | | | |
| *Kashamara* | N.E. Bean | DNF | | | | | |
| *Scorpio* | R.G. Nuttall | DNF | | | | | |

*Class V*

| YACHT | OWNER (SAILED BY) | hr. | mn. | sc. | hr. | mn. | sc. |
|---|---|---|---|---|---|---|---|
| 1 *Crazy Horse* | C. Goater | 160 | 32 | 55 | 143 | 49 | 10 |
| 2 *Silver Jubilee* | R.D. Bagnall | 160 | 31 | 10 | 144 | 35 | 45 |
| 3 *Severine* | H. Marcq | 164 | 25 | 19 | 145 | 22 | 55 |
| 4 *Tikocco* | C. Caillere | 165 | 00 | 26 | 145 | 56 | 56 |
| 5 *Flamingo II* | W. Chapman | 165 | 03 | 12 | 146 | 27 | 07 |
| 6 *Tamasin II* | R.T. Bishop | 164 | 12 | 42 | 146 | 40 | 26 |
| 7 *El Pepito* | P. Mone | 164 | 17 | 25 | 146 | 54 | 30 |
| 8 *Nimfo* | M. Fellows and D. Pye | 164 | 34 | 50 | 147 | 05 | 08 |
| 9 *Billy Bones* | Ms Boudot and Seuly | 164 | 18 | 14 | 148 | 00 | 18 |
| 10 *Twee Gezusters* | H.D.D. Zuiderbaan | 164 | 42 | 08 | 148 | 02 | 04 |
| 11 *Hurricantoo* | A.B. and N. Simms | 165 | 55 | 54 | 148 | 02 | 39 |
| 12 *Option 2* | J. Desfeux | 164 | 22 | 58 | 148 | 04 | 34 |

| YACHT | OWNER (SAILED BY) | ELAPSED TIME | | | CORRECTED TIME | | |
|---|---|---|---|---|---|---|---|
| | | *hr.* | *mn.* | *sc.* | *hr.* | *mn.* | *sc.* |
| 13 *Dael* | Y. Limoges | 165 | 31 | 02 | 148 | 06 | 17 |
| 14 *Tarantula* | P. Le Floch | 164 | 48 | 54 | 148 | 27 | 55 |
| 15 *Bigouden Express* | G. Dupuy | 164 | 57 | 14 | 148 | 35 | 26 |
| 16 *Xaviera* | A.B. Land and R. Woodbridge | 166 | 27 | 24 | 149 | 56 | 39 |
| 17 *Willem Tell* | G. Jeelof | 166 | 37 | 36 | 150 | 05 | 50 |
| 18 *Janik 2* | M. Lepine | 166 | 55 | 00 | 150 | 21 | 31 |
| 19 *Sibelius* | J. Walhain | 168 | 50 | 20 | 151 | 35 | 00 |
| 20 *Peace of Lawrenny* | Sir Julian Berney | 170 | 59 | 25 | 151 | 43 | 10 |
| 21 *Assent* | W.W. and A.W. Ker | 169 | 45 | 03 | 151 | 49 | 31 |
| 22 *Spread Eagle* | Barclays Bank Sailing Club (J. Swanston) | 171 | 32 | 27 | 154 | 00 | 33 |
| 23 *Ikan Balalang* | J.D. Drewery | 173 | 26 | 12 | 154 | 34 | 00 |
| 24 *Flecknoe* | R.C. Catesby | 176 | 48 | 30 | 155 | 36 | 32 |
| 25 *Windy of Hamble* | P. Cooke | 175 | 10 | 00 | 155 | 47 | 36 |
| 26 *Checkmate* | Mr and Mrs R. Barton | 174 | 32 | 24 | 157 | 34 | 29 |
| 27 *Obsessions* | Dr D. Oustalet | 177 | 50 | 00 | 158 | 03 | 30 |
| 28 *Mar del Norte* | Capt. R.S. Aspinall | 180 | 25 | 15 | 158 | 33 | 14 |
| 29 *Red Herring* | R. Cranmer-Brown | 177 | 07 | 00 | 158 | 47 | 06 |
| 30 *Spangle* | N. Millard and P. Warwick | 175 | 57 | 00 | 159 | 01 | 25 |
| 31 *Explorer of Hornet* | Chief P/O Hudson | 177 | 38 | 07 | 159 | 39 | 31 |
| 32 *Marelanja* | Lord Amhurst of Hackney | 176 | 52 | 53 | 159 | 41 | 19 |
| 33 *Festina* | G.P. Green | 193 | 58 | 13 | 174 | 32 | 03 |
| *Crusader of Hornet* | Walker | DNF | | | | | |
| *Gandalf* | J.P. Vadet | DNF | | | | | |
| *Comet* | A. Black | DNF | | | | | |
| *Contessa Catherine* | Brig. R.W. Dowdall | DNF | | | | | |
| *Korimako* | R.S. Kyle | DNF | | | | | |
| *Zeerob* | R. Earnshawn-Brown | DNF | | | | | |
| *Farther Bruin* | R. Manning | DNF | | | | | |
| *Meon Maid III* | HMS *Mercury* (E. Llewellyn) | DNF | | | | | |

# 1979 (11 AUGUST)

*Class Zero*

| | | | | | | | | |
|---|---|---|---|---|---|---|---|---|
| 1 *Tenacious* | R.E. Turner | 79 | 52 | 22 | 93 | 44 | 19 | (*1st overall*) |
| 2 *Condor of Bermuda* | R. Bell | 71 | 25 | 23 | 97 | 57 | 24 | |
| 3 *Kialoa* | J.B. Kilroy | 71 | 53 | 51 | 98 | 03 | 40 | |
| 4 *Mistress Quickly* | W. Whitehouse-Vaux | 76 | 02 | 00 | 101 | 01 | 59 | |
| 5 *Siska* | R.L. Tasker | 75 | 55 | 00 | 102 | 46 | 34 | |
| 6 *Gitana VI* | E. de Rothschild | 85 | 14 | 43 | 103 | 50 | 45 | |
| 7 *War Baby* | Warren A. Brown | 90 | 50 | 23 | 108 | 01 | 17 | |
| 8 *Travel* | R.T. Gustafson | 95 | 41 | 27 | 111 | 09 | 16 | |
| 9 *G3* | P. Facque and M. Loiseau | 91 | 59 | 26 | 112 | 33 | 02 | |
| 10 *Boomerang* | G.S. Coumantaros | 89 | 49 | 34 | 112 | 38 | 31 | |
| 11 *Whirlwind V* | N.A.V. Lister | 96 | 20 | 24 | 112 | 50 | 35 | |
| 12 *Il Moro di Venezia* | R. Gardini | 91 | 09 | 40 | 118 | 43 | 09 | |
| 13 *Endeavour* | J. Callow and M. Dunham | 130 | 38 | 26 | 160 | 58 | 31 | |
| *Battlecry* | J.O. Prentice | DNF | | | | | | |

*Class I*

| | | | | | | | |
|---|---|---|---|---|---|---|---|
| 1 *Red Rock IV* | E. Mandelbaum | 92 | 24 | 11 | 98 | 35 | 05 |
| 2 *Acadia* | B. Beenan | 88 | 59 | 34 | 99 | 17 | 53 |
| 3 *Gregal* | M. Peche | 93 | 36 | 21 | 99 | 52 | 39 |
| 4 *Sleuth* | S. Colgate | 87 | 53 | 08 | 99 | 53 | 27 |
| 5 *Vanina* | V. Mandelli | 93 | 31 | 38 | 100 | 12 | 52 |
| 6 *Formidable* | P.W. Vroon | 93 | 49 | 44 | 100 | 13 | 07 |
| 7 *Yena* | S. Doni | 95 | 01 | 29 | 100 | 15 | 38 |
| 8 *Ragamuffin* | S. Fischer | 93 | 12 | 13 | 100 | 17 | 47 |
| 9 *Carina* | R.S. and R.B. Nye | 96 | 08 | 06 | 101 | 14 | 58 |
| 10 *Williwaw* | S. Sinett | 93 | 51 | 32 | 101 | 38 | 23 |
| 11 *Moonduster* | D.N. Doyle | 95 | 27 | 24 | 102 | 16 | 55 |
| 12 *Rrose Selavy* | R. Bonadeo | 97 | 20 | 40 | 102 | 21 | 28 |

| YACHT | OWNER (SAILED BY) | ELAPSED TIME | | | CORRECTED TIME | | |
|---|---|---|---|---|---|---|---|
| | | hr. | mn. | sc. | hr. | mn. | sc. |
| 13 *Matrero* | T. Achaval | 97 | 14 | 26 | 102 | 29 | 30 |
| 14 *Vanguard* | D.T.V. Lieu | 95 | 55 | 54 | 102 | 47 | 27 |
| 15 *Togo VI* | Dr T. Yamada | 97 | 50 | 46 | 102 | 53 | 07 |
| 16 *Indigo* | S. Eotelho | 95 | 09 | 20 | 103 | 15 | 46 |
| 17 *Uin-Na-Mara IV* | Mr and Mrs H. Ross | 96 | 27 | 47 | 103 | 34 | 55 |
| 18 *Apollo IV* | J. Barry | 95 | 34 | 13 | 103 | 49 | 05 |
| 19 *Aries* | M. Swerdlow | 96 | 02 | 17 | 104 | 39 | 10 |
| 20 *Morning Cloud* | Rt Hon. Edward Heath, MP | 99 | 25 | 33 | 104 | 39 | 56 |
| 21 *Toscana* | E. Swenson | 97 | 14 | 00 | 105 | 05 | 23 |
| 22 *Hadar* | Y.K. Stal (Z. Perlicke) | 98 | 35 | 23 | 105 | 24 | 44 |
| 23 *Blizzard* | E.G. Juer | 94 | 08 | 03 | 105 | 25 | 49 |
| 24 *Noryema* | R.W. Amey | 95 | 43 | 56 | 105 | 34 | 59 |
| 25 *Hamburg* | Hamburgscher Verein Seefahrt | 99 | 20 | 48 | 106 | 08 | 31 |
| 26 *Cetus* | Y.K. Stal (J. Suidy) | 99 | 27 | 05 | 106 | 20 | 00 |
| 27 *Incisif* | A. Loisse | 99 | 22 | 44 | 106 | 29 | 04 |
| 28 *Dorothea* | W.C. Petersen | 103 | 18 | 29 | 109 | 03 | 44 |
| 29 *Festina* | N. Mooney | 103 | 22 | 41 | 109 | 19 | 20 |
| 30 *Midnight Sun* | J. Pehrsson | 97 | 01 | 32 | 109 | 23 | 12 |
| 31 *Alliance* | Naval Academy Sailing Squadron | 98 | 18 | 10 | 109 | 32 | 20 |
| 32 *Carat* | V. Forss | 104 | 14 | 26 | 112 | 03 | 31 |
| 33 *Nauticus* | Y.K. Kotwica (T. Slewiec) | 105 | 55 | 47 | 112 | 31 | 07 |
| 34 *Milene IV* | A. Mirlesse | 109 | 09 | 47 | 117 | 50 | 29 |
| 35 *Parmelia* | R.J. Williams | 112 | 20 | 35 | 122 | 36 | 07 |
| 36 *Lutine* | Lloyd's Yacht Club | 119 | 03 | 05 | 128 | 18 | 06 |
| *Adventure* | Ministry of Defence (Navy) | DNF | | | | | |
| *Abacus* | D.K. Clark | DNF | | | | | |
| *Big Shadow* | S. Bjerser | DNF | | | | | |
| *Quailo* | T.D. Parr | DNF | | | | | |
| *Kukri* | Ministry of Defence (Army) | DNF | | | | | |
| *Dasher* | Ministry of Defence (Navy) | DNF | | | | | |
| *Tina* | T. Friese | DNF | | | | | |
| *Tyfoon 6* | G. Versluys | DNF | | | | | |
| *Jan Pott* | N. Lorck-Schierning | DNF | | | | | |
| *Scaramouche* | H. Blane Bowen | DNF | | | | | |
| *Yeoman XXI* | R.A. Aisher | DNF | | | | | |
| *Silver Apple of the Moon* | B. Guttinger and G. Noldin | DNF | | | | | |
| *Casse Tete V* | D.H. Johnson | DNF | | | | | |
| *Marionette VII* | C.A.F. Dunning | DNF | | | | | |
| *Golden Apple of the Sun* | H. Coveney | DNF | | | | | |
| *Schuttevaer* | Dr J.C.W. van Dam | DNF | | | | | |
| *Scaldis* | S.T. Nauta | DNF | | | | | |
| *Magic Eliza* | Mr Schuldt-Ahrens | DNF | | | | | |
| *Oryx* | E. Adam | DNF | | | | | |
| *Chastanet* | N.A. Brick | DNF | | | | | |

*Class II*

| | | | | | | | |
|---|---|---|---|---|---|---|---|
| 1 *Eclipse* | J.C. Rogers | 95 | 42 | 45 | 97 | 05 | 27 |
| 2 *Jubile VI* | H. Hamon | 94 | 38 | 32 | 97 | 40 | 15 |
| 3 *Impetuous* | G. Lambert and J. Crisp | 94 | 51 | 25 | 97 | 53 | 53 |
| 4 *Police Car* | P.R. Cantwell | 94 | 26 | 46 | 97 | 56 | 26 |
| 5 *Imp* | D.W. Allen | 95 | 36 | 36 | 97 | 57 | 09 |
| 6 *Schollevaer* | W. Dearns and F. Eekels | 96 | 48 | 25 | 98 | 34 | 08 |
| 7 *La Pantera III* | C. Ostenfeld and E. de Losala | 95 | 16 | 38 | 99 | 43 | 36 |
| 8 *Assiduous* | N. Beger | 99 | 54 | 13 | 101 | 12 | 08 |
| 9 *Marloo* | Dr N.S. Girdis | 97 | 14 | 43 | 102 | 01 | 47 |
| 10 *Campsa* | J. Cusi | 98 | 22 | 35 | 102 | 08 | 04 |
| 11 *Magistri* | C. Bentley | 99 | 12 | 27 | 102 | 34 | 50 |
| 12 *Ko Teru Teru II* | T. Yamaguchi | 99 | 31 | 25 | 103 | 19 | 31 |
| 13 *Sur II* | D.P. Ramos | 100 | 08 | 42 | 103 | 28 | 47 |
| 14 *Darling Dee* | A. Nelis | 98 | 51 | 23 | 103 | 42 | 37 |
| 15 *Rubin* | H.-O. Schuemann | 100 | 28 | 22 | 103 | 49 | 07 |
| 16 *Loujaine* | Sir Maurice Laing | 101 | 51 | 32 | 104 | 13 | 56 |

| YACHT | OWNER (SAILED BY) | ELAPSED TIME | | | CORRECTED TIME | | |
|---|---|---|---|---|---|---|---|
| | | hr. | mn. | sc. | hr. | mn. | sc. |
| 17 *Dagger* | J.L. Dolk and Th. E.W. Vinke | 103 | 47 | 56 | 106 | 09 | 56 |
| 18 *Inishanier* | G. Bramwell and B. Buchanan | 105 | 02 | 04 | 106 | 32 | 49 |
| 19 *Pinta* | P.C. d'Andrimont | 114 | 37 | 57 | 117 | 58 | 06 |
| 20 *Sarabande* | J.J. Hozee | 120 | 52 | 53 | 123 | 08 | 31 |
| 21 *Tornado* | W. Singleton | 121 | 35 | 23 | 123 | 38 | 41 |
| 22 *Charlatan* | R.W. Appelbee | 125 | 00 | 48 | 129 | 38 | 20 |
| 23 *Quickstep* | S.R. Johnson | 138 | 19 | 23 | 139 | 53 | 10 |
| *Nick Nack* | N. Langley-Pope | DNF | | | | | |
| *Belita VII* | J.S. Bouman | DNF | | | | | |
| *Suca* | W. Kuhrt | DNF | | | | | |
| *Farthing* | Mr and Mrs E.T. George | DNF | | | | | |
| *Amarante* | L. Maisonneuve | DNF | | | | | |
| *Fair Judgement* | D.C. Dillistone | DNF | | | | | |
| *Caiman* | G. Jeelof | DNF | | | | | |
| *Telemaque II* | L. Delacou | DNF | | | | | |
| *Grune Sec II* | J. and J. Leguelinel | DNF | | | | | |
| *Evergreen* | D. Green | DNF | | | | | |
| *Animal* | F.D. Hogan | DNF | | | | | |
| *Gekko VI* | S. Namiki | DNF | | | | | |
| *Pachena* | J. Newton | DNF | | | | | |
| *Standfast* | J. Hass | DNF | | | | | |
| *Double O Too* | R.L. Hay | DNF | | | | | |
| *Pepsi* | A. Milton | DNF | | | | | |
| *La Barbarella* | M. Hervey | DNF | | | | | |
| *Blauwe Dolfyn II* | C. Wargnies | DNF | | | | | |
| *Sophie B* | B.H. Owen | DNF | | | | | |
| *Golden Leigh* | L. Kertesz | DNF | | | | | |
| *Wild Goose* | J. Ayres | DNF | | | | | |
| *Yachtman II* | R. Montagut | DNF | | | | | |
| *Regardless* | K. Rohan | DNF | | | | | |
| *Accanito* | S. Poli | DNF | | | | | |
| *Impromptu* | J. Ewart | DNF | | | | | |
| *Maiton IV* | K.B. Merron | DNF | | | | | |
| *Dugenou I* | J. Pajot | DNF | | | | | |
| *Lancer* | G.R. Fuller | DNF | | | | | |
| *Goodwin* | J.N. van Drongelen | DNF | | | | | |
| *Spica II* | W.L. Riviere | DNF | | | | | |

*Class III*

| YACHT | OWNER (SAILED BY) | ELAPSED TIME | | | CORRECTED TIME | | |
|---|---|---|---|---|---|---|---|
| 1 *Revolution* | J-L Fabry | 99 | 21 | 50 | 97 | 42 | 53 |
| 2 *Blue Bird* | A. Gerard | 119 | 11 | 36 | 110 | 48 | 52 |
| 3 *Ceil III* | W. Turnbull | 121 | 06 | 30 | 116 | 33 | 18 |
| 4 *Solent Oyster* | J.A.S. Bassett | 119 | 25 | 08 | 116 | 50 | 23 |
| 5 *Flycatcher* | J.W. Roome | 124 | 05 | 55 | 119 | 05 | 07 |
| 6 *Xara* | D.C. Barham | 145 | 34 | 19 | 140 | 22 | 30 |
| *Mickey Mouse* | K. Robinson | DNF | | | | | |
| *Pordin Nancq* | Dr J. Lamouric | DNF | | | | | |
| *New Brig* | Sir Frederick and Lady Coates | DNF | | | | | |
| *Innovation* | Sir Peter Johnson Bt | DNF | | | | | |
| *Moonstone* | D. Chatterton | DNF | | | | | |
| *Rock On* | P. Farrar | DNF | | | | | |
| *Ailish III* | B. Foulger | DNF | | | | | |
| *Croix du Cygne* | K. van Exter | DNF | | | | | |
| *Delnic* | L. Rousselin | DNF | | | | | |
| *Silver Apple* | G. Cryns | DNF | | | | | |
| *Cavale* | P.L. Dorey | DNF | | | | | |
| *Tai Fat* | Hamburger Regatta Gemeinschaft | DNF | | | | | |
| *Griffin* | Royal Ocean Racing Club (N. Graham) | DNF | | | | | |
| *Gorm* | S. Brandstedt | DNF | | | | | |
| *Checkmate* | R.J.C. Barton | DNF | | | | | |
| *Windswept* | I. Godfrey | DNF | | | | | |
| *Bernard II* | University of Louvain | DNF | | | | | |
| *Vigilant* | S.R.G. Jeffery | DNF | | | | | |
| *Oyster Catcher* | R.B. Matthews | DNF | | | | | |

| YACHT | OWNER (SAILED BY) | ELAPSED TIME hr. mn. sc. | | | CORRECTED TIME hr. mn. sc. | | |
|---|---|---|---|---|---|---|---|
| *Jolie Brise* | W. Jansen | DNF | | | | | |
| *Peau d'Bouc* | A. Simon | DNF | | | | | |
| *Zeehaas* | M.J.F. Vroon | DNF | | | | | |
| *Veronier II* | C.J. Vroege | DNF | | | | | |
| *Combat II* | G. Bottomley and D. Gillam | DNF | | | | | |
| *Sundowner* | B. O'Donnel | DNF | | | | | |
| *Polyhymnia* | O.V. van Tijn | DNF | | | | | |
| *Ballydonna* | R.J. Hodgson | DNF | | | | | |
| *Asterie* | R. Jeanty | DNF | | | | | |
| *Gallivant II* | W.R. Binks | DNF | | | | | |
| *Amandla Kulu* | S. Polliack | DNF | | | | | |
| *Allamanda* | M. Campbell | DNF | | | | | |
| *Andiamo Robin* | J. Harding | DNF | | | | | |
| *Samurai III* | R.G. Jordan | DNF | | | | | |
| *Zap* | W. Stewart-Ross | DNF | | | | | |
| *Live Wire* | D.D. O'Brien | DNF | | | | | |
| *Poppy II* | J.M. Dean | DNF | | | | | |
| *Juggernaut* | A. Cassell | DNF | | | | | |
| *Tam O'Shanter* | J.C. Butler | DNF | | | | | |
| *Hoodlum* | C.J. Evans | DNF | | | | | |
| *Tiderace IV* | D.E.P. Norton | DNF | | | | | |
| *Crazy Horse* | C. Goater | DNF | | | | | |
| *Good in Tension* | C.W. Billington | DNF | | | | | |
| *Festina Tertia* | N. Mooney | DNF | | | | | |
| *Pepsi* | J.J. Smith | DNF | | | | | |
| *Carmargue* | A.F. Moss | DNF | | | | | |
| *Victride* | A. Lanoue | DNF | | | | | |
| *Mutine* | Cmdr E.A. Morrison | DNF | | | | | |
| *Finndabar of Howth* | J.P. Jameson | DNF | | | | | |
| *Trophy* | A.W. Bartlett | DNF | | | | | |
| *Autonomy* | E. Bourne | DNF | | | | | |
| *Charioteer* | Drs J. Coldrey and J. Lindsay | DNF | | | | | |
| *Assassin* | N.G. Watson | DNF | | | | | |
| *Steady Tension* | R.S. and G.W. Havens | DNF | | | | | |
| *Passing Cloud* | P.B. Morgan | DNF | | | | | |
| *Angustura* | W.W. and A.W. Oliver | DNF | | | | | |
| *Palamedes* | A.J. Sheldon | DNF | | | | | |
| *Firanjo* | Group Capt. R. Wardman | DNF | | | | | |
| *Hindostan* | Royal Naval College, Dartmouth | DNF | | | | | |

### Class IV

| | YACHT | OWNER (SAILED BY) | ELAPSED TIME hr. mn. sc. | | | CORRECTED TIME hr. mn. sc. | | |
|---|---|---|---|---|---|---|---|---|
| 1 | *Black Arrow* | Royal Air Force Sailing Association | 119 | 37 | 01 | 110 | 35 | 10 |
| 2 | *Samsara* | Madame O. Tran-Van-Dom | 118 | 11 | 47 | 110 | 44 | 19 |
| 2 | *Lorelei* | M. Catherineau | | | | | | |
| 3 | *Mahuri* | G.M. Lowson | 131 | 19 | 56 | 122 | 03 | 38 |
| 4 | *Kalisana* | HMS *Sultan* (Cmdr Watson) | 137 | 34 | 52 | 125 | 49 | 06 |
| 5 | *Karimata* | E. Blokzyl | 137 | 48 | 48 | 129 | 19 | 28 |
| 6 | *Tronador* | R.M.H. Edwards | 139 | 53 | 32 | 130 | 13 | 33 |
| | *Dai Mouse III* | D.W.T. Hague | DNF | | | | | |
| | *Challenge* | F.M. Murray | DNF | | | | | |
| | *Bertheaume* | Brest Syndicate | DNF | | | | | |
| | *Kamisado* | M.J.W. Green | DNF | | | | | |
| | *Fragola* | G.I.C. des Glénans | DNF | | | | | |
| | *Golden Princess* | A. Hagnere | DNF | | | | | |
| | *Scattered Magic* | J. Chuter | DNF | | | | | |
| | *Cheesecake* | D. Hopkins | DNF | | | | | |
| | *Contentious Eagle* | Barclays Bank Ltd (B. Roberts) | DNF | | | | | |
| | *Cosmic Dancer* | R.G. Warren | DNF | | | | | |
| | *Minipyge* | M. Merfabruge | DNF | | | | | |
| | *Baradozic* | M. Ganachaud | DNF | | | | | |
| | *Nephthys II* | Y. Bodin | DNF | | | | | |
| | *Prairie Oyster* | C.F.R. Purchase | DNF | | | | | |
| | *Goniocoque* | P. Barriere | DNF | | | | | |
| | *Virginie* | Ecole Navale | DNF | | | | | |
| | *Drakkar* | R. Morelisse | DNF | | | | | |

| YACHT | OWNER (SAILED BY) | ELAPSED TIME | CORRECTED TIME |
|---|---|---|---|
| | | hr. mn. sc. | hr. mn. sc. |
| *Quixote* | E. and I.J. Watts | DNF | |
| *Signalia* | Maj. P. Scholfield | DNF | |
| *Electron II* | HMS *Collingwood* | DNF | |
| *En Passant* | M. Postma | DNF | |
| *Hullabaloo* | A.J. Otten | DNF | |
| *Cassiopee* | R. Hubert | DNF | |
| *Rhapsody* | J.A. Hughes | DNF | |
| *Cote de Beaute* | M. Amiant | DNF | |
| *Dumonveh* | G. Messink | DNF | |
| *Thunderflash* | Royal Naval Engineering College | DNF | |
| *Copernicus* | A. Morton and B. Jackson | DNF | |
| *Impetus* | D.J.C. Longstaffe | DNF | |
| *Carronade* | Mr and Mrs P. Clements | DNF | |
| *Alvena* | Y. Dreo | DNF | |
| *Scenario* | A. Fitton | DNF | |
| *Maelstrom* | M.A. Bolson | DNF | |
| *Lipstick* | C. Clarke and D. Seabrook | DNF | |
| *Sandettie II* | J. Krygsman | DNF | |
| *Fiorinda* | P.B. Eyre | DNF | |
| *Detente* | C.K. Bond-Smith | DNF | |
| *Locomotion* | E.A. and J.A. Clegg | DNF | |
| *Flashlight* | Royal Naval Engineering College | DNF | |
| *Hestrul II* | D.A. Lewis | DNF | |
| *Gringo* | A. Morgan | DNF | |
| *Callirhoe III* | P. Bouyssou | DNF | |
| *Ariadne* | F.H. Ferris | DNF | |
| *Polar Bear* | J.C. Clothier | DNF | |
| *Pegasus* | P.J.A. White | DNF | |
| *Ocean Wave* | J. Toler | DNF | |
| *Cabadah* | Capt. G. Greenfield | DNF | |
| *Odyssea* | M. Guichard | DNF | |
| *Mezzanine* | K. Hancock and L. Chapman | DNF | |
| *Elessar II* | W.P.J. Laros | DNF | |
| *Clarionet* | G. and N. Playfair | DNF | |

Class V

| YACHT | OWNER (SAILED BY) | ELAPSED TIME | CORRECTED TIME |
|---|---|---|---|
| *Assent* | W. and A. Ker | 132  12  45 | 116  58  55 |
| *Fluter* | Ministry of Defence (Army) | DNF | |
| *Spreadeagle* | Barclays Bank Ltd (F. Sanders) | DNF | |
| *Morning Rose* | Bank of England | DNF | |
| *La Negresse Blonde* | J. Cruette | DNF | |
| *Tikocco* | C. Caillere | DNF | |
| *Mosika Alma* | J. Forrester | DNF | |
| *Phynnodderee* | Dr J.K. Hinds | DNF | |
| *Sarie Marais* | Cmdr D. Gay | DNF | |
| *Rapperee* | B. Kelly | DNF | |
| *Festina* | G.P. Green | DNF | |
| *Green Dragon* | Mr and Mrs B. Saffery Cooper | DNF | |
| *Valross* | T.H. Bevan | DNF | |
| *Kate* | Mr and Mrs F. Ellis | DNF | |
| *Silver Foam* | J.A. Mehigan | DNF | |
| *Beep Beep* | G. Cornier | DNF | |
| *Morning Melody* | Y. Prieur | DNF | |
| *Esprit* | B. Lesieur | DNF | |
| *First of April* | O. Goguel | DNF | |
| *Thunderer* | Royal Army Ordance Corps | DNF | |
| *Right Royal of Upnor* | Corps of Royal Engineers | DNF | |
| *Marina* | Dr J.H. Van der Waals | DNF | |
| *Flamingo* | B. Chapman | DNF | |
| *Redskin* | P. van Tongerloo | DNF | |
| *Hurricantoo* | A.B. and N. Simms | DNF | |
| *Mordicus* | C. Volters | DNF | |
| *Gunslinger* | National Westminster Bank Ltd | DNF | |
| *Trumpeter* | Ministry of Defence (Army) | DNF | |
| *Option II* | J. Desfeux | DNF | |

| YACHT | OWNER (SAILED BY) | ELAPSED TIME<br>hr. mn. sc. | CORRECTED TIME<br>hr. mn. sc. |
|---|---|---|---|
| *Gay Gannet V* | Gen. Sir Hugh Beach | DNF | |
| *Tamasin II* | R.T. Bishop | DNF | |
| *Contessa Catherine* | Royal Engineer Yacht Club<br>(Brig. R. Dowdall) | DNF | |
| *Golden Thistle* | A.W.F. Russett | DNF | |
| *Sissytoo* | R.L. Hill | DNF | |
| *Maligawa III* | G. Foures | DNF | |
| *Alpha II* | H.S. Axton | DNF | |
| *Morning Glory* | F.A. Davies | DNF | |
| *Pinball Wizard* | P.T. Lees | DNF | |
| *Billy Bones* | Ms Boudet and Seuly | DNF | |
| *Skidbladner III* | H.A. Hansell | DNF | |
| *Xaviera* | R.A. Woodbridge | DNF | |
| *Korsar* | R.E. Mollard | DNF | |
| *Ossian* | P. Ratzel | DNF | |
| *Gan* | J. Hercelin | DNF | |
| *Magic* | P.T. Whipp | DNF | |
| *Grimalkin* | D. Sheahan | DNF | |
| *Bonadventure II* | Ministry of Defence (Navy) | DNF | |
| *Arkadina* | A.J. Boutle | DNF | |
| *Tarantula* | P. Le Floch | DNF | |
| *Little Eila* | S.R. Field | DNF | |
| *Congreve* | Maj. P. Crump | DNF | |
| *Corker* | G.T. Davies | DNF | |
| *Explorer of Hornet* | Ministry of Defence (Navy) | DNF | |
| *Humbug* | N.R. Palmer | DNF | |
| *Illusion* | K. Wason | DNF | |
| *Enia V* | M. Touron | DNF | |
| *Karibario* | J. Legallet | DNF | |
| *Skat* | Dr N. Southwood | DNF | |

# Cups Awarded and Cup Winners  1925–79

## Cups Awarded

**Fastnet Cup**
Presented by the Admiral Cmdr E.G. Martin, OBE, for the first Fastnet Race in 1925, to be held by the yacht with best corrected time in the race.

**Buckley Memorial Trophy**
Presented in 1961 by the Club in memory of Col. R. Maclean Buckley, MC, to be won outright by the overall winner in the Fastnet Race.

**Figaro Trophy**
Presented in 1969 by Mr W. Snaith, to be held by the second yacht to finish on corrected time.

**Clarke Cup**
Presented in 1969 by Capt. N.G. Clarke, to be held by the third yacht to finish on corrected time

**Norlethe Cup**
Presented in 1969 by Mr L.B. Dyball, to be held by the yacht with the best corrected time in Restricted Division.

**Clarion Cup**
Presented in 1969 by Mr D.J. Boyer, DFC, to be held by the first British yacht to finish on corrected time.

**Founder's Cup**
Presented in 1947 by the late Cmdr E.G. Martin's brother and sister, to be held by the winner of Class I.

**Hong Kong Cup**
Presented in 1937 by Mr H.S. Rouse, to be held by the winner of Restricted Division Class I.

**Bloodhound Cup**
Presented in 1953 by Sir Myles Wyatt, CBE, to be held by the winner of Class II.

**Philip Whitehead Memorial Cup**
Presented in 1969 by Sir John Power, Bt, in memory of Philip Whitehead, to be held by the winner of Class II Restricted Division on corrected time.

**West Mersea Yacht Club Trophy**
Presented in 1969 by the West Mersea Yacht Club, to be held by the winner of Class III on corrected time.

**Golden Dragon Trophy**
Presented in 1949 by Mr H.S. Rouse, for the winner of Restricted Division Class III.

**Foxhound Cup**
Presented in 1953 by the Hon. Mrs R. Pitt-Rivers, to be held by the winner of Class IV.

**Iolaire Cup**
Presented in 1953 by Mr Robert Somerset, DSO, to be held by the winner of Restricted Division Class IV.

**Favona Cup**
Presented in 1969 by Sir Michael Newton, Bt, to be held by the winner of Class V on corrected time.

**Battler Beedle Quaich**
Presented in 1969 by Mrs E. Beedle in memory of Battler Beedle, to be held by the winner of Restricted Division Class V on corrected time.

**Elizabeth McCaw Trophies**
Presented in 1939 by Mr R.J. Reynolds, for the first yacht round the Fastnet Rock (won outright).

**Erivale Cup**
Presented by Dr E.G. Greville, MC, to replace the cup lost in Germany during the war, originally given by Mr J.H. Rawlings in 1937, the first owner of Erivale. The cup is to be held by the first yacht to complete the course.

**Jolie Brise Challenge Cup**
Presented in 1933 by Mr Robert Somerset, DSO, to be held by the first yacht home in Restricted Division.

**Inter-Regimental Cup**
Presented in 1955 by Lord Astor to replace the cup originally given in 1937 by the late Maj. T.P. Rose Richards, for the yacht owned by a Regimental, Corps or Service – British or Foreign – with the best corrected time.

**Gesture Cup**
Presented in 1953 by Mr Howard Fuller, to be held by the yacht from outside Great Britain with the best corrected time.

**Iolaire Block**
Presented in 1973 by Mr D.M. Street, Jr, to be held by the oldest yacht to complete the race.

**Auscrew Trophy**
Presented in 1973 by the Auscrew Association, to be held by the first yacht on corrected time which has on board a member of the Auscrew Association.

**Erroll Bruce Trophy**
Presented in 1977 by Cmdr Erroll Bruce, to be held by the first yacht in Class IV to round the Fastnet Rock.

**David Seth-Smith Trophy**
Presented in 1977 by Mrs David Seth-Smith in memory of her husband. To be held by the best club yacht.

**Swinburne Cup**
Presented in 1979 by Mrs P. Swinburne in memory of her husband, Eric G.P. Swinburne, to be held by the best Irish yacht on corrected time.

**Alf Loomis Trophy**
Presented in 1979 by the Loomis family in memory of Alfred F. Loomis, to be held by the navigator of the winning yacht.

**Whirlwind Trophy**
Presented in 1979 by Mr N.A.V. Lister, to be held by the first Swan 57 on corrected time, or as decided by the Committee.

**Quailo Cup**
Presented in 1979 by Mr T.D. Parr, for the yacht with the best corrected times in the Channel and Fastnet races in Class Zero.

# Cup Winners

## 1925
Fastnet Cup    *Jolie Brise*

## 1926
Fastnet Cup    *Ilex*

## 1927
Fastnet Cup    *Tally Ho!*

## 1928
Fastnet Cup    *Nina*

## 1929
Fastnet Cup    *Jolie Brise*

## 1930
Fastnet Cup    *Jolie Brise*

## 1931
Fastnet Cup    *Dorade*

## 1933
Fastnet Cup    *Dorade*
Jolie Brise Cup    *Dorade*

## 1935
Fastnet Cup    *Stormy Weather*
Jolie Brise Cup    *Ilex*

## 1937
Fastnet Cup    *Zeearend*
Jolie Brise Cup    *Asta*
Hong Kong Cup    *Banba*
Inter-Regimental Cup    *Ilex*
Erivale Cup    *Elizabeth McCaw*

## 1939
Fastnet Cup    *Bloodhound*
Jolie Brise Cup    *Rose*
Hong Kong Cup    *Rose*
Inter-Regimental Cup    *Nordwind*
Erivale Cup    *Nordwind*
Elizabeth McCaw Trophy    *Nordwind*

## 1947
Fastnet Cup    *Myth of Malham*
Founder's Cup    *Myth of Malham*
St Anna Cup    *Myth of Malham*
Erivale Cup    *Latifa*
Elizabeth McCaw Trophy    *Latifa*
Hong Kong Cup    *Aideen*
Jolie Brise Cup    *Theodora*
Inter-Regimental Cup    *Gauntlet*

## 1949
Fastnet Cup    *Myth of Malham*
Founder's Cup    *Bloodhound*
Elizabeth McCaw Trophy    *Latifa*
Erivale Cup    *Latifa*
Hong Kong Cup    *Theodora*
Jolie Brise Cup    *Theodora*
Golden Dragon Cup    *Griffin*
Inter-Regimental Cup    *St Barbara*

## 1951
Fastnet Cup    *Yeoman*
Founder's Cup    *Jocasta*
Erivale Cup    *Circe*
Hong Kong Cup    *Marabu*
Golden Dragon Cup    *Iolaire*
Elizabeth McCaw Trophy    *Bloodhound*
Jolie Brise Cup    *Marabu*
Inter-Regimental Cup    *St Barbara*

## 1953
Fastnet Cup    *Favona*
Founder's Cup    *Lutine*
Erivale Cup    *Bloodhound*
Hong Kong Cup    *Kailua*
Golden Dragon Cup    *Disdaine*
Elizabeth McCaw Trophy    *Bloodhound*
Jolie Brise Cup    *Glance*
Bloodhound Cup    *Uomie*
Foxhound Cup    *Favona*
Iolaire Cup    *Larph*
Inter-Regimental Cup    *Right Royal*

## 1955
Fastnet Cup    *Carina*
Founder's Cup    *Lutine*
Bloodhound Cup    *Carina*
Gesture Cup    *Carina*
Foxhound Cup    *Mouse of Malham*
Hong Kong Cup    *Gladeye*
Jolie Brise Cup    *Gladeye*
Golden Dragon Cup    *Griffin*
Iolaire Cup    *Planet*
Elizabeth McCaw Cup    *Mare Nostrum*
Erivale Cup    *Mare Nostrum*
Inter-Regimental Cup    *Marabu*

## 1957
Fastnet Cup    *Carina*
Founder's Cup    *Carina*
Gesture Cup    *Carina*
Erivale Cup    *Carina*
Elizabeth McCaw Cup    *Carina*
Bloodhound Cup    *Myth of Malham*
Foxhound Cup    *Cohoe III*

## 1959
Fastnet Cup    *Anitra*
Bloodhound Cup    *Anitra*
Gesture Cup    *Anitra*
Founder's Cup    *Carina*
Foxhound Cup    *Danegeld*
Hong Kong Cup    *Vadura*
Jolie Brise Cup    *Vadura*
Golden Dragon Cup    *Fair Judgment II*
Elizabeth McCaw Trophy    *Anna Marina*
Erivale Cup    *Anna Marina*
Inter-Regimental Cup    *Meon Maid II*

## 1961
Fastnet Cup    *Zwerver*
Buckley Memorial Trophy    *Zwerver*
Founder's Cup – Class I    *Zwerver*
Gesture Cup    *Zwerver*
Bloodhound Cup – Class II    *Quiver III*
Foxhound Cup – Class III    *Belmore*
Elizabeth McCaw Trophy    *Stormvogel*
Erivale Cup    *Stormvogel*
Inter-Regimental Cup    *Martlet*

## 1963
Fastnet Cup    *Clarion of Wight*
Buckley Memorial Trophy    *Clarion of Wight*
Bloodhound Cup    *Clarion of Wight*
Erivale Cup    *Capricia*
Elizabeth McCaw Trophy    *Capricia*
Hong Kong Cup A Division, Class I    *Merlin*
Jolie Brise Cup A Division, Class I    *Merlin*
Golden Dragon Cup, A Division, Class II    *Christina*
Founder's Cup    *Figaro*
Foxhound Cup    *Cohoe IV*
Gesture Cup    *Pen Ar Bed*
Inter-Regimental Cup    *Blue Charm*

## 1965
Fastnet Cup    *Rabbit*
Buckley Memorial Trophy    *Rabbit*
Founder's Cup    *Quiver IV*
Hong Kong Cup    *Najade*
Bloodhound Cup    *Noryema IV*
Golden Dragon Cup    *Norlethe*
Foxhound Cup    *Rabbit*
Iolaire Cup    *Electron of Portsea*
Elizabeth McCaw Trophy    *Gitana IV*
Erivale Cup    *Gitana IV*
Jolie Brise Cup    *Sonata*
Inter-Regimental Cup    *Dambuster*
Gesture Cup    *Rabbit*

## 1967
Fastnet Cup    *Pen-Duick III*
Buckley Memorial Trophy    *Pen-Duick III*
Founder's Cup – Class I    *Pen-Duick III*
Bloodhound Cup – Class II    *Mercedes III*
Foxhound Cup – Class III    *Espirit de Reuil*
Hong Kong Cup – Class I Beta Div.    *Carina*
Golden Dragon Cup – Class II Beta
    Div.    *Caprice of Huon*
Iolaire Cup – Class III Beta Div.    *Fairwind*
Elizabeth McCaw Trophy    *Gitana IV*
Erivale Cup    *Pen-Duick III*
Jolie Brise Cup    *Gitana IV*
Inter-Regimental Cup    *Contrail*
Gesture Cup    *Pen-Duick III*

## 1969
Fastnet Cup    *Red Rooster*
Buckley Memorial    *Red Rooster*
Figaro Trophy    *Crusade*
Clarke Cup    *Ragamuffin*
Norlethe Cup    *American Eagle*
Clarion Cup    *Crusade*
Founders Cup – Class I    *Crusade*
Hong Kong Cup – Class I Beta
    Div.    *American Eagle*
Bloodhound Cup – Class II(a)    *Red Rooster*
Philip Whitehead Memorial Cup – Class II(a)
    Beta    *Zeezot van Veere*
West Mersea Yacht Club Trophy – Class
    II(b)    *Clarionet*
Golden Dragon Trophy – Class II(b) Beta
    Div.    *Pellegrina*
Foxhound Cup – Class III(a)    *Rainbow II*
Iolaire Cup – Class III(a) Beta Div.    *Hestia*
Favona Cup – Class III(b)    *Morning After*
Battler Beedle Quaich – Class III(b) Beta
    Div.    *Poinciana*
Elizabeth McCaw Trophy    *American Eagle*
Erivale Cup    *American Eagle*
Jolie Brise Cup    *American Eagle*
Inter-Regimental Cup    *Fortuna*
Gesture Cup    *Red Rooster*

## 1971
Fastnet Cup    *Ragamuffin*
Buckley Memorial Trophy    *Ragamuffin*
Founder's Cup    *Ragamuffin*
Gesture Cup    *Ragamuffin*
Norlethe Cup    *American Eagle*
Elizabeth McCaw Trophy    *American Eagle*
Erivale Cup    *American Eagle*
Jolie Brise Cup    *American Eagle*
Hong Kong Cup    *American Eagle*
Figaro Cup    *Quailo III*
Clarion Cup    *Quailo III*
Clarke Cup    *Cervantes IV*

Bloodhound Cup   *Cervantes IV*
Philip Whitehead Cup   *Clarion of Wight*
West Mersea Yacht Club
   Trophy   *Morningtown*
Golden Dragon Cup   *Sinbad of Abersoch*
Foxhound Cup   *Pioneer X*
Iolaire Cup   *Greenfly*
Favona Cup   *Morbic III*
Battler Beedle Quaich   *Salidi*
Inter-Regimental Cup   *Slipstream of Cowley*

## 1973

Fastnet Cup   *Saga*
Buckley Memorial Trophy   *Saga*
Figaro Trophy   *Recluta III*
Clarke Cup   *Charisma*
Norlethe Cup   *Apollo*
Clarion Cup   *Prospect of Whitby*
Founder's Cup   *Saga*
Bloodhound Cup   *Frigate*
West Mersea Yacht Club Trophy   *Hylas*
Foxhound Cup   *Colbart III*
Favona Cup   *Maraska*
Hong Kong Cup   *Apollo*
Philip Whitehead Cup   *Wizard of Paget*
Golden Dragon Cup   *Variag*
Iolaire Cup   *Reiver of Mersea*
Battler Beedle Quaich   *Maraska*
Elizabeth McCaw Trophy   *Sorcery*
Erivale Cup   *Sorcery*
Jolie Brise Cup   *Apollo*
Inter-Regimental Cup   *Adventure*
Gesture Cup   *Saga*
Swan Trophy   *Stuart Little*
Iolaire Cup   *Foxhound*
Auscrew Trophy   *Sorcery*

## 1975

Fastnet Cup   *Golden Delicious*
Figaro Trophy   *Polar Bear*
Norlethe Cup   *Trocar*

Founder's Cup   *Saga*
Bloodhound Cup   *Goodwin*
West Mersea Yacht Club Trophy   *Stress*
Foxhound Cup   *Golden Delicious*
Favona Cup   *Maraska*
Elizabeth McCaw Trophy   *Kialoa*
Jolie Brise Cup   *Saga*
Gesture Cup   *Goodwin*
Iolaire Block   *Brynoth*
Buckley Memorial Trophy   *Golden Delicious*
Clarke Cup   *Trocar*
Clarion Cup   *Golden Delicious*
Hong Kong Cup   *Saga*
Philip Whitehead Cup   *Nymphea*
Golden Dragon Cup   *Machichaco*
Iolaire Cup   *Trocar*
Battler Beedle Quaich   *Maraska*
Erivale Cup   *Kialoa*
Inter-Regimental Cup   *Hindostan*
Swan Trophy   *Trailblazer*
Auscrew Trophy   *Trailblazer*

## 1977

Fastnet Cup   *Imp*
Figaro Trophy   *Moonshine*
Clarke Cup   *Yeoman XX*
Norlethe Cup   *Severine*
Clarion Cup   *Moonshine*
Founder's Cup   *Moonshine*
Bloodhound Cup   *Imp*
West Mersea Yacht Club Trophy   *Variag*
Foxhound Cup   *Bertheaume*
Favona Cup   *Crazy Horse*
Hong Kong Cup   *Scaldis*
Philip Whitehead Cup   *Brynoth*
Golden Dragon Cup   *Variag*
Iolaire Cup   *Prolific*
Battler Beedle Quaich   *Severine*
Elizabeth McCaw Trophy   *Il Moro Di
   Venizia*
Erivale Cup   *Ballyhoo*

Jolie Brise Cup   *Saga*
Inter-Regimental Cup   *Velleda*
Gesture Cup   *Imp*
Swan Trophy   *Assiduous*
Iolaire Block   *Brynoth*
Auscrew Trophy   *Moonshine*
Erroll Bruce Cup   *Kalik*
Seth-Smith Trophy   *Velleda*
F.T. Clipper Race Trophy   *Ballyhoo*
Communications Prize   *Bay Bea*

## 1979

Fastnet Cup   *Tenacious*
Figaro Trophy   *Eclipse*
Clarke Cup   *Jubile VI*
Norlethe Cup   *Tenacious*
Clarion Cup   *Eclipse*
Quailo Cup   *Tenacious*
Founder's Cup   *Red Rock IV*
Hong Kong Cup   *Sleuth*
Bloodhound Cup   *Eclipse*
Philip Whitehead Cup   *Dagger*
West Mersea Yacht Club
   Trophy   *Revolution*
Golden Dragon Cup   *Blue Bird*
Foxhound Cup   *Black Arrow*
Alf Loomis Trophy   *Peter Bowker*
Iolaire Cup   *Lorelei*
Favona Cup   *Assent*
Battler Beedle Quaich   *Assent*
Elizabeth McCaw Trophy   *Kialoa*
Erivale Cup   *Condor*
Jolie Brise Cup   *Kialoa*
Inter-Regimental Cup   *Alliance*
Gesture Cup   *Tenacious*
Iolaire Cup   *War Baby*
Auscrew Trophy   *Tenacious*
Seth-Smith Trophy   *Hamburg*
Swinburne Cup   *Moonduster*
Whirlwind Trophy   *Travel*

# Index